THE ILLUSTRATED GUIDE TO

WORLD RELIGIONS

WORLD RELIGIONS

General Editor: Michael D. Coogan

METRO BOOKS
New York

METRO BOOKS
New York
An Imprint of Sterling Publishing
387 Park Avenue South
New York, NY 10016

This 2012 edition published by Metro Books, by arrangement with Duncan Baird Publishers.

Editor: Peter Bently
Managing designer: Paul Reid
Designer: Dan Sturges
Picture researcher: Cecilia Weston-Baker
Indexer: Brian Amos
Maps: Michael Taylor
Decorative borders: Neil Packer

ISBN 978-1-4351-4174-2

For information about custom editions, special sales, and premium and corporate purchases please contact Sterling Special Sales at 800-805-5489 or specialsales@sterlingpublishing.com.

Typeset in Sabon
Color reproduction by Colourscan, Singapore
Manufactured in Malaysia

2 4 6 8 10 9 7 5 3 1

www.sterlingpublishing.com

NOTE

The abbreviations CE and BCE are used throughout this book:
CE Common Era (the equivalent of AD)
BCE Before the Common Era (the equivalent of BC)

CONTENTS

INTRODUCTION

Tens of thousands of years ago, long before the invention of writing, human beings appear to have been engaged in the practice of religion. Carefully carved figurines, strikingly executed cave paintings, and elaborate burial customs can, on the basis of later parallels, be interpreted as evidence of religious activity. Since prehistoric times, therefore, a belief in the existence of a reality greater than the human has served as a definer and creator of cultures, and as an antidote to the fragility and apparent finality of human existence.

Religion has taken innumerable forms in the past and new manifestations continually appear. This book focuses on the living traditions that can accurately be called "world religions": Judaism, Christianity, Islam, Hinduism, Buddhism, Chinese Traditions, and Japanese Traditions. One criterion for selecting these seven traditions is their number of followers. Christianity (with nearly 2 billion adherents), Islam (more than 1 billion), and Hinduism (nearly 800 million) easily qualify. The number of Buddhists is more difficult to estimate, but the religion accounts for a majority of southeast Asians, and is a primary element of Chinese and Japanese traditions. Precisely how many Chinese—especially among the 1.2 billion citizens of the People's Republic—continue to adhere to traditional religious practices is also hard to judge, but even a conservative estimate must run into the hundreds of millions.

A second criterion is diffusion. Thus, while the Jewish population is numerically small—around thirteen million people—the dispersion of Palestinian Jewry from the late centuries BCE resulted in the presence of Jews in every part of the globe. In the twentieth century that spread has diminished, although two-thirds of the world's Jews still live outside Israel. Historically, Christianity and Islam in particular have been active missionary religions, spreading far beyond their places of origin. In the modern world, Muslim, Hindu, and Chinese migrants have taken their religious beliefs and practices to most areas of the world. Likewise, Buddhism has spread widely from its original heartland in India, and has profoundly shaped the religious experience of Asians and, in more recent times, of many Westerners.

The religious traditions of Japan, although still largely confined to the Japanese archipelago, also merit inclusion in this book, because of the size of the Japanese population (125 million) and the global influence of modern Japan.

The final criterion for inclusion in this survey is historical importance. Thus, despite its relatively small number of adherents, Judaism has had enormous religious, intellectual, and cultural influence. Christianity sprang directly from the Jewish tradition, and it shares many points of contact with the third great monotheistic faith, Islam. The Judeo-Christian tradition, and in many respects Islam as well, have contributed immeasurably to the formation of Western culture.

The application of these criteria means that many other traditions are not explicitly dealt with in this survey. Some are ancient, such as Zoroastrianism, while others are relatively modern offshoots of those considered in this book, such as Sikhism, Bahai, and Mormonism, or remain confined mostly to one region, such as Jainism in India. This survey also excludes any systematic coverage of the world's innumerable nonliterate sacred traditions in the Americas, Africa, Oceania, and elsewhere, or of the important belief systems of antiquity (which in many cases were supplanted by the traditions covered in this book). However, in the chapters that follow there will be occasion to note their influence on the history and doctrines of the principal living religions of today.

Each chapter presents a broad overview of one of the seven religions. At the same time, in order to enable readers to compare the seven tradi-

Indian women gather for a meal in honor of the goddess Lakshmi. Hindu celebrations are an increasingly familiar sight in many parts of the world today, and the coexistence of many religious traditions of different geographic origins is now often a regional and even local phenomenon.

A statuette of ca. 600BCE depicting the great Egyptian goddess Isis suckling her son, the god Horus. Widely cultivated throughout the ancient Near East and Mediterranean world, Isis as the divine mother provided one early model for the understanding of Mary, the mother of Christ (see illustration, opposite).

tions and to assess their similarities and differences, the material in each chapter is organized according to ten themes, each covered in an essay of two or four pages. Throughout the book, certain important topics are highlighted in "sidebars" (margin features) and "boxes" (panel features).

The thematic coverage of each tradition is preceded by an introductory essay that serves as a concise survey of the essential features of the religion and its historical and present-day significance and diffusion. This is followed by the detailed treatment of the ten themes:

ORIGINS AND HISTORICAL DEVELOPMENT

In the chapters that follow, these first two themes are treated either separately (Judaism, Christianity, Islam, and Buddhism) or combined (Hinduism, Chinese Traditions, Japanese Traditions). It is generally impossible to ascertain an exact moment when most religions truly "began," since all belief systems are intimately bound up with the development of the cultures from which they have emerged, the roots of which often lie in distant prehistory. Moreover, the sources that describe the origins of a faith may date from a much later period than the events they describe, and frequently they incorporate mythological as well as historical accounts. In addition to these complex sources, a modern religious historian may have little more to go on than the often fragmentary and elusive clues furnished by archaeologists and anthropologists.

However, for the adherents of Buddhism, Christianity, and Islam, the origin of their faith lies unequivocally in the teachings of a single revered individual, whose lifetime can be pinpointed historically with considerable certainty. For this reason, the theme of "Origins" in the chapters covering these traditions is a discrete essay that centers on the lives and careers of, respectively, the Buddha, Jesus, Muhammad, and their immediate followers. For Jews, the formative period of their faith is chronicled in a single collection of writings—the Hebrew Bible—and so the "Origins" theme in this chapter is also covered in a separate essay, focusing on the biblical history of the people and land of Israel.

ASPECTS OF THE DIVINE

As mentioned above, a central component of religion is what may be termed the "divine," or "a reality greater than the human." How this reality is defined is the subject of the book's third theme, "Aspects of the Divine." Is the reality one or many? Is it personal or impersonal? Is it without or within, far or near, transcendent or immanent? Each religious tradition approaches such questions differently, yet from a broader perspective their answers have many points of similarity.

On the question of whether the reality is one or many, the distinction between monotheism and polytheism can be more theoretical than actual. In Hinduism, for example, a very large number of gods and goddesses are the focus of religious practice, yet in one sense they are understood as manifestations of, and approaches to, a single underlying divine reality. Christianity's central doctrine of the Trinity—the godhead existing in three persons—is mysterious, but for Christians does not compromise the essential monotheism of the faith.

Even the monotheistic traditions engage in a kind of "functional polytheism," at least on a popular level, with prominent roles and powers attributed to a range of "saints" and demons. A prime example is Mary, the mother of Jesus, who for many Christians has supplied a missing feminine element within an essentially patriarchal monotheism. Moreover, in Christianity and Islam, and to some extent in Judaism, there is a continuing struggle for supremacy between God and the powers of evil.

The Madonna and Child *by the Master of San Miniato (active ca. 1460–90). The venerable, at times even goddesslike, status of the Virgin Mary is derived in part from Mediterranean traditions that Christianity supplanted. For example, the common Christian image of Mary nursing the infant Jesus can be traced directly to depictions of Isis and Horus (see illustration, opposite).*

SACRED TEXTS

One of the ways in which the divine is made accessible to humans is through divinely inspired scriptures and other writings. Every literate faith community has produced collections of texts composed, assembled, and edited within a relatively brief span or over centuries. They are used in worship and religious education and articulate the central ideals and sometimes also narrate the history of the tradition. In many religions, sacred texts are considered to be "revealed," that is, of divine inspiration or authorship. While shaped by an evolving tradition, sacred literature contributes to the subsequent stages of development through its use in ritual and study. A religion's scriptures are the repository of its essential principles and the touchstone for its formulations of doctrine.

In some traditions, the body, or canon, of sacred literature is closed, and the texts that comprise the canon are relatively ancient. This is notably true of Judaism, Christianity, and Islam: the Jewish and Christian Bibles and the Quran were each fixed at a relatively early stage of their religion's history (although Christian denominations disagree over the canonical status of a few books termed "apocrypha"). However, the three monotheistic faiths also acknowledge other, sometimes equally ancient, texts as being of special religious significance, while not of divine origin. In other traditions, the canon is more open, incorporating texts from late periods and sometimes oral compositions.

In all religions a tradition of commentary and interpretation developed around the central body of holy writings, and some of these ancillary texts themselves acquired a venerable and even canonical status.

SACRED PERSONS

Each major religion recognizes the special significance to its tradition of one or more individuals. Sometimes these are "founders," identified in some way as responsible for certain essential aspects of the tradition, or indeed its very existence. These figures may be revered as embodiments of the godhead, as in the case of Jesus and Krishna; or as recipients of a special divine revelation, such as Moses and Muhammad; or as persons who have experienced extraordinary fundamental insights, such as the Buddha and Laozi. The writings of such individuals and the narratives of their lives often form the nucleus of a religion's canon of sacred texts.

In addition to founder figures, there is in most religions an array of individuals who are respected or venerated for their exemplary lives and teachings. These persons are also sometimes understood as having attained an unusual degree of holiness or enlightenment. Some are leaders, teachers, and guides; others are celebrated for their heroic virtue, often in the face of persecution. Often a saint, sage, monk, *imam*, nun, mystic, or *guru* will be venerated by the entire tradition, but more frequently he or she will be the focus of a smaller group within the broader religious community, or the subject of localized veneration.

ETHICAL PRINCIPLES

Enshrined in sacred texts and embodied in the lives of sacred persons are the essential principles of conduct for individuals and for the community as a whole. These principles are often concisely formulated, as with the "Ten Commandments" of Judaism and Christianity and the "Noble Eightfold Path" of Buddhism. Sometimes they are codified from the scriptures, such as the total of 613 commandments that Jewish tradition identifies in the Torah.

As a religion develops, disagreements can arise over the application of older principles to new situations. Debates over questions of individual and social morality are often fierce, and can lead to schisms and ultimately to the formation of new subgroups within a tradition. Yet each community and sect is earnestly engaged in the task of formulating ethical principles that will enable their adherents to achieve the ultimate objective of the tradition—the attainment of salvation, redemption, enlightenment, and the "liberation" of the soul.

SACRED SPACE

All faiths set apart areas where the earthly and the sacred come together. Temples, mosques, churches, and public and domestic shrines serve as places for communal and private worship, life rituals (such as naming and marriage), and religious education; as focal points for festivals and other ceremonies; and as administrative centers for the religious hierarchy. Many traditions develop distinct styles of sacred building, often incorporating complex symbolism and the influence of local and regional architecture.

Followers of many faiths venerate certain natural features such as mountains, rivers, and springs, and very often the attribution of holiness to such sites is of considerable antiquity, predating the tradition itself. Other sites might be deemed sacred owing to their association with a particular sacred individual. Every holy place can become a destination for pilgrims.

SACRED TIME

All religious traditions acknowledge certain times of the day, the year, the human life cycle, and even history as times of special proximity to the sacred, occasions to be marked by private or communal acts of religious observance. The cosmic rhythms of the sun, moon, planets, and stars become enshrined in the religious calendar; dawn and sunset are widely considered times of particular holiness, and there may be liturgies setting out the devotional acts to be performed at other times of the day, week, or year. Most traditions celebrate the New Year as a time of renewal in the life of the individual and the community—a moment of

In the course of history, the same site may become sacred to succeeding religious groups. For example, the great Umayyad mosque in Damascus (below), constructed 705–710CE, was erected on the site of a Byzantine Christian church dedicated to St. John the Baptist, which itself had replaced a Greco-Roman temple to Jupiter/Zeus.

Children ritually cleanse a statuette of the Buddha at the Zenkoji temple in Nagano, Japan during the Children's Day festival. Such celebrations are an important way of involving worshippers in the religious life of their community at an early age.

optimism in which the numinous may be petitioned for blessings. The New Year is often linked with the agricultural cycle, marking the end of the harvest or the beginning of the planting season.

Sacred ceremonies ("rites of passage") also mark the key moments of transition in the human life cycle, especially birth, sexual maturity and marriage, and death. In many traditions it is also customary to perform acts in honor of one's ancestors. Such rites serve to bind individuals and families to the wider religious community of which they are a part.

Great importance is also attached to the commemoration of momentous events in the history of a religion, such as the birth or death of a founder. Pilgrimage to places associated with revered individuals, events, or objects constitutes a major form of worship in many traditions.

DEATH AND THE AFTERLIFE

Mortality is a central human concern and as such forms a major focus of religious practice and belief. The moment of death is customarily attended by some form of sacred ritual, and most belief systems anticipate that the individual will continue to exist in some manner after death. Many faiths conceive of regions beyond this world that are transitional or permanent destinations of the dead: heavens (celestial regions of bliss) for the righteous, and hells (infernal regions of suffering) for the damned. Central to the religions originating in India is the idea that a soul is reincarnated after death in a new physical form, the nature of which depends on the individual's accumulated merits or demerits.

Those who pursue the ethical dictates of their faith often do so with the express goal of achieving either freedom from death, or blessed immortality in the presence of the divine. Buddhists, who view serial reincarnation as a commitment to an eternity of human suffering, seek liberation from the perpetual cycle of rebirth and death. Judaism is exceptional in not considering questions of what happens after death to be of central religious significance; hence "Death and the Afterlife" is omitted from the thematic structure of this chapter.

His Holiness Pope John Paul II is greeted by President Fidel Castro of Cuba at Havana airport on January 21, 1998. Papal influence on the world's Roman Catholic populations has sometimes been a cause of friction between the church and national governments, particularly in Communist states, such as Cuba, which officially promote atheism.

SOCIETY AND RELIGION

The world's major religious traditions have both reflected and shaped the values of the societies of which they have been an inseparable element. Historically, religious leaders have been influential in setting national moral, social, and political agendas, and this remains true in many countries today. However, the rise of modern secular government has sometimes created tensions between the civil and religious establishments; these arise because it is sometimes assumed that the interests of "church" and "state"—or whatever equivalent terms may be used—are always distinct, and that the engagement of religious communities in the affairs of a modern state is therefore "interference." But many of the issues that face present-day societies raise ethical questions that go to the heart of central, and often longstanding, religious concerns. For example, is war in general, or a particular war, permissible? Should divorce, or abortion, or genetic engineering be prohibited?

For adherents of a particular faith, the decision whether to join with civil government or take an institutional stance independent of it may be difficult. Two questions illustrate the dilemma. The first relates to gender equality. To what extent can religions that preserve older paradigms (for example, all-male priesthoods) legitimately urge change in the status and treatment of women? Another issue is tolerance of cultural diversity. If a faith's own scripture and history have promulgated the notion that it possesses the best, or sole, path to salvation (however that term is defined), in what way can that religion encourage society in general to grant equality to other traditions with beliefs and practices perhaps antithetical to its own?

In the pages that follow, these and other complex themes are discussed and clarified by writers who are all acknowledged experts in their fields. Together they have created a vivid and authoritative survey of the profound mysteries, powerful intellectual constructs, compelling inner logic and coherence, and magnificent expressions of holiness that constitute the greatest and most lasting achievements of the world's major faiths.

Michael D. Coogan,
Professor of Religious Studies, Stonehill College, Easton, Massachusetts,
and Director of Publications, Harvard Semitic Museum

Chapter One

JUDAISM

Carl S. Ehrlich

The Tetragrammaton, the four-letter name of God (YHWH), is at the center of this illumination from a Hebrew Bible copied in Spain, 1384CE. The name is considered too holy to be uttered.

OPPOSITE *Qumran in the Judean wilderness, near the Dead Sea. The "Dead Sea Scrolls," including the earliest extant manuscripts of many biblical books, were found here in 1947. They date from before the destruction of the Temple of Jerusalem in 70CE.*

An illuminated page from the first complete printed edition (Italy, 1475) of Arba'ah Turim, *a famous codification of Jewish law by Jacob ben Asher.*

INTRODUCTION

With approximately thirteen million adherents, Judaism today is the smallest of the world religions. However, it has had an influence and a geographical distribution inversely proportional to its size. Its origins lie in the state religion of the ancient kingdom of Judah, which came to an end in 586BCE (see p.20). The surviving Judeans faced the challenge of adapting their national religion for an exiled community scattered from Egypt to Mesopotamia. Their success is indicated both by the development of Judaism itself and by the profound formative influence of Judaism on two other great faiths, Christianity and Islam.

The Diaspora ("dispersion") after 586BCE took Judaism to most corners of the world, and the religion has developed under the influence of its host cultures. The influence has been mutual, because Jews have served as great transmitters of knowledge. For example, the Arab and ancient Greek learning that Sephardic Jews (see p.24) took with them when they were expelled from Spain was a major spark for the European Renaissance.

As a religion, Judaism has three essential elements: God, Torah, and Israel. Arguably the oldest monotheistic faith, it believes in one universal and eternal God, the creator and sovereign of all that exists. God has entered into a special relationship, or covenant, with one people, the Jews, or Israel, and given them the task of being a "light to the nations" (Isaiah 49.6). There is no expectation in Judaism that all people will become Jewish, but there does exist the hope that the whole world will come to acknowledge the sovereignty of the one God. In return for God's care for Israel, Jews have a responsibility to adhere to the divine teachings, or *Torah* (see pp.30–33). This is the plane on which God and Israel meet. It contains the ethical and ritual commandments (*mitzvot*) through the performance of which one may partake of God's ethical and moral holiness.

The term "Israel" denotes a historic political entity, a people, a nation, a belief system, a social group, a culture. Its lack of a single clear definition is one reason why there continues to be so much debate among Jews on the question of who *is* a Jew (see pp.49–51). Born as the religion of a specific nation-state, Judaism has had to cope through centuries of exile with the issue of multiple identities. While the religion, with its beliefs, lifestyle, and rituals, however practiced, has served as the basis of Jewish identity, a great role has also been played by a shared historical consciousness and a global ethnic solidarity. In pointing the way toward the redemptive future, Judaism is in constant dialogue with its history.

The legendary past, recorded in the early books of the Bible, served to provide a sense of communal identity among disparate tribal elements. According to the well-known account, God, who created heaven and earth,

WORLD JEWISH POPULATIONS

Of the world's estimated total of thirteen million Jews, around one-third—4.7 million—live in Israel (which has a population of nearly six million) and two-thirds in the Diaspora, with 5.8 million in the United States and around 2.3 million in Europe. Jerusalem, with 422,000 Jews among its 603,000 inhabitants, has the world's fourth largest urban Jewish population after New York (1.75 million), Miami (0.53 million), and Los Angeles (0.49 million). (Source of statistics: World Jewish Congress, 1997.)

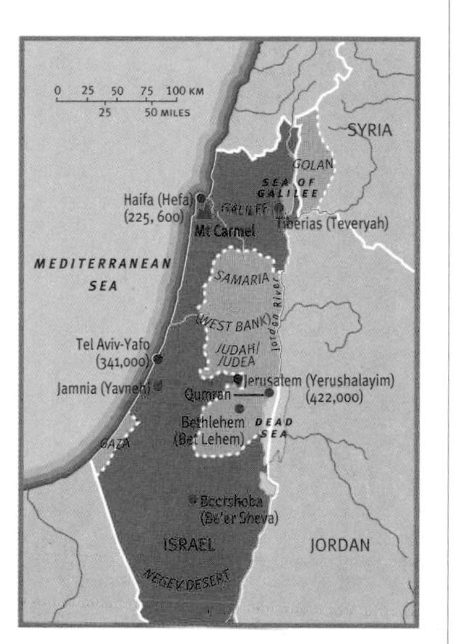

National Jewish populations

- 1 million or more
- 500,000–999,999
- 250,000–499,000
- 100,000–249,000
- 50,000–99,999
- 25,000–49,000
- 10,000–24,999
- 0–9,999

Urban Jewish populations

- City with more than 100,000 Jews
- Other town or city

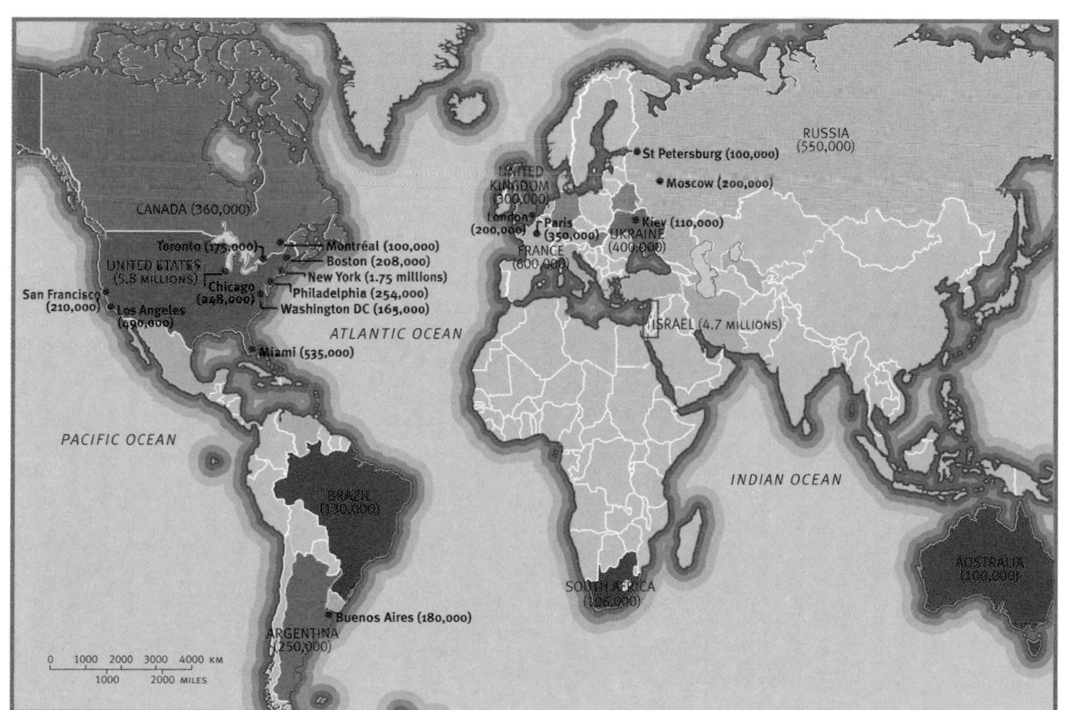

The Binding of Isaac, a mosaic from the 6th-century CE *synagogue of Beth Alpha in northern Israel. It depicts the events of Genesis 22.1–19, in which God probed the depths of Abraham's faith by commanding him to sacrifice his son.*

entered into a personal covenant with Abraham, a stateless wanderer from Mesopotamia. In return for Abraham's faith, God promised him a home in Canaan—the future land of Israel—and numerous progeny. Abraham had a grandson, Jacob (to whom God gave a new name, Israel), who with his sons and their families moved to Egypt to escape a famine. They served Pharaoh, but their descendants became slaves until God freed them. Led by Moses, the Israelites left Egypt (an event known as the Exodus) and came to Mount Sinai, where they entered into an eternal covenant with God. In Jewish tradition, this was the formative event in the history of the Jews and the birth of monotheism. But the Israelites showed a lack of faith and were condemned to wander in the desert for forty years before they entered and conquered the promised land of Canaan under Moses' successor, Joshua.

Pressures from the aboriginal Canaanites and the newly arrived Philistines forced the twelve tribes of Israel to unite, reluctantly, around a monarchy. The first king, Saul, was succeeded by David and Solomon, who ushered in a golden age that has remained the focus of Jewish aspirations ever since. However, owing to further transgressions, God was to punish the Jews with the loss of their national sanctuary and homeland. But always before them lay the hope that true repentance would lead to the restoration of their relationship with the divine. Throughout most of their history, the Jews have looked to this proud but cautionary account to give

CHRONOLOGY

Pre-1200BCE	Traditional time of Abraham, Jacob, and the other ancestors of Israel; the descent into Egypt; the Exodus; the conquest of Canaan
1200–1000BCE	Formation of ancient Israel as an ethno-religious group
ca. 1000BCE	David becomes king
ca. 960BCE	Accession of Solomon, who builds First Temple
ca. 925BCE	Israel splits into rival states, Israel and Judah
722BCE	Israel falls to Assyria; prophet Isaiah active
586BCE	Judah falls to Babylon; Temple destroyed and ruling classes exiled; Ezekiel active in exile
538BCE	Cyrus II of Persia allows exiles to return and rebuild Temple
458BCE	Ezra in Jerusalem
164BCE	Rededication of the Second Temple by the Hasmoneans
63BCE	Judea comes under Roman rule
66–73CE	First Jewish War against Rome
70CE	Second Temple razed; Yohanan ben Zakkai founds Yavneh academy
132–135CE	Second Jewish War (Bar Kokhba revolt); Rabbi Akiva martyred
ca. 200CE	Mishnah codified under leadership of Rabbi Judah the Prince
ca. 400CE	Jerusalem Talmud completed
ca. 500CE	Babylonian Talmud completed
882–942CE	Life of Saadia Gaon, head of the Academy at Sura, Babylon
1040–1105	Life of French Jewish commentator Rashi
1096	Massacre of Rhineland Jews during First Crusade
10th–12th centuries	"Golden Age" of Spanish Jewry
1135–1204	Life of Maimonides
1492	Expulsion of Jews from Spain
1648–9	Massacre of Ukrainian Jews
1665–6	Shabbetai Zvi ("Mystical Messiah") active
1789–91	French Revolution begins emancipation of western European Jews
1844	First Reform synod in Brunswick, Germany
1897	First Zionist Congress in Basel, Switzerland
1933–45	Nazi anti-Semitic policies culminate in mass murder of two-thirds of European Jews (the "Holocaust")
1948	State of Israel declared (May 14)
1967	Israel captures West Bank, East Jerusalem, Golan Heights, and Sinai in six-day Arab-Israeli war.
1972	Reform movement ordains its first woman rabbi
1973	Israel defeats Arab invasion on fast of Yom Kippur
1977	Launch of Arab-Israeli peace process
1995	Oslo Accords pave way for peaceful Arab-Israeli coexistence

them hope. As God had cared for them in the past, so too would God care for them in the present and the future.

All too often the story of the Jews has been presented as a litany of disasters. Since the Hellenistic period (330–63BCE), Jewish distinctiveness has often been subject to derision and incomprehension. Muslim regimes sometimes persecuted Jews, but Christian Europe made anti-Judaism a matter of common policy. For a faith still reeling from the effects of the Nazi persecution (1933–1945), this attention to Jewish suffering throughout the ages is understandable, but it is a precarious foundation upon which to base an identity. Hence there has been a tendency among Jews in recent years to accentuate the positive aspects of Jewish existence. Greater attention is being paid to the great literary creations of Judaism: the Bible, the Talmud, poetry, philosophy, theology, and ethics. At the same time, this is a period of great creativity, while many formerly nonpracticing Jews are rediscovering the essential joy inherent in living a Jewish life.

A major factor in the rediscovery of a "positive Judaism" has been the creation of the state of Israel. Political questions and the issue of defining a Jew and Judaism are undeniably a source of tensions between Israel and the Diaspora communities. Nonetheless, the state of Israel is one of the poles around which modern Jewish life revolves. Often more concerned with existential matters, Judaism is now confident enough to turn to internal issues of religious and ethnic importance. This attention to inner-Jewish concerns is a sign of health and hope for a fruitful future.

The traditional site of Mount Sinai, in present-day Egypt. According to the Hebrew Bible, it was at Sinai that God passed on the law to Moses and entered into an eternal covenant with Israel.

An ivory pomegranate, possibly part of the decoration of the First Temple built by King Solomon ca. 950BCE. The Hebrew inscription, not entirely legible, reads: "Belonging to [the house of YHWH?], holy to the priests."

A FAITH IN THE MAKING

The earliest known reference to the Israelites is an inscription on the so-called "Israel Stela" erected by the pharaoh Merneptah of Egypt (ruled ca. 1213–1203BCE), which indicates that in his time an ethnic entity named "Israel" existed in the central highlands of Canaan. During the ensuing two centuries, known to archaeologists as Iron Age I (1200–1000BCE), there was a marked increase in settlement in the central hill country. It seems likely that the various tribal units coalesced into a nation-state during the transition to the era known as Iron Age II (1000–586BCE), when a number of other small states also arose in the region.

An inscription of the ninth century BCE recently found at Tel Dan in northern Israel mentions David as the founder of a dynasty; but the legendary glories of the united Israelite monarchy have not been attested archaeologically. After the death of Solomon, the kingdom split into two rival states, Israel in the north and Judah in the south. Before its destruction by the Assyrians in 722BCE, Israel was the larger, richer, and more significant state. However, because the Bible was written by scribes of Judean descent, it presents a consistently negative image of the northern kingdom. Its assessment of Judah is more varied, although its judgments are based on theological rather than political criteria. For example, King Hezekiah, whose disastrous reign saw the kingdom reduced to the city of Jerusalem and its environs, is praised for his religious fidelity. Ultimately, in 586BCE, Nebuchadrezzar of Babylon conquered Judah, destroyed its religious center, the Temple of Jerusalem (see pp.40–41), and deported members of the

ISRAELITE MONOTHEISM

Texts discovered throughout the Near East have helped to place Israelite religion in a broader cultural context. Many biblical myths, as well as imagery and designations used for the divine, have parallels among Israel's neighbors. Most striking have been the connections with the religion of the Canaanites, whom the Israelites supposedly displaced.

The historical implausibility of a large-scale Exodus from Egypt has called into question the person of Moses and his role in the introduction of Israelite monotheism. While a minority of scholars continues to adhere to the biblical model, in which a pure monotheism is introduced at the beginning of the nation's history, the dominant tendency is to presuppose a lengthy development in Israel's religion. The formation of Israel as a national entity revolved around its national deity, YHWH (see p.26). However, it would appear that the early Israelites did not view YHWH as the only deity. The existence of others, serving other nations, was not explicitly denied until late in the period of the First Temple (before the Babylonian exile). In the eighth century BCE the image of a sacred marriage of Israel and God was first used by the prophet Hosea. The exclusiveness implied in such a notion—that is, that Israel owed allegiance to just one deity—may have led, in the long term, to the development of the idea that there was *only* one God, who controlled all of human destiny. Whatever its origin, this radical theological concept enabled the Judeans to hold on to their faith even after their loss of national independence.

upper classes. But the exiles retained their national religion, setting a precedent for Judaism as an exilic faith during centuries of dispersal.

In order to retain their identity, the exiled Judeans—"Judean" is the original meaning of the term "Jew"—were forced to adapt their religion. The Judean national God was definitively reinterpreted as the universal God of all human history. Hence the disasters that had befallen the Judeans did not represent the triumph of Babylon and its deities, but the punishment of the Judeans by the one God. This theology in turn led to a detailed examination of the relationship between the divine and the human and of the ritual and ethical demands this entailed. Intertwined with these issues was the need to preserve—some scholars would say to formulate—the exiles' ancient traditions. Thus began the Jewish scholarly tradition that in the first instance gave birth to many of the writings of the Bible (see pp.30–33).

The Babylonian empire fell in 539BCE to the Persians, who allowed all exiles to return home and restore their religious practices. A small number of Jews returned to Judah and rebuilt the Temple, which was dedicated in 515BCE. Judaism again had a central sanctuary and a degree of self-government, and so began the pattern whereby a Jewish presence in the land of Israel coexisted with Jewish communities in the outside world, collectively known as the Diaspora ("dispersal"). The oldest Diaspora communities were those of Babylon and Egypt. During the Persian period (539–330BCE), under the leadership of the former exiles Ezra and Nehemiah, Jewish religious law and communal law became one and the same. This regulatory structure enabled Diaspora Jews to retain a measure of autonomy within the cultures among which they lived.

Judea came under Greek rule as a result of the conquests of Alexander the Great (356–323BCE). His successors continued his policy of Hellenization, imposing Greek culture on their domains. In the religious sphere this included identifying the deities of conquered peoples with those of the Greek pantheon. Jewish society split between Hellenists, who advocated a rapid accommodation of the essentially very open and tolerant Hellenistic system, and pietists, who saw it as inimical to the exclusive monotheism of Judaism. The Greek ruler Antiochus IV Epiphanes (175–164BCE), whose kingdom included Judea, sided with the Jewish Hellenists, a move that culminated in 167BCE with a ban on many Jewish practices and the erection of an altar of Zeus in the Temple. Led by the priest Mattathias and his son Judah Maccabee (Judas Maccabeus), the pietists rebelled, won back a measure of Judean autonomy, and rededicated the defiled Temple in 164BCE (see also p.46). Ironically, the Hasmonean dynasty founded by the rebels itself became a strong advocate of Hellenic culture until, wracked by corruption, Judea fell to the Romans in 63BCE.

THE BIBLE AND ARCHAEOLOGY

The discipline of biblical archaeology was founded in the nineteenth century in order to demonstrate the veracity of the Bible. To a certain extent it has been successful: much more is now known about the world in which the biblical history of Israel is set, and certain features of that world can be seen to form the conceptual framework of the biblical account.

However, the Bible's theological interpretation of Israel's story remains at best uncorroborated and at worst actually contradicted by archaeology. For example, the thousands of ancient texts uncovered contain no mention of Abraham, Sarah, or the other ancestors of Israel, nor of Moses, nor of an Israelite sojourn in Egypt. Neither the conquest of Canaan by Joshua nor the glories of David and Solomon have been archaeologically attested. The tendency nowadays is to regard the biblical and the archaeological records as two separate entities, and the extent of their relationship remains the subject of lively debate.

King David playing the harp, from a late 13th-century Hebrew manuscript from northern France. Jews revere David as the founder of the "golden age" of ancient Israel and the author of many Psalms.

FROM HEROD TO HERZL

Judaism as it is known and practiced today has its roots in the upheavals of early Roman Palestine. Initially, the Romans governed through a Jewish client dynasty founded by Herod the Great (37–4BCE), a ruthless but effective ruler held in suspicion by many Jews as a descendant of forced converts to Judaism. His reign was marked by an ambitious building program that included rebuilding the Second Temple on a grand scale.

Herod was succeeded by his son, Archelaus, who proved so oppressive that the Romans deposed him in 6CE, from when Judea was governed for several decades by a succession of Roman prefects. The Jews finally rose up against the occupying power in 66CE, but after some initial successes, the revolt (the First Jewish War) succumbed to the overwhelming might of imperial Rome. Following a harrowing siege, Jerusalem was captured and the Temple razed (70CE). One more attempt to break Roman control over Palestine (the Bar Kokhba revolt, or Second Jewish War, 132–135CE) ended with the temporary banishment of Jews from Jerusalem. Jewish national aspirations were effectively shattered until the twentieth century.

While Jerusalem was under siege during the First Jewish War, a rabbi (teacher), Yohanan ben Zakkai, received permission from the Romans to

JEWISH LANGUAGES

In the course of their history, Jews have naturally adopted the languages of their various homelands in order to communicate with each other and with their neighbors. Distinctive Jewish tongues have developed from some of the host languages, such as Ladino from Spanish and Yiddish from German.

If the Bible is the shared foundational text of the Jews, then it is the Hebrew language that has served to bind the Jewish people worldwide. As the language of Scripture, Hebrew itself has come to be regarded as imbued with an aura of holiness. At all times, Hebrew has enabled Jews to communicate and pray together.

The rise of Zionism at the turn of the twentieth century led to the revival of Hebrew as a spoken language, no longer restricted solely to the religious sphere.

Roman troops parade furnishings looted from the Temple in 70CE. From the Arch of Titus, Rome (erected 81CE).

THE PHARISEES AND OTHER GROUPS

A number of Jewish sects existed during the last two centuries of the Second Temple period (164BCE–70CE), including the Sadducees, Essenes, Zealots, Pharisees, and the Jesus movement. The Sadducees were the priestly party of Jerusalem. The Essenes were a group that withdrew from general society and, during the First Jewish War, presumably hid the Dead Sea Scrolls at Qumran. The Zealots, as their name implies, were anti-Roman fanatics. The only groups to survive the destruction of the Temple in 70CE were the Pharisees and the Jesus movement. The latter gave rise to Christianity (see p.58), while the Pharisees, led by Yohanan ben Zakkai (see main text), were the progenitors of rabbinic Judaism.

Pharisaic Judaism was characterized by a belief not only in the written Torah (the Bible) but also in the "oral Torah," laws handed down verbally since God first vouchsafed them to Moses, and adapted to changing circumstances (see pp.30–33). The Pharisees democratized Jewish learning, in that their academies were open to all men, and their ideal of the rabbi was one trained in a trade. Their belief in an afterlife allowed them to accept their often difficult lot in this world.

Jewish visitors before the tomb of Yohanan ben Zakkai, founder of the Yavneh academy in the late 1st century CE, at Tiberias on the western shore of the Sea of Galilee in northern Israel.

found an academy of Jewish learning in Yavneh (Jamnia), near the coast between present-day Tel Aviv and Ashdod. Ben Zakkai saw that Judaism's future lay not in vainly taking arms against Rome, but in the scholastic tradition represented by the sect known as the Pharisees (see box, above).

Within a few years, the center of Jewish life and learning in the land of Israel had shifted to the Galilee, in whose academies generations of scholars debated the minutiae of Jewish custom and law, and their application to daily life. This process was mirrored outside Palestine in the great Jewish academies of Babylon, which produced an outstanding achievement ca. 500CE in the form of the Babylonian Talmud, the most influential work in Judaism over the last millennium and a half (see p.30). Judaism had entered a long period of scholarly introspection, during which its adherents for the most part lived a precarious existence as a minority among often hostile dominant cultures.

At the height of the Roman empire it is estimated that one tenth of the population of Rome was Jewish. In addition, a large number of gentiles (non-Jews) were attracted to Judaism, but did not convert because of their difficulty with such requirements as male circumcision. A Jewish offshoot, Christianity, as advocated by Paul (see p.60), did not enforce such specifically Jewish laws, and proved a more attractive alternative for gentiles

THE KHAZARS

Around the year 740CE the ruling circles of a Turkic people called the Khazars converted to Judaism. Why they did so is unknown, although it might be related to their precarious position in the Caucasus between the Byzantine Christian and the Muslim worlds.

The Khazars were able to maintain themselves as a Jewish-ruled country for around two centuries until they were conquered by Russia. About a century and a half after their demise, the Spanish Jewish poet Judah Halevi (died 1141) wrote a philosophical argument for Judaism called the *Kuzari*, which takes the form of a debate before the Khazar king on the various merits of Judaism, Christianity, and Islam. According to Halevi, the king chose Judaism because of the rational arguments in its favor.

drawn to ethical monotheism. Christianity became the Roman state religion in 392CE, and thereafter Christian rulers enacted discriminatory laws designed to make explicit God's supposed rejection of the Jews.

The history of the Jews in Christendom is one of nearly constant persecution. Massacres, expulsions, and forced conversions were common, and Jews were blamed for natural disasters such as the Black Death (1348–9). Excluded from most professions, European Jews were more often than not obliged to become merchants and moneylenders (usury was forbidden to Christians). Long restricted in their choice of domicile, from the sixteenth century Jews began to be sequestered in special town quarters, called "ghettos" after the area of Venice where the first was situated.

The position of the Jews under Islam could also be precarious, but in

SEPHARDIM AND ASHKENAZIM

An important distinction is made within Judaism between the Sephardim ("Spaniards"), who trace their origin to medieval Spain, and the Ashkenazim ("Germans"), who are descended from the Jews of medieval Germany. The Sephardim found themselves caught between the forces of Christianity and Islam fighting for control of the Iberian peninsula. Between the tenth and the twelfth centuries, under Muslim rule, the Spanish Jews enjoyed the "Golden Age," a great period of Jewish learning, creativity, and influence. This came to an end with the fanatical anti-Judaism of the Muslim Almohad dynasty in the mid-twelfth century.

The Christian reconquest of Spain brought further persecution until, in 1492, all Jews who refused to convert were expelled. Those who left went to the Netherlands, North Africa, Italy, and the Ottoman empire; some Sephardim even found their way to the Americas. The exiles played a key role in the transmission of Arab learning, an important seed of the European Renaissance.

A Sephardic boy holds the Torah scroll during his bar mitzvah *ceremony in Jerusalem.*

Jewish settlement in medieval Germany was initially concentrated along the Rhine, but these vibrant communities were devastated by the First Crusade in 1096. They reconstituted themselves, but the center of Jewish life in northern Europe shifted to the east, with Vilnius in Lithuania seen by many as the new Jerusalem. By the twentieth century, the greatest concentration of Ashkenazim was in Poland and Russia, despite a harsh and restrictive life there. Most of these communities ended with mass emigration (mainly to the US) and the Holocaust.

A third group, often wrongly included with the Sephardim, consists of Jews whose ancestors stayed in the Middle East, the Edot ha-Mizrah ("Communities of the East"). Each group has its own traditions and history. For more than a millennium, the ancient Jewish community of Babylon was Judaism's leading light, and another important group lived in Yemen. Most Jews of these communities fled or emigrated to Israel after 1948.

There are a number of other Jewish communities of ancient standing that defy neat classification. These include the Jews of China, India, and Ethiopia.

times of tolerance they flourished in a manner unthinkable under Christian rule, becoming doctors, merchants, court officials, scientists, and poets. The high point in this respect was the "Golden Age" of the Jews of Muslim Spain (tenth–twelfth centuries CE).

Jews played an important role as mediators between the cultures. Since there were Jewish communities scattered across Europe, Asia, and North Africa, Jews were an integral part of international trade, and as a consequence of their linguistic skills a major conduit of learning.

The pressures of life in western and central Europe led to the movement of large numbers of Jews into eastern Europe, where things proved little better. As their situation grew more desperate, an increasing number of Jews turned to mysticism and messianic speculation as a source of hope in a hostile world. A number of false messiahs arose, the most famous being Shabbetai Zvi (1626–76) of Smyrna in Turkey (see p.29).

From the eighteenth century, the situation of Jews as the outcasts of Christian European society seemed to take a turn for the better, during the Enlightenment and the subsequent emancipation of the Jews in many countries. For the first time, Jews were accorded equal civil rights in some western European states and in the New World. However, full acceptance came only with baptism, and many Jews purchased their entry into general society at the price of their Judaism. Those not willing to renounce their Judaism were the driving force behind the Jewish reform movement of the early nineteenth century. While some applauded the radical innovations of the reformers, others considered them to be renegades from true Judaism. The result was the division of Judaism into the three major movements of today: Reform, Conservative, and Orthodox (see pp.48–51).

In the late nineteenth century, the development of racial supremacist theories derived from Darwinian evolutionary thought gave rise to a new form of anti-Judaism, namely anti-Semitism (see sidebar, right). This baleful phenomenon reached its peak in the murder of two-thirds of European Jewry—one-third of the entire Jewish people—during the Holocaust (1941–45), the name given to the systematic mass slaughter that marked the climax of the anti-Semitic policies of Nazi Germany (1933–45).

Jewish aspirations did not end with this unparalleled disaster. Another Jewish movement, Zionism, had been founded by Theodor Herzl (see p.37) at the end of the nineteenth century and was inspired in part by European nationalist thought. Taking its name from Zion, the ancient poetic name of Jerusalem, Zionism sought a solution to the age-old "Jewish question" in the return of the Jews to their ancient homeland in Palestine and their revitalization as a nation (see also p.37). In 1948, following the United Nations Partition Plan of the previous year, a Jewish national entity was established in the land of Israel, bringing to an end nearly 1,900 years of Jewish disenfranchisement.

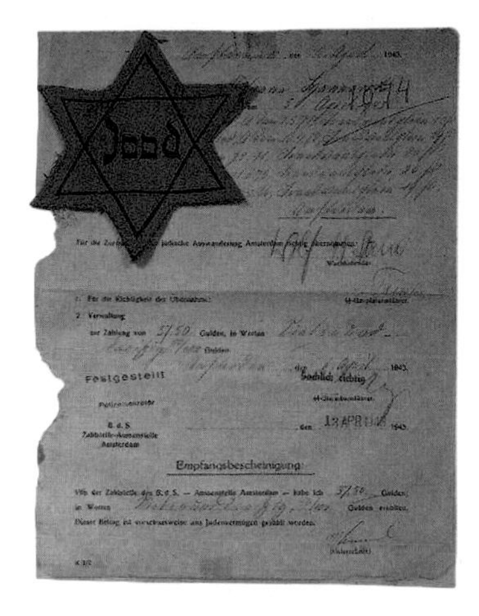

Jewish identity papers and a Star of David bearing the word Jood *("Jew" in Dutch), issued by the occupying Nazi authorities in Amsterdam in 1943. The star had to be worn on the outer clothing to identify the wearer as Jewish.*

"ANTI-SEMITISM"

The term "anti-Semitism" is now used to designate any occurrence of anti-Judaism, whether it be motivated by race, religion, or politics. In fact, this usage is often anachronistic. "Anti-Semitism" was coined in 1879 by Wilhelm Marr, a German political agitator, who redefined traditional anti-Jewish sentiment, making hatred of the Jews a racial rather than simply a religious issue. The lamentable success of Marr's views is indicated by the adoption of the term by the virulently anti-Jewish racist political movements of the late nineteenth and early twentieth centuries, including, most notoriously, Hitler's National Socialists (Nazis).

GOD THE ULTIMATE

Judaism conceives of God as transcendent, above nature and the world. However, the deity is present in the world in the sense that God communicates with people through various media. The kabbalistic tradition known as *tzimtzum* ("self-limitation") holds that God, while remaining omniscient and omnipotent, has voluntarily relinquished some control over the world, bestowing free will on humanity in order to give it the chance to prove its own level of maturity.

As the creator, God is the ultimate reality behind all earthly existence, a god of history who endows history with a moral sense. The essence of God is goodness, but Judaism is not dualistic: that is, God is the creator of both good and evil. In addressing the issue of why evil and suffering exist in the world, theologians have employed the notion of *tzimtzum* to explain the temporary triumph of the human inclination to evil. But the enormity of the Holocaust has provoked a crisis in Jewish theology, with some thinkers questioning both the nature and even the existence of God.

Judaism emphasizes that humanity is forced to resort to limiting language and metaphors to characterize a God who is inherently beyond the capacity of words to describe. The best one can do is to list, discuss, and learn from God's attributes, the two most important of which are justice and mercy. These have been likened in some contemporary Jewish circles to the male and female aspects of God. Just as God must be prepared to reward and punish his children like a father, so too must the deity exhibit compassion to her children like a mother.

The God of Israel also has a name, which was in common usage during the biblical period. This is the "Tetragrammaton," the ineffable four-letter name of God, represented in Hebrew by the consonants YHWH (see illustration on p.15). In postbiblical Judaism, YHWH was considered too holy to be uttered, and substitutes were found to avoid having to speak it. The most common is *Adonai* ("my Lord"). In some Jewish circles, *Adonai* itself has become too holy to be pronounced except in prayer, and so other circumlocutions have come to be used, such as *Hashem* ("the Name"). Alternative ways of referring to God include recitations of divine attributes (such as "the Holy One" and "the Merciful One"). God's presence in the world is designated the *Shekhinah*, a feminine noun that has been the source of much Jewish mystical speculation regarding God's male and female aspects. The *Shekhinah* has also become an important concept in modern feminist theology.

In opposition to more rational ways of approaching the divine, there have long existed strong mystical currents in Judaism. The most influential of such movements has been Kabbalah (see p.32).

AN EVERLASTING COVENANT

The Bible speaks of different types of covenant (Hebrew *brit*, also spelled *berit* or *brith*) with God. One is the personal relationship between an individual and God, marked in males by the rite of circumcision (*brit milah*, "covenant of circumcision"). Another is the covenant between a people and God, which is symbolized by the pact entered into at Mount Sinai. The Sinaitic covenant between God and Israel is modeled on ancient Near Eastern treaties in which an overlord entered into a formal relationship with a vassal. In return for God's deliverance of the Israelites from bondage, they acknowledged the suzerainty of God by observing the divine commandments. The fulfillment of the commandments is hence viewed as Judaism's obligation to God, who is in turn obliged to care for the Jews through history. The breach of this mutual relationship by either party is considered an unjustifiable transgression.

The exclusive relationship between Israel and God is expressed in the Shema prayer, which has become the central Jewish confession of faith. It is so called from the first word of Deuteronomy 6.4: "Hear (*Shema*), O Israel, YHWH is our God, YHWH alone" (or, "YHWH is our God, YHWH is one"). In the expanded version of the prayer, this single verse is augmented with other verses from Deuteronomy and Numbers.

A mezuzah *and the handwritten scroll it contains with the words of the Shema prayer. The* mezuzah *is fixed to the doorposts of a Jewish home.*

REPRESENTATIONS OF THE SACRED

Unlike the deities of the pagan world, which were depicted in various animal and anthropomorphic forms, the God of Judaism is formless, invisible, and beyond the capacity of human beings to comprehend. Since its earliest days, Judaism has been concerned to emphasize this by avoiding artistic portrayals that might be confused with attempts to depict the deity. The prohibition is codified in the Second Commandment (Exodus 20.4–6, Deuteronomy 5.8–10).

The interpretation of the commandment has caused tensions between iconoclasts—those Jews who would ban representational art in general—and those who would permit it in almost any setting. During the late Roman and Byzantine periods, rabbis who would not have allowed iconography in their divine ritual worshipped in synagogues with beautiful mosaic floors (see p.18) and, at least at Dura-Europos in Syria, walls adorned with biblical scenes. Some mosaics even depicted such non-Jewish scenes as the Greek sun god Helios. But the Jewish context was considered to deprive such images of any original religious significance and they could thus serve as representations of the universal cycle of life.

Over the centuries, the pendulum has swung between the extremes. However, as the wealth of Jewish illustration throughout history has shown, Judaism has always had some form of artistic tradition, albeit an often circumscribed one.

Part of the "Bird's Head" Haggadah, produced in Germany ca. 1300CE. The artist depicts biblical characters with the heads of birds to avert any charge of trying to create a divine image.

MESSIANISM AND REDEMPTION

The messianic idea developed in Judaism as a response to national catastrophe, offering hope to a people whose circumstances were often precarious. The word "messiah" itself is a transcription of the Hebrew *mashiach*, "one who is anointed" with oil for a specific purpose by God. In the Bible, a variety of individuals are termed "messiahs" by virtue of being anointed, including kings, priests, prophets, and even non-Israelites. But the Bible does not link these figures with the later concept of *the* Messiah who would initiate the redemptive end of time, although passages have often been employed to support one or another messianic vision.

Other biblical texts, dating to the Babylonian exile and the postexilic periods, express the hope that Israel would once more live in freedom under the glorious rule of a member of the royal house of David. Some texts also mention the desire for a second Aaron to serve as high priest, or a second Moses to inspire the land again with his gift of prophecy.

By the late Second Temple period, these diverse hopes for the future had combined in various ways with aspects of apocalyptic thought. The result was the idea of an imminent messiah who would either personally save the Jews from oppression and usher in the rule of God, or would rule in glory after God had saved the Jews. As Herodian and Roman rule grew more oppressive, a number of messianic claimants arose, such as Simeon bar

The prophet Elijah on Mount Carmel, as described in 1 Kings 18. In the rabbinic period, it was often believed that Elijah's reappearance would herald the coming of the messiah at the end of time, an idea derived from Malachi: "I will send you the prophet Elijah before the great and terrible day of the Lord" (Mal. 3.23 in the Jewish Bible; Mal. 4.5 in the Christian Bible). This wall painting of ca. 245CE comes from the synagogue in the ancient city of Dura-Europos, Syria.

SHABBETAI ZVI

Most messianic movements were confined to a particular time and place, but one convulsed the whole of the Jewish world. In 1665, Shabbetai Zvi, or Tzvi (1626–76), a wandering mystic who was born at Smyrna in Turkey, appeared in the land of Israel, where he was proclaimed as the messiah by the visionary Nathan of Gaza.

Shabbetai was hailed throughout the Jewish world, so recently demoralized by the dreadful Cossack pogroms led by Bogdan Chmielnicki in 1648–9 in the Ukraine. Jews everywhere prepared for the coming kingdom of God, but within the same year Shabbetai had been jailed by the sultan and had converted to Islam rather than be executed. Yet he still retained followers who viewed his conversion as the necessary degradation of the messiah before his ultimate glorious triumph. However, for most Jews, Shabbetai illustrates the wisdom of the first-century Rabbi Yohanan ben Zakkai, who said that if you are about to plant a sapling when someone tells you the messiah is come, of course go out to greet the messiah—but plant the sapling first.

A contemporary Dutch engraving of the 17th-century "Mystical Messiah," Shabbetai Zvi.

Kokhba, who led the Jews in a failed anti-Roman revolt (the Second Jewish War, 132–135CE). Most rabbis rejected the claims made on his behalf; an exception was the great Akiva (see p.37). It is unclear whether Jesus of Nazareth considered himself to be the messiah, but enough of his followers did so to call him *christos* ("Christ"), the Greek for *mashiach* (see p.55).

Although the Dead Sea Scrolls already mention the idea of dual (priestly and royal) messiahs, it may have been in the aftermath of the Bar Kokhba revolt that the idea developed of two messiahs, one descended from the house of the patriarch Joseph and one from the house of David. The messiah descended from David, whose rule would signal the establishment of God's kingdom on earth, would be preceded by one descended from the patriarch Joseph, who would lead the forces of good against the forces of evil in a doomed struggle. His failure and death would be the prelude to God's intervention in history, when he would establish his rule under the second, Davidic, messiah.

One tradition claims that the messiah was created at the beginning of time and is waiting with God until the moment of redemption. According to another theory, a potential human messiah walks the earth in every generation. There is even a tradition that a leprous, begging messiah sits at the gates of Rome waiting for his moment in history. The great Jewish rationalist philosopher Maimonides (see p.37) rejected the idea of a messiah who would act outside the bounds of normal human history, and fought against the apocalypticists who would have the messiah usher in the end of time. Nevertheless, he formulated a belief in the coming of the messiah as one of his thirteen articles of Jewish faith.

THE LIVING LAW

The primary religious text of Judaism is the Torah, a word often translated as "law" but originally meaning "teaching" or "instruction." In its narrow sense, the Torah is the first five books of the Bible, also known as the Five Books of Moses and the Pentateuch. They include the biblical accounts of the origins of the world, the ancestors of Israel, the enslavement of the Israelites in Egypt and their liberation, the receipt of God's commandments at Mount Sinai, and the Israelite wanderings in the desert before their entry into the Promised Land. From the Torah, the rabbis of the talmudic age (ca. second–seventh centuries CE) distilled six hundred and thirteen commandments that form the building blocks of Jewish life and custom.

"Torah" is also often taken to refer to the whole Bible, which consists of three parts. Following the Pentateuch, the second section is referred to as the Prophets (Nevi'im) and contains both historical works and works of prophecy. Thirdly, there are the eleven books known as the Writings (Ketuvim), or Hagiographa, a miscellany of poetry, wisdom, prophecy, and history. Another designation for the Bible is *Tanakh*, an acronym derived from the initial letters of Torah, Nevi'im, and Ketuvim.

The tripartite division of the Bible reflects not only the order in which it was canonized, but also the relative importance of the texts in

A DIALOGUE BETWEEN THE AGES

In a traditional Jewish context, the Bible is not read on its own. For example, rabbinic Bibles (Miqra'ot Gedolot) juxtapose commentaries from different ages and countries, beginning with that of Rashi (Rabbi Solomon ben Isaac, 1040–1105CE; see p.37) from northern France, with the text of the Bible in Hebrew and Aramaic. The reader is thus invited to become a participant in the ancient and continuing discussion of the meaning of the biblical text. Such investigation aims not to arrive at a definitive interpretation, but rather to expand one's knowledge of the interpretative possibilities, in recognition that truth is always multilayered.

THE MISHNAH AND THE TALMUD

Faced with the loss of the Temple and its rituals in 70CE, Yohanan ben Zakkai (see pp.22–3) recognized that the key to the survival of Judaism lay in the transmission of Jewish learning and the transfer of the symbols of the Temple religion to other aspects of Jewish life. In his academy at Yavneh, and in others that followed it, the rabbis developed a system of law and custom through an intense discussion of Jewish tradition and its adaptation to changing circumstances. These rabbinic decisions, or "oral law," covering all aspects of religious and secular life, were codified ca. 200CE by Rabbi Judah the Prince in the Mishnah ("That Which Is Taught"), which is divided into six "orders" and subdivided into sixty-three "tractates."

The Mishnah itself became the basis for further discussion in the various Jewish communities. The wide-ranging rabbinic debates on the Mishnah, including both majority and minority opinions, were themselves compiled in the Talmud of Jerusalem (ca. 400CE) and the Talmud of Babylon (ca. 500CE). The Babylonian Talmud became the standard collection of Jewish traditions. The two Talmuds use the same Mishnah text, but differ in their record of the debates, or Gemara. The Talmud ("Study") has attained the status of a holy text, of equal stature in the rabbinic view, to the Bible. A whole literature of additions (Tosafot), commentaries, and supercommentaries has continued down to the modern era.

Following the injunction in the tractate *Pirke Avot* ("Sayings of the Fathers") to "build a hedge [or fence] around the Torah," the rabbis attempted to safeguard it with additional regulations and customs. In theory it was considered less serious to violate one of the "hedges" than one of the primary six hundred and thirteen commandments of the Torah proper. In practice, the immediacy of the newer regulation often ensured that it was more honored.

Jewish tradition. The Pentateuch, the Torah proper, has pride of place both as the ultimate source of Jewish beliefs and practices and as an object of veneration. Each community's Torah scrolls are housed in the synagogue in a special niche or ark in one wall, toward which worshippers pray, traditionally in the direction of Jerusalem. A different portion, or *parashah*, of the Torah scroll is recited in the synagogue each week, so that the whole Scripture is read out in either an annual or a triennial cycle. After the *parashah*, a shorter passage from the Prophets is read as a complement. The synagogue reading from the Scriptures has given rise to another Hebrew term for the Bible, Miqra' ("That which is read [aloud]"), a direct cognate of the Arabic Qur'an.

The destruction of the First Temple in Jerusalem in 586BCE and of the Second Temple in 70CE, with their accompanying losses of national identity, forced the Jews in each instance to compile their traditions in written form in order to ensure their survival. This led in the first case to the redaction of large portions of the Torah and Prophets, and in the second to the compilation of the oral traditions which were eventually to find their way into the Mishnah and hence the Talmud (see box, opposite).

Rabbinic tradition places the so-called "oral Torah," the talmudic legacy, on the same level as the written Torah. Both are said to have been divinely given to Moses at Mount Sinai. The written Torah was revealed to all of Israel. The oral Torah was handed down by a circle of initiates until its compilation in writing many centuries later by the rabbis. Thus "Torah" can refer to both the biblical and the talmudic traditions and, in its widest sense, to the totality of Jewish law and custom. Because it was in book form, Jews could carry this "portable homeland" wherever they went.

In formulating the belief that the oral Torah was revealed at Mount Sinai at the same time as the written Torah, the rabbis of the talmudic age established the important and influential principle that the development of Jewish law and tradition was as much a part of the revealed message as the Torah itself. The centrality of this tenet is illustrated most graphically in the story in which Moses is said to attend the academy of the great first-century CE Rabbi Akiva (see p.37). Moses is unable to understand any part of the discussion until a student bases his argument on the Torah proper, the books written by Moses himself. It is then that Moses comprehends

THE BOOKS OF THE BIBLE

The Torah (Pentateuch)

• Genesis • Exodus • Leviticus • Numbers • Deuteronomy

The Prophets (Nevi'im)

• Joshua • Judges • Samuel • Kings • Isaiah • Jeremiah • Ezekiel • "The Twelve Minor Prophets" (Hosea, Joel, Amos, Obadiah, Jonah, Micah, Nahum, Habakkuk, Zephaniah, Haggai, Zechariah, Malachi)

The Writings (Ketuvim)

• Psalms • Proverbs • Job • Song of Songs • Ruth • Lamentations • Ecclesiastes • Esther • Daniel • Ezra-Nehemiah • Chronicles

A Torah scroll in its decorated case, produced for a Jewish community in Iraq in the 19th century CE.

At the Western Wall (see p.41), a 13-year-old Israeli boy makes his first public reading from the Torah as part of his bar mitzvah *ceremony to mark his coming of age.*

THE *ZOHAR* AND KABBALAH

A collection of late thirteenth-century Aramaic writings called the *Zohar* ("Illumination") is the foundational text of Kabbalah, Judaism's most influential mystical movement. The *Zohar* was most likely written by the Spanish mystic Moses de León (died 1305), who claimed to have compiled it from the writings of a celebrated rabbi of the second century CE, Simeon bar Yohai.

In its attempt to penetrate the mystery of the deity, Kabbalah drew on the *Zohar* to develop a complex concept of God as consisting of an unknowable central mystery (the *Ein Sof*) and ten aspects (*Sefirot*). To this was attached an intricate symbolism, the study of which led the initiate closer to understanding ultimate truth.

The Enlightenment and the rise of rationalism decreased the influence of the *Zohar*. However, there has been a rise in Jewish mystical speculation in recent years among ultra-orthodox and Hasidic Jews, as well as among Jews influenced by New Age and millennial thought or otherwise engaged in the modern quest for spirituality.

that the tradition he passed on to Israel is not monolithic and static, but subject to change and modification over time.

Many of the works of religious interpretation subsequent to the Torah and the Talmud have acquired semicanonical status in Judaism. One of the earliest such texts is actually a rendering of the Bible into Aramaic, called the Targum ("Translation").

Traditional Jewish interpretation is usually in accordance with the scholarly method known as *midrash* ("enquiry," "investigation"), the examination of a biblical text in order to derive either legal insights (*midrash halakhah*) or nonlegal ones (*midrash aggadah*). The *midrash aggadah* has been the more beloved and generally accessible. The text of the Talmud contains both of these approaches to interpretation, and the midrashic method is still employed today in reworking the tradition for a new age.

Over the centuries, the exposition of the legal aspects of Jewish tradition has spawned an extensive commentary literature, adding supercommentaries to commentaries on the traditional texts. There have also been attempts to codify Jewish legal traditions. Of these law codes the most famous and influential were the *Mishneh Torah* ("Repetition of the Torah") of Maimonides (see p.37) and the *Shulhan Arukh* ("Set Table") of Joseph Caro (1488–1575). These organize Jewish practice by subject-matter and hence can be used as reference tools. In effect they cover all aspects of life from a Jewish perspective.

Alongside these comprehensive attempts to present the totality of Jewish practice, collections were made of answers (*responsa*) given by rabbis to questions that arose from people's daily lives as Jews. This literature continues to be augmented today, most poignantly with the publication of *responsa* written during the Holocaust and reflecting the desire of Jews to continue to follow a Jewish way of life, even under extreme duress.

A passage in the Talmud concludes that the study of the Torah is equal in merit to all other ethical activities, because it is the gateway that leads to them all. This preoccupation with the study and practice of the Torah in all its aspects has ensured the continued vitality and survival of Judaism over the course of the millennia.

THE SIDDUR AND THE HAGGADAH

Two books stand out from all others owing to their importance in the context of Jewish life and ritual. The first is the Siddur, or prayerbook. There are many versions of the Siddur for daily, Sabbath, or holiday prayers. There are also differences between Ashkenazi and Sephardi versions, as well as between those of the Orthodox, Conservative, and Reform movements. However, they all share a certain basic structure and liturgy.

After the preliminary prayers, which serve to set the spiritual tone for what follows, comes the first important part of the service. This section revolves around the Shema prayer (Deuteronomy 6.4), the central Jewish confession of faith in the one God (see p.26), beginning with a call to worship. God is then praised as the creator. God's love for Israel and Israel's acceptance of the Torah provide the background for the hope in an eventual redemption. The next part of the service is known as the Amidah ("Standing"), since it is customary to stand while reciting this prayer. It consists in its weekday version of nineteen benedictions, thanking God for providing for both the individual and the community. The service ends with the Aleinu, a prayer which looks forward to a time when the world will be united in belief in one God, and the mourners' recitation of the Kaddish, a prayer extolling God, which also serves as the divider between the other parts of the service.

The second book is the Haggadah, the "Recounting" of the story of the Exodus of the Israelites under Moses from Egypt. The book serves as the basis of the family's ceremonial Passover meal (Seder), during which God's great act of liberation is recited and relived from generation to generation.

The Haggadah intersperses the biblical narrative with rabbinic interpretation and *midrash* (see main text). It is designed to be didactic and to hold the interest of children; it thus plays a major part in the formation of their Jewish identity.

An illuminated page from the Feibush Haggadah produced in Germany ca. 1470CE. It is one of the most richly decorated haggadahs to survive from this period, with illustrations by the artist Joel ben Shimon.

THE TORAH SCROLL AND SCRIBE

The Sefer Torah (Torah Scroll) is the most sacred object in Judaism. Each letter of the scroll must be painstakingly handwritten by a *sofer* (scribe), such as the Yemenite shown here, who will have trained for around seven years. The Torah is written on parchment made from the skin of a *kosher* animal and takes about a year to complete.

After being thoroughly checked by the *sofer* and other experts, an Ashkenazi scroll is covered ("dressed") in an embroidered protective "mantle," which is often richly decorated, especially with crowns. Silver finials, or *rimmonim* (Hebrew, "pomegranates") may also be placed over the scroll handles. In the Sephardic community, Torah scrolls are encased in decorated wooden or metal cylinders lined with velvet (see, for example, illustration on p.24).

The Torah Scroll remains dressed at all times when not in use for readings. In reciting from the scroll, the reader may follow the text with a pointer, or *yad* (Hebrew, "hand"), to avoid touching the scriptures. The *yad* is often made of silver, but can also be made of ivory or wood. It is usually fifteen to twenty centimeters (six to eight inches) long with, at one end, a miniature hand pointing a finger.

If even a single letter is erased over time, the scroll becomes unsuitable for use until a *sofer* has restored the letter. A scroll that has finally become too worn for restoration is taken to a Jewish cemetery for burial.

LAWGIVERS, SCHOLARS, AND FOUNDERS

In Judaism, although human beings may aspire to holiness through their actions, the veneration of mortals is generally avoided. Figures from the past are objects of emulation, but not adoration: the division between the divine and the human realms remains. There is no apotheosis in Judaism.

Two individuals tower above all others in Jewish tradition: Moses (see box, below) and King David, the first as lawgiver, prophet, and exemplary human being, and the second as political leader, poet, and flawed human upon whom God nevertheless looked with favor. The legendary golden age

Moses receiving the Ten Commandments on Mount Sinai. An illustration to the 14th-century Sarajevo Haggadah, which was produced for Jews in Muslim Spain.

MOSES

Although no firm historical statements can be made regarding the life and person of Moses, he is the central figure of the Pentateuch narrative and of subsequent Judaism. In the Bible, it is Moses whom God chooses to free the Israelites from Egyptian bondage and to lead them through the desert to the promised land. Through him the divine covenant with Israel was sealed and the commandments transmitted. Thus Moses is the key foundational figure of Judaism and the archetypal Jew. He is the only human with whom God communicated face to face and the first and greatest of the prophets. In rabbinic times, Moses became *Moshe Rabbenu*, "Moses our teacher," the prototypical rabbi. He also serves as the ideal of the compassionate leader.

Moses is perhaps best known in his function as lawgiver. However, he was not the law*maker*—he was the instrument through whom the commandments were given to Israel by God, not their actual author. Nonetheless, it was to the authority of Moses that later rabbinic Judaism appealed in its interpretation of Jewish tradition. According to the rabbis, at Mount Sinai Moses received not only the traditions written in the Torah, but also the oral traditions first recorded during the rabbinic age (see p.31). In this manner, Moses becomes the first link in the chain of tradition leading to the rabbis.

In spite of the centrality of Moses in Judaism, he always remained a human being. It was perhaps to avoid even the possibility of deification that the Bible emphasizes that the place of his burial is unknown (Deuteronomy 34.6) and hence cannot be an object of pilgrimage and veneration.

of David and his son Solomon is a great source of inspiration for Jews, and it is closely bound up with messianic hopes (see pp.28–9).

Among other biblical figures, Ezra is viewed as the second lawgiver. In the period following the Babylonian exile, he promulgated the Torah as the law of the land, and through him God bestowed on the people of Israel the blessing of a special relationship in service to the Divine.

The prototypical rabbinic Jew was Hillel (first century BCE), the exemplar of Jewish learning infused with a deep humanity and humility. Hillel strove for the betterment of the world (*tikkun olam*). The Talmud relates that when a potential convert asked to be taught the whole of the Torah, Hillel replied: "What is hateful to you, do not do to anyone else. The rest is commentary. Go and study." Rabbi Akiva (ca. 50–135CE), perhaps the greatest scholar of the rabbinic period, was an illiterate shepherd until the age of forty. A follower of the messianic claimant Simeon bar Kokhba (see p.29), Akiva was killed by the Romans, and died uttering the words of the central Jewish confession of faith, the Shema prayer (see p.26), establishing a model of martyrdom for Jews throughout the ages.

The Talmud mentions one woman, Beruriah (second century CE), whose learning equaled that of any man. Many tales are told of her wisdom and humanity, and she has inspired generations of Jewish women seeking access to the learning that has traditionally been a male preserve. Her husband, Rabbi Meir, was another famous teacher.

The two outstanding sages of the Middle Ages are "Rashi" and "Rambam," acronyms respectively of Rabbi Shlomo Yitzhaki (Solomon ben Isaac, 1040–1105) and Rabbi Moses ben Maimon (or Maimonides, 1135–1204). Rashi spent most of his life in his native Troyes in France, but he studied in Germany and represents the last flowering of Rhineland Jewry before its decimation in the First Crusade. His great achievement lay in making Jewish learning accessible to all through his commentaries on the Bible and the Talmud. Unusually, he passed his knowledge on to his daughters. Maimonides, a brilliant polymath and physician to the sultan of Egypt, is best known for the *Mishneh Torah*, an attempt to codify Jewish law and make it accessible to all (see p.32), and *The Guide for the Perplexed*, a rationalist philosophical defense of the Jewish faith that has had an influence far beyond the confines of Judaism.

Moses Mendelssohn (1729–86) was arguably the first modern Jew. A brilliant scholar and philosopher, he was the darling of the non-Jewish German intelligentsia at a time when Jews were beginning to break through the social barriers that made them second-class citizens. As a driving force behind the Haskalah (the "Jewish Enlightenment"), Mendelssohn sought to meld general European Enlightenment ideals with Judaism and was the first to confront a question that has occupied Judaism ever since: how to retain one's identity as a Jew, yet be open and receptive to modernity.

HERZL AND ZIONISM

The most influential modern Jewish intellectual and political movement draws on the age-old hope for a restoration of the people in the land of Israel, on messianism (see pp.28–9), and on modern nationalism. Theodor Herzl (1860–1904), an Austrian Jewish journalist, became convinced that the only solution to the "Jewish question" lay in the Jews again becoming a nation-state. In 1897 he organized the first Zionist Congress in Basel, Switzerland, predicting that within fifty years his dream would be realized.

Herzl's claim seemed ludicrous, but the idea took root and many Jews settled in Palestine when it was governed by the British (1918–48). In 1947 the United Nations voted to partition the land into separate Jewish and Arab states, and on May 14, 1948, the eve of the British departure, the State of Israel was declared. In 1949 the remains of Herzl, who is viewed as the spiritual founder of modern Israel, were brought from Vienna and reburied in Jerusalem.

A late 14th-century Italian manuscript of the Mishneh Torah *by Maimonides, of whom it is said "from Moses to Moses there was none like Moses."*

THE NOAHIDE LAWS

Rabbinic theology asserts that any righteous person, Jew or gentile, can attain the world to come. While Jews are expected to live according to the 613 commandments, the ethical system of gentiles must accord with the seven "Noahide laws," which God set for Noah after the legendary Flood. These ban idolatry, blasphemy, murder, sexual crimes, theft, and cruelty to animals; and recommend the building of courts of law.

In general, Judaism focuses on how to live in this world, not how to prepare for another level of existence, and the nature of the afterlife has never played a central role in Jewish theology, life, or ritual.

As the font of the Jewish way of living, the Torah occupies the place of honor in the synagogue in the Torah niche, or ark. This 17th-century ark is from Kraków, Poland.

THE WAY OF ISRAEL

In Judaism, the belief in one God is intimately tied in with the ethical principles that regulate human life. An ethical life is both a gesture of devotion to God's will and an imitation of the divine. Since God is holy and just, Jews must emulate God in these and all other aspects of the divine being. Forming the basis of an ethical life are the six hundred and thirteen commandments (*mitzvot*) that the rabbis distilled from the Pentateuch or Torah proper (see pp.30–31). These commandments, together with the enormous body of traditions based upon them, are known as the *halakhah*, literally "walk"—that is, the way in which Israel is to walk in this world.

In the Talmud tractate Pirke Avot ("Ethics of the Fathers"), the teacher Simon the Just claims that the world is founded upon Torah (the commandments and their performance), divine service (worship and praise of God), and acts of loving-kindness (good deeds toward one's fellow human beings). In the same work, Simon ben Gamliel puts it more abstractly when he claims that the world exists because of truth, justice, and peace. In neither case is the potential reward for ethical behavior the factor that motivates a life of goodness: one does good deeds for their own sake, because they are divinely ordained *mitzvot*. The performance of the *mitzvot*, especially in adversity, is seen as the sanctification of God's name (*kiddush Hashem*), while breaching them besmirches it (*hillul Hashem*).

Providing for the poor, weak, and disadvantaged thus takes on a religious significance, and the care of others has played a large part in the development of a Jewish ethic. Jewish communities have traditionally had highly organized systems of social welfare, to which all have been required to contribute according to their ability. Another factor is the concept of *tikkun olam* ("betterment of the world"), the desire to leave the world a better place than when one entered it. All these elements help to explain why Jews have often been at the forefront of the struggle for justice and social change in the modern world.

Judaism does not subscribe to the doctrine of original sin, but believes each human being to be born with the potential for doing both good and evil. The individual has to bear the responsibility for his or her actions and life becomes a struggle between the inclination to good (*yetzer ha-tov*) and the inclination to evil (*yetzer ha-ra*). One who struggles with moral ambiguity and triumphs over temptation is—according to one view—more highly regarded than one who has led a completely blameless life. Free will is an important concept in Judaism. Unlike an animal, a human being is able to choose between right or wrong. Nonetheless, God is omniscient and, hence, knows which course a person will choose.

There are two categories of ethical injunctions in Judaism: those that pertain to the relationship between humanity and God, and those that concern the relationships between human beings. On Yom Kippur, the Day of Repentance, or Atonement, the community confesses its communal transgressions against God who then forgives the community. However, atonement is not complete unless each individual has asked for forgiveness from those people whom he or she may have harmed in the past year. God cannot forgive transgressions which take place between human beings, only those which are directed against God.

KASHRUT

The Jewish dietary laws are collectively known as *kashrut*, from the Hebrew *kasher* ("suitable," "fit")—or *kosher* in the Ashkenazi/Yiddish pronunciation. *Kashrut* is little understood by outsiders, but it sheds light on three important areas of Jewish thought. To begin with, the dietary laws illustrate the nonrationality of Jewish observance. There have been apologetic attempts to imbue *kashrut* laws with a rational and scientific basis, but this ignores the basic premise behind the observance of all commandments: submission to the will of God. The commandments represent God's demands on the Jewish people, in return for God's care. As such the individual commandments require no rational foundation.

Second, the development of the laws of *kashrut* illuminates the rabbinic desire "to build a hedge around the Torah" (Pirke Avot). In order to safeguard the central teachings of the Torah, the rabbis added further regulations around the injunctions of the Pentateuch. For example, the commandment "you shall not boil a kid in its mother's milk" is clearly of great importance, since it alone, of all the Torah's injunctions, appears three times (Exodus 23.19, 34.26; Deuteronomy 14.21). Whatever it meant in its original context, the rabbis sought to prevent its transgression by extrapolating a number of additional regulations. Thus they disallowed the eating of milk and meat dishes together, required separate vessels for milk and meat, and stipulated that one must wait for a time after eating meat before consuming milk.

Third, the *kashrut* laws are an expression of the sanctity of all life. In the Jewish view, primeval humans were vegetarians, and the consumption of meat is a concession made by God after the Flood. But not all animals can be consumed, and those that are must be treated in a certain way. *Kosher* birds and mammals must be drained of all blood, since blood is considered the force of life and inappropriate for human consumption. Animals must be killed as quickly and painlessly as possible—a creature that suffers unduly is not *kosher*. Cruelty to animals in general violates basic Jewish ethical belief, hence Judaism outlaws hunting.

A kosher butcher's shop in London, England, which has the largest urban Jewish population in Europe after Paris, France.

A modern reconstruction of the central sanctuary of Herod's Temple, part of a scale model at Jerusalem's Holyland Hotel depicting the city as it may have appeared in the 1st century CE.

SANCTUARIES FOR A NATION

Judaism is at the same time community-oriented and family-oriented. In the modern world, this is reflected in two major types of sacred space: the synagogue and the home. In a sense, the precursor to both was the Temple of Jerusalem, the central shrine of Judaism in ancient times, which stood on a vast raised platform (the Temple Mount or Haram esh-Sharif), where the Muslim Dome of the Rock and al-Aqsa mosque stand today (see p.116). The Bible is the only witness to the First Temple, which was erected by King Solomon and stood from ca. 950–586BCE. It may have begun as a chapel attached to the royal palace, which was the case with a number of similar structures in other Near Eastern cultures.

Solomon's Temple was destroyed by the Babylonians, but it was rebuilt under the Persians and rededicated in 515BCE. This Second Temple was most likely an unimposing structure until King Herod the Great of Judea (37–4BCE) refurbished it on a grand scale. Its glory was short-lived, because it was destroyed in 70CE by the Romans. Nothing of the

THE LAND OF ISRAEL

According to the Bible, God's blessing for Abraham consisted of a twofold promise of descendants and of land. The Jewish people view themselves as the fulfillment of the first promise; the second is fulfilled by the people of Israel dwelling in the land of Israel. It is perhaps a uniquely Jewish paradox that a religion to which a person born anywhere in the world can belong is yet intimately bound to one small territory.

According to Jewish belief, just as there were levels of holiness in the layout of the Temple (see main text), there are also levels of geographical holiness. Israel is referred to as the Holy Land, the capital of which is Jerusalem, the Holy City. It is the navel of the world (Ezekiel 5.5, 38.12), where the divine and the human spheres are in closer contact than anywhere else. The land of Israel is the axis around which all of Jewish life revolves. The Jewish calendar (see p.45), which determines observance throughout the world, is attuned solely to the change of seasons as they occur in Israel. For centuries, the religious life of every Jew was lived in remembrance of the passage of time in a land that was often very far away.

Since the destruction of the First Temple, a sizable portion of the Jewish people has lived more or less permanently in exile. There were times during which the communities of the Diaspora, living outside the Holy Land, were the leaders in Jewish life, and times during which the Jewish community of Israel was the most important. The give and take between Israel and the Diaspora has been one of the creative tensions underlying the development of Judaism.

Yet, no matter how established they have been in the lands of their dispersion, or how loyal they may have been to the countries in which they have dwelt, the attachment to the land of Israel and the hope for a restoration to it in the messianic age (see pp.28–9) have played a central role in the identity and theology of Jews the world over. The birth of the modern state of Israel so soon after the Holocaust, and the subsequent integration into the state of Jewish refugees from all over the world, has been reckoned as one of the great miracles of Jewish history. For some, the founding of a Jewish state nearly two millennia after the end of the last one is a harbinger of the messianic age (*athalta d'geulah*).

Temple itself remains today, although part of the great platform on which it stood, extended by Herod and supported by massive retaining walls, can still be seen. The surviving Herodian masonry includes the Western Wall, the holiest site in Judaism (see sidebar, right).

The Temple precincts clearly had areas of increasing holiness and more limited access the closer one came to the central sanctuary. In Herodian times, these included the Court of the Gentiles, beyond which non-Jews could not go, then the Court of Women, the Court of the Israelites (that is, male Jews only), and the Court of the Priests. The Temple itself had a forecourt, a main hall, and finally an inner sanctum (the Holy of Holies) to which the high priest alone had access, on one day of the year (Yom Kippur, the Day of Repentance, or Atonement; see p.46). The Temple was neither a democratic nor an egalitarian institution.

The origins of the synagogue are uncertain. The Jews must have developed some way of continuing their religious and communal life in exile following the destruction of the First Temple in the sixth century BCE. However, the first archaeologically attested synagogues date from about half a millennium later, toward the end of the Second Temple period. The word "synagogue" itself, derived from a Greek rendering of the Hebrew *bet keneset* ("gathering place") indicates its communal function. Thus,

THE WESTERN WALL

After the destruction of the Temple, its ruins retained their holiness, even after all traces of them had been removed by subsequent building activity. For many centuries, Jews were denied access to the Temple Mount variously by the Romans, Christians, and Muslims, and they shifted their devotion to the extant section of the western retaining wall. The Jewish religious authorities also declared the Temple Mount off-limits, for fear that someone might tread inadvertently where the Holy of Holies had once stood. The Western, or "Wailing," Wall thus became the holiest site in Judaism.

An orthodox Jew prays at the Western Wall. Worshippers frequently place handwritten prayers in the gaps between the massive Herodian stones.

PLACES OF PILGRIMAGE

Although Judaism officially eschews personality cults, various sites have been identified as the graves of biblical figures and become objects of pilgrimage. These include the supposed tombs of the patriarchs and matriarchs at Hebron; of Rachel near Bethlehem; of David and Absalom in Jerusalem; and many others (but not Moses—see p.36). The tombs of famous rabbis and other spiritual leaders have also become sites of veneration, as have places associated with the glories or agonies of Jewish history.

However, the most popular pilgrimage destination is the Western Wall, Judaism's holiest site (see p.41).

while the Second Temple was still standing, the synagogue already existed as an identifiable and separate institution. After 70CE, with the rise and triumph of rabbinic Judaism, which had its power base in the synagogue, it can be argued that the Temple became superfluous to the continuing existence of Judaism, in spite of never-ending Jewish hopes for its rebuilding.

The loss of the Temple resulted in an expansion of the role of the synagogue from a communal center and house of study to an establishment for religious services previously provided by the Temple. Much of the Temple ritual centered on sacrifices, which in Jewish law could be offered at no other place. In the synagogue, therefore, sacrifices were replaced by further study and communal divine services. This was to have a profound effect on the development of rabbinic Judaism, which tried to keep the memory of the Temple rituals alive in the eventuality that the sanctuary would be restored, but also continued the process of reinterpreting those rituals and establishing the synagogue as an independent entity. Through the institution of the synagogue, rabbinic Judaism brought about the empowerment of the individual Jew. In the Jewish view this finally led to the realization of the biblical description of Israel as "a priestly kingdom and a holy nation" (Exodus 19.6).

While the Temple and its site are inherently holy for Judaism, it is not

The Torah ark in the 13th-century Altneu Synagogue in Prague, a great center of Jewish learning in the Middle Ages. The ark takes the place of the Holy of Holies in the ancient Temple, in which the Ark of the Covenant, containing the Ten Commandments, was deposited in the period of the First Temple (ca. 960–586BCE). The Torah ark is the feature of a synagogue most likely to be elaborately decorated (see also illustration, p.38).

a synagogue itself that is sacred, but the actions performed there and the objects deposited within its walls (the Torah scrolls, Judaism's most precious objects, and the prayerbooks; see pp.30–34). These are what make a synagogue the "small sanctuary" (Ezekiel 11.16) of Israel in exile, without a Temple. Synagogues are traditionally oriented toward Jerusalem. On the interior of the wall facing the Holy City is a niche or "ark" housing the Torah scrolls. Prominent in Orthodox synagogues is the separate seating area for women, often behind a curtain or in a balconied gallery.

With the redefinition and reapplication of Temple ritual in rabbinic Judaism, the Jewish home has also become a place for the sacred. Indicating this is the *mezuzah*, a small box containing a parchment scroll affixed to the doorposts of Jewish homes (see p.26). The *mezuzah* contains the words of the central confession of faith, the Shema prayer (Deuteronomy 6.4) and the first two of its associated blessings. It serves to show that when one crosses the threshold of the home, one is entering a space devoted to God and to a certain code of ethics. Although the rabbis of the talmudic age instituted synagogue worship to correspond to the schedule of sacrifices in the Temple, at home the sacrificial altar has been replaced by the table. In a domestic setting, eating assumes a ritual connotation and becomes for Jews a holy act of divine service of the utmost importance.

SYMBOLISM

A place of holiness to Jews may contain any of a number of significant Jewish symbols. For many, the first that comes to mind is the six-pointed "Star of David" (*Magen David*). Yet this is a relatively modern symbol, having been first employed as such in late medieval Prague. Mosaic synagogue floors from the Roman and Byzantine periods give us a glimpse of what the Jews of the formative rabbinic age viewed as their characteristic symbols. Pride of place belongs to the seven-branched candelabrum (*menorah*), which is also depicted in a famous relief on the Arch of Titus in Rome that shows objects looted from the Temple in 70CE (see illustration, p.22). This is still a clearly recognizable Jewish symbol, as in many quarters is the ram's horn trumpet (*shofar*).

Less familiar in modern times are the branches of palm (*lulav*) and citron fruit (*etrog*), which are used on the holiday of Sukkot (or Tabernacles; see p.46). An incense shovel is another common symbol, a reminder that the burning of incense was central in the rites of the Temple, which itself is depicted on ancient synagogue floors.

A menorah, *or seven-armed candelabrum, depicted in an illuminated Hebrew Bible produced in Portugal ca. 1300CE. A great* menorah *was a prominent feature of the furnishings of the ancient Temple (see p.22).*

THE RHYTHM OF LIFE

A girl recites the Haftarah (a reading from the Prophets) on the occasion of becoming a bat mitzvah *("daughter of the commandment"), at which she takes on all the obligations of Jewish adulthood. For girls this key rite of passage takes place at the age of either 12 or 13, for boys at 13 (see box, opposite).*

A traditional Jewish life is structured to express both ethical and religious concerns and a sense of connection to Jewish historical experience. It achieves this through rituals attuned to daily, weekly, monthly, and yearly cycles, as well as to the rhythm of key life-cycle events.

The individual's relationship with God and thankfulness for the divine gift of life are predominant in daily ritual. Jews are enjoined to pray three times a day, each act of prayer corresponding to one of the three daily sacrifices that took place in the ancient Temple. A sense of community is important in the individual's daily worship, and certain prayers may be recited only in the presence of a quorum (*minyan*), traditionally of ten male adults (aged thirteen or over). Great emphasis is laid upon personal hygiene as a reflection of divine perfection and purity. There are blessings for practically any situation that arises in the course of a day, thereby imbuing even the most mundane of tasks with holiness.

THE SABBATH

The scholar Ahad Ha-Am (1856–1927) said: "More than Israel has kept the Sabbath, the Sabbath has kept Israel." The observance of a universal day of prayer, study, and rest every seventh day has served to bind the Jewish people since ancient times, and already features in the first account of Creation in the Bible as part of the divine cosmic order (Genesis 2.2–3).

In accordance with the traditional Jewish reckoning of days as beginning and ending in the evening, the Sabbath (Hebrew *Shabbat*) lasts from sundown on Friday until nightfall on Saturday. Candles are lit at both the beginning and end of the Sabbath to mark the division between the mundane work week and the holy suspension of worldly time. Central to the Saturday morning synagogue liturgy is the reading of the *parashah*, the portion of the Torah assigned to that week, together with a complementary passage from the prophetic writings.

The rabbis of the talmudic age listed thirty-nine types of work forbidden on the Sabbath, deducing them from the list of activities involved in building the ancient Temple of Jerusalem. How to interpret these prohibitions of antiquity in the light of changing circumstances has been a source of inner Jewish contention over the centuries.

In ancient times in the land of Israel, weekly portions of the Torah (see p.31) were read in a cycle lasting three years, but today the Babylonian tradition of reading the whole Torah in a yearly cycle is the norm. On the Sabbath (see sidebar, opposite), the week's portion is read and studied in its entirety. It is also read in part on Mondays and Thursdays—the market days of ancient Israel, when people would be likely to congregate in large groups.

Although Nisan, the first month of the Jewish calendar, falls in the spring (March/April), the Jewish New Year (Rosh Hashanah) is not celebrated until the seventh month (Tishri, September/October). This is a result of the variation in ancient times between a year that started with the first spring harvest and one that began at the end of the agricultural

THE CALENDAR

The ancient Jewish calendar is still used in a religious context. Its starting point is the Creation, as calculated from the Bible: thus 1999CE corresponds to the Jewish year 5759–60. The annual calendar combines solar and lunar reckoning. Months are calculated by the moon, and many holidays fall on the full moon. Seven times in every nineteen-year cycle, a month is added to the year so that holidays continue to fall in the correct season.

RITES OF PASSAGE

In Judaism, great emphasis is placed on key stages of the individual's life-cycle and on their commemoration in a Jewish manner. From birth to death, there is a ritual for everything.

At the age of eight days, a male child enters into the Jewish community, and partakes of its covenant with God, by virtue of his ritual circumcision (*brit milah*, "covenant of circumcision"), during which he receives his name. A girl is traditionally welcomed into the Jewish people and given her name at a Sabbath service, but in recent times some Jews have developed ceremonies for celebrating the birth of a daughter that are intended to be more analogous to the *brit milah*. These are called *simhat bat* ("rejoicing in a daughter") or *brit bat* ("daughter's covenant").

Since the Middle Ages, a boy's attainment of religious maturity has been celebrated in the *bar mitzvah* ("son of the covenant") ceremony, at which the thirteen-year-old is called up to read from the Torah for the first time. Liberal Jews also accord this honor to girls in the equivalent ceremony of *bat mitzvah* ("daughter of the covenant").

A marriage ceremony has three main parts. First is the signing of a legally binding marriage contract (*ketubbah*), traditionally written in Aramaic. Second is the ring ceremony, or *huppah*, which takes its name from the portable marriage canopy used in the ceremony. The *huppah* is often, but not necessarily, held in the synagogue. The last stage is *yihud*, when the couple are left alone—traditionally to consummate the marriage, although today it is more often a time for a welcome breathing space in the course of a hectic day.

*An 18th-century marriage contract (*ketubbah*) from Venice. The* ketubbah *is often colorfully illustrated and found on prominent display in the home.*

A writ of divorce (*get*) must be agreed by both partners. In traditional Judaism, only a man may issue a *get*, but a woman may petition a Jewish court in order to compel her husband to do so.

It is desirable to die uttering the Shema prayer, Judaism's central confession of faith (see p.26). A week of intense grieving (*shivah*) follows the funeral, which takes place ideally within a day of death. The bereaved is then eased back into normal life during a month (*sheloshim*) of somewhat less intense mourning. The transition is complete after another ten months in mourning. The deceased is remembered on the anniversary of his or her death (*yahrzeit*). At all of these times, the traditional mourning prayer, the Kaddish ("Sanctification"), in praise of God, is recited.

Lighting the Hannukah candelabrum. For Hannukah there is a special menorah *with 9 candles—one for each day of the holiday and a 9th with which to light the others.*

year. Rosh Hashanah celebrates the annual renewal of God's creative act at the moment the cycle comes full circle. The New Year ushers in a ten-day period of reflection and introspection known as the "Days of Awe" (Yamim Noraim). This is a solemn time devoted to setting one's accounts in order with one's fellow human beings. It is believed that during this period God determines everyone's fate for the coming year. The climax of this period is Yom Kippur (see sidebar, below).

Beginning on the fifteenth day of Tishri is the weeklong celebration of Sukkot (the Feast of Tabernacles), the first of the three annual "pilgrimage festivals" (so called because in ancient times Jewish men were called upon to visit the Temple in Jerusalem on these occasions). Originally a commemoration of the end of the harvest season, it has been given an added significance in Judaism. The temporary shelters or booths (*sukkot*, singular *sukkah*) inhabited by the ancient farmers during the harvest season have been reinterpreted to represent the huts in which the Israelites dwelt during their forty years of wandering in the desert before reaching the promised land. During Sukkot it is traditional to eat or—if the climate permits—to sleep in these booths, thereby reliving the biblical past and commemorating the fragility of human existence.

At the end of Sukkot comes a double holiday. First is Shemini Atzeret ("Eighth Day of Assembly"), a biblical observance of uncertain significance. Next is Simhat Torah ("Rejoicing in the Torah"), on which the annual cycle of weekly Torah readings is completed and recommenced with the celebratory reading of Deuteronomy 34 and Genesis 1. The reading is preceded by seven rounds of whirling and dancing joyfully with the community's Torah scrolls.

The eight-day midwinter festival of Hannukah, or Chanukah ("Rededication"), is one of the few premodern holidays that is not of biblical origin. It commemorates the victory of the Jews over the Greek rulers of Syria and the rededication in 164BCE of the Temple in Jerusalem (see p.21). In origin the festival was probably a late commemoration of Sukkot, which could not be held earlier in 164BCE because the Temple had been defiled. According to a later legend, the holiday celebrates the miracle of a measure of oil that burned for eight days instead of the one day expected.

The Fifteenth Day of Shvat (Tu Bishvat), which falls in January or February, marks the annual time for planting trees in the land of Israel. Outside Israel, Jews plant trees as the weather permits. A feature of the modern festival is fundraising for reforestation projects in Israel.

A minor, but immensely popular, biblical holiday is Purim. It commemorates the miraculous rescue of the Jews from an impending massacre in the days of the Persian empire, as recounted in the biblical Book of Esther (Megillat Esther), the communal reading of which forms the centerpiece of the festival. Purim, a lesson of hope for generations of Jews,

YOM KIPPUR

The holy day of Yom Kippur (Day of Repentance, or Atonement), the tenth day of the new year, is a fast day devoted to communal repentance before God. It is traditional to dress in white, a symbol of purity, and to abstain from various activities including eating and drinking, sex, and bathing. The reading of the Book of Jonah, a meditation on prophecy and repentance, plays a central role in the ritual for Yom Kippur.

The holiday begins at sundown and ends when three stars appear in the sky the following evening (twenty-five hours later) with the sounding of the ram's horn (*shofar*), after which communal breakfasts are often held. It is only after the end of Yom Kippur that one is deemed to have been purified in order to enter the new year with a clean slate.

has assumed a carnival-like atmosphere, with parades and costumes. The giving of presents, in particular to the poor, is also a feature of Purim.

On the full moon of the first month begins the weeklong observance of Passover (Pesach). Originally a pilgrimage festival celebrating the first fruits of the agricultural year, Passover has been remodeled as a commemoration of the Exodus from Egypt. Taking place on the night on which the Angel of Death "passed over" the dwellings of the Israelites in Egypt (Exodus 12.11–12; 12.27), the ritual of the holiday revolves around reliving God's great act of salvation. The major commemoration of Passover takes place at a lavish ritual meal (Seder) at which the story of the Exodus is recounted from the Haggadah (see p.33). There are set roles for both children and adults, and all Jews are required to view themselves as personally freed from bondage.

Seven weeks after the beginning of Pesach falls the third of the pilgrimage festivals, the Feast of Weeks (Pentecost, or Shavuot), originally a commemoration of the wheat harvest. It celebrates the revelation on Mount Sinai seven weeks after the Exodus. The Book of Ruth, which is set at the time of the grain harvest, is an appropriate reading for this holiday.

The Ninth Day of Av (Tishah b'Av), in July or August, is a postbiblical fast day on which a number of disasters in Jewish history are said to have occurred, such as the destruction of the Temple in 586BCE and 70CE, and the expulsion of the Jews from Spain in 1492.

MODERN HOLIDAYS

Two new holidays have become almost universally observed by modern Jews. Holocaust Remembrance Day (Yom ha-Shoah) is observed in memory of the six million Jews murdered by the Nazis and their allies in the Second World War. It takes place about two weeks after Passover, when the doomed Jews of the Warsaw Ghetto rose up in revolt against their oppressors in 1943. It is naturally a day of mourning.

By contrast, Israel Independence Day (Yom ha-Atzmaut) is a joyful celebration of the seemingly miraculous regeneration of the Jewish people after the depths of the Holocaust, specifically culminating in the declaration of the independence of the state of Israel on May 14, 1948.

A Sephardi family celebrates the Seder (Passover meal). The head of the household holds up a matzah *(unleavened bread), symbolizing the bread that the Israelites had no time to bake properly in their haste to flee Egypt (Exodus 12.39).*

JUDAISM IN THE MODERN WORLD

For Judaism, the modern period began in the late eighteenth century with the gradual emancipation of the Jews in western Europe and the Americas from their second-class status, as a result of Enlightenment ideals. As long as Jews were excluded from society, they were able to retain their distinctive religion and identity. However, in their rush to become fully accepted members of the body politic, many chose the option of Christian baptism. The need to convert to Christianity no longer exists, but the temptation to assimilate into liberal Western society continues to exert a strong influence on many Jews. Nonetheless, a great number of other Jews have attempted to come to grips with

REFORM JUDAISM AND JEWISH IDENTITY

The Reform movement has had a major influence on other branches of Judaism, and has been to the fore in developing strategies to cope with new social realities. However, since many of the decisions of the Reform movement are reached independently of the other branches of Judaism, it often comes into conflict with its coreligionists. One striking example of this is its redefinition of Jewish identity. There are two ways in which to be Jewish. One is to convert to Judaism; the other is to be born a Jew.

Being born a Jew has traditionally meant having a Jewish mother, since Jewish identity is matrilineal. But in its attempt to be sensitive to the high rates of intermarriage among modern Jews, the American Reform movement has expanded the definition of who is a Jew to include anyone born of a Jewish parent, whether mother or father, and raised as a Jew. However, among the other branches of Judaism, only the small Reconstructionist movement (see p.51) has adopted this redefinition.

Orthodox Judaism's division of the sexes during acts of worship has applied since 1967 at the Western Wall in Jerusalem, (see p.41) where a fence separates female (right) and male worshippers.

modernity within the context of Judaism. Their diverse responses have led both to a vibrant renewal of Jewish theology and to deep religious and ideological splits within the larger Jewish community.

The first modern Jewish movement, Reform Judaism, came into being in nineteenth-century Germany as an attempt to wed Jewish ethical monotheism with the philosophies of post-Enlightenment Europe (see p.25). Reform Judaism is an eclectic theology, allowing its adherents to choose for themselves which aspects of Jewish tradition to follow. As such, it places greater emphasis on ethics than on ritual, and emphasizes social action both within and without the confines of the Jewish community (see also sidebar, opposite).

Of all the Jewish movements, Orthodoxy is the most difficult to define, because it is divided into many different currents, from the centrist modern Orthodox to the Hasidim (see box, below) and ultra-Orthodox on the right. Also, in contrast to other branches of Judaism,

HASIDISM

Originally a pietistic, mystical, and ecstatic movement, Hasidism (from *hasid*, "pietist") began as a reaction against the established orthodoxy of eastern European Judaism. It traces its origins to the teachings of the charismatic Israel ben Eleazar (1700–60), known as the Baal Shem Tov ("Master of the Good Name"). He and his followers tried to rediscover the joy inherent in simple acts of divine service and prayer. They were opposed in this by the entrenched intellectual orthodoxy of the great teacher Elijah ben Solomon (1720–97), known as the Vilna Gaon ("Genius of Vilnius," Lithuania). Elijah excommunicated the Hasidim—ironically, because Hasidism has evolved into the champion of fundamentalist Orthodoxy in Judaism. The descendants of both groups are now Orthodox allies in the battle against the supposed dilution of traditional Judaism.

Hasidic communities are organized into dynasties, centering on a charismatic rabbi or *rebbe*. The *rebbe*s are held in very great reverence. In no Hasidic dynasty is this more evident than among the group called the Lubavitch Hasidim, who have gone so far as to make messianic claims about their late *rebbe*, Menachem Mendel Schneerson (1902–94). A number of Hasidic groups can be identified by the distinctive clothes that they wear, reminiscent of the fashions of the (non-Jewish) nobles who came into contact with the Jews living in the *shtetl*s (Jewish "villages") of eastern Europe in the eighteenth century.

Hasidic Jews in conversation on a Jerusalem street. They wear the distinctive long coats and wide-brimmed hats that characterize several Hasidic groups.

HALAKHAH TODAY

For most of the history of rabbinic and postrabbinic Judaism, the authority and divine origin of the *halakhah*, the body of Jewish law (see p.38), went unquestioned. However, rationalism and historicism led to a recognition among those open to these streams of thought that *halakhah* had always been an adaptable system. The divisions among modern Jews have at their root the question of the authority of *halakhah* and whether it is to be viewed as binding in its totality or as a source of practice from which one can then choose on the basis of an informed personal judgment. According to the latter view, *halakhah* can have a vote, but no veto, on change in practice.

it lacks a central organizing body. Modern Orthodoxy was born in mid-nineteenth century Germany as a reaction to the development of radical reformist tendencies. Under the leadership of Rabbi Samson Raphael Hirsch (1808–88), it developed according to the motto "Torah combined with secular knowledge." Hirsch realized that the Jewish community could not allow itself to withdraw into a self-imposed intellectual ghetto, but had to come to grips with modernity. In contrast to the reformers, Hirsch believed that this could be achieved within the context of a traditionally observant Jewish life. Thus, modern Orthodoxy is open to the scientific investigation of all fields of human knowledge, with the exception of those areas, such as modern biblical criticism, which come into conflict with its basic religious dogmas. A fundamental belief of Orthodoxy is the divine origin of both the written and the oral Torah, so while new circumstances call for new rulings, the circumstances are interpreted within the context of the *halakhah* (the entire body of Jewish law); the *halakhah* is not tailored to fit the circumstances (see sidebar, left).

The Conservative movement in Judaism came into being as an attempt to find a middle ground between the reformers and the Orthodox. Thus it is "conservative" compared to Reform, but "liberal" in comparison to Orthodox Judaism. Although its intellectual antecedents can also be traced to Germany, the Conservative movement as such was

Beth Shalom, a Conservative synagogue in Philadelphia, Pennsylvania, designed by the (non-Jewish) architect Frank Lloyd Wright and dedicated in 1959. Such artistic interaction between the Jewish and gentile worlds has an ancient precedent in Solomon's Temple, built by Phoenicians.

born in the US. It represented a compromise between the liberal German Jewish reformers, who constituted the majority of nineteenth-century American Jewry, and the flood of traditionally raised eastern European Jewish immigrants who poured into America between 1881 and 1924. Like Orthodoxy, Conservative Judaism is based on the *halakhah*, but is generally more flexible in its interpretation of Jewish tradition. It has followed the lead of the Reform movement in according women equality in religious life (see sidebar, right), but rejects the Reform stance on patrilineality (see p.48). However, this stance has been accepted by a liberalizing offshoot of Conservative Judaism, the Reconstructionist movement, which views Judaism as a civilization that is constantly evolving. It has had a great influence on the intellectual development of Judaism in North America.

While the tragic events of the Holocaust and the creation of the state of Israel served to unite world Jewry for close to half a century, in recent years Jews have begun to turn part of their attention to internal religious issues. Because of the centrality of Israel to the Jewish people, the modern secular state has often served as the battleground between conflicting denominations. The founders of the Israeli state were for the most part secular Zionists, who were content to leave control of religious and consequent social issues to the official Orthodox authorities. This has led to the division of Israeli society into a religiously disinterested secular majority and a politically powerful Orthodox minority. In order to safeguard their influence, the religious authorities have taken steps to assure the recognition of Orthodoxy as the sole legitimate form of Judaism in Israel. Orthodox Judaism has thus become Israel's state religion, leading to a delegitimation of the other branches of Judaism. The irony is that the overwhelming majority of Diaspora Jews, who have been a mainstay of financial and political support for Israel, belong to non-Orthodox denominations.

Israel was conceived of as a haven for all Jews, and the Israeli Law of Return grants automatic citizenship to any Jew immigrating to Israel. However, ultra-Orthodox elements in Israel have sought to invalidate the authority of non-Orthodox rabbis—and indeed non-Orthodox Jews in general—in the Diaspora, particularly on the matter of defining who is a Jew (see p.48). Conservative, Reconstructionist, Reform, and liberal Orthodox Jews the world over have fought back, in an attempt to protect the rights of all Jews in Israel, and also to diversify and enrich the sometimes one-dimensional Jewish life in Israel.

Contemporary inner-Jewish ferment and turmoil, including tensions between Israel and the communities of the Diaspora, may be frustrating to those who are actively involved in those battles. But they are also a sign of the continued health and vitality of Judaism as a whole.

GENDER AND JUDAISM

Historically, Judaism developed along patriarchal lines. For the most part it was men who assumed public roles and determined the interpretation of religious texts and traditions, while women ran the household and in the first instance transmitted Judaism to their children. The rabbis interpreted this situation positively to mean that women were free from time-bound religious obligations or *mitzvot*. Thus since only men were obliged to engage in daily public prayer, this became their domain and women were exempted (or excluded, depending on one's point of view). Indeed, women had to sit apart from the men in the synagogue. Because women were not bound by the *mitzvah* to study Jewish texts, they were traditionally denied a rigorous Jewish education.

Since the advent of liberal Judaism, women have gained a greater role in Jewish public life. The Reform movement has led the way in redefining the place of women in the synagogue. Mixed seating in liberal congregations led eventually to the equal participation of women in the synagogue service, and in 1972 Reform Judaism became the first to ordain women rabbis and cantors: by 1985, all three liberal Jewish movements were doing so.

This empowerment has also had a considerable influence on Orthodoxy. The importance of women's Torah study is now acknowledged in many circles, and more attention is paid to issues of Jewish law of direct concern to women, such as divorce. Jewish feminism has led to a greater recognition of feminine aspects of God, especially the Shekhinah (see p.26).

Chapter Two

CHRISTIANITY

Rosemary Drage Hale

An illuminated Dutch prayerbook, 1475. The rich symbolism of the lefthand page includes a pelican feeding its young from her own blood (bottom), representing Christ's saving sacrifice.

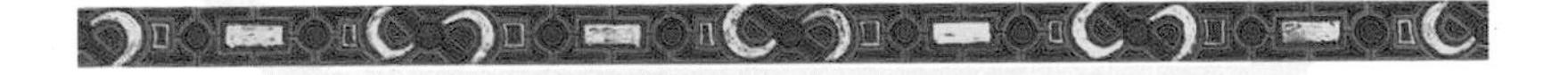

OPPOSITE *Christ in Majesty, a mosaic of ca. 1050 in the church of Hagia Sophia (Holy Wisdom) in Istanbul (formerly Constantinople), the mother-church of Orthodox Christianity. Now a museum, it was constructed in the early 6th century* CE.

INTRODUCTION

Shortly after the crucifixion (ca. 30CE) of Jesus of Nazareth, a Jewish preacher and healer, a new religious movement emerged in the Greco-Roman world that was to change that world forever. An inner circle of Jesus' disciples and many of his followers believed him to be the Christ, or Messiah, a divine redeemer of humankind, who had been resurrected after his death. They set about spreading this message, and also Jesus' teachings based on the love of God and one's neighbor. From this "Jesus movement" emerged the Christian faith, now the largest of the world's religions, with nearly two billion adherents spread over almost every country.

Essentially, Christianity is a monotheistic tradition centered on faith in one God (the eternal creator who transcends creation and yet is active in the world) and in Jesus Christ as the savior and redeemer of humankind. Christianity holds that God became incarnate—fully human—in Jesus of Nazareth. Christians believe that Jesus died on a cross and was resurrected, physically rising from the dead. The belief in the Trinity, the sacred mystery of Father, Son, and Holy Spirit as one, triune ("three-in-one") God is central to the Christian tradition.

There are hundreds of Christian groups, or "denominations," the primary ones being Roman Catholicism (the largest branch of the faith), Eastern Orthodoxy, and Protestantism. Broadly speaking, Catholics subscribe to the authority of an infallible pope (the bishop of Rome) as the head of the church. Their worship is elaborately liturgical and focuses on seven

Ethiopian Orthodox priests take part in an Easter celebration in Jerusalem to mark the resurrection of Christ. This is believed to have taken place on the third day after his crucifixion, which probably occurred at a place now within the present-day Old City, but just outside the Jerusalem of Jesus' time.

WORLD CHRISTIAN POPULATIONS

Key *(Note: "Mainly" = 80% or more; "Large" = 20% or more)*

- Mainly Roman Catholic
- Mainly Protestant
- Mainly Eastern Orthodox
- Mainly Catholic with large Protestant minority
- Mainly Protestant with large Catholic minority
- Mainly Protestant with large Orthodox minority
- Mainly Orthodox with large Catholic minority
- Mainly Orthodox with large Muslim minority
- Mainly Christian (no denomination predominant)
- Mainly Christian (no denomination predominant) with large non-Christian minority
- Christians/non-Christians evenly balanced
- Mainly non-Christian
- Mainly non-Christian with large Christian minority

- ● Seat of Western denomination
- ● Autonomous national Orthodox patriarchy
- ■ Seat of Orthodox patriarchy
- ■ Place of pilgrimage

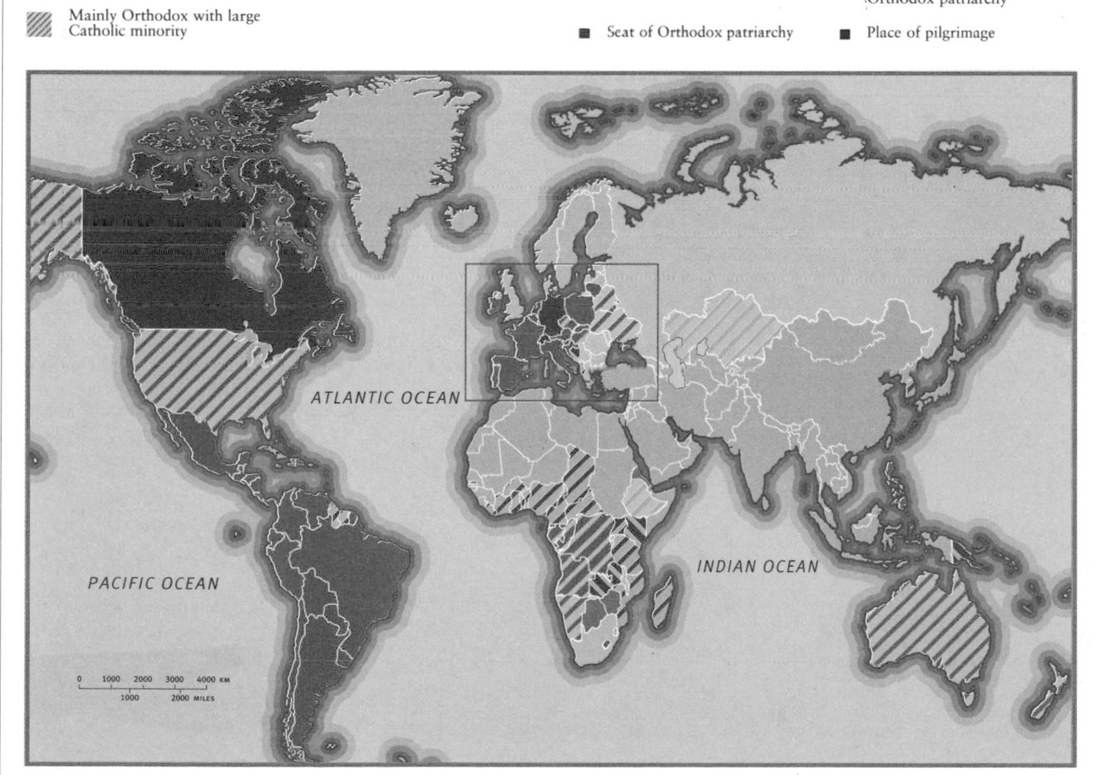

The Coronation of the Virgin, *by Lorenzo di Niccolò (active ca. 1400). The veneration of saints in the Roman Catholic church centers on devotion to Mary, the virgin mother of Christ, who is depicted here crowning her as Queen of Heaven, one of her many titles.*

"sacraments" (acts considered to confer divine grace)—baptism, eucharist (the Lord's Supper, or Holy Communion), confirmation, penance (the sacrament of reconciliation), matrimony, priestly ordination, and extreme unction (anointing the dying). The veneration of saints plays a major part in Catholic devotional practice.

Eastern Orthodoxy, in ways similar to Roman Catholicism, maintains a strong historical continuity with the early church, but resists the notion of authority vested in a single leader. Instead, the Orthodox churches are governed by bishops, patriarchs (senior bishops), and councils. In contrast to Roman Catholicism, Orthodox priests may marry if they do so before ordination. Orthodox worship also centers on the sacraments and is notable for the use of icons (sacred images) as aids to spirituality.

The Protestant movement dates from the sixteenth century, when Martin Luther and other Christian reformers rejected a great many aspects of the Roman church, including papal authority. Protestantism has developed into a hugely diverse branch of Christianity, embracing a remarkable number of offshoots and a great range of views on church governance, styles of worship, requirements for ministry, and attitudes toward the eucharist, saints, baptism, and salvation. However, all Protestants reject the authority of the pope and would agree on the primary authority of the Bible. They recognize only two sacraments (baptism and the Lord's Supper), although for some Protestant churches even these are more symbolic than sacramental. Protestants have ministers as church leaders, but gener-

CHRONOLOGY *All dates are CE, except where stated*

ca. 4BCE	Birth of Jesus of Nazareth
ca. 30CE	Crucifixion of Jesus
ca. 40–64	Ministry of Paul
ca. 70–100	New Testament gospels written
313	Edict of Milan ends persecution of Christians in Roman empire
325	Council of Nicea asserts doctrine of Trinity; Nicene Creed drafted
392	Roman empire bans paganism
354–430	Life of Augustine of Hippo, theologian
451	Council of Chalcedon
ca. 543	Death of Benedict, founder of Western monasticism
590–604	Rule of Pope Gregory the Great
638–56	Arabs conquer Egypt, Palestine, Syria, and Mesopotamia
800	Charlemagne crowned Holy Roman emperor by Pope Leo III
863	Conversion of Slavs begun by saints Cyril and Methodius
950–1000	Conversion of Europe complete
1054	Eastern (Orthodox) and Western (Roman Catholic) churches split
1095–9	First crusade to the Holy Land
1182–1226	Life of Francis of Assisi, founder of Franciscan order
1237	Inquisition established to counter heresy
1225–74	Life of Thomas Aquinas, theologian
1378	"Great Schism" in Western church, with rival popes at Rome and Avignon, France.
1414–17	Council of Constance; schism ends
1453	Constantinople falls to Turks
1492	"Reconquest" of Spain complete
1517	Martin Luther launches reform movement against church abuses
1534	Anglican church established Ignatius de Loyola founds Society of Jesus (Jesuits)
1536	John Calvin publishes *Institutes of Christian Religion*, founding work of Calvinism
1545–63	Council of Trent
1542–82	Jesuits launch missions to India, Japan, and China
1618–48	Thirty Years War
1647	George Fox begins to organize Society of Friends (Quakers)
1666	Russian Orthodox church splits between reformers and "Old Believers"
1726	Evangelical movement ("Great Awakening") begins in North America
1738	John Wesley, founder of Methodism, begins preaching
1830	Joseph Smith founds Mormonism
1869–70	First Vatican Council
1910	Edinburgh missionary conference launches modern ecumenism
1948	World Council of Churches established
1963–5	Second Vatican Council

ally uphold Luther's notion of "the priesthood of all believers," with the laity taking a much more active role than is permitted in Catholicism.

As recently as a generation ago, those who identified themselves as "Catholic," "Methodist," "Baptist," and so on, could generally be assumed to share a broad worldview with others of the same denomination. This is no longer the case. Issues such as homosexuality, inclusive language, women's ordination, and abortion are widely debated within individual congregations as well as across denominations. Today, in many churches, "fundamentalists" and "liberals" stand in opposition to each other.

However, there are also strong forces that seek to stress Christian unity, or "ecumenism." Since 1948, the World Council of Churches has sought to draw together churches that accept Jesus Christ as God and savior. This body advises such organizations as the United Nations and carries out an extensive aid program to refugees and disaster victims around the world.

Despite the differences, disagreements, and at times outright hostility and violence that have marked interdenominational relations, there are a number of issues upon which all Christians would tentatively agree, in addition to the tradition's basic theology and scriptures. All would hold that community and fellowship are vital to Christian worship. There would be accord on the essential Christian virtues—"faith, hope, and love" (1 Corinthians 13.13)—and on the belief that a life lived as far as possible in imitation of Jesus is "the Christian way." Some critics have seen in the Christian ideas of patient suffering and "turning the other cheek" a morbidity or an unhealthy renunciation of the world. But, in the main, Christianity is life-affirming. The incarnation of God as Christ is symbolized as light in the darkness of the world, and the Resurrection is regarded as a joyful affirmation of hope, demonstrating the love of God for his creation.

A Romanian Orthodox church at Humor in Moldavia. While this type of decorated exterior is unique to Romania, sacred images are a distinctive feature of Eastern Orthodox devotional practice in general.

"IN THE BEGINNING"

The foundational story of the birth, life, death, and resurrection of Jesus is chiefly preserved in the four New Testament gospels of Matthew, Mark, Luke, and John (see pp.68–9). The gospels are primarily intended as proclamations about the "kingdom of God" and about Jesus as son of God and redeemer of humankind. Hence they do not easily lend themselves to historical scholarship. Nevertheless, it is generally agreed that Jesus was born during the reign of Herod the Great (who ruled Judea 37–4BCE as a client-king of the Roman empire) to a woman named Mary and her spouse, Joseph, both of whom were pious Jews; and that he was raised at Nazareth in Galilee in northern Palestine.

The accounts of Jesus' nativity (birth) in the gospels of Matthew and Luke create an aura of divine mystery from the outset: an angel, Gabriel, appears to the maiden Mary and announces that she will miraculously conceive a divine child through the Holy Spirit; three wise men, or magi, travel to the place of Jesus' birth, following a star that they believe will lead them to the "king of the Jews." Shepherds tending their flocks at the time are told by an angel: "to you is born this day in the city of

JESUS AND JUDAISM

Christianity achieved its greatest success in the conversion of non-Jews, but it emerged unequivocally from the tradition of Judaism. Jesus was a Jew, as were his family and most of the holy figures of the New Testament, much of which reflects a Jewish Christian perspective. His message was directed at Jews, and Jews formed the core of his early followers.

What sort of Jew Jesus was is harder to answer. He has been linked at various times to several of the diverse groups that constituted the Judaism of his day (see p.23). Jesus certainly seems to have had dealings, at least, with the Pharisees, to whom the gospels often show him in opposition.

Jewish history is full of messianic pretenders (see pp.28–9) and it was not the designation of Jesus as messiah that caused the rift between his followers and Judaism. Rather, it was the Christians' abrogation of the binding nature of the Jewish law (for example, they waived the insistence on circumcision) and their belief in Jesus' divinity. Judaism holds that, just as the human cannot be divine, so God cannot be human.

In spite of the eventual triumph of gentile Christianity, a Jewish Christian community continued to exist in Palestine for a few centuries after Jesus' death.

The synagogue at Capernaum, the town that served Jesus as a base for his Galilean ministry, was built ca. 300CE on the site of the building he would have known. Synagogues were the power centers of the Pharisees, with whom Jesus is reported to have had a series of disputes on points of Jewish law, such as dietary regulations and Sabbath observance. However, their differences were within the scope of contemporary Pharisaic debate.

Jesus' triumphal entry into Jerusalem at the end of his ministry (left) and the Last Supper (right), his final meal with his 12 leading disciples before the Crucifixion. From a book of scenes of the life of Christ produced in Constantinople ca. 1650.

David a Savior, who is the Messiah [Christ], the Lord" (Luke 2.11).

The gospels recount Jesus' adult baptism (see p.82) by John the Baptist, a significant and prophetic figure who is said to have prepared the way for the disclosure of Christ's identity as Son of God. The baptism marked the beginning of Jesus' public ministry in Galilee and the surrounding area. As Jesus began his ministry, he took on twelve chief disciples, known as the apostles (Greek *apostolos*, "messenger," or "delegate," of Christ), who after his death were regarded as his successors and held responsible for spreading the belief in Jesus as messiah and redeemer. The gospel narratives tell of Jesus as a wonder-working prophet. They describe miracles of healing and raising the dead, exorcising demons, changing water into wine, multiplying loaves and fishes to feed a great multitude—all acts that his followers regarded as evidence of his messiahship.

As significant to the foundation of Christianity as the birth and ministry of Jesus is his death and resurrection. There is broad consensus that in Jerusalem, at the time of the Jewish festival of Passover, Jesus was betrayed by one of his followers and arrested. After cross-examination by the Jewish authorities, Jesus was sent before the Roman governor, Pontius Pilate, and found guilty of claiming to be king of the Jews, a claim that was blasphemous under Jewish law and treason to the Romans. Jesus was sentenced to death by crucifixion, a normal Roman punishment for criminals and traitors, and died on the cross within a few hours.

But the Jesus movement did not die out with its leader's death. Shortly after his crucifixion, a small group of Jews began to proclaim that Jesus had been resurrected, and that in his resurrection the messianic hopes of Israel had been fulfilled. They could hardly have foreseen the astounding success of their preaching.

"CHRIST" AND "CHRISTIANS"

The word "Christ" represents the Greek translation (*christos*) of the Hebrew *mashiach* ("messiah" or "anointed one of God"). While initially only a title, identifying Jesus as messiah, it soon became part of a proper name, "Jesus Christ." Hence his followers came to be referred to as "Christians," a term apparently first used of the followers of Jesus at Antioch in Syria.

The use of Christ as a name, rather than a title, occurs in one of the earliest references to Jesus by a non-Christian. The first-century CE Roman historian Tacitus writes of a "superstition" current among the Jews of Rome, started by a man whom he spells "Chrestos."

TWO MILLENNIA OF FAITH

Jesus and the disciples in the garden of Gethsemane. A late Roman mosaic in the church of San Apollinare Nuovo in Ravenna, Italy (consecrated 549CE). Christ and his 11 disciples (minus the 12th, Judas Iscariot, who betrayed him) are represented in the patrician robes of the Roman aristocracy.

In the years immediately following the Crucifixion, most believers in Jesus as messiah were Palestinian Jews. However, in the two decades from ca. 40CE, this began to alter radically as the Christians took their message to the gentiles (non-Jews). The story of this mission begins with Saul of Tarsus, a Greek-speaking Diaspora Jew and Roman citizen, who bore a Classical name, Paul, as well as his Hebrew one. Saul/Paul began as a persecutor, assisting at the stoning of Stephen—revered as the first Christian martyr—in Jerusalem. Shortly afterward, en route to Damascus to arrest other followers of Jesus, he experienced a vision of Jesus and converted (Acts 9.1–19, 22.5–16). Paul then began a zealous, lifelong, and successful mission to convert the gentiles of Greece and Asia Minor. Paul was one of the first to articulate a Christian theology distinct from Jewish practice and law.

As it spread, early Christianity faced a number of obstacles. Christians refused to sacrifice to the Greco-Roman deities or to acknowledge the Roman emperor as a god, as required by law. Hence simply being a Christian was treason and many Christians were martyred, but their example served to advertise the new religion and to unify its followers. Persecution effectively ended after the emperor Constantine's Edict of Milan (313CE) decreed tolerance for all religions. In 392CE, Theodosius I declared Christianity the sole religion of the empire.

ORTHODOXY AND HERESY

The terms "heretic" and "heresy" (from Greek *hairesein*, "to choose") refer to Christians who choose to dissent from orthodox doctrine and belief. In order to survive and flourish, the early church needed to formulate a uniform system of beliefs and a fixed canon of scripture. Ecclesiastical orthodoxy was determined by bishops and theologians meeting in councils to discuss such areas as priestly celibacy, the role of women, scriptural authority, and the form of the liturgy.

Most important, they discussed the Trinity (see p.65) and how to express the relationship between God and Christ, a complex issue that lay at the heart of early heresies such as Manicheanism, Marcionism, Arianism, and Montanism. The debate led to the formulation, at the councils of Nicea (325CE) and Chalcedon (451CE), of the creed, a statement of essential Christian belief.

THE EAST-WEST SCHISM

The break between the churches of the East (Orthodox) and West (Roman) in 1054 marked the end of a gradual process with its roots in the cultural differences between the Latin-speaking Western Roman empire and the Greek-speaking East. The basic cultural and linguistic divide was reinforced by a long history of complex doctrinal differences, including controversy over the definition of Christ's dual (human and divine) nature and over devotion to icons (Greek *eikon*, "image"), representations of holy figures such as Christ, Mary, and the saints. In the eighth century, the iconoclasts ("image breakers") of the East, who considered the use of icons in churches to be idolatry, won the upper hand for several decades and countless sacred works of art were destroyed. But the iconodules ("icon worshippers") reversed the trend and icons came to be treated in the East as not simply symbolic but as intrinsically sacred and able to confer grace on worshippers. This attitude was not accepted in the West.

What finally split the church was the question of allegiance to the Roman papacy. In the West, supreme ecclesiastical authority came to lie with the pope, the bishop of Rome, who traced his legitimacy through the apostle Peter to Christ himself. But in the East, authority rested with an episcopate made up of all the bishops. Matters came to a head in 1054, when an argument over the refusal of the Byzantine community in southern Italy to pay homage to Pope Leo IX led to the excommunication of the Eastern church, which retaliated with a counterexcommunication. Although there were attempts to reconcile the breach, the two churches have never been reunited.

Scenes from the lives of saints Florus and Laurus. A Russian icon of the early 16th century from Novgorod.

The early period of Christian history is often referred to as the "Patristic" era after the *Patres Ecclesiae* (Latin, "Fathers of the Church"), the great (male) theologians whose works helped shape Christian thought and doctrine. Perhaps the most influential of these was St. Augustine (354–430CE), bishop of Hippo in north Africa. Bishops (Greek *episkopos*, "overseer") had been instituted early in this period to act as spiritual heads of Christian communities, with those of Rome, Antioch, Jerusalem, Alexandria, and Constantinople regarded as the "patriarchs" of the church.

In the late fifth century, the secular power of the Western Roman empire succumbed to Germanic invaders. For the time being, however, the churches in the West and in the Byzantine East remained one. The feudal states that subsequently developed in medieval Western Europe were organized according to a system in which the most powerful elements were the monarchy, the aristocracy, and the church. State and church often conflicted, but it came to be accepted that the monarch would rule over temporal matters, while the pope exercised supreme authority over spiritual issues. The question of papal authority lay at the heart of the first big schism (split) in the church, between the West and East (see box, above).

Western (Roman) Christianity continued to expand during a succession of crusades from 1095—military expeditions aimed at the expulsion of

MONASTICISM

The traditional founder of monasticism is St. Antony (ca. 251–356CE), who lived a solitary life of prayer in the Egyptian desert. Countless others followed his example, becoming lone hermits or forming communities under an abbot or abbess. Those who thus renounced their worldly lives came to be revered as paradigms of Christian virtue.

One famous early monastery, at Monte Cassino near Naples, Italy, was founded by St. Benedict of Nursia (480–550CE). His "rule" (set of spiritual and administrative guidelines) served as the basis for Western monasticism for centuries (and remains so for Benedictine foundations today). Nuns and monks take vows of chastity and obedience, and devote themselves mainly to prayer and the daily chanting of the Divine Office (see p.82). Benedict's rule includes regulations for the hours of sleep, manual work, reading, and mealtimes.

Muslims from the Holy Land. The interaction with Islamic civilization also brought Western culture into contact, via Arab scholarship, with the lost philosophical traditions of ancient Greece, especially Aristotle. This rediscovery brought both a challenge and renewed vigor to Christian philosophy, reflected in the work of theologians whose collective approach is referred to as "scholasticism." The greatest scholastic thinker was probably St. Thomas Aquinas (1225–74) (see p.64), for whom questions of reason, knowledge, and revelation were at the forefront of the attempt to reconcile ancient philosophical systems with Christian theology.

The medieval flowering of Christian scholarship coincided with the rise of universities in Europe, and with the reform of the long tradition of Benedictine monasticism (see p.61). This reform resulted in the emergence of several new orders as well as the formation of the mendicant ("begging") orders of the Dominicans and Franciscans, who originally sought to lead poor and humble lives in close imitation of Jesus and his disciples.

Prior to the Protestant reformations in the sixteenth century, reformers such as John Wyclif (or Wycliffe, 1330–84) in England and John (Jan) Hus (1373–1415) in Bohemia had begun to question the traditional authority of the ecclesiastical hierarchy and to oppose what they regarded as corrupt church practices. Both men were condemned as heretics, but their criticisms and reforms continued to garner support among the laity.

Discontent came to a head in 1517, when Martin Luther (1483–1546), an Augustinian friar of Wittenberg, Germany, publicly posted ninety-five "theses," statements criticizing Rome for selling "indulgences"—promises to reduce one's time in purgatory (see p.85)—to raise funds. In spite of church opposition, the German reform movement quickly gathered pace and within just a few years the split in Western Christianity had become irrevocable. In 1529, the signatories to one formal protest against the suppression of reformers were dubbed "Protestants," and this name stuck.

Protestantism, which essentially advocated the authority of scripture over that of an ecclesiastical hierarchy, developed along several distinct lines. Radical reformers such as Ulrich Zwingli (1484–1531) and John Calvin (1509–64) opposed the veneration of images, certain aspects of the Roman liturgy, and clerical celibacy. Unlike those who followed Luther's notion of salvation through faith and not through deeds, Calvin believed in predestination: some of the faithful were destined to be saved, others were not. Today, the term Protestant covers an extraordinary proliferation of denominations (see sidebar, opposite).

Secular rulers took up the cause of reform for a variety of reasons. Many agreed with the criticisms of the reformers; others saw an opportunity to seize church wealth. The origins of one of the largest denominations, Anglicanism (the Church of England and its affiliates, such as Episcopalianism), was linked with the marital problems of the monarch,

THE COUNTER-REFORMATION

The Protestant Reformation prompted a renewal of Roman Catholicism that is known as the Counter-Reformation. Fostered by the Council of Trent (1545–63), the Catholic reform movement not only saw the ending of many of the practices (such as the sale of indulgences) that had fired the reformers, but also the founding of new orders such as the intellectually rigorous Jesuits (the Society of Jesus), who, under the guidance of their founder, Ignatius of Loyola (1491–1556), sought to lay new emphasis on pastoral care and missionary work.

The Counter-Reformation also led to a reaffirmation of the supremacy of priests, the sacraments, and the authority of the papacy in those areas where it remained dominant. The new optimism within Catholicism was reflected in a great flowering of sacred art.

A portrait of Martin Luther, the leader of the German reform movement, painted in 1529 by one of his early followers, the artist Lucas Cranach (1472–1553).

Henry VIII (ruled 1509–47), who was refused a divorce by the pope.

With its new emphasis on the holiness of marriage and the family, Protestantism had a negative influence on monasticism and in many of the reformed areas monasteries and convents all but disappeared.

The era of the Reformation and Counter-Reformation (see sidebar, opposite) coincided with the beginnings of European colonialism. As Europeans expanded their horizons to the Americas and elsewhere, missionaries zealous to "make disciples of all nations" (Matthew 28.19) had a profound impact on the worldwide spread of Christianity. While missionary activity continues today, it does so altered by ecumenism, a movement that began with an international and multidenominational missionary conference at Edinburgh in 1910. The movement aimed to foster cooperation and dialogue across denominational boundaries and to end centuries of suspicion and hostility among Christians of different traditions.

As Christianity moved into the modern period, powerful rationalist and skeptical influences were exerted on the faith by the eighteenth-century Enlightenment, the Industrial Revolution and the emergence of industrial capitalism, and advances in science from the seventeenth century to the present. Urbanization and secularization, particularly in the West, were among the factors that changed traditional roles and functions performed by the church and its community in earlier historical periods.

Nonetheless, like any living religious tradition, the vitality of the Christian faith is evidenced in a continual process of reform and internal pluralism. Today, over four hundred denominations all identify themselves as Christian. Many regard this worldwide religious diversity as one of the greatest challenges facing Christianity in the modern world.

A service in the "Crystal Cathedral," a modern evangelical Protestant church in Orange County, California.

PROTESTANT DENOMINATIONS

The major organized churches of Protestantism include Lutherans, Baptists, Methodists, Presbyterians, Anglicans (or Episcopalians), Friends United Meeting (Quakers), Mennonites, Mormons, and Christian Scientists. Anglicanism has the most elaborate liturgy, basing its worship throughout the world on *The Book of Common Prayer*. Baptists, one of the largest Protestant churches (with many subgroups), stress personal religious experience and adult baptism. Among other groups, Seventh-Day Adventists celebrate the Sabbath on Saturday and adhere to some of the dietary laws of the Old Testament. Denominations such as Jehovah's Witnesses are called "millennialist," because they believe that Christ will soon return for the final apocalyptic battle of Armageddon, after which he will reign for a thousand years.

Evangelicalism is common to several Protestant churches. Evangelicals typically regard themselves as "born again" in Christ, stress personal conversion, and often dedicate themselves to evangelizing the world. Evangelical preachers are strongly biblical in orientation.

Stimulated by television evangelists and worldwide missions, one of the fastest growing movements is Pentecostalism, a phenomenon that has also had some currency among Roman Catholics. It has a strong focus on evangelism (proclaiming the word of God) and is essentially charismatic, that is, ecstatic experiences such as "speaking in tongues" are considered a vital element of worship. The term Pentecostalism refers to the descent of the Holy Spirit among the apostles at the time of Pentecost (Whitsunday) (Acts 2.1–4).

REVELATION AND TRUTH

Christian theology is a profoundly complex subject and has a great many forms and methods—natural theology, practical theology, systematic theology, mystical theology, pastoral theology, speculative theology, and, more recently, liberation theology (see p.87), to name a few. However, it can be broadly divided into two types: dogmatic theology and moral theology. Dogmatic theology, the science of the theoretical truths of God, seeks to establish fundamental doctrines and articles of faith. Drawing on scripture and tradition, dogmatic theology generally deals with issues relating to the concept of the Trinity (see box, opposite). Moral theology, while grounded in Christian dogma, is the science of practical moral truths and aims to explain the divine laws and the relationship of humankind to God.

Christian theological inquiry has had a lively history that goes back to the very beginnings of the church. Within an expansive general brief—"the nature of God"—theologians systematically treat a wide range of topics relevant to doctrinal concerns, such as "Christology" (the study of the person and nature of Jesus); "Mariology" (the study of Mary's role in the Incarnation); "soteriology" (revelation pertaining to redemption and salvation); and "eschatology" (revelation concerning the end of the world).

There is theological discourse in the New Testament, but the distinct discipline of theology emerged only with the "Church Fathers," such as St. Augustine, who was the source of the basic Christian notions that humanity suffers from a hereditary moral disease derived from the original sin of Adam (see p.74), and that only God's grace can offer salvation.

Later, with the development of European universities in the Middle Ages, theology was placed at the pinnacle of studies as "Queen of the Sciences." This was the period of "scholastic" theology, a systematized manner of deriving theological conclusions on the basis of "syllogism" (deductive reasoning). Foremost among the scholastic theologians is Thomas Aquinas (1225–74), author of *Summa Theologica* ("The Sum of Theology"), a work of profound influence that attempts to synthesize reason and faith in the light of Western Europe's rediscovery, via Muslim scholarship, of ancient Greek philosophy, particularly that of Aristotle. Still authoritative in modern Catholicism, the study and continuation of Aquinas' work is referred to as "Thomism."

After the Protestant Reformations and the Enlightenment, theological inquiry diversified and the plurality of thought was compounded by the emergence of various denominational perspectives. Critical reason and scientific advancements further challenged theological thought. Friedrich Schleiermacher (1768–1834), hailed as the founder of Protestant theology,

THE WORD MADE FLESH

"In the beginning was the Word, and the Word was with God, and the Word was God ... And the Word became flesh and lived among us, and we have seen his glory." While modern scholars may contest the authenticity and authorship of the opening lines of the gospel of John, few would question their importance for understanding the origins of Christianity. They echo the opening of the Hebrew Bible, the Christian Old Testament—"In the beginning God created the heavens and the earth" (Genesis 1.1)—but also reveal a critical difference between Christianity and its parent religion, Judaism. Here, in John's words, the divinity is created in the flesh, in the human nature of Jesus of Nazareth, and this divine person is regarded as the Son of God, redeemer of humankind.

St. Augustine preaching to his disciples. An English illustration of ca. 1100 to Augustine's work De Civitate Dei *("The City of God").*

argued that theology could not be circumscribed by reason and morality, but rather by the human feeling of dependence upon an infinite being. Ludwig Feuerbach, author of *Essence of Christianity* (1841), claimed that God is a mental projection whose purpose is to respond to human hopes and satisfy human needs. In the twentieth century, Paul Tillich (1886–1965), saw Christian theology in the context of the modern world, maintaining that Christian faith is one of many ways of dealing with the "ultimate concern" of existence and God. Overall, the history of Christian theology is an elaborate story of varied translations, interpretations, and reconstructions of the mysteries of the faith.

THE HOLY TRINITY

The Trinity is a central doctrine of Christianity and has challenged theologians throughout the history of the religion. The doctrine holds that there is one God but that God comprises three elements—Father, Son, and Holy Spirit—worshipped as a unity. The idea of God as "one-in-three and three-in-one" remains one of the most sacred mysteries for both the Eastern and Western churches.

It is generally agreed that the Bible contains no explicit teaching of the Trinity. The gospels of Matthew, Mark, and Luke emphasize Christ's humanity, while the gospel of John stresses his divinity. Early theologians were keen to stress Jesus' divine nature, but debated how Christianity could remain monotheistic if both Jesus and God were to be regarded as divine. As early as the second century CE, Tertullian (155–222CE) used the term *trinitas* (Latin, "trinity") in theological discourse, teaching that God is "one substance" comprised of "three persons." Origen (185–254CE) insisted that Christian faith is founded on the unity of a transcendent God (who created humanity), coeternal with the Son (who redeemed humanity) and the Spirit (who sanctified humanity). By the fourth century CE, theologians had consolidated the orthodox position of God as three persons in one nature and placed this doctrine in the opening lines of the statement of faith known as the "Athanasian Creed."

The Cappadocian Fathers—theologians of Asia Minor whose writings remain vital and doctrinally sound for Eastern Orthodoxy—differed on the issue of the generation of the Son and the "procession" of the Holy Spirit. One doctrinal issue at the center of the East-West schism (see p.61) was the East's insistence that the Spirit "proceeded" (originated, or arose) from the Father *through* the Son, while the West insisted on procession from the Father *and* the Son.

The Holy Trinity, *by a 14th-century Hungarian painter known as the Master of the Trinity. God the Father, enthroned, holds the crucified Son, above whose head hovers the Holy Spirit in the form of a white dove. Medieval theologians compared the Trinity with the three human faculties of memory, intellect, and will that reside in one personality.*

A MYSTIC UNION

Christian mysticism is essentially theistic, that is, it centers on the transcendent reality of God and typically emphasizes divine love. Overall, it is shaped by Christian notions of God and reflects God's relationship to the soul. The expansive writing of Christian mystics is often divided into two strands: the intellectual discussion of mystical philosophy and the experiential descriptions of practical mysticism. Regardless of type, a common theme in Christian mystical literature is that of the inexpressibility or ineffability of the mystic union with God. Philosophical mysticism analyzes the nature of divine union while practical mysticism tends to use metaphorical language to describe the experience itself.

While personal narratives of Christian mystical experience vary widely, all Christian mystics describe in some way or another a direct awareness of the presence of God, generally defined by scholars and theologians as

"EMBODIED MYSTICISM"

Christian mystical literature recounts an array of what are termed "embodied" spiritual experiences. These include physical appearances of Christ or Mary; "auditions" (hearing the voice of God or angels); mystical pregnancies; and miraculous lactation in devotion to the infant Jesus.

There are innumerable reports of devotees attaining a state of mystic ecstasy accompanied by other physical manifestations such as swooning, levitation, weeping fits, and trance. Such states are said to arise from divine activity within the soul and are attended by alienated or heightened senses. In the thirteenth century, when devotion to the suffering Christ was especially cultivated, St. Francis of Assisi (1182–1226) became the first mystic to receive stigmata, the marks of the five wounds of the crucified Christ.

St. Theresa of Avila, a sixteenth-century Spanish mystic, reformer, and organizer of the Carmelite order, maintained that ecstatic experience was one stage on the way to mystical union with God. Her autobiographical writings and treatise on the mystical path, *The Interior Castle*, were composed during the tumultuous times of the Spanish Inquisition and so offer only cautious descriptions of the stages of ecstasy and rapture.

The Ecstasy of St. Theresa, *by Gian Lorenzo Bernini (1598–1680). The sculpture depicts what Theresa called "Transverberation," the experience of the soul being pierced with God's love (here represented as Cupid).*

"mystical union" (Latin, *unio mystica*) with God. Mystical union often involves a lengthy preparation, a life path beginning with an "awakening," followed by a period of purgation, an "illumination," and finally the experience of union. For others, it is a transcendent experience that comes suddenly, without preparation, but utterly transforms their lives. The mystic's spiritual path is reflective and inward, turned away from the world.

The roots of Christian mysticism are scriptural. Paul, in particular, taught that through the love of Christ, the Christian may experience the presence of God. Nonetheless, while early Christian mysticism included a prominent contemplative element, it was essentially intellectual and philosophical and drew on Greek and Roman thought. For example, the pagan philosopher Plotinus (205–270CE) wrote at length on the notion of the Absolute, maintaining that world-renunciation and contemplation provided the most perfect path to union with God. Augustine (354–430CE), attempting to reconcile Greek philosophy with Christian theology, saw God at the center of all reality, transcending thought and concrete being. The first to use the term "mystical theology" was the writer known as Pseudo-Dionysius the Areopagite (ca. 500CE), who placed early Christian asceticism on an intellectual plane. He spoke of God's hidden presence and claimed that knowledge of God was only achieved through self-denial accompanied by an emptying of the mind of all thought.

The medieval church saw a flourishing of mystical experience. Mystics perceived themselves as instruments of God, and while they led contemplative lives, popes and secular rulers solicited their counsel. The many famous mystics of the period include the remarkable Hildegard of Bingen (1098–1179), a German abbess who recounted her prophetic and apocalyptic visions using allegorical symbols. The French mystic St. Bernard of Clairvaux (1090–1153) employed the imagery of the Song of Songs in the Bible to portray the union of the soul and Christ in terms of a metaphorical marriage. In Italy, St. Francis of Assisi (1181–1226), founder of the Franciscan monastic order, practiced a mysticism based on the "imitation of Christ" (see also box, opposite). In her account of her revelations on the mystery of the faith, Julian of Norwich (1342–ca. 1415), one of many medieval English mystics, focused on the infinity and immeasurability of divine love and employed the metaphor of Christ as mother.

Following the Reformation, Protestant views of mysticism were generally negative, but some Protestants, such as Jakob Boehme (1575–1624), did recount experiences of mystical divine union.

In more recent times, mystics have drawn on mystical traditions outside Christianity. Thomas Merton (1915–68), for example, was inspired by Buddhism. The appeal of mysticism remains vibrant today as Christians continue to find inspiration in their efforts to communicate the profound and intense mystery of the soul's union with God.

THE JESUS PRAYER

Contemplative mysticism is central to Eastern Orthodoxy and is based on a meditative technique for divine union that involves the constant repetition of "the Jesus Prayer": "Lord Jesus Christ have mercy on me a sinner." The prayer dates from the fifth century CE and is still recited in Orthodox churches.

The devotional practice of repeating the Jesus Prayer is called "hesychasm" (from the Greek for "quietness"). Practitioners report that it produces a state of spiritual stillness in which they have an experience of holy wisdom, a partaking of the nature of God. A famous Greek saint and mystic, Gregory of Palamas (1296–1359), was among those to recount this direct communion with the divine.

By saying the prayer, the worshipper also hopes to experience a vision of the Divine Light, thought to be identical with the light of the Transfiguration (Matthew 17.1–9 and parallel passages in Mark and Luke).

A 17th-century engraving of Jakob Boehme, one of the most influential of Protestant mystics. A Lutheran, Boehme claimed to have experienced knowledge of the nature of the Trinity (see p.65).

THE CHRISTIAN CANON

The Bible is regarded by Christians as having been inspired by God and is thus Christianity's holiest text. It consists of two parts: the "Old Testament," essentially the Hebrew Bible (see pp.30–31), which for Christianity represents God's first covenant ("testament") with humankind; and the "New Testament," the covenant of Jesus Christ, in whom God's promises to Israel were fulfilled. The twenty-seven books of the New Testament, composed in the century following Christ's death, record his birth, ministry, passion ("suffering"), and resurrection. They also contain "Acts of the Apostles," including an account of Paul's mission to the gentiles, and letters by Paul and other figures in the early church (see box, opposite). The last book, Revelation, is an apocalyptic vision of the end of time.

The core of the compilation are the four "gospels" (an old English word translating Greek *euaggelion*, "good news") attributed to authors called Matthew, Mark, Luke, and John (the "evangelists"). Since the late eighteenth century, scholars have referred to the first three gospels as "synoptic" ("viewed together"), because when looked at in tandem they are seen to contain many significant parallels of form and content. The gospel of John, or the "Fourth Gospel" (ca. 95CE), is markedly different in style and tone. Collectively, the four books are called simply "the Gospel."

How the Old and New Testaments came to constitute the authorized scripture of Christianity is a complex story. Christians and Jews share most of the texts of the Hebrew Bible, but the early church reordered them in order to conclude the Old Testament with the books of the prophets. The Old Testament thus ends with the book of Malachi, whose reference to the prophet Elijah as precursor of the messiah was understood by the gospel writers to apply to John the Baptist (Matthew 11.7–15 and Luke 1.16–17).

LANGUAGES OF THE BIBLE

The Hebrew Bible (the Christian Old Testament), originally written mainly in Hebrew, was translated into Greek in the third century BCE for the use of Greek-speaking Diaspora Jews. This version, the Septuagint, was considered authoritative by the early church and remains so for the Greek Orthodox church. The New Testament was composed in Greek.

Following the establishment of the canon, the pope commissioned Bishop Jerome of Dalmatia (340–420CE) to translate the Christian Bible into Latin, the language of Western Christianity. Jerome's work (382CE), the Vulgate (Latin *Versio Vulgata*, "Common Translation"), was the standard Bible of Roman Christendom until the Reformation and remains the official source for Catholic translations.

Latin had ceased to be spoken by the Middle Ages, when only priests and educated laypeople could read the Bible. A number of glosses, paraphrases, and even complete Bibles appeared in various languages, but it was only with the Reformation that vernacular Bibles proliferated as Protestant churches insisted that the scriptures should be accessible to all. Today, every branch of Christianity encourages worshippers to hear and read the Bible in their native tongue, and it has been translated into more than two thousand languages.

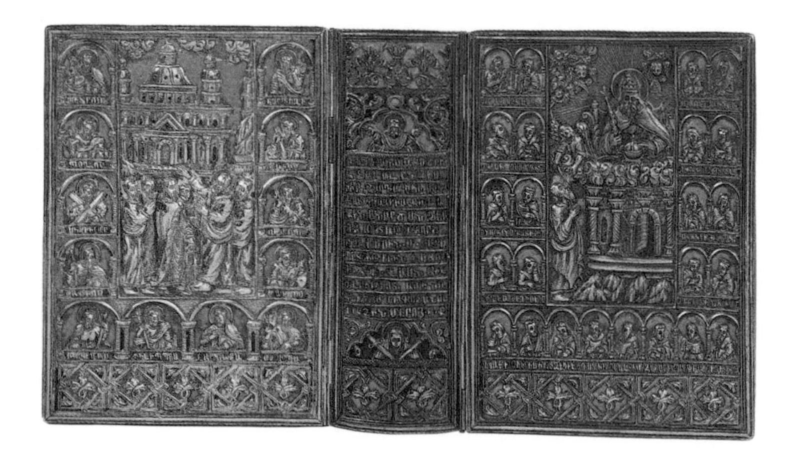

An Armenian enameled silver gospel cover of 1658. The front (right) depicts God enthroned above the Temple, with portraits of Old Testament prophets; the back (left) shows Jesus before the Temple and portraits of the twelve disciples.

The canon of the New Testament consists of writings that the early church considered to have been inspired by God, and saw as best communicating the religious experience of Christians. It was not the work of a single individual or a church council, but evolved piecemeal over several centuries. As early as 160CE, the theologian Tertullian used the phrase "New Testament" to refer to a collection of first-century writings recalling Christ. But it was not until the early fifth century that the twenty-seven books of today's New Testament gained universal acceptance and that the Christian canon attained a form recognizable to modern worshippers.

From the very beginning, the church acknowledged a number of texts as "apocryphal" (literally "hidden away"), meaning that they possessed special spiritual or historical merit but were not to be regarded as divine revelation. The status of some of these writings is the source of disagreement among the Protestant, Catholic, and Orthodox churches.

The Bible is open to a wide range of interpretations and has been used to justify opposing practices, such as polygamy and monogamy. For many Christians, particularly those who belong to fundamentalist congregations, the Bible is all revelation: every word is inspired by God and hence literally true and without error. Some communities apply a more allegorical interpretation. There are scholars who read the Bible as literature and apply literary critical methods to understanding its merit, attempting to unravel the threads of authorship and genre. Biblical interpretation is also directly related to the manner of translation, a tendency that goes back to the German Bible of Martin Luther and beyond. New translations (see sidebar, opposite) continue to reflect the variety of interpretative perspectives.

An early printed edition (1561) of Luther's German Bible. The Catholic church accused the reformer of "mistranslating" certain passages to reflect Lutheran doctrine, for example Paul's words on justification by faith (Romans 3.28).

THE LETTERS OF THE NEW TESTAMENT

The literary genre of the epistle, or letter, is an important element in the writings that constitute the New Testament. While the gospels are narratives concerned with the events of Jesus' life and his teaching, the letters are public communications directed at the new communities of converts (four are addressed to individuals). They were, in effect, a means of carrying on missionary activity. Hence they often employed the rhetorical style of the day and were read aloud as sermons.

The letters also provided a way to respond to opponents of the Jesus movement. While they refer to particular situations in the places to which they were addressed, the theologians who decided on the canon of the New Testament perceived in the letters a timeless quality and considered them as essential to the formation of faith as the gospels and Acts.

Forming the core of the epistles are the thirteen "Pauline" letters, those traditionally attributed to Paul (although scholars now question the attribution of some of these). Originally written in Greek, like the rest of the New Testament, they reflect Paul's mission to gentile communities and establish his authority as an apostle of Christ. His two letters to Corinth, Greece, outline his views on the doctrinal and ethical concerns of the community there, such as celibacy, eating food sacrificed to a pagan god, and the nature of the Resurrection.

In his letter to the Galatians (a Christian community in Asia Minor), Paul confronts the controversial issue of whether a gentile must be circumcised before becoming a Christian. His response—no—marked a major divergence in Christian practice from that of its Jewish heritage.

MARTYRS, SAINTS, AND ANGELS

In Christianity, men and women who are deemed to have lived lives of extreme virtue or to have died a martyr's death are revered as "saints" (Latin *sanctus* or *sancta*, "holy [man, woman]"). Reverence for such an individual involves cherishing his or her memory as well as venerating, and aspiring to imitate, the spirituality of a life that exemplified religious and moral ideals. Devotional practices associated with the cultivation of saints include making offerings, invocations, and vows, and petitioning for cures and miracles. Because they reside in heaven in close proximity to God, saints are thought to possess special power to intercede with the

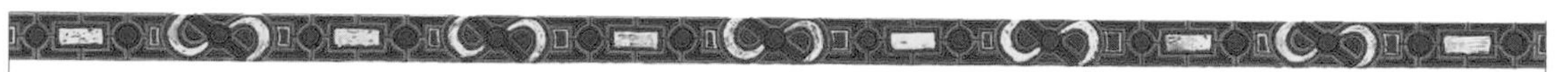

THE VIRGIN MARY

A 16th-century Cretan icon of the Virgin and Child. The Eastern church's special reverence for Mary is reflected in the Akathistos, *a 5th-century hymn still used in worship, and in her Greek title* Theotokos *("Bearer of God").*

Throughout the centuries, a popular cult of veneration of Mary, the mother of Christ, has grown up in both Eastern and Western strands of Christianity. "Marian" devotion developed first in the East, and can be traced to the fourth century CE. Later, the second council of Nicea (787CE) determined that while full adoration was reserved for God alone, Mary was due a greater degree of veneration than other saints.

In the Western church, the veneration of Mary developed much later, but remains especially vibrant in Roman Catholicism. By the twelfth century, she was commonly called simply "Our Lady" or "My Lady" (Notre Dame, Madonna) and hundreds of churches were dedicated to her. For centuries, theologians debated such doctrines as the "Immaculate Conception" (which asserts that Mary, as well as Christ, was conceived without original sin; see p.74) and the "Assumption," when she was taken bodily to heaven. In modern times there are many instances of Marian apparitions at places such as Lourdes, France, that have become great pilgrimage sites (see p.76).

Devotion to Mary, like that to other saints, is based on her intercessory powers, faith in which arises from the belief that as her son, Jesus cannot refuse his mother's pleas. There are countless stories of her compassion for all those who invoke her name. For this reason she is often portrayed as a merciful and benevolent mother of all worshippers.

In Protestantism, Mary is honored as the mother of Christ, but does not occupy as important a position as she does in Eastern Orthodoxy or Roman Catholicism. She is not actively venerated and has no significant place in Protestant worship.

Deity on the petitioner's behalf. The veneration of saints involves a reciprocal relationship: the believer declares loyalty and devotion, and the saint offers protection and intercession in return.

Devotion to saints began as early as the period of persecution in the Roman empire. The belief in the intercessory powers of saints was a cultural extension of Greco-Roman practices, in which those who had died heroic deaths were thought to exert supernatural power from their graves. The word martyr (Greek *marturos*) means "witness" (that is, for Christ) and the women and men who went to their deaths in this period were the exemplars and heroes of early Christianity, those who had followed most closely the example of Christ. The names of the martyrs of this period, such as Perpetua and Felicitas (who both died in 203CE), were included in the liturgy of the early Christian communities. In later centuries their remains would be venerated as relics and as testimony to the foundational period of the faith. Instead of being interred in cemeteries, the bodies of the first martyrs and saints came to buried under church altars.

Healings, exorcisms, and a variety of miracles were associated with the reverence of saints' remains, and as this practice grew, from the fourth century into the Middle Ages, so also did the demand for holy relics: bones and other objects associated with the saint. Under the guidance of church leaders, Christendom thus evolved a network of sacred tombs and "reliquaries" (relic shrines). For many centuries, devotion to a host of saints was a fundamental element of private and public Christian worship. A calendar of saints' days provided worshippers with a daily guide for meditation.

Popular devotion to saints was central to medieval Christianity. To the saints' relics were added written accounts, or "hagiographies" (Greek *hagios* or *hagia*, "saint," and *graphia* "writing"), of their lives and miracles that encouraged devotion to the saints and portrayed their relics as living instruments of divine power. Particularly popular was *The Golden Legend*, a thirteenth-century collection of miracle stories by James of Voragine. Later, in the eighteenth century, Alban Butler's *Lives of the Saints* covered 2,565 saints arranged in calendrical order of their feast days.

Some saints were only venerated locally, while others have enjoyed widespread veneration. Foremost among the latter are Mary (see box, opposite) and her husband, Joseph the carpenter. Described

A silver, silver-gilt, and bronze reliquary from the Vatican. Made for Pope Pius II (reigned 1458–64) in order to house relics believed to be those of St. Andrew the Apostle, it incorporates over 200 precious and semiprecious stones.

in the gospels as "a righteous man" (Matthew 1.19), Joseph is revered as a compassionate and caring husband and protector of the infant Jesus, whom his wife conceived through the Holy Spirit. His piety and obedience to God are essential aspects of his exemplary character.

As the practice of devotion to saints expanded and developed, so too did the notion of "patron saints," still accepted in the popular devotions of Roman Catholicism and Eastern Orthodoxy. According to this idea, the lives and legends of saints, and the particular miracles attributed to them, came to be seen as evidence of specialized assistance. Thus St. Lucy (died 304CE), who was said to have had her eyes miraculously restored after being blinded by her persecutors, became the patron of eye complaints. The aid of St. Sebastian, a Roman soldier who recovered from being shot with arrows, was sought for protection against the plague and other diseases, which in Greco-Roman times were believed to be caused by the arrows of the gods (Sebastian later suffered a painful martyr's death).

As the protector of Christ, Joseph, the husband of Mary, came to be venerated as the patron of the universal church (from 1870) and of fathers, carpenters, and workers. Because it is believed that he died peacefully, some time before the Crucifixion, in the company of his beloved family, Joseph is also regarded as the patron saint of the dying.

Religious associations and communities often take a saint as their special patron, and it is customary in Roman Catholicism to name chil-

CANONIZATION

The Roman Catholic process of adding new individuals to the official list of saints is known as "canonization." While the pope maintains the sole right to confer sainthood, a group of experts in church law at the Vatican in Rome review all the evidence relating to any candidate for canonization. The complex and lengthy procedure has remained largely the same for four hundred years, although it has notably speeded up since the accession of Pope John Paul II in 1979. First, the candidate's life is submitted to a rigorous investigation in order to ascertain his or her reputation for holiness and orthodoxy. Reports of divine signs—inexplicable events that might be regarded as miracles—are verified. The holy person is then "beatified" (declared "blessed") and local veneration is permitted. Subsequent evidence that God has continued to work through the intercession of the beatified individual leads to a repetition of the process. At the end of this the pope may declare the candidate a saint, worthy of universal veneration.

Canonization is relatively rare, with only around three hundred new saints having been created in the last eight centuries. Over the years, the Vatican has also decanonized numerous saints, evidence for whose claims to sainthood have been found wanting. These include some quite popular and familiar figures, such as St. George and St. Christopher.

St. Michael the Archangel, a Russian icon of the Stroganov school, ca. 1600. Revered as the protector of the church against the forces of evil, Michael is often depicted as a warrior.

dren after saints, believing that this will assure the child of the holy person's special patronage and protection.

Eastern Orthodox worshippers venerate far fewer saints and devotion tends to focus on devotion to the Church Fathers (see p.61) and the early martyrs, icons of whom are widely displayed in churches and homes. Protestant churches grant special reverence to the prophets of the Old Testament and to the apostles, but otherwise they generally regard the veneration of the saints as an idolatrous practice, and deny the intercessory powers of anyone but Christ. But both the Anglican and Lutheran churches recommend certain names for remembrance and thanksgiving.

The Roman Catholic church is the only Christian denomination that has a formal procedure for identifying saints (see box, opposite), and it imposes specific regulations for their cultivation. While the veneration of saints is encouraged, neither they nor their relics may be objects of adoration, which is reserved solely for the persons of the Trinity (Father, Son, and Holy Spirit).

ANGELS

The title of saint is applied to a number of angels—supernatural beings who are believed to reside in heaven and possess extraordinary powers. Angels occur frequently in the Bible, where they praise God and protect the faithful. But biblical angels, as their name (Greek *aggelos*, "messenger") suggests, primarily act as divine messengers, intermediaries between heaven and earth; among them are the archangels ("leading angels") Gabriel, Raphael, and Michael. In the Old Testament, angels announce the births of Ishmael, Isaac, and Samson, and in the gospels they announce those of John the Baptist and Jesus, as well as proclaiming the Resurrection and advising Joseph of Nazareth in his dreams.

In the early sixth century CE, the writer Pseudo-Dionysius the Areopagite spoke of angels as part of a hierarchy of celestial forces, each with a specific cosmic function. Charged with overseeing aspects of human affairs, angels act as rescuers, admonishers, and encouragers. The idea of the guardian angel—a protective angel assigned by God to each person—derives from scripture (notably Psalm 91.11) and also the Greco-Roman belief in protective deities. In Roman Catholicism, October 2 is a feast day for guardian angels, and the feast of St. Michael falls on September 29 (celebrated by Anglicans as the feast of St. Michael and All Angels).

Interest in angels is widespread and found among all branches of Christianity today, but Protestantism has generally downplayed belief in their supernatural power, or indeed existence.

THE WAY OF CHRIST

Throughout the history of Christianity there has been little variation in the fundamental principles intended to guide believers in a Christian way of life. Christian ethical injunctions often take the form of divine imperatives, or commandments. The authoritative sources for Christian ethics are essentially the Ten Commandments, which Moses is said to have received from God on Mount Sinai (Exodus 20.2–17; Deuteronomy 5.6–21), and the teaching of Jesus. In both cases, the scriptural sources have remained relatively constant, although Roman Catholics and Lutherans on the one hand, and the Eastern Orthodox and Protestant Reformed churches on the other, differ slightly in their ordering of the Ten Commandments. The interpretation of scripture has also varied within different historical, social, and geographical contexts and from one denomination to another. The same set of principles has been used, for example, to justify both the maintenance of the status quo by the old Inquisition and the promotion of a radical social agenda by present-day liberation theologians (see p.87).

The Ten Commandments, or Decalogue ("Ten Words," or "Sayings"), articulate fundamental religious and social obligations and in the Bible are explicitly the word of God. They cover the individual's correct relationship to God, parents, spouse, and community. The first four commandments deal with one's relationship to the Deity—one must worship God alone (avoiding idolatry), keep the Sabbath, and honor God's name. Following an admonition to honor one's parents, the remaining five commandments focus on ethical behavior within society, with imperatives not to steal,

SIN AND VIRTUE

Early Christian theologians interpreted the failure of Adam and Eve to obey God's command not to eat from the fruit of one of the trees in the garden of Eden (Genesis 2.17) as the fall from grace of humankind, and as symbolic of human inadequacy in the face of moral freedom. According to Paul, the fall of Adam introduced sin into the world; Augustine developed this idea into the doctrine of "original sin," whereby every human being (except Christ and Mary; see p.70) inherits Adam's sinfulness. This doctrine remains valid in Roman Catholicism.

Medieval Christianity recognized "Seven Deadly (or Capital) Sins"—pride, covetousness, lust, anger, gluttony, envy, and sloth—as the source of all other sins. Pride was considered at the core of all vice, and evidence for this was found in the apocrypha, in the passage "the beginning of pride is sin" (Ecclesiasticus 10.13). The seven sins were personified in sermons, art, and religious literature, and were often presented in battle with their opposites—humility, generosity, chastity, meekness, temperance, fraternal love, and diligence.

Prudence, temperance, fortitude, and justice are called the "Cardinal ['pivotal'] Virtues," while "faith, hope, and love" (as expressed by Paul in 1 Corinthians 13.13) are the "Theological Virtues." The Theological Virtues constitute what Acts 9.2 calls the (Christian) "Way." It is generally agreed that the prime Christian virtue, as Paul says, is love—both of God and of one's fellow creatures.

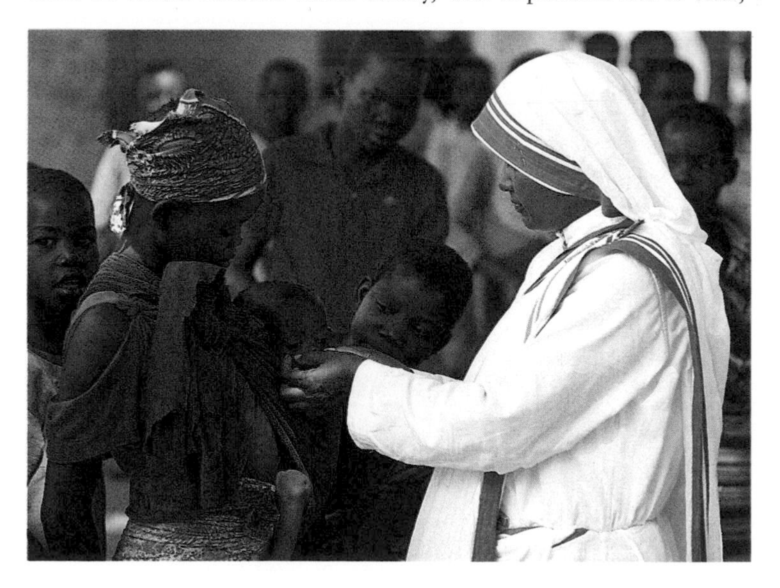

One of the Missionaries of Charity, a Roman Catholic sisterhood founded in India by the Albanian nun Mother Theresa (1910–97) and dedicated to aiding the sick and destitute, treats young war victims in Mozambique. Selfless acts of charity (Latin caritas, *"love," "affection") are among the highest expressions of Christian virtue.*

THE BEATITUDES

In the Sermon on the Mount (see main text), Jesus presents a list of nine blessings for right behavior, for example: "Blessed are the meek, for they will inherit the earth" (Matthew 5.3–12). These are referred to as "the Beatitudes" (Latin *beatus*, "blessed") in the Western churches and as the "Commandments of Blessedness" in the East. Unlike the Ten Commandments, the Beatitudes are not formulated as ethical imperatives. Rather, they state qualities to which Jesus' followers should aspire in order to attain blessedness and eternal life in heaven. These qualities echo the key Christian virtues of humility, simplicity, an active desire for righteousness, purity of heart, mercy, peacemaking, and a readiness to suffer persecution for the Christian faith.

Luke 6.20–26 presents a different version of the Beatitudes that includes a contrasting series of "woes" or curses.

The Mount of the Beatitudes, traditional site of the Sermon on the Mount, on the northwestern shores of Lake Galilee. The Roman Catholic Church of the Beatitudes (foreground) was built in 1936.

covet another's goods, bear false witness, murder, or commit adultery.

Matthew's gospel has a lengthy account of a discourse that Jesus preached to a crowd on a hillside. The so-called "Sermon on the Mount" (Matthew 5–7) is crucial to the ethical foundations of Christianity. Jesus begins by telling the crowd that he has not come to abolish the Jewish law of Moses but to fulfill it, and warns them that anyone who breaks the commandments or teaches others to do so will be "least in the kingdom of heaven" (Matthew 5.17–20). He goes on to set out a new ethical system that extends the Mosaic law in a way that became central to the formation of a distinctly Christian morality. Jesus broadens the commandment not to kill to include even the nurturing of anger against another; expands the commandment against adultery to include lustful desires; and intensifies the injunction against taking the Lord's name in vain to include swearing by heaven, earth, or oneself. (See also box, above.)

However, the heart of the Christian ethic lies in Jesus' reevaluation of the commandments of love. Later in Matthew's gospel, when a lawyer asks him what the greatest commandment is, Jesus quotes the Bible: " 'You shall love the Lord your God with all your heart, and with all your soul, and with all your might' [Deuteronomy 6.5]. This is the greatest and first commandment. And a second is like it: 'You shall love your neighbor as yourself' [Leviticus 19.18]. On these two commandments depend all the law and the prophets." (Matthew 22.36–40; also Mark 12.29–31 and Luke 10.25–28). On a personal level, people must love not only those who return that love, but they must also love and be reconciled to their enemies.

THE GOOD SAMARITAN

Jesus' famous parable of the Good Samaritan (Luke 10.29–37) offers his interpretation of the concept of "neighbor" as used in the commandments, and exemplifies the moral behavior that he expects from his followers.

In the story, a man is left to die by robbers. His plight is ignored by the supposedly holy men of (it is implied) his own nation, and he is aided by a Samaritan—an adherent of a religious tradition found in Samaria (between Judea and Galilee) and related to, but distinct from, Judaism. Most of Jesus' hearers would have regarded Samaritans with suspicion or hostility. But in the parable, Jesus says, the Samaritan represents the true "neighbor": not just someone who belongs to the same family, nation, or even religion—but anyone who extends love to all from a pure heart and with no expectation of reward.

THE LORD'S HOUSE

The term "church" is used to refer to the entire body of the Christian faithful, and to any individual denomination. It also denotes the place where God is believed to reside on earth and where Christians gather for private devotion or public worship. These functions are reflected in the words for this holy space in many languages—*church*, *Kirche*, *église*, *iglesia*, and so on—which derive either from Greek *kuriakos* [*domos*] ("[house] of the Lord") or *ekklesia* ("gathering").

The proliferation of Christian denominations today is reflected in a huge variety of architectural styles and internal arrangements. But during the early years of Christian history, in the period of Roman persecution, churches as distinct buildings cannot be said to have existed at all: Christians met in private homes ("house churches") for worship and gathered secretly in underground catacombs to bury their dead. With an end to persecution in the fourth century CE, Christians were able to gather publicly. Under emperors such as Constantine the Great pagan temples were torn down or converted to Christian use, and magnificent new churches were constructed, often honoring the earthly ruler as well as God. Many housed

PLACES OF PILGRIMAGE

Every year, thousands of Christian pilgrims visit places associated with the life of Christ, such as Bethlehem, Jerusalem, and sites in Galilee. There are many other Christian pilgrimage sites outside the Holy Land, most associated with the relics of saints, which are revered for the sacred power they are believed to possess. Pilgrimages are primarily intended as acts of devotion, to ask or thank a saint for intercession, or as penance.

Among the most famous pilgrimage sites (see map, p.55) are Santiago de Compostela, Spain (home of the reputed relics of St. James the Apostle), and Canterbury cathedral, England (which houses the tomb of St. Thomas à Becket, an archbishop of Canterbury murdered in 1170). In the Middle Ages, Santiago rivaled Rome as a pilgrimage destination. The pilgrimage to Canterbury inspired *The Canterbury Tales* by the fourteenth-century English author Geoffrey Chaucer, a collection of stories supposedly told by pilgrims traveling to Becket's shrine.

Numerous pilgrimage centers have arisen around sites of visions of the Virgin Mary, especially in Roman Catholic countries. Some of the most notable are at Fatima (Portugal), Lourdes (France), and Czestochowa (Poland). Lourdes is perhaps the best known. Here, in 1858, a peasant girl claimed to have had visions of Mary at a grotto where a spring appeared that has since been regarded as a source of miraculous cure. Each year thousands of the faithful flock to the Church of the Rosary built above the grotto.

One of the prime pilgrimage sites in the Holy Land is the Church of the Nativity in Bethlehem, constructed over a cave in which Jesus is said to have been born. The church, which follows the Roman basilican plan, was built by the emperor Constantine in 326CE and restored in the 6th century CE after a fire.

the bones of martyrs or other revered relics, unifying the early Christian landscape into a network of sacred pilgrimage sites (see sidebar, opposite).

The earliest originally Christian churches in the West were in the style of the *basilica* (Latin, from Greek *basilike*, "royal"), the chief public building in every Roman town or city, which functioned as both a meeting hall and a law court. A basilican church has a dominating longitudinal axis leading from the main door to the chancel (or sanctuary), the area in the front (eastern) end of the church where the altar is situated and from which the service is conducted. By the fifth century, every major city in Christendom possessed at least one church on the basilican plan, providing ample room for growing congregations.

In the early Middle Ages, another architectural type emerged, the cruciform church, named because its plan was in the form of the cross, with two side areas or "transepts" leading off the "nave" (Latin *navis*, literally "ship"), the long main axis. In the Eastern Orthodox church, both ancient and modern places of worship are normally constructed on a square plan and surmounted by distinctive domes.

Regardless of how humble or lavish, a Christian church is a sacred place of reverence and awe, intended to communicate Christian mysteries and the drama of salvation to its congregants. This intention is apparent

CHRISTIAN SYMBOLISM

The early Christians often denoted the sacred use of houses or catacombs by carved or painted symbols such as a fish (representing baptism, Christ, and the Resurrection); a shepherd carrying a lamb (an image of pagan origin); the letters A and Ω (the first and last letters of the Greek alphabet, signifying Christ as the beginning and end of all things; see Revelation 1.8); and the Chi-Rho, a monogram of the Greek letters X and P (the first two letters of "Christ" in Greek).

Christians rarely used images of the crucified Christ or the cross alone before the emperor Constantine the Great (306–337CE) abolished crucifixion, from which point memories of its status as a degrading penalty for criminals began to recede. Christianity's pagan opponents themselves sometimes employed images of the cross in order to mock Christ and his followers.

THE ALTAR

The focal point of most Christian churches—at the eastern end or in the center, depending on the plan—is the altar, an intricately carved piece or a simple table of wood, marble, or stone. Its focal position indicates its special role: in the early church, and to this day in Roman Catholicism, Eastern Orthodoxy, and Anglicanism, this is where the Eucharist (see pp.82–3) is celebrated. The altar is infused with a special religious mystery, and the area around it is often reserved solely for the clergy.

With the establishment of the doctrine of transubstantiation (the belief, later rejected by Protestants, that the bread and wine of the Eucharist miraculously become the body and blood of Christ), the altar came to be viewed as the dwelling place of God. Worshippers would show reverence by genuflecting before it.

In Roman Catholicism and Eastern Orthodoxy, a "tabernacle," an ornamental receptacle for the "host" (consecrated bread), is found on the main altar or on a side-altar, and in both traditions a lamp or candles are kept burning near it. Also on the altar, during the liturgy, is an ornate chalice for serving the wine and a silver or gold paten (dish) for the bread. On special feasts in the Roman Catholic church, the consecrated bread is displayed for veneration in a portable shrine called a "monstrance" (from Latin *monstrare*, "to show").

The altar is normally surmounted by a crucifix and sometimes a decorated panel called an "altarpiece." In Protestant churches, the altar (frequently referred to as the Lord's Table) is usually far plainer, with just a simple cross placed on or above it.

A monstrance from the 13th-century cathedral of Toledo, Spain. It reflects the soaring, pinnacled Gothic style of many western European churches of the period.

in the great artistic triumphs of the Romanesque (ca. 1000–1150), Gothic (ca. 1150–1550), and Baroque (ca. 1550–1750) styles of Western Christian architecture. Solid stone and exquisitely crafted or painted ornamentation, vaulted ceilings and soaring spires, and translucent light and color honored the divine and inspired the worshipper.

With an emphasis on light and uplifting space, the design of the medieval church was based on an interaction of theological symbolism and geometric harmony. Spatial orientation was an essential consideration for the construction of a church. The entrance was in the west, the place of the setting sun, darkness, and death, which the worshipper symbolically left behind on entering the sanctuary and approaching the altar in the east end of the church, the direction of the rising sun, light, and resurrection. The north side of the church represented the Old Testament and the south the Last Judgment and the Christian paradise on earth, the New Jerusalem.

Irrespective of period or denomination, certain significant elements of church design have remained more or less constant, such as the altar (see p.77), chancel, nave, pulpit, and (in the West) pews. In many churches, three steps mark the boundary between the sanctuary and the nave, where

IMAGES OF THE SACRED

Throughout the history of the Christian tradition, its sacred stories and mysteries have been expressed in stone and wooden sculptures, intricate mosaics, frescoes, carved altarpieces, and colored glass (see sidebar, opposite). For the illiterate mass of medieval worshippers, religious images served a didactic purpose as well as being aids to spiritual awareness and contemplation. The subject matter of ecclesiastical images naturally includes God, Christ, Mary, saints, and events from scripture and Christian history.

Some Christians at various periods have been strongly opposed to the veneration of images in churches, at times seeking to rid them of sacred images altogether (usually with the exception of the cross), on the grounds that they breach the biblical commandment against idolatry (Exodus 20.4). In the eighth century, the iconoclasts ("image-breakers") of the Eastern church succeeded in officially banning all icons for several decades, and the more radical Protestants of the sixteenth and seventeenth centuries stripped many churches of their decoration, replacing stained windows with plain glass and whitewashing over frescoes. The austere grandeur of many medieval cathedrals in Protestant Europe today is usually the result of such action; in the Middle Ages they would probably have been places of breathtaking color.

The sanctuary of a Russian Orthodox church at Harbin in Heilongjiang province, China. At the top of the steps, the iconostasis *(see main text) is adorned with icons of Christ, Mary, and saints. Entrance to the area behind the screen, where the altar is located, is permitted only to priests.*

The rose window in the north transept of the cathedral of Notre Dame in Chartres, France. The enthroned Virgin and Child (center) are ringed by images of angels and the Holy Spirit (in the form of a dove), Israelite kings, and Old Testament prophets.

the congregation gathers, but in Orthodox churches there is a screen, or *iconostasis* ("place of images"), richly decorated with icons (see box, opposite). Anglican churches usually have a communion rail, where worshippers traditionally kneel to receive the Eucharist from the priest.

The pulpit is an elevated stone or wooden dais used for scripture readings and sermons. In Protestant churches, where the reading of scripture is central to the service, the pulpit may be in a very prominent position. Pews (long benches or chairs for worshippers) were a medieval innovation in the West: for many centuries, Christians stood during the liturgy, as is still the case in the majority of Eastern Orthodox churches.

While most Christian places of worship are called churches, other terms are also used. Historically, a "cathedral" (short for "cathedral church") housed the *cathedra*, the official seat or throne of the local bishop. In Roman Catholicism, the pope confers on certain churches the privileged title of *basilica* indicating that the church contains an altar solely for the use of the pope himself or his delegate (the use of the term *basilica* here is distinct from its purely architectural sense; see p.77). A small, subsidiary, or private church or worship space is often called a chapel (Latin *cappella*, literally "little cloak"—the word derives from a famous medieval shrine near Tours, France, containing the cloak of St. Martin). A chapel may be to one side of the main nave or chancel of a larger church; within a private institution such as a school, hospital, or even an airport; or within a royal or aristocratic residence. Many Protestant denominations employ the term to denote their principal places of worship.

TRANSFORMED LIGHT

Among the remarkable architectural achievements of the Romanesque and Gothic cathedrals of western Europe was the development of the medium of stained (colored) glass, suffusing the internal space with light and color. Stained-glass windows may record biblical or saintly portraits or narratives, or they may be more geometrical and abstract in design.

The shape and proportions of some windows, such as the "rose" windows of Chartres cathedral, France, may possess sacred numerological significance (for example, groups of three represent the Trinity, of four the gospels, and so on).

The concept of the church as the house of God led in medieval times to the idea that the physical fabric of the building represented the Virgin Mary, the vessel in which God became incarnate. Abbot Suger, a twelfth-century French churchman, commented that stained-glass windows demonstrated the nature of the great mystery of the Virgin Birth, since the light came through them and was made glorious without breaking the glass.

LITURGY, SACRAMENTS, AND FESTIVALS

A worshipper is blessed by the officiating archbishop during a Russian Orthodox Christmas service in Moscow.

In Christian tradition the word "liturgy" has two distinct applications. Generally speaking, it applies to all communal church services, in contrast to a wide array of private devotions. The term also refers to a specific ritual event, which for Roman Catholics and Eastern Orthodox worshippers is synonymous with the celebration of the Eucharist (Holy Communion or Lord's Supper) and for Protestant denominations is called the "Liturgy of the Word" and denotes the celebration of Scripture. The term "liturgy" itself (Greek *leitourgia*, "work of the people") connotes the highly congregational aspect of much Christian worship, in which the faithful gather to participate in the liturgy by speaking, singing, or praying in unison.

Christians observe a liturgical calendar, or yearly cycle of holy days, that moves between two principal festivals that are central to all branches of Christianity: Christmas, a celebration of the nativity, or birth, of Jesus (see sidebar, left) and Easter, celebrating his salvific resurrection (see box, opposite). They are preceded by two seasons of special holiness, Advent and Lent respectively. Advent (Latin *adventus*, "arrival") anticipates both the celebration of Jesus' birth and also his expected Second Coming. In Western traditions, it takes in the four Sundays preceding December 25, while in Eastern Orthodoxy it is the forty days before Christmas. However, all churches recognize the first Sunday of Advent as the beginning of the liturgical year.

Easter is preceded by Lent (an old English word for "springtime"), a forty-day preparatory period of repentance, fasting, and self-denial that begins on "Ash Wednesday." The days immediately before Lent are commonly marked by a final round of merrymaking that ends on "Shrove Tuesday" or "Mardi Gras" (French, "Fat Tuesday"), traditionally the last time one could eat meat before Easter, hence the term "carnival" (from Italian *carne*, "meat").

After Easter comes Pentecost (Greek *pentekoste*, "fiftieth [day]"), or Whitsunday, commemorating the descent of the Holy Spirit to Jesus' disciples (Acts 2.1–4). In the New Testament account, this event was marked by *glossolalia* ("speaking in tongues"), a phenomenon characterizing present-day Pentecostalism (see sidebar, p.63).

In Eastern Christianity, two other holy days are of vital importance: the feast of the Transfiguration (August 6), which recalls Jesus' appearance in glory with Moses and Elijah (Matthew 17.1–13; Mark 9.2–13; Luke 9.28–36), and the Feast of the Assumption of Mary (August 15), which commemorates her being taken ("assumed"), body and soul, into heaven.

CHRISTMAS

The New Testament provides few clues as to the time of Jesus' birth, although it has been noted that Palestinian shepherds would have watched their flocks in the hills at night in summer rather than winter. In the Roman empire, the winter solstice was observed on December 25 as the celebration of the Invincible Sun (Sol Invictus), and this was also the time of Saturnalia, an exuberant and popular festival. In the late fourth century, with Rome's abolition of pagan festivals, the date of Sol Invictus was adopted as the birthday of Jesus, who is hailed as the "light of the world" in the gospels (John 8.12).

Taking December 25 as a starting point, the church was able to calculate other Christian celebrations, such as the Annunciation (Luke 1.26–38) on March 25; the Circumcision (Luke 2.21) on January 1; and the Epiphany, or Theophany, marking the homage of the eastern wise men to the messiah (Matthew 2), on January 6.

EASTER

Easter, the commemoration of Jesus' redeeming death and resurrection, is the church's holiest festival. As an observant Jew, Jesus went to Jerusalem to celebrate the Passover, or Pesyach (see p.47)—whence the name for Easter in many churches (Greek and Latin *Pascha*). Matthew, Mark, and Luke describe his final meal with his disciples—the "Last Supper"—as a Passover meal, after which he was arrested, tried, and condemned. Jesus was executed on the following day, marked by Christians as "Good Friday" and the faith's most solemn festival. He died within a few hours and because of the approaching Sabbath (Friday evening to Saturday evening; see p.44) he was entombed in haste.

According to the gospels, a group of women found the tomb empty on the following Sunday; a divine messenger proclaimed to them that Jesus had been raised from the dead. The Resurrection is commemorated on Easter Sunday, the most joyous day in the Christian calendar. Many early Christians celebrated the occasion at Passover (which falls on the fourteenth day of the Jewish month of Nisan, the time of the spring equinox), but the church later fixed upon the Sunday following the first full moon after the equinox.

The week preceding Easter Sunday is known as Holy Week. In Eastern Orthodoxy and Roman Catholicism it includes the liturgies of Maundy Thursday (marking the Last Supper and Christ's washing of the feet of his disciples; [John 13]); Good Friday (the Crucifixion and the end of Lent); Holy Saturday (the resting of Christ's body in the tomb); and "Paschal Vigil," in which worshippers await the arrival of Easter Sunday at midnight.

A procession in Mompox, Colombia, on Palm Sunday, the Sunday before Easter and the first day of Holy Week. It marks Jesus' entry into Jerusalem on a donkey, when people scattered branches (of palm, according to John 12.13) before him.

A Russian Orthodox worshipper lights a candle in a Moscow church. This private act of devotion would normally be accompanied by a moment of quiet reflection and personal prayer.

Over the centuries, local saints' festivals and other regional feasts, such as the dedication of a church, brought considerable variation and confusion into the liturgical calendar. In 1582, as part of a wide reform of the calendar, Pope Gregory XIII systematized the holy days for the Roman Catholic church. Protestant churches eliminated the majority of these feasts, regarding them as having no foundation in the Bible, but by the mid-eighteenth century most of the churches and states of western Europe had adopted Gregory's adjustment to the old Julian calendar, which had become out of step with the solar year by twelve days since being established in Roman times.

However, while most Orthodox countries adopted the Gregorian calendar for secular use, the Orthodox church itself has continued to observe the Julian calendar. Hence there is an enduring discrepancy with regard to the dates of Easter and Christmas between Roman Catholics and Protestants on the one hand, and the Eastern Orthodox church on the other. For example, December 25 in the Julian calendar falls on what in the Gregorian calendar is January 6, while the different Orthodox date for the spring equinox similarly affects the timing of the Orthodox Easter (see p.81).

Christianity has numerous rituals that recall and honor the life of Christ and bring the worshipper into direct proximity with the sacred. These include the sacraments; the reading of the Bible; prescribed prayers; vigils; fasts; and pilgrimages (see p.76). For many monks, nuns, and priests, daily ritual includes an obligation to chant the "Divine Office," which involves a series of communal acts of daily worship called "hours"—lauds, prime, terce, sext, none, vespers, compline, and matins. Otherwise, churches may observe daily matins (morning service) and "vespers" or "evensong" (evening service).

Central to Christian ritual is the celebration of sacred acts known as "sacraments." Most Christians would agree that Christ himself instituted two sacraments, that of baptism (a ritual of initiation into the body of the faithful that also usually involves naming) and that of the Eucharist, or Lord's Supper, a ritual remembrance of the Passion. Both sacraments have been the focus of intense disagreement and today account for some of the major differences between denominations. Baptism, which involves immersion in or pouring on of water, is a ritual which in several denominations initiates infants into the religion and is accompanied by the naming of the child. For other Christians, it is reserved exclusively for adults.

The meaning and significance of the Eucharist (Greek *eucharistia*, "thanksgiving"), for many the foundational sacrament of Christianity, have also been a source of great controversy. For Roman Catholic, Eastern Orthodox, and some Anglican worshippers, the bread ("host") and wine given to believers are literally transformed into the body and blood of Christ through the act of consecration by the priest. This mystery of

PRIVATE WORSHIP

Liturgical observances, such as the celebration of sacraments, are the traditional rituals of Christian worship, but a wide range of nonliturgical rituals, often unstructured and spontaneous such as prayer, form a significant part of the ritual life of many Christians. For Eastern Orthodoxy this would include devotion to icons. These occupy a special place even in the home, where a lamp, candle, or incense is burned before the icon during prayer. Many Roman Catholics, too, light candles and pray in churches outside service times. In private, they may recite the "Hail Mary" (Latin *Ave Maria*), a devotional prayer to the Virgin, and the Lord's Prayer, while counting off a string of beads, or rosary. Taught by Jesus to his disciples, the Lord's Prayer (Matthew 6.9–13; Luke 11.2–4) is central to the devotions of all Christians.

faith is called "transubstantiation." Lutherans accept a modified notion called "consubstantiation," meaning that the substances of bread and wine coexist with the body and blood. Calvinists and many Anglicans believe that there is no physical change in the bread and wine but that they convey to the worshipper the power of the body and blood (a notion called "virtualism"). Most other Protestant denominations believe that the Eucharist is purely a memorial rite and that there is no transformation of the bread and wine.

In Roman Catholicism and Orthodoxy, only the baptized may partake of the Eucharist. In these churches five other sacraments are also held to bring divine power into the life of the believer. These are confirmation (a renewal of baptism with holy oil); penance (atonement for sins); marriage; ordination (investment with priestly powers); and extreme unction (anointing of the sick and dying). Both traditions hold that the sacraments are necessary to guarantee salvation, but most Protestant denominations feel that baptism and the Eucharist are obligatory due to scriptural authority, but are not essential for salvation.

THE LORD'S DAY

By the second century CE the Christian Sabbath, or the "Lord's Day" (Revelation 1.10), had moved to the first day of the week (Sunday) rather than the last (Saturday), not only to distinguish it from the Jewish Sabbath (see p.44) but also, and principally, because this was the day on which Jesus' resurrection occurred. On Sundays, Christians regularly gather to re-create or remember the Lord's Supper. In the liturgy of the Eucharist, this is done by the communicants partaking of bread and wine; in the Protestant liturgy of the Word, readings of the Bible are accompanied by homilies or sermons. Roman Catholics refer to the liturgy of the Eucharist as the Mass, a term derived from the Latin words *missa est* ("it is the dismissal"), spoken by the priest at the conclusion of the service.

Rituals associated with the Lord's Day primarily remember and celebrate what Christians regard as Jesus Christ's sacrifice of body and blood. The following gospel passage (Luke 22.19–20), often spoken by a priest or minister, is incorporated into most Christian rituals celebrating the Eucharist: "And he took bread, and when he had given thanks he broke it and gave it to them, saying: 'This is my body which is given for you; do this in remembrance of me.' And likewise he took the cup after supper, saying, 'This cup which is poured out for you is the new covenant in my blood.' "

A worshipper at an open-air evangelical Protestant service in Manila in the Philippines receives the consecrated bread of the Lord's Supper from a minister. Catholics, Anglicans, and Eastern Orthodox worshippers use the term "Eucharist," but other Christian communities use the term "Communion" or "the Lord's Supper," directly recalling the gospel story of the Last Supper, Jesus' final meal with his disciples before his arrest and crucifixion.

THE DEARLY DEPARTED

At the heart of Christianity lies the belief in an eternal life after death. Its basis is God's redemptive activity to save sinful humankind, manifested in the incarnation and resurrection of Christ and extended to all believers. As with other essential elements of Christianity, worshippers find authority for the doctrine of immortality in the Bible. One of the most quoted passages is John 3.16: "For God so loved the world that he gave his only Son, so that everyone who believes in him may not perish but may have eternal life." Ritual acknowledgment of the belief in eternal life is included in a number of Christian liturgies through the recitation of a creed (statement of belief). The last line of all Christian creeds affirms the worshipper's faith in the resurrection of the body and "life everlasting."

Salvation, the term for the state of redemption and reconciliation with God, is a primary spiritual goal of Christians. Aside from the Calvinist notion of predestination, which holds that only an elect body of worshippers is saved, in most Protestant communities salvation is guaranteed solely by the worshipper's faith, the acceptance of Jesus Christ. For Roman Catholicism and Eastern Orthodoxy, salvation is also dependent upon faith in the mysteries of the church, and on the fulfillment of sacraments (see pp.82–3). Interpretations of the nature of and path to salvation vary, but the view that humans have an immortal soul is generally accepted in Christianity.

As he judges a dead person's soul in the balance, an angel fends off the Devil; by Guariento di Arpo (ca. 1310–70).

While distinctions exist among Christians about what qualifies one for salvation or damnation, it is a tradition of all denominations that the saved will spend eternity rewarded in the paradise of heaven while the damned will be punished forever in hell. The precise location of the everlasting life is a complex issue for theologians and worshippers alike. In the Middle Ages, Christians envisaged four possible locations for the soul after death: heaven, hell, purgatory, or limbo. In the Old Testament the term "heaven" refers to the blue firmament, the region above the clouds where God resides, and the New Testament repeatedly refers to the "kingdom of heaven" or the "kingdom of God" (terms that encompass various other meanings) as a place where believers are gloriously present with God. For Christians today, heaven is conceptualized as a state of triumphant glory and joy, a blissful paradise in the presence of the beatific vision of God.

Enmity with God leads to the state of damnation in hell. Throughout Christian history, hell has been envisioned as a place of unspeakable punishment, an eternal inferno, presided over by the Devil, or Satan. The damned are eternally estranged from God; hence their abode is said to be as remote as possible from heaven, located in a fiery darkness. Biblical authority for the image of hell is found in a vivid account of the great final day of judgment in Matthew's gospel. Christ sits in majesty separating the saved from the damned, and says to the latter: "depart from me into the eternal fire prepared for the devil and his angels" (Matthew 25. 41).

For medieval Christians, purgatory (from Latin *purgare*, "to purge, make clean") was the place where souls that were neither damned nor free of sin would suffer for a time after death and be cleansed of their sins. This belief was founded on the notion that sin and God cannot coexist and consequently the soul must become sinless in order to enter into the eternal heavenly paradise. In modern Roman Catholic teaching, purgatory is a state or condition of punishment for those whose souls at death are not free of sin or whose sins have not been remitted by God through the sacrament of penance (see p.83). Protestant reformers rejected the belief in purgatory as without biblical foundation.

Some Roman Catholic theologians still regard limbo, a peaceful state but without the possibility of the presence of God, as the destination for unbaptized infants.

BURYING THE DEAD

The traditional manner of caring for the dead in Christianity is burial. Customs vary historically and include a wide range of regional differences. Burial practices are an expression of Christian belief in immortality. As with other religious traditions, disposal of the deceased is a rite of passage, leaving one world for another. Care of the dead requires ceremonial rituals. The body is prepared and displayed for farewell followed by burial or cremation. Funeral services and traditional wakes have a comforting aspect and are often concluded with a common meal shared by the mourners.

HONORING THE DEAD

Many denominations commemorate the dead in special masses, prayers, and festivals. The dates of such feasts vary: in Greek Orthodoxy, the dead are remembered on the eve of Sexagesima (the second Sunday before Lent) or on the eve of Pentecost, while the equivalent Armenian Orthodox feast falls on Easter Monday. The Roman Catholic festival, All Souls' Day (November 2), has its origin in the medieval cult of the dead and in the Middle Ages, with All Saints' Day (November 1), ranked after Christmas and Easter in importance. It is a highly charged holy day in many countries, a time to pray for and remember the departed.

In colonial Mexico, Spanish missionary priests combined an indigenous pre-Hispanic religious festival of the dead with All Souls' Day to produce the famous "Mexican Day of the Dead." As in many parts of Europe, Christians visit the graves of their deceased relatives, and decorate them. Mexicans also prepare picnics at the cemetery, and after eating a sumptuous meal they tell stories about the lives of the dead and leave special offerings. At an evening meal the family shares a loaf of bread called *pan de muerto* ("bread of death"). It is regarded as a sign of luck to be the one who bites into the plastic toy skeleton hidden inside.

Graves decorated by relatives with flowers, candles, and special offerings such as gifts of food, during the Day of the Dead festival on Juanita Isle, Mexico.

CHURCH, STATE, AND COMMUNITY

The Bible calls upon Christians to obey the laws of the state, notably in Jesus' instruction to "give to the emperor the things that are the emperor's, and to God the things that are God's" (Mark 12.17). However, the relationship between the ecclesiastical and secular authorities has varied at different times and in different countries. The later Roman emperors played a vital role in church affairs, convening counsels, prosecuting heretics, and determining church leadership. These functions were inherited in the East by the Byzantine emperors and in the West by the rulers of the Holy Roman empire (a confederation of central European states originally founded by Charlemagne in 800CE and abolished by Napoleon in 1804).

In the Middle Ages, the political power of the clergy increased, especially in the West, after the twelfth-century "Investiture Controversy"—a dispute over the extent of the authority sovereigns could exercise in ecclesiastical affairs—from which the church emerged with sole authority over spiritual matters. The sixteenth-century Protestant Reformation saw a further entrenchment of the principle of the separation of church and state. In Protestant countries, all legal and political authority came to lie with secular leaders (except in England, where the monarch is "supreme governor" of the Church of England).

In recent centuries and in the modern era, anticlerical and antiecclesiastical movements have arisen owing largely to criticisms of ecclesiastical wealth and the perceived abuse of clerical privilege. In the twentieth century, several governments, including those of France, Mexico, and Spain, have pursued expressly anticlerical policies, placing restrictions on the clergy and taking over church property. In Communist states, anticlericalism has been pursued as part of a general antireligious ideology extending to the prohibition of the public practice of the religion.

While all Christian denominations claim a status distinct from the state, many Christians are keenly interested in engaging in society and actively pursuing social change. Modern Christian thinking includes the concepts of "social gospel" (see sidebar, left), and a number of radical approaches, or "liberation theologies" (see sidebar, opposite), that rethink theological foundations in terms of the poor and oppressed, and maintain that theology, by its nature—especially its concern with God's relationship to humanity—has practical and political implications.

In the twentieth century, bitter disagreements have continued to pit Christian groups against one another. Many interdenominational

SOCIAL GOSPEL

As Christianity entered the twentieth century, several Christian thinkers and activists brought a challenging social vision to their faith. Protestants and Catholics alike argued passionately —as do today's liberation and feminist theologians (see sidebar, opposite)—that Christianity has an obligation to engage with social problems, to speak out against violations of human rights. The notion of a "social gospel" was founded on the belief that humanity suffers from problems only religion can resolve. Social gospel movements such as the Salvation Army, established in 1878 by William Booth (1829–1912), worked to establish hospitals, orphanages, homeless shelters, and soup kitchens as well as employing overtly political strategies aimed at economic justice and racial equality.

The Salvation Army is particularly evangelical in its rescue work, but most Christian social movements today are less concerned with the salvation—or even Christianity—of those they help than with their physical and social wellbeing.

Movements that subscribe to the social gospel idea are challenged by conservative and fundamentalist groups primarily concerned with evangelizing and with maintaining traditional Christian values.

A convoy from the international charity Christian Aid brings relief to drought victims in the west African state of Mali.

Anglican women priests and deaconesses in a special ceremony at Canterbury cathedral. Female ordination is a major issue dividing the main denominations: most Protestant churches now have women priests, while Roman Catholicism and Orthodoxy remain firmly opposed.

conflicts date back to the Reformation or, like the Roman Catholic-Orthodox clash in the former Yugoslavia, even further. The policies of segregation in the southern United States and of apartheid in South Africa both found support from local denominations in those regions but met with fierce opposition from churches outside.

Christianity confronts other, outside challenges in the modern world. Since the sixteenth and seventeenth centuries, science has called fundamental Christian teachings into question and continues to raise new doctrinal, moral, and ethical issues. Creationism and evolution still split believers after more than a century, to which must now be added bioethical debates on questions such as cloning and genetic engineering.

Other issues facing Christians as they enter the third Christian millennium include environmentalism versus material development; the use of capital punishment; abortion; and the complex questions of sexuality and the family. While Protestant churches do not regard marriage as a sacramental bond, unlike the Roman Catholic and Eastern Orthodox churches, all Christians liken the institution of marriage to the relationship of the church and Christ (see Ephesians 5.22–33). Historically the church has regarded the family as vital for the transmission of Christian values, and both progressive and conservative theologians of all denominations uphold the social importance of marriage and the family. However, there is wide disagreement over the laws that govern marriage, sexuality, and the raising of families. Bitter controversies, often fought on the lines of the political ideologies of the Left or Right, over issues such as the equality of marriage partners, family planning, and sexual orientation, show little sign of ending their tendency to divide the faithful.

"LIBERATION" THEOLOGIES

The term "liberation theologies" covers a variety of radical Christian strands, including liberation theology proper and feminist theology. Liberation theology, which originated among Catholics in Latin America, looks for radical social change to eliminate poverty and portrays Jesus as the chief liberator of the oppressed. Its advocates hold that suffering humanity constitutes God's elect, and they highlight the books of Exodus (the account of one nation's liberation) and Job (the story of an innocent individual's suffering).

Some Roman Catholic leaders have criticized liberation theology, maintaining that, because it incorporates Marxist theory, it reduces faith to politics. However, it might be observed that there has been a long tradition of Christian political engagement, even in Catholic countries, as seen in the Christian socialist and Christian democratic movements of Italy, Germany, and elsewhere.

Feminist theology is founded on the belief that traditional theology is fundamentally patriarchal, that is, it has been formulated almost exclusively by and for men. The primary goal of feminist theologians is the elimination of oppression based on gender, race, or class, and the promotion of a full humanity for all Christians. In seeking to address a perceived systematic oppression of women in Christian history, theology, and practice, feminist theologians use scripture and tradition in their critique of patriarchal theology and their quest to recover the lost experiences of women.

Chapter Three

ISLAM

Matthew S. Gordon

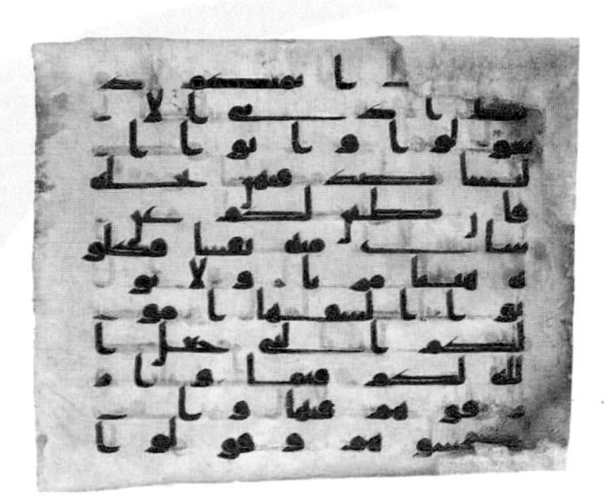

A folio from a massive Quran (54x66cm [21x26in]) produced in north Africa in the early 8th century CE. *This style of Arabic calligraphy is known as kufic, from the Iraqi town of Kufa.*

OPPOSITE *The magnificent tiled interior of the Shah mosque in Isfahan, Iran, built 1612–30 by Shah Abbas the Great. The decoration consists almost entirely of symbols and calligraphy, in accordance with Islamic views on representational art* *(see p.100)*.

INTRODUCTION

Islam is the third major monotheistic tradition to emerge in human history. The term *Islam* itself, often translated as "submission," refers to the decision by the Muslim ("One who submits or surrenders") to abide both in mind and body by the will of God (in Arabic *Allah*, "The One God"). To submit to the divine will, as articulated in the sacred texts of the tradition, is therefore to bring about a harmonious order in the universe. In this sense, Islam refers not only to the act of submission but to its consequence, that is, peace (*salam*).

The Islamic tradition dates its origins to events which unfolded in the early seventh century CE in the Arabian town of Mecca. The tradition teaches that a forty-year-old merchant, Muhammad ibn Abdallah—commonly referred to simply as the Prophet, or Messenger, of God—received a series of revelations from God beginning in 610CE and ending soon before his death in 632CE. These revelations, collectively known as the Quran, are held by Muslims to be God's direct and inalterable word and are the principal source of Islamic belief and practice. The Quran is both the symbol and embodiment of the intimate relationship between God and humankind.

Complementing the Quran is the vast and complex record of Muhammad's life, known as the Hadith (see p.105), which embodies the *Sunna*, or "Tradition," of how the Prophet thought, spoke, and conducted his affairs. The Quran and the Hadith are the two most important sources of Islamic religious and legal thought. Those with the task of interpreting the Quran and the Hadith are known as *ulama*, religious

Palestinian men at prayer in Manger Square, Bethlehem, a largely Muslim town of sacred significance to Jews and Christians. The interaction of the three monotheistic traditions throughout their history has been both contentious and mutually enriching.

WORLD ISLAMIC POPULATIONS

Numbering over a billion souls, Muslims today form the majority in more than fifty countries and a substantial minority in many others. There are vibrant growing communities in Europe and both North and South America. However, the greatest number of Muslims live in the developing regions of the world, including Arabic-speaking north Africa and the Near East, and countries of east and west Africa and central, southern, and southeast Asia.

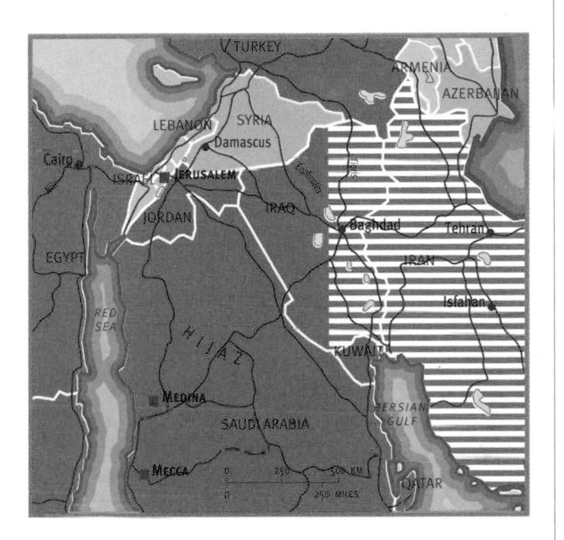

Muslims as percentage of population

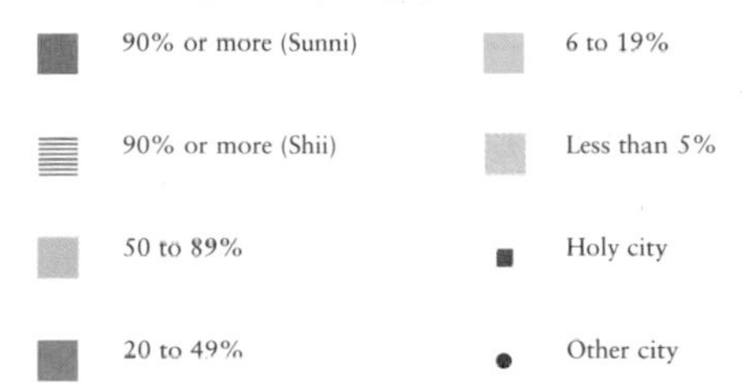

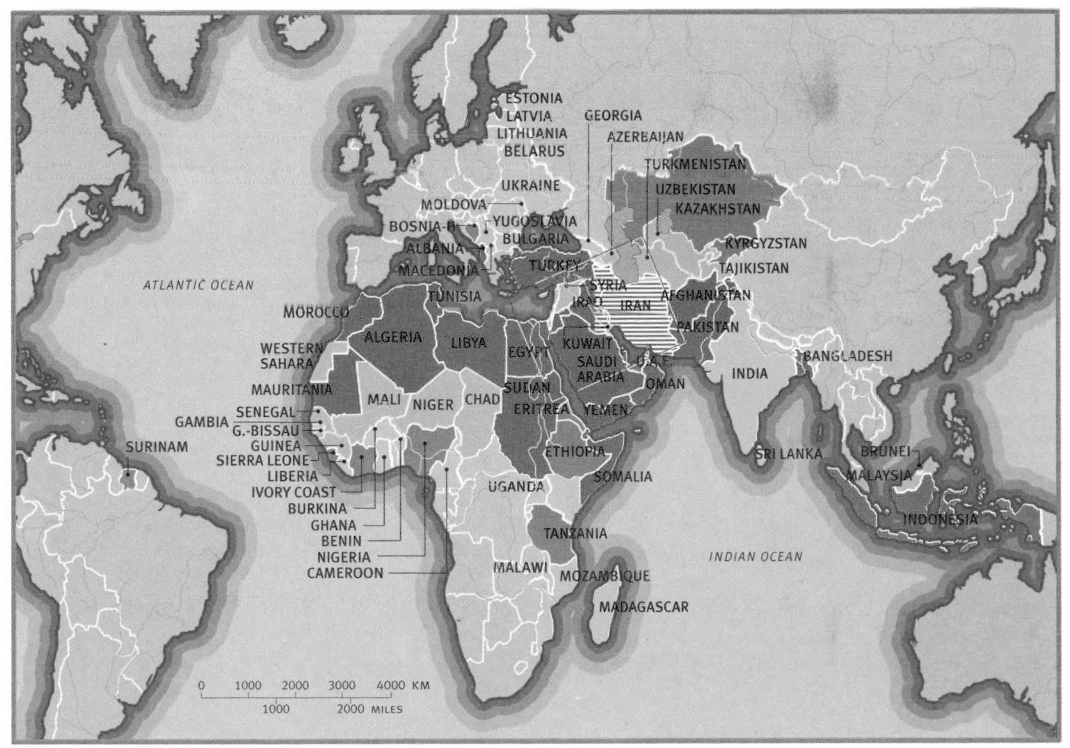

scholars, from the Arabic for "learned ones." From their efforts emerged the code of regulations known as the Sharia, which in turn gave rise to Islamic law (see pp.110–11).

The majority of contemporary Muslims are members of the Sunni community. The Sunni variety of Islam (see p.98) had emerged by the tenth century CE from the urban scholarly circles of Cairo, Damascus, Baghdad, and the major Iranian cities, such as Nishapur. While thinking of themselves as members of the single worldwide community of Islam, Sunni Muslims recognize internal social and cultural differences born of the encounter between Islamic teaching and local and regional practices in the Near East and elsewhere. There are also distinctions arising from doctrinal and especially legal interpretation.

Sunni Islam took shape partly as a result of an inevitable tendency among organized religions to establish what one might term an "orthodoxy," and partly as a reaction to the growth of other branches of the Islamic tradition. Chief among these is Shiism, sometimes referred to as the "minority" community of Islam (see p.97). Of the various branches of Shii Islam, the largest are the "Twelver" Shiis (see pp.108–9), who form a majority in Iran and southern Iraq and a substantial minority in Lebanon, Kuwait, Pakistan, and elsewhere; the Ismailis (see p.109), who themselves have several offshoots, and are mainly located in India, East Africa and, increasingly, in urban Canada and the United Kingdom; and the Zaydis, represented principally in Yemen.

Islam took shape in a Near Eastern context. In its early period, the faith

CHRONOLOGY *All dates are* CE

570–632	Lifetime of the Prophet Muhammad
622	Muhammad migrates to Medina; Muslim calendar begins (July 16)
632	Death of Muhammad; Abu Bakr elected first caliph
632–661	Rashidun caliphate extends Islamic rule to north Africa, Persia, Jerusalem, Damascus, the Caucasus, and central Asia
ca. 640–660	Beginnings of Shii Islamic tradition
732	Muslim advance into Europe halted at Poitiers, France, by Christian armies
750–925	"Golden Age" under the unified Islamic empire of the Abbasids
969–1171	Ismaili Fatimid dynasty rules from Cairo
1055–1220	Seljuq sultans rule from Baghdad
1096	First Crusade launched
1099	Jerusalem falls to Crusaders
1250–1517	Mamluks rule from Egypt
1258	Baghdad sacked by Mongols; end of the Abbasid empire
1291	Islamic forces seize Acre in Palestine, last Crusader stronghold
1453	Constantinople (Istanbul) falls to the Ottoman Turks
1492	Fall of Granada ends Muslim rule in Spain
1502–1736	Safavid dynasty rules Iran
1520–66	Sultan Sulayman the Magnificent expands Ottoman overlordship of southeastern Europe, north Africa, and the Near East
1526	Establishment of Mongol (Mughal) rule in India
1683	Turks besiege Vienna
1798	Napoleon invades Egypt
1832	French occupy Algeria
1857	Direct British rule begins in India as Mughal empire abolished
1885–98	Mahdists rule Sudan
1920	Mandate system establishes European colonial government in ex-Ottoman lands of Iraq, Syria, Lebanon, Palestine, Transjordan
1923	Secular Turkish state declared by Kemal Atatürk; caliphate abolished
1932	Foundation of Saudi Arabia
1947	Foundation of Muslim state of Pakistan
1948	Establishment of state of Israel and first Arab-Israeli war
1949	Independence of Indonesia
1967	Second Arab-Israeli war
1973	Third Arab-Israeli war
1979	Islamic revolution in Iran
1991	Independence of former Soviet republics of central Asia
1993 and 1995	Oslo Accords lead to creation of Palestinian political entity in Gaza and West Bank

encountered Judaism and Christianity together with Zoroastrianism in Iran (Persia), and the legal and political traditions of the Byzantine empire, Iran, and the largely Turkic central Asian steppes. As Islam spread beyond these core regions, it inevitably came into contact with a host of other cultures. The worldwide Islamic community today represents an enormous range of national, ethnic, socio-economic, and linguistic backgrounds.

Islam is a faith to which a steadily growing proportion of the world's population adheres. The figure of one billion is most often cited, although accurate figures are hard to come by in several regions where Muslims predominate. One common misconception among non-Muslims is that most Muslims are Arabs, an idea derived from the fact that most Arabs are Muslims, and the Arabian origins of the tradition itself. Moreover, Arabic is the language in which the Quran itself claims to have been revealed. However, most contemporary Muslims reside outside the Arab regions of the Near East and north Africa. The nation with the largest Muslim population is Indonesia, followed by Pakistan, Bangladesh, and India. Most Iranians and Turks are Muslims, as are significant populations in China, Russia, and sub-Saharan Africa. Europe and North America are home to relatively small but vibrant and rapidly growing Muslim communities. For example, there are large numbers of Pakistani and Indian Muslims in the United Kingdom and sizeable communities of north African Muslims in France and of Turks and Iranians in Germany. The Islamic populations of the United Kingdom and the United States includes converts as well as immigrant families and their descendants.

Worshippers in the Haydar mosque in Kulyab, southern Tajikistan. In the medieval period Islam penetrated deep into central Asia as far as western China (Chinese Turkestan). A revival in Islamic activity followed the independence of much of the region from Russia in 1991.

The modern Faisal mosque (constructed 1976–88) in Islamabad, Pakistan, is a monument to Islamic internationalism. The gift of Saudi Arabia (and named for the Saudi king Faisal ibn Abd al-Aziz Al Saud), it was designed by a Turkish architect as a centerpiece for the new Pakistani capital city. Pakistan itself was created in 1947 from the mainly Muslim regions of northwestern and eastern India, an area that once formed the heartland of the Mughal empire that dominated the subcontinent from the 16th–18th centuries.

THE ARABIAN CRUCIBLE

The Islamic tradition traces its origins to the Hijaz, the northwest region of the Arabian peninsula, and specifically to the towns of Mecca (or Makkah) and Yathrib, subsequently known as Medina (from the Arabic *Madinat al-Nabi*, "the city of the Prophet"). Sixth-century CE Mecca was the scene of the first revelations that form the basis of Islam, which were given to a forty-year-old merchant called Muhammad ibn Abdallah. Influential members of Muhammad's clan, the Banu Hashim, a branch of the powerful Quraysh tribe, dominated a trade network serving the Hijaz and linked to southern Syria, Mesopotamia (Iraq), Yemen, and east Africa.

"Arabia" in the sixth century CE encompassed nearly the entire Arabian peninsula, as well as areas of Transjordan, southern Syria, and Mesopotamia. Scattered throughout the peninsula were small commercial centers such as Mecca and also agricultural communities such as Yathrib. There was a common language, Arabic, but no political unity.

The tribe was the principal form of social and political organization. Most Arabs at this time were pastoral nomads, living a rough and demanding existence based on the rearing of camels, sheep, and goats, and the tribe, headed by its chief, provided both a sense of identity and physical security.

The patterns of Arab life were influenced by political, economic, and religious developments in the Near East. It is likely that Christian merchants and itinerant preachers traveled around the Arabian peninsula and that Muhammad therefore had some contact with the traditions of Christianity. There was also a substantial Jewish presence in the Hijaz, particularly in Yathrib, where at least three Jewish tribes lived. The Near East itself was dominated by two rival superpowers, the Byzantine and

THE HARAM

Pre-Islamic Mecca was the site of an ancient sanctuary, called the Haram, from the Arabic for "sacred, inviolable." At the time of Muhammad's birth, perhaps in 570CE, the Quraysh tribe controlled access to the Haram, which was the focal point of local religious practice and a place of pilgrimage. At its heart was the Kaba, an ancient sacred structure (see p.112), in and surrounding which were a large number of stone idols representing a variety of deities, chief among them Hubal, perhaps a war god, and the three daughters of Allah, the divine lord of the Haram. It was in the name of Allah—originally the Arabic for "the god" (*al-ilah*)—that Muhammad would initiate his teachings, although at this time Allah was clearly accompanied by "associate" divinities.

The use of the Haram by pilgrims overlapped with its use by merchants: it was considered neutral ground, where goods could be exchanged and meetings held without fear of violence. The role of the Quraysh was thus a complex one, involving diplomacy, the protection of sacred sites, and participation in an active local commerce.

A view of Medina, where the first Muslim community was consolidated. The city, in present-day Saudi Arabia, is Islam's second holiest after Mecca. A painting of ca. 1750CE.

Sassanian (Persian) empires. In the early seventh century CE, both were debilitated by war and internal discontent.

The Islamic community, or *Umma*, to use the Quranic term, dates its foundation to a specific event in the life of Muhammad. Prompted by divine revelations, he began his prophetic mission ca. 610CE (see pp.106–7). The response of the Meccans, and the Quraysh in particular, was initially tolerant, but quickly changed to hostility when Muhammad gradually turned to a pure monotheism and criticized the pagan cult centered on the Haram (see sidebar, opposite). In 622CE, the persecution of his followers led the Prophet to move them to Yathrib (Medina), an agricultural town to the north. Muhammad and a close follower and kinsman, Abu Bakr, were the last to depart. The Prophet's journey in 622 is known as the Hijra and is held by the Islamic tradition to mark the *Umma*'s founding moment and the beginning of its calendar.

THE PROPHETIC TRADITION

In one sense, Muslims regard the teachings of divine revelation on the part of Muhammad as the founding moment of their tradition. But in another sense, the tradition articulated through the Prophet is held to be as old as humankind itself.

Muslims believe that the one true God, omnipotent and eternal, first revealed his Word in a pristine, unaltered form to Adam, the first man, then to the ancient patriarch Abraham (in Arabic, Ibrahim). That same primordial message, and the unique relationship with humanity that it embodies, was later given to Muhammad. Thus Islam sees itself as the original and only true religion, that of Abraham.

An angel intervenes with a sacrificial ram as Abraham, in a divine test of faith, is about to sacrifice his son. Islamic scholars differ over whether the son was Isaac (Ishaq) or Ishmael (Ismail). A Turkish painting of 1583.

Between Abraham and Muhammad, according to the Quran, there lived many other prophets (*nabis*), of whom twenty-eight were chosen to propagate the divine Word; these are known as *rasuls*. Among the most important *rasuls* are Noah (Arabic, Nuh), David (Dawud), Moses (Musa), and Jesus (Isa). Through the latter two, the divine message was brought to the communities of the Jews and Christians, and so both groups belong, like Islam, to a common "Abrahamic" tradition. The Quran terms Jews and Christians "Peoples of the Book" and accords them particular respect.

But the Quran also contains polemic against the two other "Abrahamic" religions. According to Islamic teaching, every moment of revelation represents the start of a new cycle of prophecy, which culminates in a willful or careless corruption of the original primordial idea—at which point a new prophet appears. Thus the cycle initiated by Jesus ended in the "corruption" represented by the Christian insistence on the Trinity and the divinity of Christ (see p.64).

For each successive prophet, therefore, the degeneration of the divine message necessitated a dual responsibility: to warn and to renew. In the Islamic view, Muhammad stands in this prophetic tradition but is unique, in that he is the "seal" of the prophets: with him the prophetic cycle ceases. He reminds humankind of the original true message and brings its final and perfect form: the Quran.

AN AGE OF EMPIRES

In Medina, Muhammad continued his preaching and consolidated his following, drafting a "Constitution of Medina," announcing the existence of the *Umma* (see p.95). Over the next ten years Muhammad exercised religious, political, and military control over a dynamic new community. Attempts to win the backing of Jewish tribes in Medina ended in tragedy, with the exile of two tribes and the violent suppression of a third. However, a military campaign to capture Mecca was a success, and at his death, on June 8, 632CE, Muhammad controlled much of the Arabian peninsula and had sent forces to probe Byzantine defenses in southern Syria. Within another two decades, Arab armies under Muslim command had destroyed the Persian empire of the Sassanians completely and driven the Byzantines out of Syria and Egypt. Subsequent conquests took Muslim armies into central Asia, northern India, the rest of north Africa, and Iberia.

Rule over this rapidly growing empire was exerted at first by close companions of the Prophet, who were succeeded, following internecine warfare, by an élite of Muhammad's tribe, the Quraysh, headed by the Umayyad family. The political successors to the Prophet bore the title

THE TRAVELS OF IBN BATTUTA

One important source for our knowledge of the medieval Islamic world is the travel account of a fourteenth-century scholar, Ibn Battuta (1304–ca. 1370). Crossing the world from north Africa to Egypt and the Hijaz, from Palestine to Persia, central Asia, India, southeast Asia, and perhaps China, Ibn Battuta encountered a range of Islamic societies representing a rich array of languages, cultures, and histories. He records the devastating effects upon Persia and central Asia of the Mongol invasions of the thirteenth century; the spread of Islam among the Turks who were gradually occupying the Anatolian peninsula; and the growing presence of the faith in the lands bordering the Indian Ocean and within Africa.

CONQUERED PEOPLES

Conversion among the subject peoples of the Arab-Islamic empire took place steadily over the first few centuries of Islamic history, with sizeable majorities emerging in the Near East and north Africa. But significant Christian, Jewish, and other communities remained in Egypt, Iraq, and elsewhere. Incidents of forced conversion are recorded, but appear to have been rare. Some Christian churches were converted into mosques, but this practice was exceptional.

As "Peoples of the Book"—that is, peoples to whom God had sent his prophetic message—Jews and Christians came to be defined by the *ulama*, the Muslim religious scholars, as *dhimmi*s or "protected" peoples. This meant that their traditions and practices were to be respected and they were largely to be left to govern their own internal affairs. Later, mainly for political and fiscal reasons, *dhimmi* status was also extended to Zoroastrians.

For *dhimmi*s, security of person, property, and religious sites was guaranteed and usually in practice maintained. On the other hand, the status of *dhimmi*s was definitely secondary to that of Muslims. In many places and at many times, the *dhimmi* was required to wear distinguishing clothing and was often prohibited from bearing arms. More significantly, *dhimmi*s were forbidden to propagate their faith or to build new houses of worship, and were obliged to pay a special poll tax, the *jizya*, that was imposed on non-Muslims. It appears to have been the stigma that was attached to *dhimmi* status that in the end compelled many non-Muslims to convert to the new faith.

The Byzantine church of Hagia Sophia in Constantinople became a mosque after the city fell to the Turks in 1453.

"Caliph," from the Arabic *khalifa* ("deputy" or "successor"). From 661CE to 750CE, following a transfer of the Islamic capital to Damascus from Medina, the Umayyads controlled the caliphate and took significant steps toward both the arabization and islamization of the conquered regions. In 750CE, the Umayyads were overthrown by the Abbasids, another branch of the Banu Hashim (the Prophet's clan). Based in Baghdad, the Abbasid caliphate ruled over a period of steady growth in the Islamic community, with conversion sweeping north Africa, Spain, and the Near East.

In the wake of their conquests, Arabs settled in the main urban centers of the Near East, while new Arab garrisons such as Basra, Kufa, and Fustat steadily evolved into towns and cities. In this urban environment, during the ninth and tenth centuries CE, the Arab encounter with Jewish, Christian, Persian, and Zoroastrian traditions, coupled with the demands of administering a vast empire, prompted a remarkable flowering of Islamic legal, religious, and political thought. The scene of greatest activity was the thriving imperial capital, Baghdad. Among the prominent figures of this period were the renowned scholars Jafar al-Sadiq (700–765CE) and al-Shafii (767–819CE), the historian and exegete al-Tabari (838–923CE), the philosopher Ibn Sina (known in Europe as Avicenna; 980–1047), and perhaps the most influential of all, al-Ghazzali (1058–1111; see p.103).

In the mid-ninth century, however, the Abbasids began to lose their grip on power. The dynasty had already lost Spain a century and a half earlier to a survivor of the Umayyads, and now political setbacks and the growing prominence of the *ulama* contributed to a loss of legitimation. No less serious was the rise of two sectarian communities that represented what would come to be known as the Shii branches of Islam (see sidebar, right). The

The Court of the Lions in the Alhambra palace, seat of the Muslim rulers of Granada in southern Spain. The last remnant of a great Arab civilization in Iberia, Granada was captured by Spanish Christian forces in 1492.

SHII ISLAM

The roots of Shiism go back to a conflict over the succession to the Prophet. A handful of respected Muslims chose Abu Bakr, Muhammad's close follower, as the first caliph, to the dismay of those who saw Ali ibn Abi Talib, the Prophet's son-in-law, as his rightful successor. While Ali did later become caliph (656–661CE), his followers argued that an injustice had been committed. The Shiite movement arose from the Alid (pro-Ali) faction. Shii Muslims hold that only a descendant of Ali and his wife Fatima, the Prophet's daughter, can serve as leader, or Imam, of the *Umma*, the Muslim community. In 680CE, the Alid cause was taken up by his son, al-Husayn, in a brief uprising that ended with the massacre of al-Husayn and his male followers by troops of the caliph Yazid I (680–683CE).

The two major divisions of Shiism, the Twelvers and the Ismailis, arose as a result of disagreements over who could claim the title of Imam (see pp.108–9). Centered on Baghdad, the Twelvers were led by a fairly apolitical scholarly élite and were well integrated into Islamic urban society. Ismaili Shiism, rurally based and politically radical, emerged as a dynamic missionary movement, winning followers throughout the Islamic world. In the early tenth century, an Ismaili state, the Fatimid caliphate, was established in north Africa. From 969 to 1171CE, the Fatimids ruled an empire with Egypt at its center.

SUNNI ISLAM

Most Muslims adhere to the Sunni branch of Islam. Its emergence can be traced to disputes between Shiism (see p.97) and majority communities in the early caliphate, as well as to the challenges that face all new faiths in developing coherent systems of practice and thought. Sunnism stresses consensus and community, based on the Quran and the Prophetic model. The term "Sunni" derives from the Arabic for "people of the tradition [*sunna*] and the community." The "tradition" is the example of Muhammad, the model for Muslim conduct. Key steps in the formalization of Sunnism include the development, by ca. 1000CE, of four major legal schools (see p.110).

Abbasid empire was gradually replaced by regional power centers. The Fatimids, established in Tunisia since 909CE, conquered Egypt in 969CE and established their imperial capital at Cairo. Abbasid principalities in Iran and the lands beyond the Oxus (Amu Darya) river yielded to nomadic Muslim Turkic armies, notably those led by the Seljuq family. The Seljuq rulers, or sultans, seized Baghdad and ended what was now only a puppet caliphate in 1055. A brief period of imperial unity across much of the Near East under the Seljuq Turks ended in fragmentation, but the stage was set for further Turkic invasions and ultimately the arrival of the Mongols in the thirteenth century.

The Seljuq period saw a flourishing of Persian and Turkish intellectual and artistic traditions, furnishing a new source of inspiration for Islamic thought. The Seljuq minister Nizam al-Mulk (died 1092) is particularly associated with Seljuq patronage of the *ulama*, the religious establishment, through appointments to religious and legal posts and sponsorship of the *madrasa* (theological college) system. This uneasy, if mutually beneficial, relationship between a ruling Turkic military élite and the religious community also characterized the Mamluk dynasty (1250–1517) that succeeded the Fatimids in Egypt. The efforts of the *ulama*, in part as the result of such official patronage, led to the emergence of a shared system

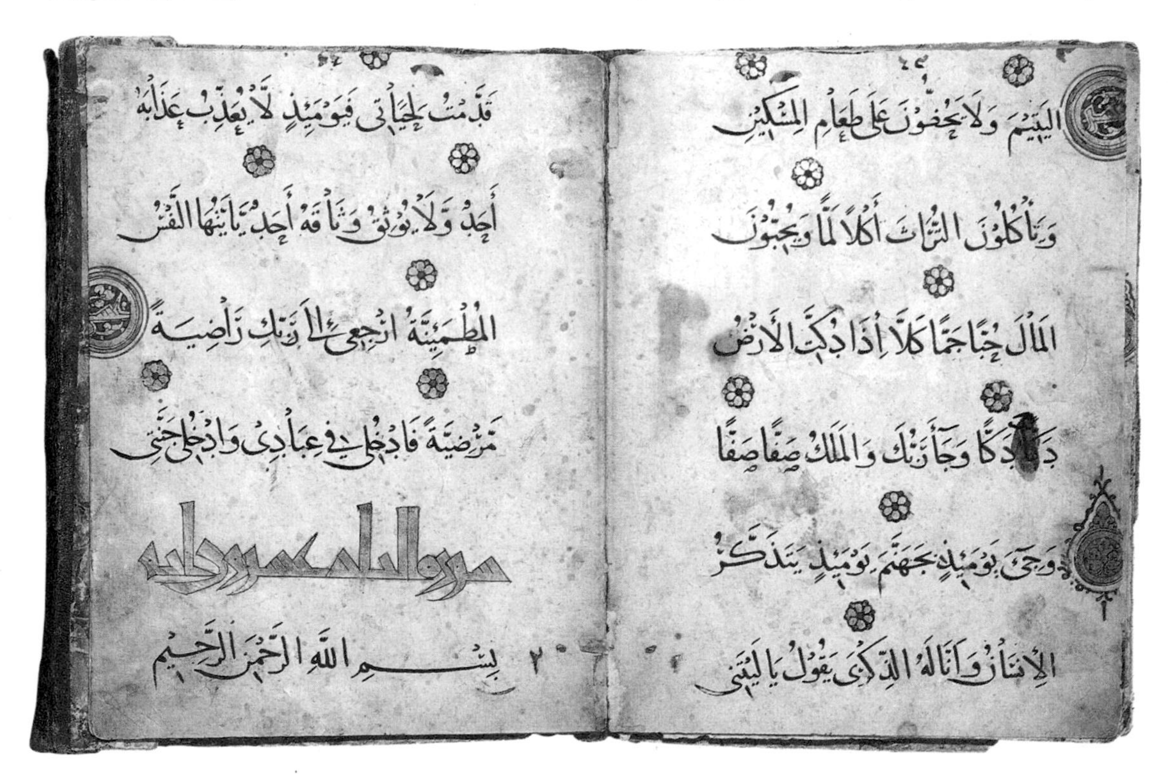

Two folios of a Seljuq-period Quran. They are written mostly in a script called muhaqqaq, *with* sura *headings in angular "kufic" script.*

of symbols, rites, traditions, and attitudes across the Islamic world.

Islamic rule first came to India with the early conquests, but an extensive presence arrived only in the early thirteenth century with the establishment of the "Sultanates of Delhi" (1206–1526), principalities ruled by Turkic and central Asian warlords. Muslim merchants, missionaries, and especially mystics (Sufis; see pp.101–3) shared in converting the Indian peoples to Islam. The thirteenth and fourteenth centuries witnessed the peaceful spread of Islam, via Sufi travelers and merchants, from India into southeast Asia. Gradually, Islam came to be accepted by a majority of people in what are now Indonesia and Malaysia. Merchants and Sufis were also critical to the spread of Islam from north Africa through the western Sahara and along the coasts of present-day Somalia and Tanzania. From the late medieval period Islam slowly spread into sub-Saharan Africa, but its principal advances in this region only took place in the nineteenth and twentieth centuries.

The fifteenth to seventeenth centuries saw three dynamic and prosperous empires emerge in the Islamic world. Ruling from Istanbul (formerly Constantinople, the Byzantine capital), the Ottoman sultans, at the height of their authority, controlled a domain embracing north Africa, Egypt, the Near East, Anatolia, and much of southeastern Europe. The Safavid dynasty of shahs brought about a fundamental change with the conversion of Iranian society from Sunni to Twelver Shii Islam. In India, the equally centralized empire of the Mughal dynasty was officially an Islamic state, but drew legitimation from its patronage of Hindu culture (see p.132).

However, the period from the eighteenth century to the present has witnessed rapid and often wrenching change within the Islamic world. To begin with, the three great empires of the Ottomans, Safavids, and Mughals were beset by internal troubles and challenges from the increasingly imperialistic states of Europe, notably Britain, France, and Russia. The encounter of Christian Europe and the Islamic world can be dated to at least the Crusades undertaken by Latin (that is, Roman Catholic) Christian forces beginning in the eleventh century, a conflict that led to a permanent end to Muslim rule in Spain by 1492. In this more recent period, several phases of European imperialism led to the occupation, by the 1920s, of nearly the entire Islamic world from west and north Africa to the East Indies.

In the eighteenth century, the pressing concerns of Muslim scholars and writers had mostly to do with the dislocation and disunity caused by the fragmentation or weakening of the three Islamic empires. Social and political renewal movements that arose in response to this lack of cohesion throughout the Islamic lands (see sidebar, right) helped to lay the groundwork for the twentieth-century reemergence of Islam on the modern world stage with extraordinary vigor and vitality.

A Quranic school in Timbuctu in the Saharan state of Mali. Islam was brought to this part of Africa along trade routes between ca. 1250 and 1500CE.

EARLY REVIVAL MOVEMENTS

The diverse responses to Muslim disunity in the eighteenth century (see main text) all sought a solution to perceived crises through a restructuring of Islamic social and religious life. In the Arabian peninsula, Ibn Abd al-Wahhab (died 1792) articulated a strict, even authoritarian, vision of Islamic society. An alliance with Prince Muhammad ibn Saud (died 1765) eventually led to the founding of modern Saudi Arabia in 1932. Uthman dan Fodio (1754–1817), a popular Nigerian teacher and activist, led his followers against political foes and, especially, what he saw as forces corrupting Muslim society. His movement aimed to shape a properly Islamic society and a theocratic state that would direct the process of revival. In India, Shah Wali Allah (1702–62) called for reform of traditional Islamic legal thought and practice. His ideas were shared by Muhammad ibn Ali al-Sanusi (1787–1859), a north African scholar and founder of the Sanusiyya Sufi order.

By the mid-1800s, the issue of European imperialism had come to overshadow that of revitalizing Islamic society. For example, in what is now Libya, the Sanusiyyas led armed resistance to French and Italian colonialism.

ART AND DIVINITY

The claim that Islam has always forbidden representational art is exaggerated if not simply false, as demonstrated by the rich Islamic tradition of illustrated manuscripts (although they are never of the Quran or other purely religious texts). While the Quran itself contains no explicit ban, a predominantly hostile attitude developed among scholars toward any sort of representational imagery, based on the theory that to form images of living beings challenges the creative genius that God alone possesses. No representational art appears in mosques: here, the great Islamic traditions of calligraphy and symbolic art continue to flourish.

APPROACHES TO GOD

Islam conceives of Allah, God, as that from which all else emanates. He is, first and foremost—and as the concept of *tawhid* (see box, opposite) makes clear—utterly One. In the words of the Quran: "God bears witness that there is no god but He, as do the angels and those possessing knowledge. He acts with justice. There is no god but He, the All-powerful, the All-wise" (*Sura* 3.18). Affirming the oneness of God is the first part of the Shahada, the Islamic profession of faith: "There is no god but God."

To violate the principle of *tawhid* is to commit *shirk*, often translated as "association," that is, associating any aspect of the world with the holy or divine when it does not possess these qualities. As the Quran puts it: "Serve God and do not associate anything with Him" (4.36). The term can be applied in a variety of ways. Naturally, it is a grievous sin to worship any other force or being in the universe. Muslims may also interpret a preoccupation with material wealth, or impulsive and arrogant behavior, as examples of *shirk*, corrupting as these do the individual's attitude and behavior both toward God and within the community.

Islamic writers often write of faith, or *iman*, as being composed of five doctrines. The first is belief in *tawhid*. Second is the belief in creatures linked to God and his presence in the universe, and in the work they perform on behalf of God; this includes angels and the beings known as *jinn* (a collective noun, the origin of the term "genie"). Third is the belief in the prophets and in the prophetic message which communicates the divine will to humankind. This belief encompasses all the books of divine revelation, including the Torah of Moses and the Gospel of Jesus. The fourth concerns the belief in the Final Judgment and the eternal reward or suffering that ensues (see box, opposite). The fifth doctrine is the belief in predestination.

A key Quranic notion is that God reveals himself through "signs," for which the Quran uses the term *aya* (plural *ayat*), a word also used for each verse of the Quran. In the sense that it alerts and instructs, the Quran itself is such a sign.

Muslim scholars from the earliest period have wrestled with the issues surrounding knowledge, or awareness, of God. The intellectual history of the Islamic tradition is shaped, in part, by the pursuit of various approaches to theology and by the tensions generated between these approaches. For example, a debate erupted in the ninth century CE over whether God was discernible through the use of reason, the result of a long period of translation and commentary by Muslim scholars of Greek works of philosophy and science.

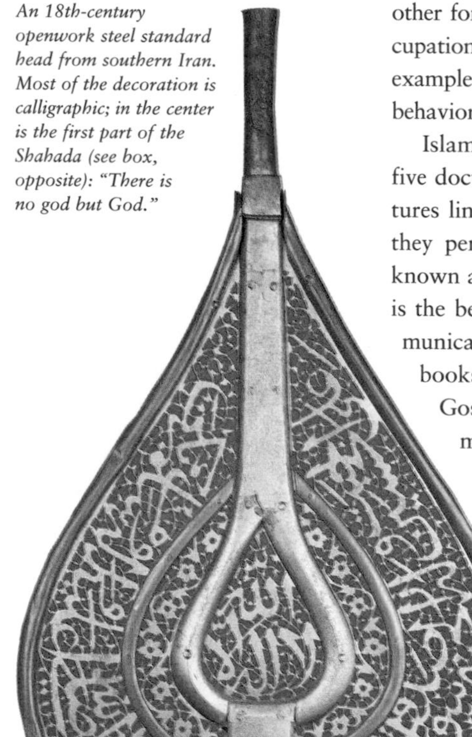

An 18th-century openwork steel standard head from southern Iran. Most of the decoration is calligraphic; in the center is the first part of the Shahada (see box, opposite): "There is no god but God."

Mysticism, the quest for a heightened spiritual experience and awareness of the Divine, is represented in Islam by Sufism. The term may derive from the Arabic *suf* ("wool"), and thus is perhaps a reference to the rough, simple garb worn by ascetics in the formative period of Islam.

In the Muslim context, the search for inner spirituality should be seen as an integral dimension of Islamic life rather than as something pursued apart from the mainstream practices and doctrines of the tradition. Sufism draws much of its inspiration from the Quranic idea of "friendship" (*wilaya*) with God, and therefore "Sufis" are often referred to in Islamic letters as "friends" (*awliya*, singular *wali*), those who are sincere and utterly trusting in their relationship with God.

The origins of Sufism extend back to the practice of the Prophet and his companions. Literature on Islamic spirituality tells of Muhammad's ascetic lifestyle and how his example inspired even the élite of the early Islamic empire, including the caliphs. In Sufi letters, Muhammad emerges as the exemplar of the inner, spiritual life, and later Sufi thinkers and poets cited as their best evidence for this the miraculous journey (Miraj) of the Prophet from Mecca to Jerusalem and thence to heaven (see p.107).

Drawing on the Prophetic example and the teachings of revelation, the early Sufis began to articulate ideas that later scholars would develop into

THE NAMES OF GOD

The Quran provides a long series of names for God, each of which expresses a different dimension of the infinitely complex and ultimately indescribable divine presence. In a famous Hadith (see p.105), the Prophet refers to ninety-nine names of God, although the Quran can be read as listing many others. These are not simply a list of characteristics but constitute one way in which the Quran underscores the idea of God's perfection: each quality may be partially possessed by humans but only God can possess them all, perfectly and completely.

Two names perhaps stand out: *al-Rahman* ("the Compassionate") and *al-Rahim* ("the Merciful"). The two terms often occur together, as in the invocation known as the *Basmala* (see p.104).

THE AFFIRMATION OF GOD

The Muslim's relationship with God focuses on three central Islamic principles that derive directly from the Quran. The first, *tawhid*, might be rendered conveniently as "the unity of God." This conveys the key Islamic idea that God is utterly and inevitably One, a perfect unity and unique unto himself. However, a more accurate translation would be "the affirmation of divine unity," which encompasses the crucial obligation for Muslims to structure their faith (*iman*) and its practice (*islam*), according to their belief in the divine unity. Thus *tawhid* is a summons to an attentive and pious life.

Nubuwwa, or "prophecy," refers to the manner in which God makes clear his will to humankind. Prophets are designated by God to bring the message of *tawhid* to the world and to summon humanity to proper obeisance and worship. Islam accords Muhammad a special role as the "seal" of prophecy (see p.95).

The complex ideas of *tawhid* and *nubuwwa* are expressed in brief in a statement known as the Shahada ("Bearing Witness"): "There is no god but God [Allah], and Muhammad is His messenger." Uttering the Shahada is all that is required in order to convert to Islam, and it is traditionally whispered into the ears of a newborn child. It is also the first of what is known as the "Five Pillars," the five acts upon which the ritual system of the Islamic tradition rests (see pp.114–17).

The third principle concerns the concept of the "Last Days," or the end of the world. It is often expressed with the term *maad*, which conveys the idea of "return," that is, the return of everything created by God to its divine source. According to the Quran, the Last Days will be accompanied by the Final Judgment. In often vivid terms, the Quran makes clear the inevitability of divine judgment and the certainty that everyone will be assessed on the character of their response to the prophetic summons.

The Shii tradition adds two further principles. The first is the "imamate," the idea that Muhammad's social and spiritual leadership was carried on by a line of his divinely inspired descendants, the Imams (see pp.108–9). The second principle concerns the "Divine Attribute" of perfect justice, or *adl*. Medieval Shii scholars selected this particular attribute of God as the basis of their arguments on Divine Judgment, the justice upon which it is based, and the responsibility of humans for their actions.

theoretical Sufism, a key branch of late medieval Islamic letters. These ideas are associated with such early figures as Hasan al-Basri (died 728CE), Rabia al-Adawiya (died 801CE), al-Tustari (died 896CE), and Junayd (died 910CE). The first two stressed the need for asceticism, a deep and unwavering trust in the divine purpose, and self-awareness. The later Sufis articulated notions such as the union of the self with the divine presence, sometimes called the annihilation of the self (*fana*), through discipline and contemplation, which became a central idea of formal Sufism. Among other early Sufi thinkers was Jafar al-Sadiq (died 765CE), held to have been the Sixth Imam by Shii Muslims.

As the reputation of these early figures grew, they and other like-minded individuals attracted followers. In the ninth and tenth centuries CE, there emerged informal circles of teachers, or "guides" (*shaykhs*), and their students (*murids*). Their experience generated the key idea that the inner life was shaped by a disciplined progress through a series of

EARLY SUFI ORDERS

Historians usually see the Qadiriyya as among the first of the major Sufi orders to emerge. The name derives from Abd al-Qadir al-Jilani (1077–1166), a Persian scholar and preacher, whose sermons in Baghdad are said to have attracted a wide following. His sons and other early disciples laid the groundwork for the order, and for the growth in Abd al-Qadir's reputation, which is reflected in the numbers of pilgrims who still visit his tomb today.

Other early orders include the Suhrawardiyya and Shadhiliyya groups, the first important today in India, Pakistan, and Bangladesh, the second traditionally prominent in north Africa and the Near East. The Bektashiyya, a Turkish order closely associated with the military of the former Ottoman empire, was known for its esoteric practices, as was the Rifaiyya, a branch of the Qadiriyya, whose members, for example, sometimes ate glass and walked on hot coals. These large orders played a critical part in winning converts to Islam in many regions of central Africa, the Indian Ocean region, and central Asia.

Certain élite orders were joined only by educated urbanites, or were closely associated with certain sectors of society, for example the military or urban guilds. Other orders had a broader social base and often overlapped with the popular cults of Muslim saints that emerged throughout the medieval Islamic world. A Sufi master might be the inspiration of a specific order and also the object of veneration, expressed through festivals held at his tomb.

The mausoleum of Rukn-i-Alem, a Suhrawardiyya Sufi saint, at Multan in Pakistan, built in the 13th–14th centuries. Originally founded in Baghdad, the Suhrawardiyya order acquired many adherents in the Indian subcontinent, where its followers are concentrated today.

spiritual stages, to each of which the student or disciple was led by the teacher or master. Just as the master derived knowledge and guidance through trust in God, so too would the student from his or her *shaykh*.

Central to the spiritual search of Sufism is the practice of *dhikr*, often translated as "remembering" or "invoking" God and his names (see sidebar, p.101), either in silent meditation or quiet chanting. The origin of *dhikr* lies in the Quran and in the Hadith of the Prophet (see p.105), and is epitomized in the ritual prayer, or *salat*, in which Muslims invoke the presence and names of God.

Early Sufism was largely confined to small, ascetic circles, but by the tenth and eleventh centuries its ideas had begun to spread into the broader community. Sufi orders, or "brotherhoods," began to take shape (see box, opposite), accompanied by the appearance of Sufi lodges (*khanqahs*) in ever greater numbers. Within several centuries, the Sufi orders became an everyday feature of Islamic life, and remain so today in many regions.

A devotee in a mosque belonging to the Khalwatiyya Sufi order at Baqal Gharbiyya, Israel.

GOD IN ISLAMIC LITERATURE

Sufism has generated a large body of often very difficult writings concerning spiritual knowledge and mystical union with the divine presence. Among the most important are works by Ibn al-Arabi (1165–1240), who wrote partly in Muslim Spain (al-Andalus). For many Sufi writers the task of expressing complex and deeply felt ideas found its most suitable expression in poetry. Farid al-Din al-Attar (died 1230) and Ibn al-Farid (1181–1234) are among the greatest such poets, while Jalal al-Din al-Rumi (died 1273) is today widely popular in translation in Europe and North America. He produced a body of mystic poetry that is considered among the gems of medieval Islamic letters.

God and the many divine characteristics are the subject of an extensive body of writings by medieval and modern theologians, mystics, poets, and novelists. Among the great medieval thinkers is Abu Hamid Muhammad al-Ghazzali (1058–1111), whose works remain widely read today. Of Persian origin, he pursued a lifetime of teaching and writing, interrupted by a decade of contemplation and travel occasioned by a spiritual crisis. His best-known work, and a significant expression of Sunni Muslim faith, is the voluminous *Ihya Ulum al-din* ("The Revival of the Religious Sciences"). In this and other works, including his famous spiritual biography, *al-Munqidh min al-Dalal* ("Deliverance from Error"), al-Ghazzali achieved a kind of synthesis of rational and mystical approaches to the worship of God.

THE *BASMALA*

With one exception, every *sura* of the Quran begins with the invocation known as the *Basmala* or *Bismillah*: "In the name of God, the Compassionate, the Merciful" *(Bismillahi al-Rahman al-Rahim)*. This phrase is also spoken at the beginning of every act of worship and is frequently uttered by Muslims throughout their daily lives. The Quran devotes much attention to the quality of divine mercy, the greatest expression of which is the Quran itself, for the light it sheds and the guidance it provides.

THE WORD OF GOD

The Islamic tradition reveres the Quran as the literal word of God, directly transmitted to the Prophet over the course of his adult life. Muslims acknowledge the Quran as the extension of the divine into the earthly realm, the embodiment on earth of God's mercy, power, and mystery.

The verses of the Quran were given to Muhammad, who in turn recited them to his followers. The word *Quran* itself means "recitation," and can refer to a part or the whole of the sacred text. According to the tradition, the Quran achieved its present, written form during the caliphate of Uthman (644–656CE), who ordered a group of respected Muslims to create a definitive version. It is composed of one hundred and fourteen chapters known as *suras*, each of which bears both a number and a title, the latter usually a word or phrase occurring early in the *sura*; for example *Sura* 2, *al-Baqara* ("The Cow"). While Western scholars tend to cite Quranic chapters by number, Muslim writers generally refer to their titles.

The *suras* are composed of individual verses (*ayat*, singular *aya*), literally "signs" from God of his presence and mercy. The tradition teaches that the first *sura* revealed was *Sura* 96, *al-Alaq* ("The Blood-Clot"), spoken to the Prophet by the angel Gabriel. It represents the announcement to Muhammad of his mission: "Recite: in the name of your Lord who created, who created Man from a blood-clot" (96.1–2, that is, *Sura* 96, *ayat* 1–2).

THE QURAN IN ISLAMIC LIFE

The Quran is present in the lives of Muslims in a variety of ways. It was the focus of traditional Islamic education, with young Muslims learning to read and write Quranic verses, and, ideally, memorizing the entire text. While this practice has fallen victim over the past century to the spread of largely secular public schooling, parents today still generally ensure that their children receive Quranic learning.

The Prophet's own example of oral transmission of the word of God to his followers helps to explain the great value attached to the memorization and oral recitation of the Quran down to the present day. Quranic recitation remains a highly cherished art form, and recordings by noted reciters are readily available throughout the Islamic world.

The Quran possesses a physical sacredness. Muslims prefer to approach and handle the holy book only in a state of ritual purity, and it has a divine power or grace (Arabic: *baraka*) that can, in more popular usage, even be employed as a means of healing.

Boys at the Fouad Islamic Institute, a Quranic school in Assyut, Egypt. Instruction in the Quran continues to form an important part of the education of most Muslims.

Sura *1*, al-Fatiha *("The Opening") (right) and the first page of* Sura 2, al-Baqara *("The Cow"), from a decorated Quran produced in Mughal India ca. 1700.*

The *suras* are ordered according to length, with the longest at the beginning of the Quran, the shortest at the end. The one exception is *Sura* 1, *al-Fatiha* ("The Opening"), which has seven verses.

The *suras* are also identified as either "Meccan" or "Medinan," depending on whether they were revealed before or after the Hijra, Muhammad's departure for Medina in 622CE. The Meccan verses center on God's majesty and unity and the certainty that he is to bring his compassion and judgment to bear upon humanity and the world. In this context, Muhammad's role in the Meccan period, as he himself proclaimed, was to bring glad tidings of God's compassion, and to warn of the coming judgment that would separate the righteous from the wrongdoers. As *Sura* 35 states: "For those who disbelieve will come a fearsome punishment, for those who believe and do good will come forgiveness and reward" (35.7). The Meccan verses are often short and succinct, with vivid, intense imagery.

The Medinan verses contain similar ideas and language, but reflect the new challenges facing Muhammad and the nascent Islamic community. The verses are generally longer and more complex and often express a concern for religious, moral, and social order. Most importantly, they prescribe the central duties of Islam: prayer, alms, fasting at Ramadan, and the pilgrimage to Mecca (the Hajj). Also addressed are such varied matters as marriage, divorce, adultery, gambling, and the waging of war.

Muslim scholars, from very early in the tradition, have dedicated enormous effort to elucidating the complex teachings of the Quran. Quranic interpretation, or *tafsir*, forms part of the core of Islamic learning. Works of *tafsir* abound; one of the earliest, and greatest, is the multivolume opus of al-Tabari (839–923CE), who also wrote an influential history.

HADITH: THE WAY OF MUHAMMAD

To guide them in interpreting the Quran, the religious scholars (*ulama*) relied on traditions about Muhammad himself. On his death, the Islamic community set about collecting his teachings, words, and deeds. The Prophet's "way," or "tradition" (*sunna*—hence the term Sunni; see p.98), was subsequently assembled in a series of reports known collectively and individually as Hadith. Each Hadith was headed by a list of those through whom the report was transmitted, which ideally extended back to Muhammad or to a close companion to whom he had spoken directly.

The key period of Hadith collection and commentary was the late eighth to early ninth century CE. The Hadith generated much debate in early medieval times since it became clear to scholars that individual Hadith often reflected opinions or doctrinal positions that postdated the Prophet's lifetime. From ca. 850CE a number of critical collections of Hadith were produced in the Sunni Muslim world, the most respected being those of al-Bukhari (810–870CE) and Muslim ibn al-Hajjaj (died 875CE).

Shiism, from an earlier period, also generated a large and complex body of Hadith going back through the Imams (see pp.108–9). For Shii scholars, the Hadith of the Imams play an identical role to that of the Sunni Hadith, namely to elucidate the Quran and to serve as a source of religious and legal thought. Of four early collections of Hadith held as canonical in Shiism, perhaps the central one is that of al-Kulayni (died 939CE).

A 19th-century "Hand of Fatima," a popular type of amulet for warding off the "evil eye." Fatima was reputedly the Prophet's favorite daughter and a woman of exemplary goodness.

THE PROPHET AND MESSENGER

It is impossible to overestimate the importance of Muhammad not only to the formation of Islam but also to the daily lives of Muslims ever since. He is revered as the perfect Muslim, the prime exemplar of how to live an Islamic life, and his career is set out in a series of writings, primarily from the first centuries of Islam, that form the basis of a later, and vast, body of work. The early writings include biographies of the Prophet and his family, historical works such as that by al-Tabari (838–923CE), and the Hadith, the body of reports of the Prophet's words and deeds (see p.105). The Quran, of course, is a unique source for the Prophet's life, both as the record of the revelation he received from God, and as a valuable—if often difficult to interpret—source of references to Muhammad's career.

Such works bring together information that is both clearly legendary and grounded in actual events. According to Muhammad ibn Ishaq and other biographers, Muhammad was born in Mecca ca. 570CE into the Banu Hashim clan of the Quraysh tribe, and orphaned at an early age. Reared by his uncle, Abu Talib, and his extended family, he is said to have acquired, even as a youth, a reputation for probity that earned him the nickname *al-Amin* ("the Trustworthy"). It is also said that a series of predictions marked the young man out as a future prophet. His reputation caught the attention of an older woman, Khadija, a merchant who was to become his first wife and the mother of four of his daughters, including Fatima, who is especially revered by Shii Muslims (see sidebar, left).

Muhammad's prophetic mission began during one of his frequent periods of solitary meditation. In 610CE, in a cave on Mount Hira overlooking Mecca, the angel Gabriel is said to have appeared to him with a summons to prophethood. Overcoming his initial fears, Muhammad began teaching the monotheistic message that was revealed to him, attracting a small number of close followers at first, then a larger public.

Initially, Muhammad enjoyed the protection of his uncle and the support of Khadija in the face of growing opposition from the pagan Meccans. But the death of both in 619CE left him increasingly vulnerable to attack, and he emigrated with his followers from Mecca to Yathrib. This journey (the Hijra, or Hejira), traditionally said to have begun on July 16, 622CE, marks for Muslims the beginning of their communal history (see p.95).

In Yathrib (later Medina), Muhammad quickly assumed new and complex responsibilities. In Mecca, he had been a prophet and teacher, the founder of a new religious movement, but now he had to oversee and run a community that looked to him both to organize physical protection

THE FAMILY OF THE PROPHET

The term *ahl al-bayt* (literally, "family of the house [of the Prophet]") refers to Muhammad's immediate family and his descendants. Among both Sunni and Shii Muslims, the members of his household are revered for their blood ties to the Prophet and for having lived their lives within his presence. For Shii Muslims, Ali ibn Abi Talib, his wife Fatima (the Prophet's daughter), and their sons Hasan and Husayn are significant as the source of the line of the Imams (see pp.108–9).

Several women who played a crucial role in the Prophet's life are held up as especially venerable and praiseworthy. Khadija, his first wife, is remembered in part for encouraging the Prophet during the initial period of revelation, when he is said to have been nearly overcome by the vision of the angel Gabriel. A later wife, Aisha, is more controversial. Sunnis recognize her as Muhammad's favorite wife after Khadija, but Shiis claim she committed adultery and took part in civil strife some time after the Prophet's death.

from its opponents and offer guidance in all its religious, social, and legal affairs. His followers, the Muslims, were principally of two groups: the Muhajirun, or those who had come with him from Mecca, and the Ansar, or "Helpers," those from Medina. Convincing the two groups to work in harmony was among Muhammad's tasks in this period.

Armed conflict with the Meccans ended with the surrender of Mecca in 630CE. On reentering the city, Muhammad is said to have made his way directly to the Kaba (see p.112), which he purged of pre-Islamic pagan idols. He also strove to forge alliances with powerful tribes throughout the Arabian peninsula, or else to bring about their submission. Following the Prophet's death in 632CE, many of the alliances collapsed, obliging Muhammad's immediate successors to wage campaigns to bring these tribal groupings back into the Islamic fold.

Following his last pilgrimage to Mecca, a few weeks before his death, the Prophet is said to have delivered a final address to his followers at a place called Ghadir Khumm, where he urged unity on the community of his followers. His alleged words on this occasion about his son-in-law and cousin, Ali ibn Abi Talib, are one source of the division in Islam between the Sunni majority and the Shii community.

WRITING THE LIFE OF THE PROPHET

Biographies of Muhammad constitute a genre known as Sira. The earliest and perhaps most important is by the eighth-century scholar Muhammad ibn Ishaq (died ca. 770CE), which survives only in a later edition by Abd al-Malik ibn Hisham (died ca. 834CE).

Over the course of Islamic history, the early biographies and the Hadith served as the basis of increasingly elaborate accounts, in a variety of contexts, of the Prophet's life and achievements. "Popular" accounts include a large body of songs and poetry, which are performed to mark Muhammad's birthday (*mawlid al-nabi*).

MUHAMMAD'S MIRACULOUS JOURNEYS

For Sufi writers and poets, one central event in Muhammad's career in itself furnishes sufficient proof of his remarkable status. According to Islamic tradition, shortly before the Hijra (see main text), the Prophet went on a miraculous journey from Mecca to Jerusalem in the company of the angel Gabriel (Jibril). This event is known as the Isra.

In the Holy City, it is said, the Prophet led a session of prayer with a group of earlier prophets, including Abraham (Ibrahim) and Jesus (Isa), affirming their place as prophets and also as Muslims. Then, astride a strange winged beast named Buraq, he ascended to heaven and into the divine presence. The accounts of the Isra and the ascension (Miraj) recount that at this point the number of prayers required of Muslims in the daily cycle was fixed at five.

The journey, as explained in a host of writings and collections of verse, stands as an indication both of Muhammad's relationship with God and of the possibility of achieving, in mystical terms, proximity to God.

Muhammad (on right of picture) ascends to heaven on Buraq, a part-horse and part-human creature, guided by Gabriel (left). A miniature painted in Herat, Afghanistan, in 1436.

IMAMS AND "SAINTS"

Husayn (top left) and Hasan (mounted) at the battle of Karbala, an event that Shiis commemorate to this day as an act of martyrdom. An Iranian poster, ca. 1900.

The chief difference between the Shii and Sunni traditions is Shiism's belief in, and veneration of, a line of divinely inspired leaders known as Imams. This belief is grounded in a particular understanding of events in the early history of Islam. In his last address to his followers at Ghadir Khumm (see p.107), Muhammad is said to have spoken of his son-in-law, Ali ibn Abi Talib. According to Sunni interpretation, Muhammad praised Ali and commended him to the community. But Shii commentators claim that Muhammad in fact designated Ali as his successor and that Ali therefore had the only legitimate claim to succeed the Prophet as leader (*imam*) and spiritual guide of the young Islamic community. In the Shii view, the Muslim leadership violated the Prophet's wishes in not selecting Ali ibn Abi Talib as Muhammad's immediate successor. The term Shii, or Shiite, derives from *Shiat Ali*, "partisans, or followers, of Ali."

Following Ali's death in 661CE, the Shiis turned their loyalties to Ali's son Hasan, then to Hasan's brother, Husayn. In 680CE, Husayn attempted to join his partisans in the southern Iraqi town of Kufa, an act that his kinsman, the Umayyad caliph, viewed as a bid to seize power. Troops loyal to the caliph killed Husayn and his male companions at Karbala, near Kufa.

Building on this early tragic history, Shii scholars and activists developed a complex system of belief and practice centered on the office of the imamate. The person of the Imam, as described by the elaborate literature of the Shii tradition, is a link in the chain of prophecy stretching back through Muhammad and Jesus to Abraham and Adam (see p.95). He must be a direct descendant of the Prophet Muhammad and the designated heir of the Imam before him, just as Ali, in the Shii view, was the designated suc-

TWELVER GOVERNANCE

Initially, the Twelver *ulama* (religious scholars), in the absence of the Imam himself, were content to play a limited role as teachers and spiritual guides to their community. However, it became increasingly clear that the *ulama* would also have to carry out, if only temporarily, the Imam's functions as leader of the community and source of legal and doctrinal rulings. Over the course of centuries, the Twelver *ulama* have elaborated a definition of their role as the representative of the "Hidden Imam." As a result, the Imam's full legal and religious authority came to be bestowed upon the leading scholars of the day, and the community was obliged to pay alms, sometimes referred to as religious taxes, to the leading members of the *ulama*. The combination of economic power with high moral and religious standing endowed these men with considerable influence within the Twelver community.

cessor of Muhammad. The Imam, therefore, is the only legitimate authority on earth, and obedience to him is required of humankind. He is held to be infallible, without sin, and in possession of a body of knowledge transmitted by God through the Imams.

By far the largest Shii branch is "Twelver" Shiism, so called because its doctrines center on the person of the Twelfth Imam, a boy named Muhammad who is said to have disappeared a short while after the death in 873CE of his father, the Eleventh Imam, Hasan al-Askari. The Twelfth Imam's disappearance became the basis of a complex body of doctrine. Most fundamentally, it is held that he did not die, but entered a miraculous state of concealment (the doctrine of "Occultation"), the nature and duration of which is known only to God. He therefore remains a living being to whom veneration and obedience are due from adherents of the tradition. The "hidden" Twelfth Imam is also a messianic figure who will return shortly before the Day of Judgment to lead the forces of good against those of evil in a final apocalyptic battle. He is often referred to as the "Imam Mahdi," *mahdi* being the most common Islamic term for messiah.

THE ISMAILIS

The Ismaili branch of Shiism arose following the death of Jafar al-Sadiq, the Sixth Imam, in 765CE. While many of his followers supported his son, Musa, to succeed as Seventh Imam, others backed his eldest son, Ismail, hence this branch is known as the Ismailis, or "Seveners." The Ismailis believe in an unbroken line of Imams to the present day, unlike the Twelvers who await the return of the "hidden" Imam (see main text). Ismaili Shiism encompasses a variety of subsects. An offshoot is the Druze community, originally an Ismaili group which, in the eleventh century, ascribed divine status to a Fatimid caliph. Attempts to eradicate this heresy failed, and the Druze persist in remote areas of Lebanon, Syria, and northern Israel.

"FRIENDS OF GOD"

Throughout the Islamic world persists the belief in individuals and family lineages privileged with special spiritual powers or a proximity to the holy. There is considerable overlap between the veneration of such "saints" and the more popular side of Sufism (see pp.101–3), including the use of the Quranic term *wali Allah*, "friend of God," for both Sufis and Muslim "saints" alike.

Muslim religious scholars have often displayed an uneasiness, or even hostility, toward such beliefs, partly on the grounds that holiness can be ascribed only to God, not human beings. But many ordinary Muslims find the idea of "saints" unobjectionable, and the veneration of such figures forms a significant part of their experience as Muslims to the present day. These beliefs can center on the "saint's" piety and moral standing or on his or her ability to transform the physical world (for example, through healing) or to summon the natural elements. Other "saints" are more like folk heroes, renowned for their resistance to oppressive rulers.

Devotees at the tomb of Abd Shah Ghazi, an Islamic "saint," in Karachi, Pakistan. Many parts of the Islamic world share the notion of baraka, *a spiritual or divine blessing or boon that can be transmitted to the follower from a "saint" or a "saint's" relic (such as his or her tomb).*

Cults may be local or international. For example, the southern Moroccan city of Marrakesh—often referred to as "the tomb of the saints" owing to the large numbers of holy persons buried there—is associated with seven "saints" whose birthdays are celebrated only locally in small neighborhood festivals. In contrast, the Egyptian "saint" Sayyid Ahmad al-Badawi (died 1276) is renowned throughout Egypt and neighboring countries, and is celebrated by several annual festivals, the biggest of which, at Tanta in Egypt, brings together very large numbers of people.

SHARIA AND THE LAW OF ISLAM

The Islamic tradition, based on teachings of the Quran and Hadith (see pp.104–5), and as articulated by the Muslim religious scholars (the *ulama*), directs Muslims to abide by the divine will not simply as individuals but also as a community. According to this view, humankind was chosen by God to serve as his representative (*khalifa*) on earth and, to use a variation of the Quranic formula, "to bring about the good, and forbid the wrong" (*Sura* 3.110). All Muslims, therefore, bear the responsibility to see that a just and moral social order is created and maintained.

Forming the basis of this moral order and social wellbeing are, of course, the teachings laid out in the Quran (the principal source of Islamic legal and ethical practice), Hadith, and the religious-legal traditions developed by the *ulama* (see sidebar, left, and box, below). This body of teachings is collectively known as the Sharia, the "Islamic way." From it derive the laws by which Muslim scholars have sought to put the ideal Islamic social system into practice. The study of the Sharia is known as *fiqh*, perhaps best translated as "jurisprudence." Scholars who study the Sharia are known as *fuqaha* (singular *faqih*).

From early on in the development of the legal tradition, the laws that govern Islamic life were perceived as essentially divided into two categories: those that concern the relationship between humankind and God; and those that relate to the integrity of the human community. In each of

THE FOUR PATHS

In the medieval period, four legal schools or traditions emerged in Sunni Islam. Each tradition (*madhhab*, literally "path" or "route") developed its own interpretations of Quranic and Hadith teachings.

The four traditions—the Hanafi, Maliki, Shafii, and Hanbali schools—are named for their ostensible founders, all towering figures in early Islam: Abu Hanifa (died 767CE), Malik ibn Anas (ca. 715–795), Muhammad ibn Idris al-Shafii (767–820), and Ahmad ibn Hanbal (died 855). The most significant was al-Shafii, whose arguments on religion and law are set out in his treatise *al-Risala* ("The Epistle"). It was largely as a result of his influence that the Hadith was codified as a source of legal guidance, and the sources of the law were formalized (see box, below).

The schools are distributed throughout the Sunni world. The Maliki predominates in north Africa; the Shafii in Egypt, Indonesia, and Malaysia; the Hanafi in central Asia and the Indian subcontinent; and the Hanbali in Saudi Arabia.

THE SOURCES OF ISLAMIC LAW

Sunni scholars discern four sources of Islamic law. First and foremost is the Quran, the direct expression of the divine will. From very early on, Muslim scholars dedicated themselves to Quranic exegesis or *tafsir*, an intense scrutiny of the sacred book from both a linguistic and religious point of view.

To help elucidate the often complex meanings of the text, scholars turned next to the Hadith, the second authoritative source for the law. Containing as it does the teachings of the Prophet himself (see p.105), the Hadith provided explications and elaborations of the Quranic verses.

The third source for Sunni legal scholars is *ijma*, usually translated as "consensus," that is, an agreed interpretation of a given issue, either on the part of a majority of scholars of a particular region, or as understood from the work of earlier generations of scholars. *Ijma* was an effective means of establishing and maintaining conformity of opinion over a given issue or problem.

The fourth source of law, developed roughly at the same time as *ijma*, is *qiyas*, "reasoning on the basis of analogy." This proved to be a useful tool with which scholars could reach decisions over problems for which the Quran and Hadith provided no clear instruction.

Where Shii scholars differ from their Sunni colleagues is in placing greater value in the exercise of human reason and intellect; therefore, instead of *qiyas*, the Shiis have *aql* or *ijtihad*, "individual reasoning."

The main courtyard of the madrasa *of the al-Azhar mosque in Cairo, Egypt, a principal center of Sunni legal teaching.*

these spheres there are in turn five categories of human ethical behavior: "required," "recommended" (or "not required"), "indifferent" (or "permissible"), "reprehensible," and "forbidden." Thus, in the sphere of human relationships with Allah, five acts of devotion to God (*ibadat*, singular *ibada*) are "required" practice for Muslims. These acts are often referred to as the "Five Pillars" of Islam and constitute the Islamic ritual system (see pp.114–17).

The body of Islamic laws concerning the social and political realm is far larger. One key Quranic area of concern to the legal scholars is family law. The Quran speaks of an array of issues in this regard, which include marriage, divorce, adultery, inheritance, the treatment of wives and children, and financial matters. As far as Islamic teachings on marriage are concerned, the question of polygyny (having more than one wife) remains controversial. The Quran is clear that a Muslim man may be married to up to four women at the same time (*Sura* 4.3). However, as modern apologists are quick to point out, this and a later verse (4.129) also exhort men to treat each of the women equally in all respects—a demand that has been understood as a practical limitation, if not an outright ban, on the practice.

THE *MADRASA*

As the many branches of Islamic learning —jurisprudence first and foremost—took shape, and teachers began to accumulate disciples, the need developed for buildings in which to house students and hold classes. The *madrasa* (religious college) is believed to have emerged in eastern Iran in the tenth century CE, whence it spread rapidly eastward and westward to become a common feature of the Islamic urban landscape, especially under the Seljuqs (see p.98). The *madrasa* can be thought of as an extension of the mosque, in that formal worship often takes place there as well as study and instruction.

MECCA AND THE KABA

The most sacred place for the Islamic tradition is the holy city of Mecca and its immediate surroundings, at the very heart of which stands the central shrine of Islam, the Kaba.

The environs of Mecca, and the city itself, are forbidden to non-Muslims. Within its limits, Muslims are expected to comport themselves in a particular manner. Fighting, hunting, and all other forms of bloodshed are banned, and in general the entire city is considered to be a sanctuary.

The Kaba is referred to in the Quran as the "House of God." The tradition holds that this venerated cubic structure was built by Adam and then rebuilt and purified by Abraham, an act repeated by Muhammad when he destroyed the idols of what Muslims call the Jahiliyya, the pre-Islamic "Age of Corruption."

The Kaba plays a central part in Islamic practice. In their cycle of five daily prayers (see p.114), Muslims turn in the direction of the Kaba. At the climax of the great pilgrimage, the Hajj (see p.117), the faithful walk around the sacred shrine three times. In one corner of the Kaba is a black stone, perhaps a meteorite, held to be a physical symbol of the primordial bond joining God to humankind.

MOSQUES AND SHRINES

The remarkable unity of faith and practice that has characterized the diverse cultures that make up the Islamic community since the medieval period is expressed in physical form in the principal site of Islamic worship: the mosque (Arabic *masjid*, "place of prostration"). All mosques have the same basic plan (see box, opposite), yet many possess additional features that reflect their particular cultural and historical settings.

The mosque is traditionally believed to have its origin in Muhammad's own house at Medina. Although repeated attempts to reconstruct the site have not satisfactorily revealed the original plan, the Prophet's house is said to have contained a large open space for prayer; a covered area to protect worshippers from the elements; and some indication of the *qibla*, the proper direction in which to pray (that is, toward Mecca).

Over the course of Islamic history, Muslim builders and architects have worked with these elements in a wide variety of styles and materials. The early Muslims, following the conquests, either took over existing structures, such as Christian churches, or built what were probably rather rudi-

The Selimiye mosque in Edirne, Turkey, built 1569–75 by Sinan. In it, he fulfilled his ambition to be the first Muslim architect to create a dome greater than that of Hagia Sophia in Istanbul (or Constantinople; see illustration, p.96).

mentary mosques. Quite early on, the distinction emerged between small, local mosques and larger, congregational ones used not only for private prayer and study but also for the Friday communal prayer session and weekly sermon (*khutba*). Reflecting Byzantine and Persian influences, new architectural features began to appear, such as the *mihrab* and the *minbar*.

Among the most impressive examples of early mosques are the Umayyad mosque in Damascus, the al-Aqsa mosque in Jerusalem, and the two congregational mosques built in Samarra, the ninth-century CE capital of the Abbasid caliphate, neither of which unfortunately survives today. From a later period, Ottoman mosques are widely held to be among the finest examples of Islamic architecture, and of these the structures designed by the great Ottoman architect Sinan (1499–1588) stand out. The finest of Sinan's mosques is perhaps the Selimiye mosque in the Turkish city of Edirne (Adrianople; see illustration, opposite).

The mosque is not the only place where Muslims may pray. For daily prayer (see pp.114–15), it is expected simply that they will choose a spot that is quiet, clean, and free of distractions, and thus worthy of the act of worship. It is common for Muslims to use a mat or small rectangular rug upon which to pray, emphasizing the notion of a special place.

SUFI LODGES

The Sufi lodge, often known as the *khanqah*, can hardly be distinguished from a *madrasa* (see p.111) in terms of both function and architectural form. It also developed in eastern Iran in the tenth and eleventh centuries CE as a place in which a Sufi master could instruct and accommodate followers and served as a hospice and inn for travelers.

In time, the bigger Sufi orders came to be represented by networks of lodges across the Islamic world. The celebrated Moroccan scholar and pilgrim Ibn Battuta (see p.96) mentions coming across large numbers of *khanqahs*.

THE ARCHITECTURE OF THE MOSQUE

The characteristics of the mosque emerged at various times in early Islamic history. The most essential feature is the *mihrab*, or prayer niche, often the mostly carefully decorated element of the mosque. It indicates the *qibla*, the direction in which the Muslim is to pray. It orients the worshipper toward Mecca and the Kaba (see sidebar, opposite).

Other important elements include the *minaret*, or "tower," which began as a quite separate building with no connection to the mosque and of uncertain purpose. Today it is the place from which the call to prayer (see p.114) is commonly made, although it seems that originally this was not its main function, since the call may be, and often is, made from the roof of the mosque itself.

A fountain provides the water required by Muslims for the ritual cleansing (*wudu*) that precedes each of the five sessions of daily prayer. The *dikka*, or raised platform, a later addition to mosque architecture, was traditionally used by assistants to the *imam* (in this context, the *imam* is the person who delivers the Friday sermon from the "pulpit," or *minbar*). The *dikka* is often an elaborate and decorated structure that incorporates a flight of steps.

A Turkish tiled mihrab *of ca. 1570. The Quranic inscription (from* Sura 3*) in the top band is common on prayer niches and is the source of the term* mihrab*: "Every time Zachariah entered her chamber [al-mihrab] he found provisions with her. He said 'O Mary, where is this from?'" (Mary's reply is: "From God.")*

JIHAD

The opinion that *jihad*, a Quranic concept widely discussed in Islamic letters, constitutes a "Sixth Pillar" of Islam has been expressed at various times during the development of the Islamic tradition. *Jihad* is a complex term that has too often been reduced in the Western media and popular imagination to but one of its meanings, namely "holy war," the slogan of modern radical Islamic movements. In the Quran, and in the tradition, it is understood as "striving in the path of God," that is, working to achieve a perfect moral order in society as well as in each individual life. It thus contains an imperative for every Muslim and for the community at large to struggle against all that might corrupt God's word and cause disharmony.

Jihad probably originated in close association with Islam's early conquests, in which case it certainly meant the spread of the true faith, thus lending itself to the present-day use of the term by those with a militant vision of the Islamic tradition.

Men at prayer outside a mosque in Jamma, India. The mats and cloths on which they kneel denote the sanctity of the space where they pray (see p.113).

DUTIES OF WORSHIP

Muslims are expected to learn and perform five ritual duties, often referred to as the "Five Pillars of Islam," although the tradition itself regards them more as acts of worship, known by the Arabic term *ibadat* (singular *ibada*). The Quran mentions all five duties but none in much detail, so that Islamic scholars and teachers turned to the Hadith for further guidance. Islamic literature, in both its scholarly and more popular forms, treats the five duties at great length, an indication of the emphasis placed upon the physical dimension of Islamic religious life.

The first of the five duties is uttering the Shahada, the Muslim profession of faith: "There is no god but God, and Muhammad is His messenger." These are essential beliefs for the Muslim, and the phrase is widely used in Islamic daily life.

The second—and in the opinion of many, central—duty is prayer, *salat*. This obligation is made clear by the Quran and the Prophet himself. In one of many Hadith in which he speaks of prayer, Muhammad is quoted as saying: "When each of you performs his prayer, he is in intimate communication with his Lord."

The Quran makes a number of references to prayer, and it is clear that it refers to several kinds. The "required prayer," the major type, consists of a cycle of prayers performed by Muslims five times daily at designated times, following the proper rite of ritual cleansing. Other forms of prayer are not considered obligatory. The five sessions of prayer take place at sunset, during the evening, at dawn, midday, and in the afternoon. Daily life in Muslim regions and neighborhoods is punctuated by the call to prayer (*adhan*), which is made before each of the five times of worship by the *muadhdhin* (often pronounced "muezzin"), usually from the mosque "tower," or *minaret*.

While it is desirable for all Muslims to congregate at the mosque for prayer, a requirement to do so applies only to males, who are obliged to attend midday prayers on Friday. The Friday session includes a sermon (*khutba*) delivered by a preacher, or prominent member of the community, and usually consists of commentary on a specific religious or social topic, and discussion of a specific Quranic verse or set of verses. The worshippers form straight lines with the *imam*, the person chosen to lead the session, standing alone at the front, facing the *mihrab* (see p.113). It should be noted that in the context of prayer the term *imam* is distinct in meaning from its specific use by Shii Muslims for the line of successors from the Prophet (see pp.108–9).

Before prayer, whether in the mosque, at home, or at the workplace, Muslims must prepare themselves both mentally and physically by

A worshipper in Istanbul. Muslims are encouraged to pray together, but are not obliged to do so, and individual prayer outside the 5 prescribed daily times is considered highly commendable.

focusing upon the act at hand and its significance. Physical purity is achieved by the ritual cleansing that must take place prior to each session of prayer.

The prayer cycle begins with the *takbir* ("*Allahu akbar*," "God is most great") and the opening *sura* of the Quran, *al-Fatiha*. The worshipper then performs a cycle of four physical postures—standing, bowing, prostrating, and sitting—which are accompanied by a set of utterances, some obligatory, others voluntary. Each cycle is called a *raka* and the number of cycles varies depending on the daily prayer being performed.

Alone or in a group, the worshipper concludes each session by uttering the "Peace," a phrase known as the *taslim*: "Peace be upon you and the mercy and blessing of God." This is said to all fellow Muslims and, according to some interpretations, to angels perched upon the shoulders of the worshipper.

The third of the five central Islamic duties is *zakat* or "required almsgiving." It is mentioned in the Quran and is spoken of both there and in the Hadith as the means by which Muslims provide for one another. It is distinct from voluntary alms and traditionally has been calculated as a percentage of income, although levels of wealth and thus actual ability to pay are duly recognized.

The fourth duty is to participate in the fast (*sawm*, or *siyam*) that occurs each year during Ramadan, the ninth month of the Islamic calendar. The fast applies to daylight hours, during which Muslims must

THE MUSLIM YEAR

The Islamic calendar has twelve months, the first being Muharram and the last Dhu al-Hijja, when the Hajj (see p.117) is performed. It is a lunar calendar and falls behind the solar year by around eleven days annually. Thus every month passes through all the solar seasons in a cycle lasting approximately thirty-two and a half years. Days of celebration and commemoration include the Prophet's Birthday (Mawlid al-Nabi) on the 12th of the third month (Rabi al-Awwal). The two great feast days, Id al-Fitr and Id al-Adha, respectively mark the end of the ninth month, Ramadan (a period of fasting), and the occasion of the Hajj.

Muslims washing at a designated area for ritual ablutions near the Dome of the Rock on al-Haram al-Sharif (the Temple Mount of Jewish tradition), Jerusalem.

refrain from eating, drinking, sexual activity, and smoking. Ramadan is a remarkable display of communal worship throughout the Islamic world. It is marked not only by a heightened religious sense but also by a great emphasis upon social and family ties.

The fifth and final duty for Muslims is the pilgrimage to Mecca, the Hajj (see box, opposite).

The state of ritual purity, such as that required of Muslims prior to the five daily sessions of prayer, is known as *tahara*. Purification rituals accompany prayer, the major pilgrimage rites, and such activities as handling and reading the Quran, which a Muslim must not do without being in a state of purity.

Other types of purification ritual include circumcision, which, while not mentioned in the Quran, is universally performed on boys and, in some regions, on girls as well. For boys, it usually occurs at the age of ten or, in some societies, when he has demonstrated his ability to recite the Quran. The controversy both within and outside the Islamic world surrounding female circumcision continues to grow. Muslim scholars disagree as to the requirement of female circumcision, with many arguing against the rite on the grounds that it is largely a local cultural practice with no basis in either the Quran or Hadith. It has been outlawed in some Muslim countries.

Before purification, a worshipper may be in a state of either "greater" or "lesser" pollution or impurity. The first demands a full cleansing of the body (*ghusl*), which must follow, for example, menstruation, childbirth, and the emission of semen. Lesser pollution requires a ritual ablution (*wudu*), which is performed following sleep, using the lavatory, fainting, and at other times.

Until fairly recently, Muslim and non-Muslim scholars studying the Islamic ritual system sometimes came into conflict over their views on the centrality of these ritual acts to the religious life of Muslims. For example, in now badly outdated Western studies, one finds a near dismissal of Islamic ritual as mechanical, even lifeless.

Such a reading of the "Five Pillars" misses Islam's central preoccupation with the inner attentiveness and focused intention on the part of the Muslim engaged in acts of worship. The term *niyya*, or "intent," is used quite often in this context by Muslim writers. As al-Ghazzali (see sidebar, p.103), a key figure in the development of Islamic religious thought, understood it, ritual of any kind is without meaning unless the Muslim is alert and mindful of what he or she is doing: "Far from seeing or witnessing Him, the careless worshipper pays no mind to Whom he is speaking, moving his tongue simply out of habit." And, to cite the Quran itself, "woe to the praying ones, who are unmindful of their prayers, and who [pray only] to be seen" (*Sura* 107.4–7).

RITES OF PASSAGE

In devout households, a newborn child will be given a name with historical or sacred significance, such as Muhammad or Husayn for boys and Khadija or Fatima for girls (see p.106). Other names might be formed from those of God, such as Abd Allah and Abd al-Rahman. Verses of the Quran, usually *Sura* 1 (*Al-Fatiha*), may be read to the child as a blessing.

Circumcision takes place in childhood but is universal only for boys (see main text). Many marriages remain arranged, but this practice is changing, particularly in urban areas. Polygyny is permitted, but is now rare (see p.111).

After death, prayers are said for the deceased as the corpse is washed and prepared. Burial usually takes place on the morning after death. In many regions funeral processions are common, but the Hadith record the Prophet's disapproval of elaborate or emotional obsequies.

THE PILGRIMAGE TO MECCA

The Hajj, the pilgrimage to the sacred city of Mecca, constitutes the fifth ritual duty for Muslims. All believers are called upon to perform the Hajj at least once, but only if they are able to afford the journey and can ensure that their families will be provided for in their absence. In practice, therefore, most Muslims never make the Hajj, but they are not considered the lesser on that account. Some countries operate schemes aimed at enabling Muslims to save for the Hajj; one example is Malaysia, which also runs a national lottery with an expenses-paid Hajj as the first prize.

The pilgrimage takes place in the last month of the Islamic year, Dhu al-Hijja ("Month of the Hajj"). Even in the age of modern communications, the Hajj remains both physically and spiritually demanding. It begins with the donning of the *ihram*, a white garment; this is a rite of ritual purification that symbolizes a turning away from worldly concerns. Subsequent rituals emphasize the centrality of Abraham to the Muslim idea of humanity's relationship with God, as well as the link between Abraham and Muhammad. On entering Mecca, the pilgrim circles the Kaba (see p.112) seven times, then runs seven times the distance between two hills, Safa and Marwa, reenacting the search by the biblical Hagar (Hajir) for water to give to her son Ishmael (Ismail).

Further rituals take the pilgrim outside Mecca: these include standing on the plain of Arafat to commemorate Abraham and Ishmael; hurling stones at pillars to represent Satan's temptation of Ishmael; and the sacrifice of animals.

A final *tawaf* (circumambulation) of the Kaba helps conclude the sacred rites. Many pilgrims then proceed to Medina to visit the Prophet's tomb, a ritual not formally part of the Hajj, but nevertheless a highly cherished act.

The Kaba stands today in the center of a vast mosque, the size of which is a testimony to the huge numbers of pilgrims who now make the Hajj (ca. 3 million annually compared with ca. 1 million in 1970). The kiswa, *a black veil embroidered in gold thread with Quranic inscriptions, is hung over the Kaba.*

THE RETURN TO GOD

The Quran treats death not so much as an ending as a return to God, the source of all things, Creator (*al-Khaliq*), and sole possessor of true and perfect reality. Just as God creates, so too he decrees the moment at which all things cease to be. "Every soul must taste of death. We [God] test and try you with the evil and with the good. To Us you will return" (*Sura* 21.35).

Death is thus the taking away by God of the temporary life led by human beings on earth, a shift from one mode of being to another. The earthly life is fleeting, incomplete, and—because only God can be perfect—inevitably flawed. Death is likewise an impermanent state. The physical body crumbles and disappears, as the soul (Arabic *nafs*), now freed of physical constraints, moves on to a different plane. The Islamic tradition thus holds to the idea of an afterlife, knowledge of which may be gained only through divine revelation, the Quran. Believing in the afterlife is seen

ANGELS, *JINN*, AND IBLIS

A *16th-century Turkish manuscript illustration depicting the angel Gabriel transmitting the word of God to Muhammad (right).*

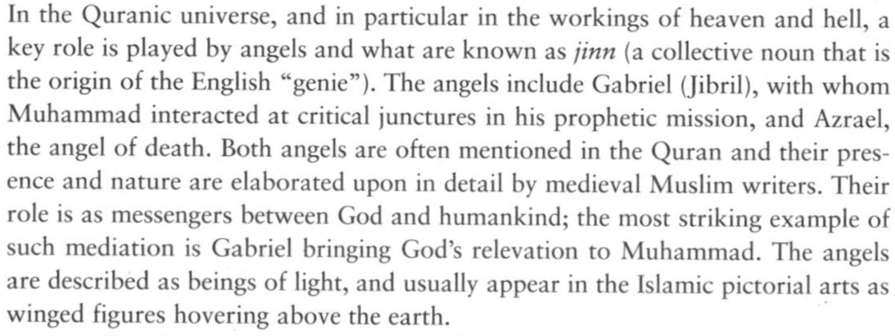

In the Quranic universe, and in particular in the workings of heaven and hell, a key role is played by angels and what are known as *jinn* (a collective noun that is the origin of the English "genie"). The angels include Gabriel (Jibril), with whom Muhammad interacted at critical junctures in his prophetic mission, and Azrael, the angel of death. Both angels are often mentioned in the Quran and their presence and nature are elaborated upon in detail by medieval Muslim writers. Their role is as messengers between God and humankind; the most striking example of such mediation is Gabriel bringing God's relevation to Muhammad. The angels are described as beings of light, and usually appear in the Islamic pictorial arts as winged figures hovering above the earth.

Angelic light, which bears the symbolism of both illumination and wisdom, stands in contrast to the fire of which the *jinn* are said to be made. The *jinn* are often portrayed as a rank beneath the angels, and are more ambiguous figures in the Islamic universe. They are capable of serving God in both positive and destructive ways: for example, the great Arab musician al-Mawsili (767–850CE) claimed that the *jinn* inspired his music; but it is also from the ranks of the *jinn* that Iblis, the Islamic Satan, is said to have emerged.

The account of Iblis's experience before God is among the relatively few detailed narratives to be found in the Quran. Initially accepted by the angels, and God, as a pious figure, Iblis is described as having stood against God at the moment of Adam's creation. When commanded by God, the angels prostrate themselves before the newly created human being; Iblis refuses, however, and is banished from heaven for his pains. In response, he vows to dedicate himself to the corruption of humankind (*Sura* 2.28–34).

as an essential aspect of Islamic faith, because in doing so Muslims affirm God and his awesome presence. It also serves to explain the significance and purpose of this life, with its manifold trials and demands.

Islam believes both in the judgment of each individual after death, and in a final apocalyptic judgment of all souls. In the Hadith literature, scholarly commentaries, and more popular accounts, the fate of the individual is usually described as taking place in several phases. At first, the body ceases to function, thereby releasing the soul, which undergoes an examination by two of God's angels (see box, opposite), Munkar and Nakir. From this point, the soul occupies the grave until the world ends and all humankind is resurrected from the dead to face the final Day of Judgment. God will judge humans (in one popular image, he uses a set of scales) according to their response to the prophetic message brought by Muhammad and the prophets who came before him. This response is understood largely in terms of obedience to the divine will: the unbeliever rejects the conduct codified in the Quran and Hadith, and thus earns a place in Hell, while the true believer, whose acts conformed to the Prophetic tradition (Sunna), is brought into paradise. The Quran reminds its readers time and again of these rewards and punishments, and provides detailed, striking images of both Heaven and Hell.

Among the more notable ideas that occur in the descriptions of the end of time in the Quran and various commentaries is that of the "Straight Path" (*al-sirat al-mustaqim*) of true devotion, with the wrongdoers straying from it and believers remaining true. For example: "Surely God is my Lord and your Lord, so worship and serve Him. This is the straight path" (*Sura* 19.36). At the Final Judgment, the path narrows to a razor-sharp edge along which all humankind must walk. Believers will make their way with ease, but sinners will stumble, falling into the eternal fires of Hell.

A Muslim funeral in Kashgar, China. The Prophet opposed all but the simplest of grave markers, and while there have been exceptions—such as the monumental tombs of the Mamluk rulers of Egypt (1250–1517)—most graves, as here, are plain and unadorned.

FREE WILL AND JUDGMENT

A central problem for Islamic theologians, as for their Jewish and Christian counterparts, is the definition of free will and responsibility. On what basis can humans be judged if all is preordained by God? Debates on this issue among early Muslim scholars reflected contemporary political divisions, with opponents of the Umayyad caliphate (see pp.96–7) arguing strongly for the existence of human free will and the requirement for all humans to accept responsibility for their actions. But supporters of the Umayyads espoused the idea of predestination, arguing that all is ordained beforehand by God—including, of course, the rule of the Umayyads.

The emphasis on human free will was taken up in the ninth century CE by a group of scholars, the Mutazilites, who sought to promote the idea that evil in the world could never be of divine origin but was the product of humans alone. Later Sunni theologians, principally al-Ashari (died 935CE), sought a middle position. Al-Ashari argued that God, while retaining his omnipotence, also provides humankind with a "modicum" (or, in other readings, "a brief moment") of freedom and thus responsibility.

ISSUES AND DISPUTES

Kemal Atatürk ("Father of Turks"), whose radical reforms in post-Ottoman Turkey proved to be the most enduring program of secularization in the Islamic world.

In the past century or so, responses within the Islamic world both to Western imperialism and to the spread of new technologies and ideologies have naturally been quite varied. For example, in the military and political circles of some lands the ideas of secular nationalism with its emphasis upon a centralized, dynamic state proved popular. In Iran and, especially, Turkey following the collapse of the Ottoman empire after the First World War, ambitious military men rose to power and initiated programs of radical secular reform of the state. Mustafa Kemal Atatürk (1881–1938), the founder of the modern Turkish state, sought to separate Islamic practice and law from the public sphere. His measures included the abolition of the caliphate as well as the Sharia, and ending the education system based on the *madrasa*s (religious colleges). In Iran, the Pahlavi dynasty of shahs (ruled 1925–79) attempted similar policies, but with much less success owing to strong opposition from the Iranian Twelver Shii religious establishment (see pp.108–9) and its supporters.

Other influential figures and movements also attempted to shape what was conceived of as a modern, forward-looking society founded on Islamic principles. Those who contributed to, and often argued over, the ideas known as "Islamic reform" included such vocal members of the Muslim intellectual community as Jamal al-Din al-Afghani (1839–97), Sayyid Ahmad Khan (1817–98), Rashid Rida (1865–1935), Muhammad Abduh (1849–1905), and Abd al-Hamid ben Badis (died 1940). However, their attempts at reform were generally frustrated by the emergence of nationalist, largely secular élites. They also encountered often bitter opposition from the more conservative *ulama*, who were alarmed at the reformers' willingness to reexamine even the most basic structures of Islamic tradition and law—borrowing from Western legal and political thought in the process—and their call for a shakeup of the traditional, *madrasa*-based Islamic education system. Abduh felt the conservative opposition at first hand. Trained at Cairo's famous al-Azhar university, he struggled largely in vain to revamp the curriculum of this and other institutions of Islamic learning. He is credited with helping to found a new style of higher education institution, the University of Cairo, in 1914.

Issues that confront the contemporary Islamic world are, of course, rooted both in the recent and distant past. Responses to these issues reflect the variety of ways in which modern Muslims, scholars and laity alike, understand and apply the patterns of a complex and deep-seated religious and social tradition. The Islamic community continues to grow, both in regions where it has long existed and in those where its presence is more recent, chiefly Europe and North America. Questions unique to

Islam, of both a local and transnational character, jostle with problems of the modern period in general, whether related to the expansion of new technology and communications, shifting political currents rooted in post-Cold War realities, the global spread of Western popular culture, or the profound impact of the transformation of world economic structures. However, any consideration of the problems facing the present-day Islamic world can only be fruitful if due recognition is given to the meaning furnished by the tradition to the lives of its adherents, on the individual as well as communal levels.

To the questions confronting Islamic society, a number of contemporary Muslims would offer a straightforward response: "Islam is [or "provides"] the solution." The phrase is commonly used by what are often termed "Islamist" or, more crudely, "Islamic fundamentalist" movements. The latter term implies that such movements seek a return to some idealized Islamic past, or are a throwback to "medieval" patterns. Mostly, however, these movements present a *new* vision of both Islam and Islamic society, even when they do refer to the achievements of Islamic history. For example, many observers have pointed out that the sharply political manner in which Islamic vocabulary and symbols—be it the veil or other forms of dress, or the Quran itself—are used by both the leaders and supporters of Islamist movements actually has little precedent in the Islamic past.

What is also termed "political Islam" is a phenomenon of great complexity, too often reduced by the media and academic observers to such seismic political events as the 1979 Islamic Revolution in Iran that ousted the shahs and brought Ayatollah Ruhollah Khomeini (1902–89) and his followers to power; the 1981 assassination of President Anwar Sadat of Egypt by radical Islamists; and the activities of such organizations as Hizballah in

THE NATION OF ISLAM

Islam has been the seedbed of socio-religious movements with doctrines and practices that strike the mainstream Muslim as beyond the pale, their Islamic roots notwithstanding. Two prominent examples are the Druze (see p.109) and, in modern times, the Nation of Islam movement in the United States.

The Nation of Islam began during the Depression of the 1930s in African-American neighborhoods of Detroit and Chicago. Its founders, Fard (Farrad) Muhammad (died 1934) and his disciple Elijah Muhammad (1896–1975), preached a militant, separatist African-American nationalism to the poor and politically dispossessed inhabitants of the urban ghettoes of the northern states. The Nation's strong racialist message and its ascription of divinity to Fard Muhammad are unacceptable to mainstream Islam.

A key role in the Nation's history was played by the radical leader Malcolm X (1925–65), an early follower of Elijah Muhammad. Malcolm X subsequently broke with the Nation to embrace Sunni Islam. Divisions in the Nation in the 1970s and 1980s led many members to follow Malcolm X's example; others took up with a reinvigorated Nation led by Louis Farrakhan (born 1933).

Women on their way to a mosque in central Bosnia. "Political Islam" among Bosnia's largely secular Muslims was an unexpected phenomenon that arose mainly as a consequence of the pressures from non-Islamic extremist nationalism in the former Yugoslavia.

Lebanon, Hamas in Israel-Palestine, and the various Islamist groupings that emerged in the Algerian civil war from the early 1990s. Too often ignored is the fact that overt political activity is but one expression of a renewed commitment to the faith on the part of many Muslims. In addition, it should be recognized that most Islamist groups are political opposition movements and therefore cannot fairly be understood without consideration of their particular ideals and perceived grievances.

The ideas and movements of "political Islam" have their roots, to a large degree, in the early twentieth-century response to Western imperialism and debates over the manner in which to revitalize Muslim society. In this sense, they are a radical answer to the ideas of Islamic reform and to the rise of nationalist, largely secular states throughout the Islamic world. In this context, three movements are significant. In Iran, developments in

Algerian women wearing the traditional full veil. In Algeria the conflict between a secularizing ruling élite and Islamist radicalism had particularly tragic consequences in a bloody civil war that erupted in the last decade of the 20th century.

WOMEN IN ISLAM

The role of women in Islamic society is a hotly debated topic both within and outside the Islamic world. Efforts by Muslim writers and activists to address the public and private lives of women have been varied. The arguments partly concern the specific treatment of women and gender roles as expressed in the Quran, Hadith, and elsewhere.

Well-known modern Islamic thinkers such as Mawdudi (see main text, opposite) and the Egyptian writer Qasim Amin (died 1908) called, in their different ways, for a reexamination of these issues. More recently, arguments have centered on women in the public sphere, specifically in the workplace and institutions of higher education. The increased wearing of the "veil" (*hijab*) or modest, austere clothing, by female Islamists indicates the extent to which Western feminist arguments are seen as irrelevant to Muslim women.

However, the issues regarding women have frequently been seen as a problem involving Islamic society as a whole. In other words, the debate surrounding gender roles has often formed just one part of arguments regarding marriage, divorce, inheritance, and other areas of Islamic law pertaining to the family.

Family law has often been the subject of intense activity and debate among those concerned with the place of women in Islamic society. Efforts to rewrite traditional family, or personal status, codes have had a very mixed record, with reform being achieved in Atatürk's Turkey and in Tunisia under the leadership of President Habib Bourguiba (1903–), but meeting with varying results in, for example, modern Egypt, Kuwait, and Pakistan.

the nineteenth century, particularly the decline of the Qajar state (1794–1925), strengthened the influence of the Twelver Shii *ulama*. This set the stage for tensions in later decades between the shahs and more vocal members of the *ulama*, a conflict which culminated in the rise of the militant movement led by Khomeini. In India, the ideas of Abu Ala Mawdudi (1903–79) led to the creation in the 1940s of the Jamaat-i-Islami ("Islamic Association"), which remains very active in Pakistan today. In Egypt, the activism and ideas of Hasan al-Banna (1906–49) prepared the ground for the emergence of the Muslim Brotherhood in that country. Subsequent decades witnessed the emergence of a number of offshoots of the Brotherhood in the Near East, including Hamas and branches in Syria and Jordan.

Much like the reformers of earlier periods, modern Islamists frame some of their arguments in social and moral terms. Islamic society, they claim, has been corrupted by its acceptance of Western culture, which generally they perceive as morally lax. In particular, they express concern about the increasing public role of women, a move seen by many Islamists as undermining the social order and Quranic principles (see box, opposite).

Islamists today also tend to be interested in political reform. In the writings of Khomeini and, for example, Sayyid Qutb (died 1966), a member of the Muslim Brotherhood executed by the Egyptian government for his views, one finds a powerful critique of the political élite of the Islamic world and a call for both social justice and revolutionary change. Qutb's writings remain a major source of influence upon militant Islamist groups. The central theme sounded by the Islamists is the need for an Islamic state, that is, an entity whose sole foundation is the Sharia or Divine Law (see pp.110–11).

ISLAM AND ISRAEL

The Palestinian-Israeli conflict has been a great source of concern and debate within the Islamic world, especially the Arab Near East. The creation of Israel in 1948 led to the departure of hundreds of thousands of Palestinian Arabs from their homes and properties.

For the Arabs, the conflict was fueled by the war of 1967, with the capture by Israel of East Jerusalem, the West Bank, Golan Heights, and Gaza Strip. Jerusalem is the third holiest city in the Islamic tradition, largely because of its association with the Prophet Muhammad (see box, p.107) and the formative period of Islamic history.

To this religious factor one should add that, for many Arabs, the losses of 1967 underscored what they saw as the corrupt nature of several Arab regimes and of Arab secular nationalism. Many Arabs, therefore, see the defeat as justifying the rise of more militant forms of Islamism.

The conflict entered a difficult new phase with the Oslo Accords of the 1990s, which led to the establishment of a degree of Palestinian autonomy in the West Bank and Gaza. Widely seen as a way forward in the tangled web of Arab-Israeli relations, the accords nevertheless faced militant opposition from both sides.

A new mosque in Brunei, southeast Asia, a small Islamic state flourishing as a result of the discovery of oil. Muslim countries control some two-thirds of the world's oil reserves, bringing a prosperity and economic muscle that have been key factors in the 20th-century reassertion of Islam on the international stage.

Chapter Four

HINDUISM

Vasudha Narayanan

*A sandstone figure of ca. 800*CE *from Madhya Pradesh depicting the god Shiva in his important manifestation as Nataraja ("Lord of the Dance").*

OPPOSITE *Colorfully painted images of gods, goddesses, and other divine beings adorn the exterior of Kadirampuram temple, Hampi, in Karnataka province.*

INTRODUCTION

Eighty percent of India's population of almost one billion are Hindu, and there are Hindus in every part of the world today. Yet the term "Hinduism" is somewhat difficult to define. The religion has no single founder, creed, teacher, or prophet acknowledged by all Hindus as central to the religion, and no single holy book is universally acclaimed as being of primary importance.

The use of the word "Hindu" itself is complex. Both "India" and "Hindu" derive from *Sindhu*, the traditional name of the Indus river. In ancient inscriptions and documents, "Hindu" refers to the people of "Hind," the Indian subcontinent. In the Muslim-ruled empires of medieval India, it was used for all non-Muslim Indians, of whatever faith. Only after the late eighteenth century did the term come to refer to the dominant religion of the Indian people.

"Hinduism" is not a term most Hindus have applied to themselves in the past, or use with great specificity even now, although the term "Hindutva" ("Hinduness") has received political currency in recent years. Hindus identify themselves with reference to their caste, community, region, and language. The phrase *sanatana dharma* ("eternal faith") has become popular in the last two centuries, but it applies more to philosophical interpretations of the religion than to its colorful local manifestations. In early texts, *sanatana dharma* meant the ideal religious obligations of human beings, but did not express the idea of a faith community.

In Indian law, the term "Hindu" may even include those who belong to traditions usually thought of as theologically distinct from Hinduism. It is

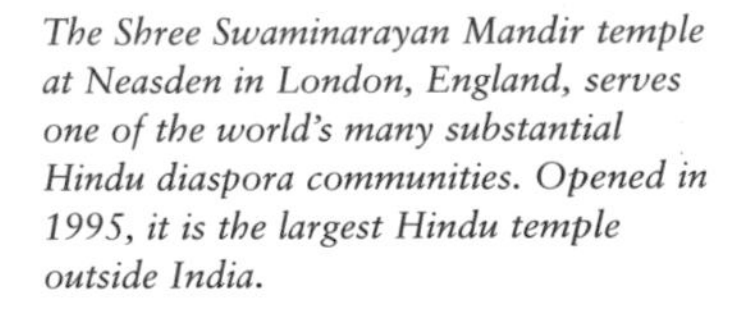

The Shree Swaminarayan Mandir temple at Neasden in London, England, serves one of the world's many substantial Hindu diaspora communities. Opened in 1995, it is the largest Hindu temple outside India.

HINDU SACRED SITES

This map indicates many of the major holy sites of Hinduism, including towns, mountains, and rivers. Most towns shown are sacred to one or more deities (such as Ayodhya, the birthplace of Rama); others, such as the Harappa cities, Ellora (the site of Hindu caves), and the temples of Khajuraho, are of historical rather than present-day significance. Other towns are marked for reference; but while they may possess no specific religious importance, most will possess a multitude of holy places, from temples to roadside shrines.

Key

- Hindu sacred site
- Other towns
- Sacred mountain
- Harappa civilization site

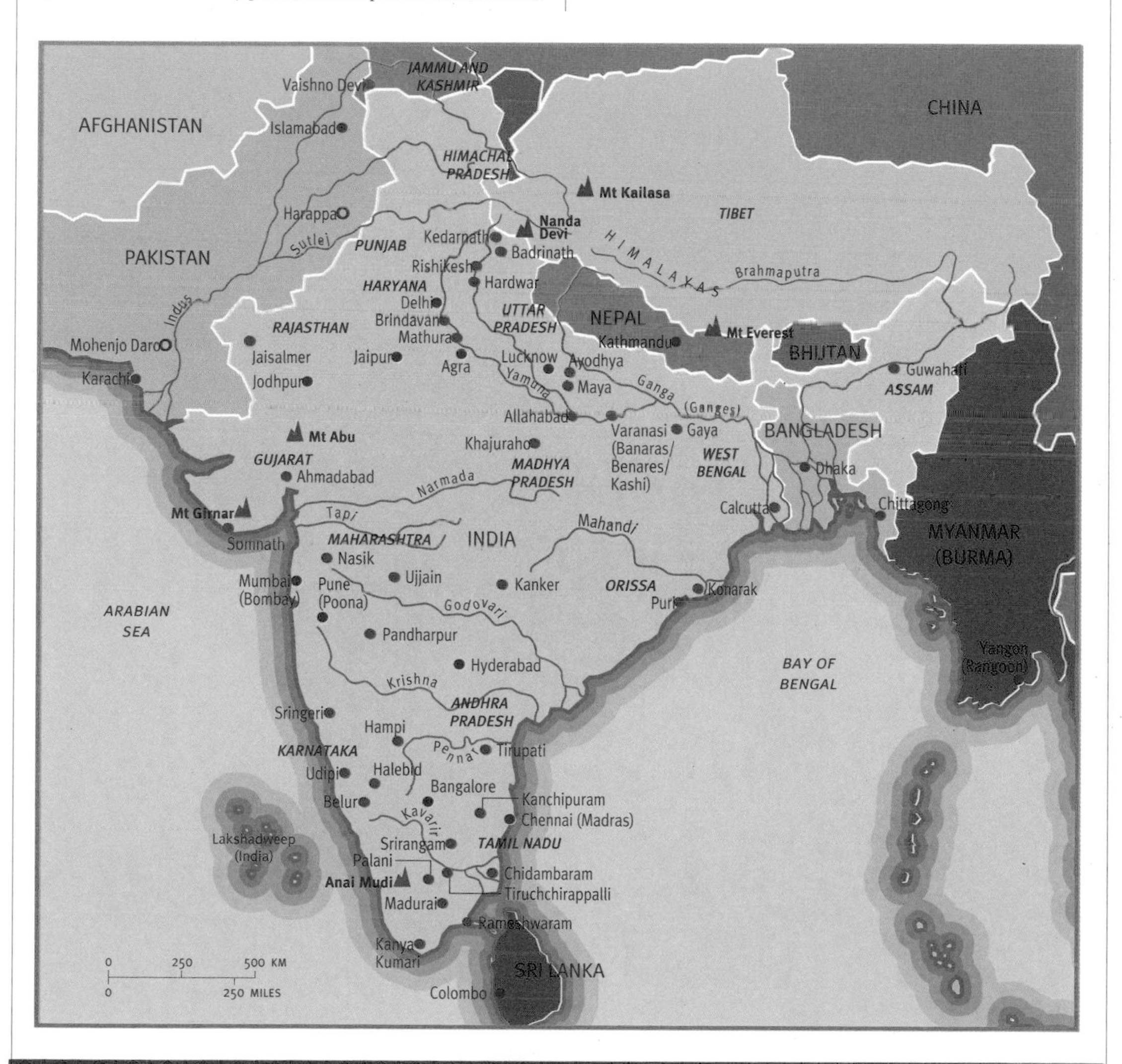

generally applied to anyone who lives in India and accepts the Hindu tradition—which is not defined—in any of its forms or developments. This therefore embraces Buddhists, Jains, and Sikhs. The term also applies to anyone else who is not a Muslim, Christian, Parsi (Zoroastrian), or Jew.

On the other hand, "Hinduism" has been a problematic label even for some traditions that many people would generally consider to be Hindu. At different times several Indian sects and movements have gone to court to argue against their official "Hindu" status.

Hinduism has been portrayed in the last two centuries as being a more or less unified religion. However, it is important to note that there are hundreds of internal divisions created by caste, community, language, and geography. Regional manifestations of a deity or a local sacred text may sometimes be more significant to a particular group of worshippers than any pan-Hindu concept. Many such groups may extensively share common texts, deities, traditions, and patterns of ritual, even though they interpret them variously; but there may be other groups with whom they have very little in common. Yet there are also threads that run geographically throughout the subcontinent and historically across thousands of years. At certain times, therefore, it may be more useful to talk of many Hindu traditions, and at others, of one tradition.

Is Hinduism a religion, a culture, or as many Hindus would say, a way of life? It is all three, but what in the West might be viewed as the boundaries between the sacred and nonsacred spheres do not apply to the Hindu

CHRONOLOGY *All dates are CE, except where stated*

- **ca. 3000–1750BCE** • Indus Valley (Harappan) civilization
- **ca. 1500BCE** • Aryan invasions of northern India
- **ca. 800BCE** • Compilation of oral *Vedas*
- **ca. 600BCE** • Production of the *Upanishads*
- **326BCE** • Greek armies under Alexander the Great reach as far as India
- **ca. 272BCE** • Accession of Mauryan emperor Ashoka
- **ca. 100BCE** • Composition of *Bhagavad Gita*
- **ca. 200CE** • Compilation of *Laws of Manu*
- **ca. 500** • Hindu Tantric tradition established
- **ca. 700** • *Alvars*, Tamil *bhakti* (devotional) poets, including Nammalvar, active
- **ca. 800** • Philosopher Shankara produces *Advaita Vedanta*, key work of nondualist philosophy
- **1137** • Death of Ramanuja, Vaishnava theistic philosopher
- **ca. 1175** • Life of the *bhakti* poet Jayadeva
- **1206** • Muslim sultanate established at Delhi
- **1450?–1547** • Life of Princess Mira, *bhakti* poet
- **1483–1530** • Reign of Babur, founder of the Mughal empire
- **1483–1563** • Life of Surdas, great Krishna devotee
- **1486–1583** • Death of Chaitanya, Bengali Vaishnava *bhakti* leader
- **1518** • Death of Kabir, north Indian *bhakti* poet
- **1543?–1623** • Life of Tulsidas, north Indian *bhakti* poet
- **1556–1605** • Reign of Mughal emperor Akbar
- **1757** • British rule established in Calcutta
- **1772–1833** • Life of Hindu reformer Ram Rohan Roy, founder of Brahmo Samaj ("Society of Brahman"), 1828
- **1824–83** • Life of Hindu reformer Dayananda Sarasvati, founder of Arya Samaj ("Society of Noble Ones"), 1875
- **1857–8** • Abolition of Mughal empire and establishment of direct British rule
- **1875** • H. Blavatsky and H. S. Olcott found Theosophical Society, drawing on Hinduism and Buddhism
- **1893** • Vivekananda, founder of Ramakrishna Mission, Hindu devotional order, attends World Parliament of Religions, Chicago
- **1914** • Sri Aurobindo (1872–1950) founds first *ashram* (religious retreat) at Pondicherry
- **1920** • M. K. ("Mahatma") Gandhi (b.1869) launches anti-British campaign based on *ahimsa* (nonviolence)
- **1947** • India gains independence from Britain
- **1948** • Gandhi assassinated
- **1966** • A.C. Bhaktivedanta founds the International Society for Krishna Consciousness, New York
- **1992** • Hindu militants destroy 16th-century mosque at Ayodhya

traditions. While many Hindu holy texts and practices are intended to provide the devotee with spiritual paths to liberation from the repeated cycle of life and death, many other aspects of Hindu life and ritual do not lead directly to such transformation, but are perceived to enhance one's quality of life on earth. Thus such activities as tree-planting, singing, dancing, medicine, archery, astrology, sculpture, architecture, and building a home might all be considered part of the religious domain.

In studying the many Hindu traditions, therefore, the words "secular" and "sacred" have to be used with caution. More meaningful terms in a Hindu context are *dharma* and *moksha*. *Dharma*, a Sanskrit word from a root meaning "to sustain," is truth, righteousness, duty, law, and justice. *Moksha* literally means "liberation," that is, liberation from the cycle of life and death that every soul is believed to undergo (see pp.156–7) and which is repeated endlessly, until such time as the soul achieves liberation into a state of bliss. While not unique to Hinduism, the belief in this process is perhaps the one thing that all "Hindus" can be said to share.

A woman and child enter the Hoysala temple at Halebid, Karnataka. The temple is dedicated to Hoysaleshvara ("Lord of the Hoysala dynasty or people"), a regional manifestation of Vishnu, one of the great pan-Hindu gods.

FIVE MILLENNIA OF TRADITION

The Hindu tradition has no founder figure and cannot date its origin to a particular year or century. It is generally believed that its beginnings lie in the ancient indigenous culture of India and of the Indo-European people, who appeared in India some four thousand years ago. The stages of early Hindu history are marked not by remarkable personalities (although there must have been many) and great proselytizing movements, but rather by the composition of orally transmitted sacred texts expressing central concepts of what we now call Hinduism.

The earliest known Indian civilization existed ca. 3000–1750BCE in a broad area around the region of the Indus river and probably elsewhere. Entire cities have been excavated at Harappa and Mohenjo Daro. The people of this civilization (often called "Harappan") were literate but their script remains undeciphered. Some Harappan seals bear images of figures that share characteristics with the later Hindu deity Shiva. The "Great Bath," a huge pool complex at Mohenjo Daro incorporating porticos and side rooms, may have had a religious function. From such fragmentary evidence we can tentatively state that some features of the present-day Hindu religion may be nearly five thousand years old.

The Harappan culture was followed by the "Age of the *Vedas*," so called from the sacred compositions of the Indo-European people. It is widely held that Indo-Europeans moved into India from central Asia

The remains of the "Great Bath" at the ancient Indus Valley site of Mohenjo Daro, Pakistan. Built of brick, the bath may have been a sacred pool for ritual ablutions, much like similar structures at later Hindu temples.

ca. 2000BCE, although some scholars think that India was the original homeland. The work of archaeologists, anthropologists, and linguists suggests that it was a peaceful process, undertaken in pursuit of new lands to farm. The Indo-Europeans referred to themselves as "Aryans" or "Noble Ones." Their speech was the ancestor of the ancient Indian language of Sanskrit, which is closely related to all the other tongues referred to by linguists as "Indo-European," including Latin, Greek, and English.

In India, the Indo-Europeans composed many sacred poems and, later, entire manuals on rituals and philosophy. The earliest such compositions are known collectively as *Veda* (Sanskrit, "Knowledge") and form the core of India's ancient "proto-Hindu" Vedic religion (see box, below).

The sacrifice-based worldview of the early Vedic age gave way to philosophical inquiry and discussion in the later texts known as the *Aranyaka*s and *Upanishad*s (see p.138). These were composed around the early sixth

VEDIC RELIGION

A dominant feature of religious life in the Vedic period was ritual sacrifice. Most rituals involved fire (see p.155) and were conducted by ritual specialists and priests who also supervised the making of altars and the recitation of hymns. Many sacrifices involved the use of *soma*, an intoxicating liquid.

Vedic religion perceived a delicate connection between the performance of rituals and the prevalence of *rita* ("truth," "justice," and "rightness"). *Rita* makes harmony and peace possible on earth and in the heavens and was upheld by early Vedic gods, such as Varuna. According to Vedic hymns composed before ca. 1000BCE, the world itself may have come into being through an act of cosmic sacrifice. One creation hymn explicitly mentions the beginnings of the social divisions referred to today as "caste" (see pp.158–60).

An 18th-century CE manuscript of part of the Rig Veda *("Wisdom of the Verses"), a collection of over 1,000 hymns to ancient Vedic gods that refer to various sacrificial rituals.*

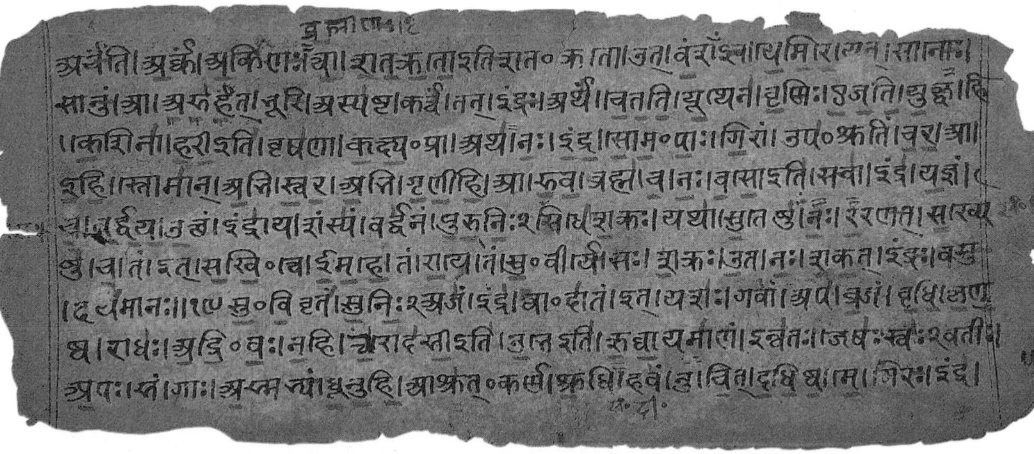

century BCE, a time of great intellectual speculation, when Siddhartha Gautama (the Buddha; see pp.168–71), Mahavira (the founder of Jainism), and others questioned and even rejected the authoritarian structures of traditional Indian religion, such as the religious leadership of the priestly caste (the *brahmins*), the caste system itself, and the status of the *Vedas* (see sidebar, left). The *Upanishads* seek liberation from the cycle of life and death and introduced the notion of immortality as reality. The ultimate quest of the Hindu tradition, as it subsequently developed, has been to achieve the immortality of the soul and, in this life, happiness and peace.

Most of the later literature in Sanskrit deals directly or indirectly with *dharma* (a word with multiple layers of meaning, including "righteous behavior," "truth," and "law"). The *Bhagavad Gita* emphasizes that *dharma* should be performed without expectation of reward but with devotion to one God. The "supreme being," conceived of in the *Upanishads* as *brahman*, an abstract concept (see pp.134–5), is referred to in the *Bhagavad Gita* as the deity Krishna or Vishnu. Devotionalism (*bhakti*)—the intensely personal worship of, and surrender to, this supreme being, whether it be manifest in the form of Vishnu, Shiva, the Goddess, or any other divine being (see pp.134–7)—has been one of the most common features of many Hindu communities in the last two millennia.

Two factors contributed to the spread of such devotion. One was the use of vernacular languages, rather than Sanskrit. The other was its appeal across all social classes. Some of the most famous devotional poet-saints, such as Nammalvar in the eighth century CE and Tukaram in the fifteenth, were perceived as being from very low castes. Yet their influence cut across all levels of a highly stratified society, their simplicity of

HINDUISM, THE BUDDHA, AND MAHAVIRA

The sophisticated philosophy of the *Upanishads* was contemporaneous with the spirit of critical enquiry in many parts of northern India. Siddhartha Gautama (the Buddha) and Mahavira the Jina ("Victorious One," whose followers are today's Jains) both challenged the notion that the *Vedas* were divine revelation. They, and others, relied on their own spiritual experiences to proclaim a path to liberation that was open to all, not just to the higher castes of society.

Both Siddhartha and Mahavira emphasized nonviolence (*ahimsa*), and this virtue has been very significant in Hinduism and many other south Asian traditions. In modern times, it informed the strategy of Mohandas Karamchand Gandhi (known as the Mahatma or "Great Soul"), who led India's struggle for independence in the twentieth century.

An 18th-century miniature illustrating an ancient Hindu creation story in which the god Vishnu (center) presides over the churning of a vast primordial ocean of milk to produce the sacred liquid called soma. *To turn the great churning-paddle, deities (left) and demons (right) pull the head and tail of a cosmic serpent.*

HINDU REFORMERS

Ram Mohan Roy (1772–1833) was born into an orthodox *brahmin* family, but became familiar with Western social life and the Christian scriptures, and met members of the Unitarian movement. Following his study of the *Upanishads* (see p.138) and other texts, Roy came to the conclusion that certain Hindu practices were not part of "classical" Hinduism. In 1828, he established a society to debate the nature of *brahman*, the supreme being (see p.135). This organization came to be called the Brahmo Samaj ("Society of Brahman").

Roy translated some of the *Upanishads* and other Sanskrit texts and distributed them for free. An educational pioneer, he also set up new periodicals and teaching institutions, and worked to improve the status of Hindu women.

Dayananda Sarasvati (1824–83) considered only the early hymns of the *Rig Veda* (see p.131) to be the true scripture. He was impressed by the joy of living they expressed and their concern for the individual, the family, and the community. In 1875 Dayananda founded the Arya Samaj ("Society of the Noble Ones"). It was based on the teachings of the *Rig Veda* and advocated a life of education and vigorous work. For him, the ideal person served other human beings and thus lived a full life, not one of renunciation. A good society, he asserted, is one in which people work to uplift humanity; this in itself leads to the welfare of body and soul.

worship appealing to the élite and masses alike. Other popular *bhakti* poets came from a wealthier social milieu. One of the most famous, Mira (1450?–1547CE), was a Gujarati princess who wrote passionate poetry about her love for the god Krishna. According to some legends, at the end of her life Mira merged with Krishna's icon in a temple.

The sixteenth century saw the emergence of Sikhism under its Gurus, beginning with Guru Nanak (1469–1539), and the zenith of the Muslim-ruled Mughal empire under the emperor Akbar and his successors (see sidebar, right). In this period, the Portuguese, Dutch, English, and French began to establish trading settlements in India. In time, as Mughal power disintegrated, their agenda came to include the possession of territory, and in the eighteenth century large parts of the subcontinent became loosely unified under British control. Many social and religious practices of the Hindus—in particular "idolatry" and the caste system—came in for severe criticism from European missionaries and others, and some practices, such as *sati* (the cremation of widows with their husbands), were banned. One response to external criticism came in the shape of reform movements that arose within Hinduism in the early modern period (see box, above).

The many traditions that make up the tapestry of Hinduism continue to flourish in the diaspora. Hindus who migrated to southeast Asia in the first millennium CE sought to transmit their culture through the building of the great temples of Cambodia and Java. Similarly, Hindu emigrés to Britain and the United States in the past few decades have sought to perpetuate their culture into the next millennium through the religious and cultural nuclei of their own community temples.

HINDUISM UNDER THE MUGHALS

Five centuries ago, much of India's Hindu population came to be governed by the Mughals ("Mongols"), a Muslim dynasty of central Asian origin. However, the social and the doctrinal gulf that existed between Hinduism and Islam could be transcended by devotional spirituality. Hindu devotionalism (see main text) had its counterpart in Islam's own mystical tradition, Sufism (see pp.101–3). Where Hindus lived in contact with Muslims, their piety could be seen as having much in common.

The tolerant rule of the emperor Akbar (1556–1605) even led to attempts to synthesize the two faiths, or at least identify their common ground, notably by Akbar himself and Prince Dara Shikoh, a son of the emperor Shah Jehan (ruled 1627–58). Dara Shikoh was executed by his brother, Aurangzeb (ruled 1658–1707), whose reign brought a return to strict Islamic orthodoxy at the Mughal court.

GODS AND GODDESSES

The towns and cities of India may have dozens of temples and shrines dedicated to many deities. But images of gods and goddesses are also prominently displayed in stores, hospitals, government offices, and on altars and shrines in Hindu homes.

Hindus may acknowledge many deities, but consider only one to be supreme; or they may consider all gods and goddesses equal, but worship one who is their favorite. However, most Hindus view all divinities to be manifestations of a single godhead. For many, to say that this God is male or female, one or many, is to limit it, to impose human ideas of gender and number on the divine.

The *Upanishads*, Hindu sacred texts composed ca. 600BCE (see p.138), refer to the supreme being as *brahman*, which is considered to be ineffable and beyond all human comprehension (see sidebar, opposite). However, the texts called the *Puranas* ("Ancient [Lore]") claim that this divine entity assumes a form and name to make itself accessible to humankind. Hence Hindus speak of the supreme being as both *nirguna* ("without attributes")

SACRED IMAGES

Hindus worship the supreme being in temples in the form of an "image," a word often used (together with "idol") to translate the Sanskrit *murti*, which, however, is more accurately rendered as "form," "embodiment," or "incarnation." Most Hindus think of a sacred image as an actual incarnation of the supreme being, a form taken by the godhead in order to receive worship.

During a consecration ritual called *prana pratishta* ("establishment of life"), an image ceases to be gross matter and becomes an actual presence or incarnation of divinity on earth. The divine spirit is believed to remain in the icon for as long as devotees wish.

THE DIVINE FEMALE

Hindus have continuously venerated the divine in female form—very often referred to simply as the Goddess—for over two thousand years. The tradition may even go back to the pre-Hindu Harappan civilization (see p.130). The Goddess, sometimes called Devi in Sanskrit literature, is usually seen as a manifestation of Parvati, the wife of Shiva. As a beneficent deity, she is frequently called Amba or Ambika ("Little Mother"), and is widely venerated as Shri or Lakshmi (see p.136). As Kali, the Goddess is dark, dishevelled, and awe-inspiring, with a necklace of skulls. Even in this form, she is called "mother" by her devotees.

An 18th-century painting of the fearsome—but much adored—goddess Kali bestride the god Shiva, a popular image that represents the union of the female and male divine principles.

As a warrior goddess, she is Durga, depicted with a smiling countenance but wielding an array of weapons. Durga, riding a tiger or lion, is one of the most popular goddesses in India. Strong and beautiful, the weapons in her hand show her readiness to assist her devotees. In one celebrated story, she manifests herself with the energies of all other deities in order to combat a buffalo-demon, Mahisa Asura. She emerges victorious after nine nights of struggle, commemorated by the festival of Navaratri ("Nine Nights") in the fall (see p.153).

There are many other goddesses throughout India. In some regions a goddess may be known only by a local name and celebrated in stories with a local setting; elsewhere she may be identified with a pan-Hindu goddess. Some communities may offer animal sacrifices to their local village goddesses or Kali.

and *saguna* ("with attributes," such as grace and mercy). Texts identify the supreme being variously as Vishnu ("All-Pervasive"), Shiva ("Auspicious One"), or the Goddess in one of her many manifestations, such as Shakti ("Energy"), Durga, and Kali (see box, opposite).

Although Vishnu, Shiva, and the Goddess are the most important deities in Hindu texts, other very popular deities include the elephant-headed Ganesha (a son of Parvati), Kartikkeya/Murugan (a son of Shiva), and Hanuman (a divine monkey-devotee of Rama, an incarnation of Vishnu). Many roadside shrines are dedicated to Ganesha and Hanuman. Ganesha is depicted as riding a mouse and is also called Vigneshwara ("He who overcomes all obstacles"). Hindus worship him before embarking on any task, project, or journey.

Gods and goddesses all have their own iconographic characteristics, and every position of the hands or feet, every associated animal, plant, or bird, has a special significance. Many deities have several hands, each carrying a weapon or a flower to protect his or her devotees from harm. Some Hindus interpret the numerous arms of a deity as representing omnipotence. Most deities are associated with one or more animals or with birds. Although sacred texts give specific mythological reasons for

A statue of the monkey-deity Hanuman is paraded through Mysore during a festival. The deity is shown tearing open his breast to reveal his beloved Rama and Sita (see p.138) in his heart.

BRAHMAN AND HIGHER WISDOM

For centuries the definition of *brahman*—the supreme being, according to the *Upanishads*—has been the subject of intense speculation. *Brahman*, according to the *Taittiriya Upanishad*, is truth (*satya*), knowledge (*jñana*), and infinity (*ananta*). Beyond this, all that can be expressed about *brahman* is that it is existence (*sat*), consciousness (*chit*), and bliss (*ananda*). Ultimately, *brahman* cannot be described, since to describe is to confine, and with the infinite, this is impossible. The sage Yajñavalkya said that one may come close to describing *brahman* only by stating what it is not.

A similar difficulty surrounds any definition of the relationship between *brahman* and *atman* (the human soul). In a famous dialogue in the *Chandogya Upanishad*, a father asks his son to dissolve salt in water. He says that *brahman* and *atman* are united in a similar manner and ends his teaching with a famous dictum: "*Tat tvam asi*" (Sanskrit, "You are that"). "That" (*tat*) refers to *brahman* and "you" (*tvam*) to *atman*. The philosopher Shankara (eighth century CE) believed this statement to imply that *brahman* and *atman* are identical. But Ramanuja (eleventh century CE) saw it as indicating that *brahman* and *atman* are inseparable, but not identical.

THE DIVINE IN NATURE

Many Hindus attribute divine status to natural features and phenomena. For example, the rivers Ganga (Ganges), Kaveri, Yamuna, and others are personified and worshipped as mother goddesses. Hindus also revere heavenly bodies and propitiate the *navagraha* ("nine planets"—the sun, the moon, Venus, Mercury, Mars, Jupiter, Saturn, and two mythical entities called Rahu and Ketu) in rituals. Many temples in south India and in the diaspora incorporate images of the planets.

their presence, believers may understand them more metaphorically. Thus Ganesha's elephant head and mouse companion represent his power to overcome hindrances: an elephant crushes large obstacles, and a mouse gnaws through little ones. Like Ganesha, many deities have specific functions, so a person may worship one god or goddess in order to achieve success in their career, another to cure illness, and so on.

In addition to the pan-Hindu deities, there are many local gods and goddesses who may have distinctive histories and functions. Many are regarded as local incarnations of the great divinities. Thus Vishnu is known in many parts of south India by specifically regional names.

Devotees of a deity may perceive him or her to be the supreme being. Some early writings express the idea of a divine trinity (*trimurti*) of Brahma (the creator), Vishnu (the preserver), and Shiva (the destroyer), but this concept was never widely popular. In time, Brahma became marginal and the functions of creation, preservation, and destruction were combined in one deity—either Vishnu, Shiva, or Devi (the Goddess), depending on the individual devotee.

The manifold aspects of Shiva's power are expressed in his often paradoxical roles: he is both threatening and benevolent, creator and destroyer, exuberant dancer and austere *yogi*, lone ascetic and husband of the god-

SHRI, THE GRACIOUS GODDESS

An image of Shri-Lakshmi among other deities on a domestic altar decorated for the Dipavali festival (see pp.152–3).

Perhaps the best known manifestation of the Goddess in the Hindu and Jain traditions is Shri, more popularly known as Lakshmi. She is the goddess of wealth and good fortune and her picture graces millions of homes, shops, and businesses. Shri-Lakshmi is called the mother of all creation, bestower of wisdom and salvation and grace incarnate. Many teachers have composed hymns celebrating her compassion and wisdom. She brings good fortune on this earth, but above all she is instrumental in granting liberation from the cycle of life and death.

Lakshmi is said to bestow wealth and saving grace just by glancing at a person. One of her hands points to the ground in what Hinduism refers to as the *varada* ("giving") position. In Hindu art, she may be portrayed giving wealth to her devotees, with a shower of gold coins emanating from her hand. The other hand may be held upright, denoting her protection of the devotee. While she is depicted as an independent goddess, and has her own shrine in many temples, she is often also portrayed as the inseparable consort of Vishnu.

Shri-Lakshmi is persistently associated with the lotus. She is all-pervasive, latent in everything, but manifests herself only in auspicious places, of which the lotus is a great example. She may be depicted holding these flowers, and is said to dwell on a resplendent lotus or even in "a forest of lotuses." She shares their hue and their fragrance: the scent of the lotus is as inseparable from its source as Shri's grace is from the goddess. The flower reminds humans of how to regard their relationship to the world: it rises from mud and dirty water, yet is never tainted by them.

dess Parvati. Stories of his powers of salvation present him as granting wisdom and grace to his devotees. Iconographically, Shiva and Parvati are portrayed in the abstract form of a shaft (*linga*) within a womb (*yoni*), which represent their creative powers.

Krishna among the cowherd maidens. A painting of ca. 1710.

Vishnu is portrayed as having several incarnations, or *avatars* (Sanskrit *avatara*, "descent"). It is believed that over the ages he has descended to earth several times in animal and human form to overthrow evil and establish *dharma*, or righteousness. By the fifth century CE, ten incarnations had come to be considered the most important. Vishnu's first *avatar* was as a fish that saved Manu (the progenitor of the human race), his family, and many animals from a flood. Vishnu was subsequently incarnated as a tortoise, a boar, a creature half lion and half man, and a dwarf-being.

The fully human incarnations of Vishnu follow: the warrior Parasurama; Rama (the hero of a great epic, the *Ramayana*; see p.138); Balarama; and Krishna. It is believed that the tenth incarnation will come at the end of the present world age, which according to some reckonings began ca. 3102BCE and will last 432,000 years. Some texts omit Balarama and introduce the Buddha as the ninth incarnation, after Krishna. The progression of the incarnations from fish to full human is understood by some Hindus today as anticipating evolutionary theory. But the more prevalent explanation is that Vishnu takes the form most suited for the crisis on hand.

Vishnu's ninth incarnation, Krishna ("the Dark One"), is one of the most popular Hindu gods, celebrated in folksongs, narratives (such as the *Bhagavad Gita*; see p.139), sculpture, painting, and performance. While Krishna is generally perceived to be an incarnation of Vishnu, several traditions, such as that of Chaitanya and the International Society of Krishna Consciousness (see sidebar, right) think of him as the supreme deity. To some extent, most Hindus accept Krishna's supremacy among the incarnations of Vishnu, considering him to be what is termed the "full" descent of the deity, the lord of grace, mercy, and peace. Krishna is also the alluring lover, dancing moonlit nights away with adoring *gopis* (cowherd maidens). Their dances are reenacted in many communities: the Gujarati *raas lila* dances are particularly renowned. Sanskrit texts such as Jayadeva's *Gita Govinda* (twelfth century CE) identify the *gopi* Radha as Krishna's lover, and the two are commonly depicted together (see illustration, p.141).

"KRISHNA CONSCIOUSNESS"

In 1966 A. C. Bhaktivedanta (born Abhaycharan De, 1896–1977) launched the International Society for Krishna Consciousness (ISKCON) in New York. Both its theology, attributing divine grace to Krishna, and its emotive, devotional chanting, may be traced back directly to the great *guru* Chaitanya (1486–1583). Members of ISKCON study the *Bhagavad Gita* (see p.139) and the stories of Vishnu in the *Bhagavata Purana*. The name "Hare Krishnas," often given to ISKCON members in the West, derives from their practice of chanting the devotional *mantra* "*hare Krishna, hare Krishna, Krishna Krishna, hare hare*" ("hail to Krishna").

ISKCON followers are vegetarians and also avoid garlic, onions, and other foods considered impure in Vaishnava ("Vishnu-following") traditions.

THE *RAMAYANA*

This great epic focuses on the young prince Rama, who is born in Ayodhya, the capital of the Kosala kingdom. On the eve of his coronation, his father Dasaratha exiles him. In the forest, Sita, the beautiful wife of Rama, is captured by Ravana, the demon king of Lanka, and the epic focuses on Rama's struggle to win her back. After a protracted battle, Rama kills Ravana and is reunited with Sita. They eventually return to Ayodhya and are crowned.

Revered as the seventh incarnation of Vishnu (see p.137), Rama is held to be an ideal just king. While many Hindus have traditionally viewed Sita as the perfect wife who follows her husband into exile, others see her as a model of strength and virtue. She complies with her husband as he does with her, and their love is worthy of emulation. Yet she also stands her ground when asked by Rama to prove her virtue. Once, in Lanka, she acquiesces, but the second time, in the act of proving her purity, she rules out any possibility of a reunion—she asks Mother Earth to swallow her up if she is pure.

There have been many vernacular versions of the *Ramayana*, and the story has been understood in many ways. In one thirteenth-century interpretation, Sita voluntarily undergoes captivity and suffering to rescue other human beings and the world from evil. In a metaphorical reading, the human soul (Sita) is captured by the material body (Ravana), which is defeated by Rama, who saves the soul from the clutches of the senses. Some versions of the tale, called the *Sitayana*, tell the story from Sita's viewpoint.

WORDS OF DEVOTION

The oldest Indian sacred texts are the *Vedas*, first collected ca. 800BCE, although some are centuries older in origin (see p.131). Each of the four Vedic collections (*Rig Veda*, *Sama Veda*, *Yajur Veda*, and *Atharva Veda*) comprises hymns and ritual treatises, together with *Aranyakas* ("Compositions for the Forest") and *Upanishads* ("Sitting Near [the Teacher]"), philosophical works composed ca. 600BCE or a little later.

Many Hindu traditions consider the *Vedas* to be transhuman, that is, not authored by human beings. They are said to be eternal in nature and revealed in every cycle of time. The Vedic reciters, or "seers" (*rishis*), did not invent or compose the *Vedas*; they "saw," or "envisaged," them. For centuries, to write the early Vedic texts down was considered defiling and hence taboo. The seers transmitted them to their disciples, starting an oral tradition that has come down to the present. The order of the sacred words must remain fixed, and committing them to memory is an elaborate and disciplined process involving the use of many mnemonic devices to ensure accurate pronunciation, rhythm, and diction.

The Vedic corpus was followed by a body of works called *smriti* or "remembered" literature. Although of human authorship, *smriti* was nonetheless considered inspired, and while of lesser authority than the *Vedas*, it has played a far more important role in the lives of the Hindus over the last two and a half millennia. The *smriti* is sometimes divided into the categories of epics, ancient stories (*Puranas*), and codes of law and ethics (*dharmashastras*; see p.159).

The two *smriti* epics, the *Ramayana* ("Story of Rama"; see sidebar, left) and the *Mahabharata* ("Great Epic of India" or, alternatively, "Great Sons of Bharata"; see sidebar, opposite), are the best known works of the Hindu tradition. They have been interpreted, commented

An illustration to the Ramayana *from Rajasthan showing various incidents in the life of Rama and Sita during their exile in the forest.*

THE *BHAGAVAD GITA*

One of the holiest books in the Hindu tradition is the *Bhagavad Gita* ("Song of the Blessed One"), or the *Gita* for short. Just as the war of the *Mahabharata* (see sidebar, below) is about to begin, Arjuna, one of the Pandava brothers and hitherto portrayed as a hero who has emerged victorious from several battles, becomes distressed at the thought of having to fight against his cousins, uncles, and other relatives.

Krishna (left) converses with Arjuna in his chariot in this illustration to a 19th-century manuscript of the Bhagavad Gita.

Putting down his bow, Arjuna asks his cousin Krishna (who is now portrayed as an incarnation of Vishnu) whether it is correct to fight a war in which many lives, especially of one's own kin, are to be lost. Krishna replies in the affirmative: It is correct if we fight for what is right. One must fight for righteousness (*dharma*) after trying peaceful means. The conversation on the field of battle between Krishna and Arjuna takes up about eighteen chapters. It is these that constitute the *Bhagavad Gita*.

The *Gita* speaks of loving devotion to the lord and the importance of selfless action. In the *Gita*, Krishna instructs Arjuna—who is generally understood to represent any human soul who seeks spiritual guidance—on the nature of the soul, God, and how one can reach liberation.

One may reach Vishnu/Krishna/God through devotion, knowledge, or selfless action. Later interpreters think of these as three paths, while other commentators consider them to be three aspects of the one path of loving surrender to the supreme being.

upon, and enjoyed for over two thousand years and form the heart of Hindu sacred literature. Their popularity down the centuries has cut across sectarian and social divisions, and for children, the narration of the epics is invariably their first and most lasting encounter with Hindu scripture. For many Hindus, the phrase "sacred books" connotes these epics in particular. The *Ramayana* especially has been a source of inspiration for generations of devotees in India and in many parts of the world. When the epic was televised in sixty weekly episodes, it drew the largest audience in the history of Indian television. The *Ramayana* is danced out and acted in places of Hindu (and Buddhist) cultural influence in southeast Asia, and its characters are well known as far away as Thailand and Indonesia.

The epics and the *Puranas* are written in Sanskrit, the ancient "perfected" language, which, rather like Latin for many centuries in Europe, was largely the province of male members of the social élites. However, in India, men and women of other castes voiced their devotional passion and quest for divine compassion in local tongues. Today, India has over eighteen official languages and hundreds of dialects, and many of them have a long and rich history of religious literature.

THE *MAHABHARATA*

With around one hundred thousand verses, the *Mahabharata* is considered the world's longest poem. It is the story of the great struggle among the descendants of a king called Bharata (whose name is used by many Indians to mean "India").

The main part of the story deals with a war between two families, the Pandavas and the Kauravas. The Kauravas try to cheat the Pandavas out of their share of Bharat's kingdom, and a great battle ensues that forces every kingdom to take sides. The Pandavas emerge victorious, but at great cost—all their sons and close relatives die in the battle.

Few Hindu households will have the complete *Mahabharata*, but many will have a copy of one celebrated episode, the *Bhagavad Gita* (see box, above).

In this modern poster of the temple complex on Omkareshvera island on a lake in northern India, the roads (in red) take the form of the written syllable Om.

As early as the sixth century BCE, Siddhartha Gautama (the Buddha) and Mahavira, the founder of the Jain tradition (see p.132), had rejected Sanskrit and started to address their followers in the vernacular language. However, the devotees of the *Vedas* and the epics—people whom we call Hindu today—retained Sanskrit as the medium for religious communication until well into the Common Era.

The earliest Hindu religious texts in a vernacular language are in Tamil, a south Indian language spoken by about seventy-five million people today. A sophisticated body of literature in Tamil existed two thousand years ago. The oldest works, usually referred to as *Sangam* ("Academy") poems, are secular texts about kings and chivalry or love and romance. These became the model for later devotional literature, where the deity was cast in the role of a ruler and lover.

The Hindu *bhakti* (devotional) movement began in south India around the sixth century CE. Saints traveled from temple to temple singing hymns in Tamil (language not related to Sanskrit) in praise of Vishnu or Shiva. These hymns, Hinduism's earliest sacred works in the vernacular, draw on earlier Tamil poetry and address the deity in highly personal, intimate, and tender language. In the vernacular literature, Vishnu and his incarnations (see p.137) and Shiva are cast in several roles by the devotee, who considers the deity to be a father or mother, lover, bridegroom, protector, innermost soul. Often the deity is even portrayed as a young child, to whom the devotee sings with maternal love.

After the tenth century, Tamil devotional poems were introduced into temple liturgy in Tamil-speaking areas and were regarded as equivalent in status to the Sanskrit *Vedas*. Devotionalism spread to the west and north of India after the eleventh century CE, transmitted through sacred texts such as the *Bhagavata Purana* as well as the figure of Ramananda (1299?–1400), a famous and influential Hindu saint and charismatic. In the thirteenth century, the poet Jñaneshvar discussed the ideals of the *Bhagavad Gita* in a famous treatise that bears his name, the *Jñaneshvari*, composed in Marathi, the language of the Maharashtra region.

Two features contributed to the spread of vernacular devotion. One was the use of contemporary living languages. The second was its appeal across all social classes, as demonstrated by the "low" caste devotional poet Tukaram (1598–1649) and the "high" caste Princess Mira (1450?–1547). Mira composed hundreds of songs which remain very popular and are sung in homes and at shrines in India and the diaspora.

One of the most celebrated poets of northern India was Surdas (ca. 1483–1563), a blind singer and poet who settled just south of Delhi near Agra. He composed in a dialect of Hindi. In his *Sursagar*, the youthful Krishna is celebrated in lyrics popular among many Hindus.

Puri, in Orissa to the east, is famous as the setting of the annual

OM: THE SACRED SYLLABLE

The syllable *om* is recited at the beginning and end of all Hindu and Jain prayers and recitations of scripture, and is also used by Buddhists, particularly in Tibet. *Om* is understood to consist of three sounds, *a-u-m*. The sound of the word begins deep within the body and ends at the lips; this is claimed to be auspicious.

The history of *om* in Hinduism is ancient, and its meaning and power are discussed in the *Upanishads*. All Hindus believe that *om* is the most sacred sound, but they disagree on its meaning. Some derive the word from a Sanskrit verbal root, *av-*, to mean "that which protects." It is said to represent the supreme reality or *brahman*. According to many Hindu philosophers, *om* was the first sound and contains the essence of true knowledge. Some say that its three sounds represent the three worlds: earth, atmosphere, and heaven; for others they represent the essence of three of the *Vedas* (*Rig Veda*, *Yajur Veda*, and *Sama Veda*; see p.138). Among Vaishnavas (Vishnu devotees) it is claimed variously that *a-u-m* represents Vishnu, the human being, and the relationship between the two; or Vishnu, Shri, and the devotee.

Jagannatha street procession featuring a massive float or wheeled cart (whence the word "juggernaut"). Probably associated with this cult was the poet Jayadeva (ca. 1175CE?), author of the Sanskrit *Gita Govinda*, a famous work extolling the love of Radha and Krishna. However, later eastern Indian Krishna devotees wrote in the local language, Bengali.

Another important vernacular devotional writer was Tulsidas (1543?–1623), who settled in Varanasi. His *Lake of the Deeds of Rama* was more than a recounting or translation of the *Ramayana*. Its widely known verses have their own beauty, inspiring hundreds of traditional storytellers and millions of Rama devotees in Hindi-speaking areas.

VERNACULAR WRITINGS AND VEDIC TRADITION

With the spread of the *bhakti* movement all over India (see main text), the status of Sanskrit works as scripture was diminished, since the presence of vernacular lyrics in temple liturgy challenged the orthodox claim that Sanskrit was the exclusive vehicle for revelation and theological communication. While some *brahmins* have always learned and hence kept alive large sections of the Sanskrit Vedic tradition, others may know only a few Sanskrit hymns. Almost all Hindus have heard the stories from the great epics, although they may not be able to read them in the original Sanskrit.

However, overwhelming numbers of Hindus can recite devotional verses written by Hindu saints in their own languages. The Hindi poems of Surdas on Krishna (see main text), the songs of Princess Mira, and the Tamil poems of Nammalvar and Andal (eighth–ninth centuries CE), may serve as scripture for a particular community. In this sense, vernacular poems and songs guide, inspire, console, and offer hope and wisdom to the mass of the faithful more directly than the *Vedas* and other Sanskrit writings.

This is not to say that the vernacular literature is considered to be at variance with the message of the *Vedas*. Rather, in most communities, there is a belief that the holy people who composed in the living tongues gathered the truth from the incomprehensible *Vedas* and made it accessible to everyone, inspiring devotion and hastening the attainment of divine, saving grace.

The vernacular *bhakti* poets came from different castes—one was apparently an outcaste—and were held up as ideal followers of the gods and goddesses they revered. The *bhakti* poets, venerated irrespective of their sex or caste, call into question the hierarchical caste system, which sometimes denied saving knowledge to the "lower" castes, women, and outcastes (see pp.159–61).

Krishna plays the flute for his lover, Radha, in this illustration from an early 18th-century vernacular text from Himachal Pradesh. The couple's rapturous physical union became an important way of depicting the union between a human soul and the divine in later devotional poetry and classical dance. In the Hindi-dialect poems of Surdas (see main text), Krishna is a mischievous butter thief, but also a seductive flute player, who dances in the moonlight with Radha. Surdas celebrates Radha's affection for Krishna as a model of devotion, and his distinctive poetry served to reinforce Krishna veneration throughout northern India.

TEACHERS AND LEADERS

Indians of the Hindu, Buddhist, and Jain traditions have long looked to holy men and women to instruct them on how to attain peace in this lifetime and, eventually, liberation from the cycle of life and death (see pp.156–7). For many Hindus, the primary religious experience is mediated by a teacher who may be called *acharya*, *guru*, or *swami*. The term *acharya* usually denotes the formal head of a monastery, sect, or subsect, or a teacher who initiates a disciple into a movement. Sometimes the word is used simply as a synonym for *guru*, which, like *swami* ("master"), is a looser and more widespread word for any religious teacher. For many Hindus, the paradigmatic *guru* is the god Krishna, who instructs his cousin Arjuna in the *Bhagavad Gita* (see p.139). For others, Shiva (see pp.135–7) is the ultimate *guru*. As well as teachers, there are thousands of ascetics, individuals possessed by a deity or spirit, mediums, storytellers, and *sadhus* ("holy men"), who all command the veneration and sometimes obedience of their followers.

Each of the many Hindu philosophical traditions forms a distinct sect and has its own leader. At any given time there are many influential theologians, and new sects with substantial followings arise under the inspiration of charismatic *gurus* (see box, below) in almost every generation. Often the leadership of such schools has passed from teacher to teacher

WOMEN *GURUS*: ANANDAMAYI MA

Many female *gurus* today have acquired a large following of devotees. Among the most famous is Anandamayi Ma (1896–1982), a Bengali, whose name means "Bliss-Filled Mother." She was married but led a celibate life, and her husband became her devotee. After a number of spiritual experiences, she heard an inner voice, telling her that she was divine and should bow to no one. Many charismatic teachers who do not come from a lineage of institutionalized *gurus* undergo a similar transforming experience.

Anandamayi Ma attracted thousands of followers who saw her not simply as a *guru*, but as a manifestation of the Goddess: one disciple recalled seeing her as a beautiful deity, illuminating a room like the sun at dawn. While she did not explicitly manifest magical phenomena, her devotees saw her as quietly working miracles for their own good.

CHARISMATIC LEADERS

Sai Baba (right) and some of his devotees, who are believed to number upward of 50 million worldwide.

Although the distinction may not be clear in the minds of followers, it is possible to distinguish between those spiritual leaders who belong to ancient or more recent lineages, and charismatic teachers who attract devotees through "supernatural" phenonomena ranging from the "magical" manifestation of objects to faith healing. Such leaders defy straightforward classification, and each has a large following. Devotees sometimes consider these *gurus* to be an incarnation of a divinity, who has descended to earth in the form of their teacher for the welfare of humanity. This is the case with Sri Satya Sai Baba (born Satya Narayan Raju, 1926), a charismatic leader from Andhra Pradesh, who is believed by his followers to be an incarnation of the deities Shiva and Shakti (the Goddess).

In other cases, devotees revere their teachers simply as spiritually elevated and highly evolved souls, beings who have ascended above the cares of human life to a state of self-realization or perfection. Occasionally, a charismatic religious leader may have a title such as *rishi* ("seer"), like the composers of the *Vedas*. One well-known example is Mahesh Yogi (born 1911), the founder of the Transcendental Meditation movement—popularly referred to in the West as "TM"—who is known as the Maharishi, or "Great Seer."

in a line of succession that has continued for centuries down to the present day. This is the case with, for example, the schools founded by Shankara (ca. 800CE; see sidebar, right), Ramanuja (eleventh century), Madhva (thirteenth century), and Chaitanya (sixteenth century). Schisms often occur in such communities, with complementary or competing leaders vying for the loyalty of the disciples. In the Ramanuja school, as part of a complex initiation ritual, the leader brands a new member lightly on the shoulders and gives him or her a new name and a personal *mantra* for meditation. However, membership in other devotional communities may be much more informal.

In the *Taittiriya Upanishad*, a departing student is exhorted to consider his mother and father as God, and also his teacher; this placing of spiritual teachers on a par with the godhead has continued to the present day. Adherents of the philosophical traditions founded by Ramanuja, Chaitanya, and others, venerate their religious teachers almost as much as the deities that are the focus of their worship. In their pious writings, the living, human teacher is seen to be of more immediate importance than God, and absolute surrender to him or her is said to be one path to liberation.

Many teachers are celibate ascetics. Sanskrit scriptures suggest that "high" caste male *brahmins* traditionally go through four stages of life: student, householder, forest dweller, and ascetic. Shankara apparently went from the first stage directly to the last. Following his example, initiates into the Ramakrishna Mission, a popular order founded by Swami Vivekananda in the nineteenth century, become ascetics without marrying.

Today, many *gurus* have Internet sites maintained by devotees (see p.149); their itineraries, sermons, and songs are broadcast through these web pages, creating a worldwide Hindu "cyber-community."

THE LINEAGES OF SHANKARA

One of the most important Indian theologians, Shankara (ca. 800CE), is said to have established four or five monasteries in different parts of India: at Dvaraka (west), Puri (east), Sringeri and Kanchipuram (south), and Badrinath (north). In each of these monasteries there is an unbroken lineage of teachers, all of whom bear the title "Shankara the Teacher" (Shankaracharya). They have often engaged with social and political issues, and exercise considerable leadership among the educated urban population, as well as influencing those who adhere to the philosophy of their founder. A similar role is played by intellectual philosophical commentators such as Swami Chinmayananda, whose followers have been active in the preservation of traditional scriptures in print and electronic media.

The sage Sukadeva (center), a famous rishi *("seer"), at the court of King Parikshit, a ruler who claimed descent from Arjuna, the warrior advised by Krishna in the* Bhagavad Gita. *A painting of ca. 1760.*

PATHS TO LIBERATION

The religious traditions originating in India have portrayed human beings as caught up in a continuous cycle of life and death (see pp.156–7). Hindus, Jains, and Buddhists have spoken of this predicament in terms of perpetual suffering and being trapped on earth. However, the traditions differ on how to attain liberation from the cycle.

Within Hinduism itself, among several possible routes to liberation two broad perspectives stand out. The first characterizes Hindu traditions that believe the human soul (*atman*) to be identical with the supreme being (*brahman*) (see pp.134–5). Because there is only one supreme being and we are identical with it, liberation is the final experiential knowledge that we are divine. This worldview, best described by the teacher Shankara (see p.143), emphasizes the importance of human effort and striving in achieving the necessary transforming wisdom. The second perspective comes from the schools that speak of an ultimate distinction, however tenuous, between the human being and God. Proponents of this outlook advocate devotion to the supreme being and reliance on God's grace.

In the course of the *Bhagavad Gita* (see p.139), Krishna describes three ways to liberation: the way of action; the way of knowledge; and the way of devotion. Some Hindus view these as multiple paths to the divine, others as aspects of one discipline. The way of action (*karma yoga*) is the path of unselfish action; a person must do one's duty (*dharma*), such as studying or good deeds, but not out of fear of blame or punishment, or hope of praise or reward. In thus discarding the fruits of one's action, one attains

HINDU TANTRA

Tantra began to gain importance in the Hindu tradition around the fifth century CE and influenced many sectarian Hindu movements. Shaiva and Vaishnava temple liturgies are in large measure derived from Tantric usage. For example, when images of deities are installed in temples, geometric drawings (*mandalas*) representing the deity and the cosmos are drawn on the floor for use in meditation and ritual.

The Tantric tradition advocated its own form of *yoga*, known as *kundalini yoga*. Literally "the one with earrings," *kundalini* refers to Shakti or the power of the Goddess, which is said to lie coiled like a serpent at the base of one's spine. When awakened, this power rises up through the body, passing through six cosmic centers known as *chakras* ("wheels") to the final center, located under the top of the skull. This center is envisaged as a thousand-petaled lotus.

The ultimate aim of this form of *yoga* is to awaken the power of the *kundalini* and make it unite with Purusa, the male supreme being, who resides in the lotus. This union grants the practitioner visions and psychic powers and leads eventually to emancipation from the cycle of life and death.

Holy men meditating, Varanasi. In Hindu tradition, meditation (dhyana) *is one path toward the acquisition of "true wisdom."*

abiding peace. A related concept is the idea of "detached action" as the best way to acquire liberation. This entails acting altruistically for the good of humanity and performing all actions in a compassionate manner.

According to the way of knowledge (*jñana yoga*), by attaining scriptural knowledge one may achieve a transforming wisdom that destroys one's past *karma* (see p.156). True knowledge is an insight into the real nature of the universe, divine power, and the human soul. This wisdom may be acquired through the learning of texts from a suitable and learned teacher (*guru*), meditation, and physical and mental control in the form of the discipline called *yoga* (see box, below).

The third way is the one most emphasized throughout the *Bhagavad Gita*: the way of devotion (*bhakti yoga*). This path may be the most popular one among Hindus of every walk of life. Ultimately, as Krishna promises to Arjuna, if one surrenders to the Lord, he forgives all sins and eradicates *karma*. Such complete devotion to a god or goddess, leaving oneself open to divine grace, is considered by many Hindus the only way to salvation. The paths of striving with wisdom and with the many other forms of *yoga* are considered laudable, but are not widely practiced.

PATAÑJALI AND *YOGA*

The Sanskrit term *yoga* (literally "yoke") refers to the practice of various disciplines whereby a devotee "yokes" his or her spirit to the divine. It is held in high regard in Hindu texts, and has had many meanings. Its origins are obscure, but are generally thought to be pre-Indo-European. Many Hindus associate *yoga* with Patañjali (ca. third century BCE), author of the *Yoga Sutras*, a series of brief, aphoristic sentences.

Patañjali's *yoga*, as interpreted by commentators, involves moral, mental, and physical discipline, and meditation. This form of *yoga* is described as having eight "limbs," or disciplines, the first two being *yama* (restraint from violence, falsehood, and other negative practices) and *niyama* (positive practices such as equanimity and asceticism). Patañjali also recommends bodily postures (*asanas*) for meditation, and the practice of breath control (*pranayama*) and mental detachment from external stimuli (*pratyahara*). Perfection in concentration (*dharana*) and meditation (*dhyana*) lead to *samadhi*, the final state of union with the divine and liberation from the cycle of life and death; it is a state that cannot be adequately described in human language.

While Patañjali's *yoga* is considered the classical form by many scholars, *yoga* was probably an important element of Indian religious life for several centuries before his text was written, and there are many other varieties. In the past century a distinction has been drawn between *raja yoga* and *hatha yoga*. *Raja yoga* deals with mental discipline; occasionally this term is used interchangeably with Patañjali's *yoga*. In *hatha yoga*, which largely focuses on bodily postures and control, the human body is said to contain "suns" and "moons"; final liberation can be attained only after one harmonizes different centers in the body with the cosmos. It is this form of *yoga* that has become widely popular in the West.

A posture for meditation, from an 18th-century hatha yoga *handbook.*

A LAND OF HOLINESS

Millions of Hindus regularly visit sacred towns, worship in temples, bathe in holy rivers, and climb sacred mountains, in order to pray for happiness in this life and in the next. According to some Hindu texts, all of India is holy, as it is the place where the actions that form the basis of *karma* come to fulfillment. The idea of India as a sacred land began around the beginning of the Common Era. Manu, the author of a book on *dharma* (see p.129) and ethics, defined a region south of the Himalayas and between the eastern and western oceans as the holy Aryavarta ("Country of the Noble Ones"). In time, the concept of the sacred land was extended to cover the whole subcontinent. From the late nineteenth century, India came to be personified as a divine mother. In many songs, "Mother India" (Bharata Mata) is extolled as a compassionate mother goddess. This image has had political overtones: during the struggle for freedom from British rule, Mother India was portrayed as being held captive by foreign forces.

The map of India is filled with holy places. Although there are many standard Hindu pilgrimage itineraries—for example, all the famous temples of Vishnu or Devi—thousands of other towns, villages, and sites across India are also held sacred. Pilgrimage routes are often organized thematically: devotees might visit the one hundred and eight places where Shakti, or the power of the Goddess, is said to be present; the

HOLY TOWNS

Hindu holy texts, especially the epics and the *Puranas*, extol the sanctity of many individual sites. For pious Hindus, to live in such places, or to undertake a pilgrimage to one of them, is enough to destroy one's sins and *karma* and assist in the attainment of liberation from the cycle of life, death, and rebirth (see pp.156–7). There are numerous lists of sacred cities and villages, many regional and some spanning the entire subcontinent. A short verse known by millions of Hindus draws attention to seven of the most famous holy towns:

> "Ayodhya, Mathura, Maya,
> Kashi, Kanchi, Avantika
> And the city of Dvaraka;
> These seven [cities] give us
> Liberation."

*The Lakshmi Narayan temple in New Delhi, also known as the Birla temple after the family who constructed it in 1938. It is principally dedicated to the deities Vishnu and Lakshmi. Hindu temple exteriors are often brightly decorated, and the towers (*shikharas*) are typical features of north Indian sacred architecture. They represent the cosmic mountains where the gods and goddesses are believed to dwell.*

HOLY RIVERS

The Ganga (Ganges), Yamuna, Kaveri, and Narmada rivers are believed to be so holy that merely by bathing in them one's sins are said to be destroyed. Confluences of two rivers or of a river and the sea are particularly sacred. Pilgrims journey regularly to bathe at Triveni Sangama ("Confluence of Three Rivers") at Prayag (Allahabad), where the Ganga, the Yamuna, and a mythical underground river, the Sarasvati, all meet. Small sealed jars of holy water from the Ganga are kept in homes and used in domestic rituals to purify the dead and dying.

The water from the Ganga or another holy river in the north may be taken to a sacred site in the far south, such as the coastal town of Rameswaram, and sand from Rameswaram may be taken back to the Ganga and immersed there. This practice serves to mark the completion of a circular pilgrimage and demonstrates one way in which the various holy places and traditions of Hinduism can be interlinked. When temples are consecrated in Hindu communities outside India, water from Indian sacred rivers is mingled with water from rivers in the host country and poured onto the new temple, physically and symbolically connecting it with the sacred motherland.

A worshipper performs morning prayers in the Ganga at Varanasi. Immersion in the sacred waters of the river is held to be a great act of spiritual purification.

sixty-eight places where emblems of Shiva are said to have emerged "self-born"; the twelve places where he appears as the "flame of creative energies" (*jyotir lingas*); the eight places where Vishnu spontaneously manifested himself; and so on.

Almost every holy place is associated with a *sthala purana*, a text that details the site's antiquity and sacredness. The temple itself is like a "port of transit," a place from where a human being may "cross over" (*tirtha*) the ocean of life and death. In fact, many temples and holy places are also located near the sea, a lake, a river, or a spring. When such a body of water is not close by, there is usually an artificial ritual well or pool, a feature that may date back to the time of the Harappan civilization (see p.130)—the "Great Bath" of Mohenjo Daro resembles the pools attached to hundreds of Hindu temples in south India today. Pilgrims cleanse themselves physically and spiritually in these pools before praying in the temple.

Many holy sites are near mountains and caves, places where Hindu deities are said to reside in *Purana* stories. For example, Shiva lives on Mount Kailasa in the Himalayas, which for the devotee is represented by every Shiva temple. In some regions, particularly in the north, large temple towers (*shikharas*) represent these cosmic mountains (see illustration, p.146). The innermost shrine of a Hindu temple is traditionally a windowless space, like the sacred caves that were among the earliest Hindu places of worship.

Although there is evidence of worship at temples dating from the beginning of the Common Era, large sacred complexes were built only after the sixth century CE. Migrants to southeast Asia also built temples to preserve and transmit their religion. Temples were major religious, cultural, and economic centers and were constructed according to elaborate rules to represent the whole cosmos. Some of the larger ones have seven enclosures, representing the seven layers of heaven in Hindu cosmology.

Many of the temple complexes in India are associated with the major sects—that is, they enshrine Vishnu, Shiva, or the Goddess and their entourages. In many of them, the deities are known by their local or regional names. A typical temple may have separate shrines for the deity, his or her spouse, other divine attendants, and saints. For example, an

TIRUMALA-TIRUPATI

India's richest temple—and one of the wealthiest religious institutions in the world—is the temple of Tirumala-Tirupati in Andhra Pradesh. Referred to in ancient literature as Tiru Venkatam, it is dedicated to Vishnu, who is popularly known as Venkateshvara ("Lord of the Venkatam hills"). Devotional literature addressed to Venkateshvara dates back to the seventh century CE, but pilgrims are known to have been visiting the site of the temple for almost two millennia. The temple is located in the scenic Tirumala hills and until 1965, when the government took them over, it owned more than six hundred surrounding villages.

The central shrine of the Tirumala-Tirupati temple complex. The temple has spawned offshoots dedicated to Lord Venkateshvara in Pittsburgh, Atlanta, New York, Chicago, and other major cities in the US.

Tirumala-Tirupati enjoyed the patronage of Indian royalty for over a thousand years, but has become a destination for large numbers of pilgrims only in the past century. The popularity of the temple is said to have increased phenomenally following a major reconsecration in 1958. The enormous wealth of the temple is also frequently reported and commented upon in the Indian media. In the temple's offering container devotees regularly leave diamonds among donations of jewelry and gold that amount to around twenty kilograms (forty-four pounds) every month. Gifts to the temple of cars and trucks are not unknown. Annual donations of cash by pilgrims can amount to tens of millions of dollars.

The Tirumala-Tirupati temple employs its huge financial resources to fund a range of projects and enterprises, including charities, hospitals, universities and other educational institutions, housing developments, and publications. One major objective of the temple in recent years has been to contribute to the solution of India's considerable ecological problems, to which end it has subsidized massive reforestation projects.

eighth-century CE temple in Tiruvanmiyur, a suburb of Chennai (Madras), has shrines for the main god, Shiva, his wife Parvati—known locally as Tripura Sundari ("Beautiful Lady of the Three Worlds")—and their children, Ganesha and Murugan. The temple also incorporates images of other manifestations of Shiva, such as Nataraja (the cosmic dancer; see illustration, p.125), and icons of his devotees. Temples in the diaspora generally cater to a broader community of worshippers and have images of Shiva, Vishnu, the Goddess, and other deities enshrined under one roof.

Most Hindus attend their local temple or other holy place that has been important to their families for generations, or they may save for an extended pilgrimage to a famous distant sacred site. Émigrés and other devotees who cannot physically go on such a pilgrimage may watch the rituals that take place there on specially commissioned television programs or videos. At all times, Hindus can also worship at home, where a special area will be designated as the family's domestic worship space.

The human body itself is sometimes spoken of as the "temple of the supreme being." Some Hindu traditions, such as the Virashaivas (a community organized ca. 1150CE), explicitly denounce temple worship and revere every human being as the temple of the supreme being, Lord Shiva. Other traditions, for example the communities that worship Vishnu and Lakshmi in south India, uphold the practices of temple worship, but also think of the human body as divine. In one song, the eighth-century CE poet Periyalvar declared: "Build a temple in your heart. Install the lord called Krishna in it; Offer him the flower of love."

DEVOTIONAL "CYBERSPACE"

A holy space in the Hindu tradition is one in which devotees come to see the enshrined deity and hear sacred words from holy texts. In the past, religious teachers were careful about whom they imparted their teachings to, and screened their devotees carefully. But now, the Internet allows anyone to see images of deities, teachers, and *gurus*, and even hear the recitation and music of sacred texts and songs.

Important *gurus* may have as many as fifty websites set up by their devotees. Some organizations portray their home pages as "electronic *ashrams*." An *ashram* was a traditional place of hermitage or learning. Other websites, such as "Om Sweet Om," are dedicated to the sacred syllable "*Om*" (see p.140).

Internet images of deities are taken seriously by devotees; some websites remind Internet surfers that it would be disrespectful to download such images. The sermons of *gurus* and recitations of prayers are all available on audiofiles accessible to the "cyber-devotee."

A man tends the shrine in his home in Puri, Orissa. Hindus worship in temples and also at home, where an altar, a shelf, a cabinet, or even an entire room, may be set apart for devotion and filled with images of gods and goddesses.

अखाड़ा वापसी
मार्ग

गुलाबबैण्ड
ज्वालापुर
गुलाबबैण्ड
ज्वालापुर
गुलाबबैण्ड
ज्वालापुर

PREVIOUS PAGE *The Kumbh Mela ("Festival of the Jar," or "Aquarius") at Hardwar, where the Ganga river enters the plains of northern India, is one of the largest religious gatherings of human beings on earth. It takes place every twelve years, when close to 15 million Hindu pilgrims may descend on the city at an astrologically propitious time to bathe in the river—an act that is said to destroy one's previous sins. The last full-scale Kumbh Mela was celebrated at Hardwar between February and April of 1998 (this photograph was taken at the previous festival in 1986). Smaller versions of the Kumbh Mela take place every four years, rotating among the cities of Hardwar, Nasik (on the Godavari river), Allahabad (the confluence of the Ganga and Yamuna), and Ujjain (on the Sipra river). These celebrations are attended by hundreds of thousands of Hindu ascetics.*

REJOICING IN THE DIVINE

Hindu festivals are filled with color and joy and almost always associated with feasting and pleasure, although they usually also involve periods of ritual fasting. The birthdays of the gods Rama, Krishna, and Ganesha are widely popular throughout India, while important regional festivals include Holi (a jubilant spring festival held in parts of northern India to celebrate the new colors of the springtime flowers), Onam (a harvest festival celebrated in the southern state of Kerala between August and September in honor of the fifth incarnation of the god Vishnu (see p.137), and Pongal (a mid-January harvest festival in Tamil Nadu).

Other festivals, such as Navaratri (see box, opposite) and Dipavali (known colloquially in some areas as Diwali) are pan-Hindu festivals and generally mark the victory of the forces of righteousness over evil. Dipavali ("Necklace of Lights") is probably the most widely observed Hindu festival. It falls on the new moon between mid-October and mid-November and is celebrated by decorating the home with lights, setting off fireworks, and wearing new clothes. Presents may be exchanged and festive meals are eaten. In south India, it is believed that Dipavali marks the day on which Krishna killed a demon, Narakasura, thus ensuring the triumph of light over darkness. In the north, it celebrates the return of the god Rama to Ayodhya and his coronation (see p.138). In Gujarat, it heralds the beginning of the New Year. In many parts of India, people rise before dawn on Dipavali for a ritual bath, because it is believed that on this day the holy waters of the Ganga river are present in all other water.

A painting of ca. 1780 from Himachal Pradesh depicting Krishna (center) celebrating the jubilant spring festival of Holi. As shown here, people throw brightly colored powder over each other as part of the festivities.

Temple worship forms a key element in Hindu religious life. In most temples, worship is traditionally not congregational in the sense that people do not gather for communal worship at fixed times. There is no seating in the temple: devotees usually stand for a few minutes while they view the deity in its shrine. The closest thing to a religious congregation in Hinduism is when people gather to listen to a religious teacher—although in most cases this will take place in a public hall rather than a temple—or to sing traditional religious songs together at home and in other public places. This type of group worship is common in the diaspora, particularly on weekends.

Footwear is always left outside the temple precincts, a custom that symbolizes the worshipper's temporary abandonment of the dust and grime of worldly thoughts and passions. The simplest act of temple worship is to make the deity an offering of camphor, fruit, flowers, or coconut, all of which may often be bought at stalls outside the temple. In a small temple, the devotee may make the offering directly to the image of the deity, but in most places the worshipper first hands the gift to a priest, who then presents it to the god or goddess. In many north Indian temples,

HINDU CALENDARS

The many Hindu calendars and systems of reckoning time are all connected with the phases of the moon. These calendars are adjusted to the solar cycle regularly so that the festivals fall within the same season every year. The different parts of India celebrate New Year at different times of the year. In the state of Gujarat, for example, it falls a day after Dipavali (see main text). Elsewhere it may fall on the new moon closest to the spring equinox, or in the middle of April.

NAVARATRI

The festival of Navaratri ("Nine Nights") is celebrated all over India and begins on the new moon in the lunar month from mid-September to mid-October. In many parts of the country it is dedicated to the worship of the goddesses Sarasvati, Lakshmi, and Durga. In general, however, it is a time when people acknowledge with respect the tools of their trade, whatever it may be. In some regions, cars and buses are decorated with garlands, and in recent years typewriters and computers have been blessed with sacred powders and allowed to "rest" for a day.

The ninth day of Navaratri is dedicated specifically to Sarasvati, the patron of learning and music. In south India, all the musical instruments in the house, any writing implement, and selected educational textbooks are placed before the image of the goddess in order to receive blessings for the coming year.

The last day of Navaratri is dedicated to Lakshmi, the goddess of good fortune (see p.136). On this day, after ritually writing the auspicious word "Shri" (a name of Lakshmi), people traditionally embark on ventures, open new business account books, and take up courses of learning. To mark the day, new prayers, pieces of music, and items of knowledge are learned, and great Hindu teachers are honored.

Worshippers parade a framed stucco portrait of the goddess Sarasvati through the streets of Calcutta to celebrate the festival of Navaratri.

SACRED PERFORMANCE

For Hindus, two of the most important ways of attaining a religious experience are through dance and music. These are more than just entertainment: both singer and dancer are considered to be emulating the great devotees of the past and in doing so may achieve liberation from the cycle of life and death (see pp.156–7)—even if they follow no other route to salvation.

While folk dancing has always been widely performed, for centuries classical Indian dance was confined to the dancers of India's royal courts and the temples. It is only in the twentieth century that men and women from all walks of life have had access to this ritual path to liberation.

The elements of dance are contained in a book called *Natya Shastra* ("Treatise on Dance") of ca. 200CE. This work is highly revered, to the extent that it is considered by many Hindus to constitute a fifth *Veda* (see p.138), created to make the paths to the divine accessible to all human beings. Sacred dances are frequently performed in Hindu temples for the deity to enjoy.

Worship in the Hindu tradition has included the performance of music since the time of the *Veda*s. Music is believed to be divinity manifest on earth as sound, and some Hindu texts say that Vishnu and Shri may be present as Nada Brahman—*brahman*, the supreme being (see pp.134–5), in the form of sound.

The great Hindu religious narratives (see pp.138–41) are transmitted not so much through the medium of books as through song and dance, and stories from sacred texts—especially those about the gods Krishna and Rama—are dramatized all over India. In the most celebrated of these sacred dramas, the *Ramayana* (see p.138) is performed annually in a huge park near the city of Varanasi as part of the celebrations known as Ramalila. The actors who take part in this performance are actually considered to be divine for the duration of the play.

Colorfully costumed dancers celebrate the spring festival of Holi (see p.152) at a temple near Sadri, Rajasthan.

ordinary worshippers may enter the innermost shrines, but in the south access to these areas is restricted to priests and other initiates.

To the devotee, the most meaningful part of temple worship is the experience of seeing the deity (in the form of an image; see p.134) and being in his or her presence. After the offering has been presented to the divine image it is considered to have been "blessed" by the deity and to contain its "favor" (*prasada*). It is then returned to the worshipper. This simple act of viewing the deity, making an offering, and getting the sanctified offering back is the most popular of all Hindu votive rituals.

As in the temple, a deity worshipped at home is considered to be a royal ruler and is treated accordingly. Members of the family may regularly light an oil lamp or incense sticks before the divine image, and make offerings of fruit or other foods (see illustration, p.149).

When a group of devotees prays at home or in the temple, the ritual may end with an *arati*, or "waving of lamps." The attendant priest or one of the worshippers will light a piece of camphor in a plate, and sanctify it by waving it clockwise in front of the deity. The burning camphor is then shown to the worshippers, who briefly, but reverentially, place their hands over the flame and then touch their eyelids, as if to absorb the light of spiritual knowledge emanating from the supreme deity.

Single and married women—but not widows—frequently perform special votive observances called *vrata*. Many of these rituals are domestic in nature and observed for the welfare of the husband, the extended family, or the community. Sanskrit manuals claim that these rites enable a woman to attain liberation from the cycle of birth and death, but most women perform them simply for happiness in the home. After prayers to a domestic deity, women may eat together and distribute auspicious substances, such as bananas, coconuts, turmeric, and *kum kum* (a red powder that is daubed on the forehead). A *vrata* may last from a few minutes to five days, with periods of fasting alternating with communal meals.

In northern India, many women's rites focus on the welfare of male relatives. For example, in the lunar month from mid-October to mid-November, women undertake two fasts on the fourth and eighth days of the waning moon for the benefit of their husbands and sons. In much of south India, spiritually empowering women's rituals take place in the lunar month from mid-July to mid-August. *Brahmin* women pray to the goddess Lakshmi (see p.136) for domestic well-being. Non-*brahmin* women may take special pots of water and milk to temples of a local goddess as offerings on behalf of their family, or they may cook rice and milk dishes and then distribute them. At the temples of the powerful regional goddess Draupadi Amman (a principal character in the *Mahabharata* epic), women and men alike may enter a trance and walk over hot coals in a ceremony euphemistically called "walking on flowers."

RITES OF PASSAGE

The Hindu tradition, like other religions, possesses numerous rituals marking an individual's transition from one stage of life to another. In some sacred texts, the life-cycle sacraments begin with the birth of a child, while in others they begin with marriage, for it is then that the life of a person is believed truly to begin. While some life-cycle rites are pan-Hindu, many are purely local celebrations, particularly women's rituals (see main text).

Like all significant Hindu sacraments, rites of passage must take place in the presence of a sacred fire. The importance of fire (Sanskrit *agni*) can be traced as far back as the Vedic period. Early Vedic rituals (see p.131) were performed around an altar of fire, and fire was thought of as the master of the house.

Offerings are made to the sacred fire during prenatal rites, when a child is one year old, during weddings—indeed the ceremony is valid only if the couple is married before a fire, which is deemed to be the cosmic witness to the sacrament—and when a man reaches the ages of sixty and eighty. Finally, when a person dies, his or her body is offered up to the flames. Annual rites to commemorate one's ancestors are also performed before a fire.

Auspicious times are chosen for the conduct of all life-cycle sacraments. These times are in accordance with a person's horoscope, which is cast at birth.

KARMA, DEATH, AND REBIRTH

The author's son, Venki Narayanan, takes part in his "sacred thread" ceremony at Chennai (Madras), a ritual that will permit him to study and teach the ancient Vedic scriptures (see p.159). Study of the holy texts is one way in which to pursue moksha *(the liberation of the soul), since it enables the devotee to acquire supreme knowledge. Hindu philosophers have said that just as fire reduces firewood to ashes, so too the fire of knowledge eradicates all* karma.

One distinctive characteristic of the religions that began in the Indian subcontinent is the belief in *karma*, an idea first occurring around the seventh century BCE. *Karma* literally means "action," especially ritual action, but after the *Upanishads* (ca. 600BCE) it came to mean the concept of rewards and punishments attached to various acts.

Underlying the theory of *karma* is the idea of the immortality of the soul. Although the early *Veda*s contain a nebulous notion of an afterlife, by the time of the *Upanishads* it was claimed that the human soul existed forever, and that after death it underwent rebirth or reincarnation (*samsara*). The "law of *karma*" thus refers to a system of cause and effect that may span several lifetimes. It dictates that human beings gain merit (*punya*) or demerit (*papa*) from every action they perform. Good deeds and bad deeds do not simply cancel each other out; one has to experience the fruits of all actions in the course of many lives. The balance of *punya* and *papa* acquired in one lifetime determines the nature and quality of one's next existence.

Liberation (*moksha*) from this pattern, according to the *Upanishads*, comes from a supreme, experiential wisdom. In acquiring this transforming knowledge, one has a profound insight into one's own immortality (*amrta*), from which point the soul ceases to possess the ability to be reborn. Rebirth and its connection with *karma*—notions central to the later Hindu tradition—are thus clearly articulated in the *Upanishads*, as is the ultimate goal of every human being—liberation from the unending cycle of birth and death and the attendant human suffering implied by experiencing multiple lifetimes (see pp.144–5).

Since the time of the *Upanishads*, Hindus have taken the notions of *karma* and *amrta* for granted. However, the various Hindu traditions differ on what happens to the soul when it is ultimately liberated from the cycle of life and death. For some, the soul experiences a joyous devotional relationship with the supreme being. Other schools, such as that of Bengali Vaishnavism, think of the ultimate liberation as a state of passionate separation of the human soul from God. In this tradition God is thought of as Krishna, and the soul is cast in the role of the young female cowherd with whom the deity consorts.

A number of writings describe the soul's journey after death. A soul that has achieved liberation and will not be reborn may enter the abode of Shiva or Vishnu (see box, opposite). As for unemancipated souls, none of the Hindu sacred texts discuss the details of what happens immediately after death or even between lifetimes. While it is clear that one's *karma* accumulated from previous lifetimes is believed to influence what sort of life will follow, the holy books offer no theories about how long it takes before a soul is reincarnated. Nor is there any discussion or explanation of why people do not remember their past lives, although in popular belief it is claimed that many people do indeed recall small pieces of previous existences. Only the truly evolved souls, the great spiritual leaders and teachers, are said to remember all their past lives.

Many texts speak of the repellent nature of this life and urge human beings to seek everlasting "real" life through the liberation of the soul. Others, however, state that by glorifying God on earth one can achieve the experience of heaven in one's present lifetime. To this end, sacred pilgrimage centers offer a break from the daily rhythms of earthly existence and the opportunity for divine revelation. Some Hindus consider that a life lived in praise of the divine is a truly joyful experience that is not merely an imitation of a state of liberation, but that state itself.

HINDU HEAVENS AND HELLS

Although reincarnation and liberation (see main text) are the most frequently discussed aspects of the afterlife in Hinduism, the *Puranas* talk of many kinds of heavens and hells. In some writings, seven underworlds and seven heavens are described in detail, while accounts of the various paradisiacal regions typically refer to dancing girls and trees that grant wishes—fairly generic imagery of a (male-centered) place of delight.

In the Hindu tradition, a soul's sojourn in a hell or paradise is generally seen as being temporary. A soul is reborn in such a region if it has accumulated certain kinds of good or bad *karma*; but once this *karma* is exhausted, the soul moves on into a different form of existence.

According to some texts, a soul that has attained emancipation from the cycle of life, death, and rebirth crosses a river called Viraja ("Without Passion") and enters a heavenly paradise, either Vaikuntha (the abode of Vishnu) or Kailasa (the mountain abode of Shiva on the borders of India and Tibet). Devotees of these gods imagine their heavenly dwellings as places filled with other devotees singing his praises. Vaikuntha is sometimes described as an enormous palace with a thousand pillars and filled with light.

The family of the god Shiva and his consort, Parvati, with their children Ganesha and Skanda, in their dwelling on Mount Kailasa (a Himalayan peak in southwestern Tibet). Other deities and worshippers look on in adoration.

DIVISION AND IDENTITY

Until recently, the word "Hindu" has seldom been used as a signifier of identity in India. A person's position in society has depended much more intimately on his or her social "class" (*varna*, literally "color"), "subclass" (*jati*, literally "birth group"), religious sectarian community, and philosophical allegiance.

There are four major *varna*s and, today, over a thousand *jati*s. The earliest mention of distinct social classes within Indian society occurs in the *Veda*s. In discussing a cosmic sacrifice, in which the various elements of the universe arise from the body of a primordial cosmic man, the *Rig Veda* declares: "From his mouth came the priestly class, from his arms, the rulers. The producers came from his legs; from his feet came the servant class" (*Rig Veda* 10.90). While some have seen these verses as the origin of what eventually came to be called the "caste system" (Portuguese *casta*, "social division"), it is probable that the stratification of Indian society had begun long before the composition of the text.

These initial four broad *varna*s were the priests (*brahmins*), the rulers and warriors (*kshatriya*s), the merchants and producers (*vaishya*s), and the servants (*shudra*s). The latter two, at least, were always broad groupings, and while in time it came to be expected that members of all classes would, in theory, pursue the vocation associated with their particular group, it is likely that this prescription was not far-reaching. Today, while some *jati*s can be fitted loosely into the ancient fourfold division, hundreds more cannot be defined easily as "merchants" or "servants."

Basketmakers in Jodhpur, Rajasthan. There are many jatis *whose occupational specialty is basketmaking. In many parts of India they are considered to be of "low" social status.*

Members of the priestly, warrior, and merchant groups were sometimes known as the "upper" castes, and their male members were known as the "twice born" because of their traditional initiation ritual of spiritual rebirth called *upanayana*. Through this, they become invested with a "sacred thread" that grants them the power to study the *Vedas* (see illustration, p.156, and below). Women and members of the *shudra* class are traditionally prohibited from reading the *Vedas*, even though some of the Vedic hymns had female authors.

Underlying the hierarchical social system is the fundamental Hindu idea that people are born into an existence that is the fruit of their past *karma* (see pp.156–7). One's social status in this life is therefore traditionally considered predetermined and immutable, and the individual must adhere to

THE DUTIES OF THE FOUR CASTES

By the first centuries of the Common Era, many treatises on righteousness, moral duty, and law had been written. Known collectively as the *dharmashastras* ("texts on righteous behavior"), of which the most famous is the *Manava Dharmashastra* (*The Laws of Manu*), these formed the basis of later Hindu laws.

The *dharmashastras* outline the duties and privileges of the four main *varnas* (classes) of society. The *brahmin* (priestly) class retained sole authority to teach and learn the *Vedas*. For centuries, the *brahmins*—who included teachers and counselors as well as priests—jealously guarded this monopoly, and forbade the *Vedas* to be written down.

The former kings and princes of India belonged to the *kshatriya* ("royal," or "warrior") class that traditionally held the reins of secular power. *Kshatriya* men were allowed to learn, but not teach, the *Vedas*; their duty was to protect the people and the country. Most *kshatriyas* traced their ancestry back to primeval divine progenitors of humanity—in Hinduism, to this day, claimed lines of descent are highly important—and later Hindu rituals explicitly emphasized their connection with divine beings.

The mercantile class (*vaishyas*) were in charge of trade, commerce, farming, and thus potential possessors of great wealth and economic power. According to the law codes, the *vaishyas*, too, possessed the authority to study the *Vedas* but not teach them.

The law texts state that the duty of a *shudra* is to serve the other classes, especially the *brahmins*. *Shudras* are not allowed to accumulate wealth, even if they are well able to do so, and a *shudra* may be respected on account of his or her advanced years but for no other reason.

Brahmin *priests reciting from the* Vedas, *photographed by the author at a temple in Kanchipuram, Tamil Nadu. Each wears the "sacred thread" that denotes his status as one qualified to learn and teach the ancient Sanskrit scriptures.*

The caste system was—and is—far more complex and flexible than the behavior the *dharmashastras* advocate, and historical evidence suggests that their prescriptions on class, like Manu's pronouncements on women (see p.160), were probably not taken too seriously by many classes of society and apparently not followed at all in many areas. For instance, the *jati* called Vellalas were technically a *shudra* caste but in practice they were wealthy landowners who wielded considerable economic and political power in the south. The *dharmashastra* prohibitions seem to have had no effect on their fortunes.

Eventually, various groups of "outcastes" emerged who were not covered by the law codes. These arose either from mixed marriages or more often from association with professions deemed inferior (see p.160).

A Vaishnava (devotee of Vishnu) at Sri Rangam temple, Tamil Nadu. Vaishnavas are identifiable by the distinctive markings painted on their foreheads.

the particular ritual practices and dietary rules of his or her *jati*. In past centuries, any deviation from caste practices may well have resulted in a person being excluded from the *jati* and being forced to live as an outcaste.

It has been widely debated whether caste originally depended on birth or simply on a person's qualifications. The Sanskrit word *jati* implies the former, but some discussions in the epic *Mahabharata* (see p.139) imply that the situation may once have been less clear cut. This discussion has not been prominent in subsequent Hindu practice, and today one's social status is entirely dependent on which group one is born into. However, historically there has always been a degree of caste mobility. For example, members of "low" *jati*s have usurped thrones and declared themselves to be of divine descent, thus raising their caste to *kshatriya* status.

To this day, people continue regularly to identify themselves by their *jati*, and the entire Indian caste system is such a strong social force that non-Hindu communities such as the Christians, Jains, and Sikhs have absorbed parts of it. For instance, Nadar Christians in the south of India will only marry people of the same heritage.

While various texts and practices do clearly imply the hierarchy of the castes (see box, p.159), some Hindus have interpreted the traditional system as an equal division of labor, with each major group being responsible for a particular area of activity essential to society. But even in the modern era, the strength of the caste system has proved an obstacle to social reform. Mahatma Gandhi, for example, especially sought to overcome the prejudice against some of the most disadvantaged people in Indian society, the so-called "Untouchables"—those who pursued occupations considered "unclean" and "defiling" to the "higher" castes.

WOMEN IN HINDU WRITINGS

On the whole, Hindu literature has expressed paradoxical views on the role and position of women. *The Laws of Manu*, written at the beginning of the Common Era, implies that contemporary women were accorded a low status, for example: "Though destitute of virtue ... a husband must be constantly worshipped as a god by a faithful wife"(*Manu* 5.154). Although Manu goes on to say that women must be honored if the gods are to be pleased, on balance, the negative statements outweigh the positive ones.

Underlying many of the attitudes expressed by male religious writers is the concept of "auspiciousness." Essentially, a person or thing is auspicious if it promotes the three goals of *dharma* (duty), *artha* (prosperity), and *kama* (sensual pleasure). Thus, in the *dharmashastras* (see box, p.159) and in Hindu practice to this day, it is auspicious for a woman to be married and thus a full partner in *dharma*, *artha*, and *kama*. Only a married woman may bear the title *Shrimati* ("Possessor of Auspiciousness"). She is *Grhalakshmi*, "the Goddess Lakshmi of the Home" and the most honored woman in Hindu society, especially if she bears children.

The dictates of Manu and others were not necessarily followed. Even in the Vedic age, women composed hymns and took part in philosophical debates. After the eighth century CE, there were women poets, temple patrons, philosophers, religious commentators, and writers of scholarly works. They were respected, honored, and in some cases even venerated.

A modern painting depicting Chaitanya (1486–1583), a great Bengali saint, among his followers. The adherents of Chaitanya, a devotee of Krishna, form one of the most prominent Hindu "philosophical communities," whose ideas are also fundamental to the International Society of Krishna Consciousness (see p.137).

Such occupations included dealing with animal hides and corpses, because dead skin and flesh are considered polluting (the use of the Tamil word *pariah*—"drummer"—to mean "outcaste" derives from the fact that drumskins were made of "unclean" animal hides). Gandhi called the outcastes Harijans ("Children of God"), and the postindependence Indian constitution makes discrimination against them illegal. But so far such official declarations have had little effect in practice.

Sectarian, philosophical, and regional allegiances cut across caste lines and provide a different basis for social identification. Hindu sects are determined by the god they worship—Vaishnavas are devotees of Vishnu, Shaivas of Shiva, and so on. Philosophical communities—followers of such great thinkers as Shankara (eighth century CE), Ramanuja (eleventh century CE), and Chaitanya (sixteenth century CE)—also form distinct groups in many parts of India. Regional identity is important, too: Hindus tend to marry partners who come not only from the same *jati*, sectarian community, and philosophical group, but also from the same geographical area.

In general, the Hindu wife is traditionally expected to be monogamous, faithful to her husband in life and to his memory after he has died. Some of these notions are still adhered to in Hindu society, and while a man may abandon his wife, social pressures still make it difficult, in some communities, for a woman to leave her husband. However, while Manu (see box, opposite) may have been quoted with enthusiasm by male writers on Hindu law—whose works have informed many Western notions of Indian womanhood—many Hindu women have always enjoyed, as they do today, a degree of religious and financial independence and have made an important contribution to the culture of their homeland.

Chapter Five

BUDDHISM

Malcolm David Eckel

A 14th-century Nepalese gilt bronze figure of Maitreya, one of several celestial beings who feature prominently in the Mahayana Buddhist traditions of Asia (see pp.176–7).

OPPOSITE *Buddhist prayer flags—strips of material bearing sacred texts—in the Kambala Pass in central Tibet. The motion of the wind is believed to activate the prayers.*

INTRODUCTION

Buddhism takes its name from Siddhartha Gautama (ca. 566–486BCE), who was revered by his disciples as the Buddha, or "Awakened One." In the course of only a few centuries, his teaching spread across the Indian subcontinent and into many other parts of Asia. Although it later almost died out as a living religion in the land of its origin, Buddhism has had a profound impact on religious life and cultural development outside India, from Afghanistan in the west to China, Korea, and Japan in the east, and through southeast Asia from Myanmar (Burma) as far as the Indonesian islands of Java and Bali. Today, Buddhism is also a vibrant part of the religious landscape of Europe and North America.

In the course of their migrations, Buddhist practices and teachings have shown a remarkable flexibility and capacity for adaptation to meet the needs of new host cultures and traditions. In fact, Buddhism has produced so many different varieties that it is sometimes difficult to recognize particular practices or beliefs as being distinctively "Buddhist."

At the heart of the tradition is the figure of the Buddha. Born an Indian prince, he renounced his royal life to seek release from *samsara*, the eternal cycle of birth, death, and rebirth (see p.192). After long study, meditation, and self-scrutiny, he experienced the enlightenment or "awakening" (*bodhi*) that made him a *buddha* (it should be noted that while Siddhartha is called *the* Buddha, he was not the first, or the last, to attain "*buddha*-hood"). Eventually he began to preach and to win his first disciples. He went on to summarize his insights in the doctrines of the "Four Noble Truths" (see p.171) and the "Noble Eightfold Path" (see pp.184–5).

The Buddhist tradition evolved in many complex ways, but it has

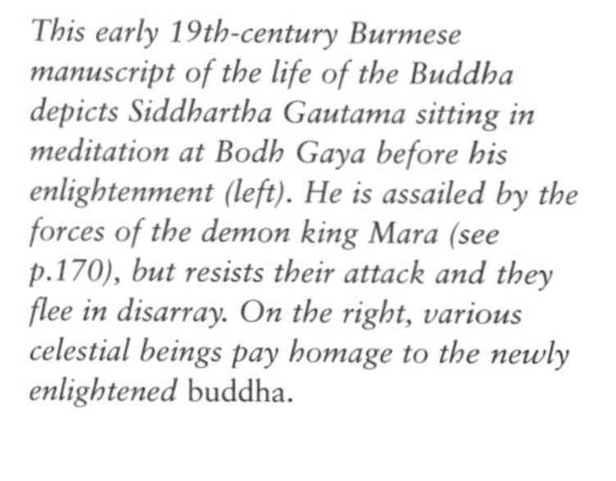

This early 19th-century Burmese manuscript of the life of the Buddha depicts Siddhartha Gautama sitting in meditation at Bodh Gaya before his enlightenment (left). He is assailed by the forces of the demon king Mara (see p.170), but resists their attack and they flee in disarray. On the right, various celestial beings pay homage to the newly enlightened buddha.

BUDDHISM IN ASIA

Key

- Ancient Buddhist heartland
- Early area of Buddhism
- Mahayana Buddhism
- Theravada Buddhism
- Tantric Buddhism
- Former Sino-Tibetan border
- Main transmission routes of Buddhism
- Site of special Buddhist significance
- Site of significance in the life of the Buddha
- Other town or city
- Sacred mountain
- (PAEKCHE) Historical region

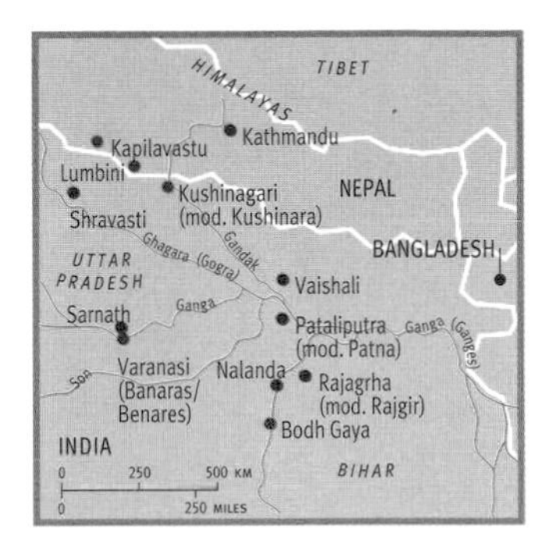

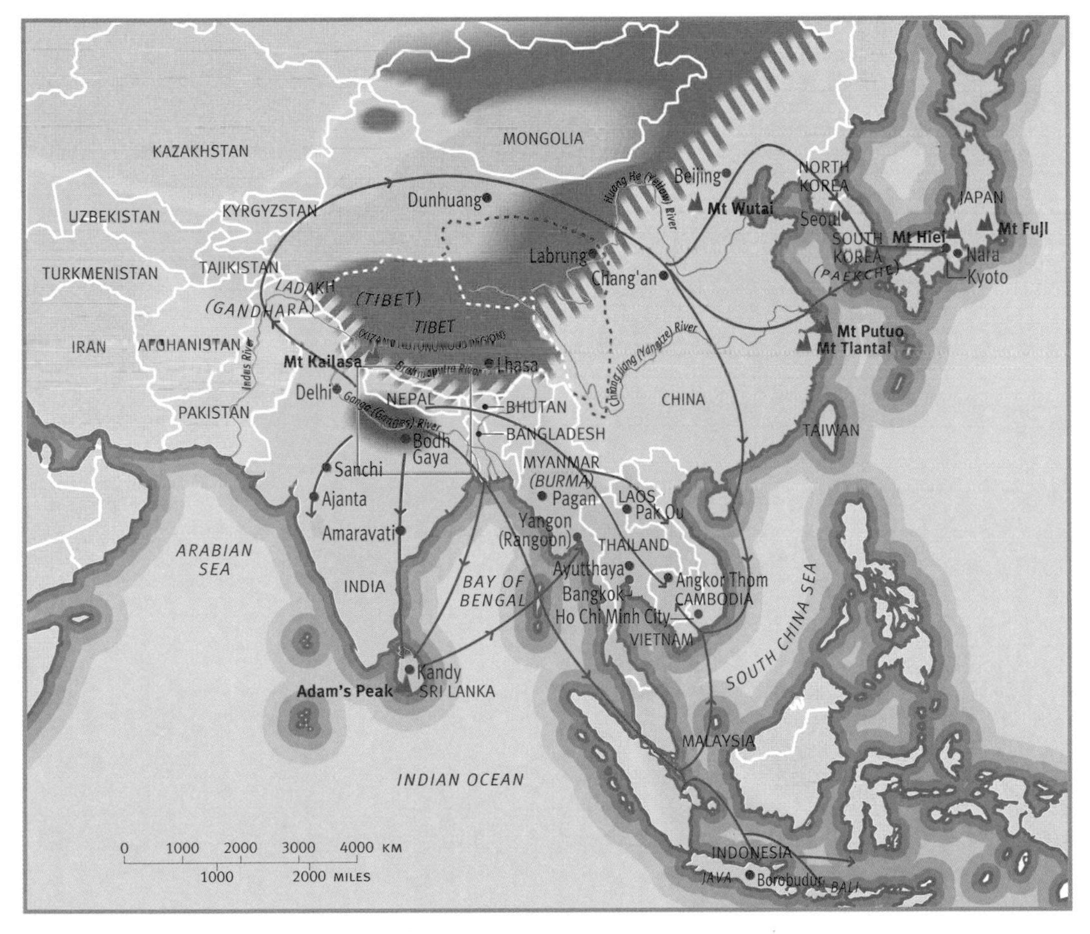

retained its practical focus. The Buddha was not considered to be God or a supernatural being, but a man who had found the answer to the deepest dilemmas of human life and had made that answer available to others. For millions of Asians and for many Europeans and Americans, Buddhism conveys a sense of the sacred and a sense of social and cultural cohesion without reliance on the concept of a creator God.

About a century after the Buddha's death, disputes over discipline led to the first splits in the Buddhist community. Eighteen rival "schools" (*nikayas*) arose, of which only Theravada, the dominant tradition of present-day southeast Asia, survives. In the third century BCE, the patronage of the Indian emperor Ashoka brought Buddhism to Sri Lanka, whence it traveled to southeast Asia, including Indonesia. In the second century CE, monks took Buddhism along the Silk Road to China, from where it passed to Korea and thence to Japan. Tibetan Buddhism took root in the seventh century CE and today is one of the most recognizable Buddhist cultures, largely through the figure of the Fourteenth Dalai Lama (see p.194).

The success of Buddhism in northern and eastern Asia was enhanced by the emergence of the Mahayana, or "Great Vehicle" movement, in India, around the beginning of the Common Era. The Mahayana brought with it a new body of scriptures (the Mahayana *sutras*); a new emphasis on the importance of laypeople alongside monks and nuns through a reinterpretation of the ideal of the *bodhisattva*, or "future *buddha*" (see pp.176–7); and a new way of thinking about the Buddha himself. Tantric Buddhism,

CHRONOLOGY *All dates are CE, except where stated. See also Chronologies on p.202 (China) and p.240 (Japan).*

ca. 566–486BCE	Life of Siddhartha Gautama, the Buddha
ca. 486BCE	First Buddhist Council; formation of the nucleus of Buddhist canon
ca. 383BCE	Second Buddhist Council; first splits in Buddhist community
327–325BCE	Greeks under Alexander in India
268–239BCE	Reign of Ashoka, who sends Buddhist missionaries to Sri Lanka
ca. 100BCE	First Mahayana *sutras* appear
1st century	Buddhism arrives in China
220–236	Buddhism flourishes under south Indian Satavahana dynasty
320–540	Time of the Gupta dynasty, the "classical age" of Indian Buddhism
4th century	Buddhism arrives in Korea; Buddhaghosa codifies foundations of Theravada Buddhism
6th century	Buddhism arrives in Japan
7th century	Emergence of Tantric Buddhism
606–646	Reign of Harsha in north India
7th–8th centuries	"First Diffusion of the Dharma" in Tibet; first Tibetan monastery founded at bSam-yas
800–1200	Time of the Pala Dynasty; great monastic universities in eastern India
838–842	Reign of Glang-dar-ma of Tibet
10th century	"Later Diffusion of the Dharma" in Tibet
11th century	Emergence of the four major schools of Tibetan Buddhism
1040–1123	Life of Tibetan saint Mi-la-ras-pa
1100–1200	Monasteries in eastern India destroyed; Buddhism declines in India
1173–1210	Reign of Narapatisithu in Sri Lanka
12th–14th centuries	Theravada adopted from Sri Lanka by Indochinese peoples
1357–1419	Life of Tsong-kha-pa, founder of Tibetan dGe-lugs-pa school
1391–1475	Life of Tibetan monk dGe-'dun-grub, (retrospectively "1st" Dalai Lama)
1543–88	Reign of bSod-nams rGya-mtsho of Tibet, who gains title Dalai Lama
1617–82	Reign of Ngag-dbang-blo-bzang rGya-mtsho, "Great 5th" Dalai Lama; Potala built in Lhasa
1801–52	Life of Eugène Burnouf, pioneer French translator of Buddhist texts
1844	First Buddhist text published in US (translated from French by H. D. Thoreau)
1881	Pali Text Society founded, England
1864–1933	Life of A. Dharmapala, Sri Lankan reformer
1891–1956	Life of B. R. Ambedkar, who revives Buddhism in India
1893	Leading Asian Buddhists at World Parliament of Religions, Chicago
1935	Birth of bsTan-'dzin rGya-mtsho (Tenzin Gyatso), 14th Dalai Lama
1950	Chinese invasion of Tibet
1966–76	"Cultural Revolution" in China: Buddhists in Tibet persecuted

an offshoot of Mahayana, appeared in the seventh century CE. With its emphasis on symbolism and ritual and its vision of *buddhas* as "wrathful" deities, Tantra is one of the most striking and intellectually challenging varieties of Buddhism. Schools of Tantric Buddhism are found in China, Korea, and Japan, and Tantra is the predominant tradition in Tibet and Nepal.

Sacred Buddhist writings in silk wrappings, part of the library of the monastery of Gompa, Ladakh, in the western Himalayas.

The institutional and intellectual expansion of Buddhism was fostered by a series of remarkable personalities, beginning with the Buddha's early followers, called *arhants* ("worthy ones"). Both Mahayana and Theravada produced a series of scholar-monks, such as the Theravada scholar Buddhaghosa, who gave intellectual shape to the monastic tradition of southeast Asia. Buddhism has produced religious and social reformers such as Shinran and Nichiren in Japan (see pp.254–5), and it has a tradition of political engagement, from the ancient emperor Ashoka to the two recent Buddhist recipients of the Nobel Peace Prize, the Fourteenth Dalai Lama (see pp.183, 194) and Myanmar's Aung San Suu Kyi (see p.197).

There have also, of course, been generations of ordinary Buddhists whose stories have not been preserved but who have given meaning to their lives through the simple gestures of Buddhist worship; by observing the "Five Precepts" (see p.185); by offering food to monks; by celebrating rites of passage; by participating in celebrations of the Buddha's birthday or of Buddhist "saints"; or by going on a pilgrimage. All of these aspects of Buddhist practice seem to express, in one fashion or another, the same fundamental impulse: to find serenity in a world of suffering and change.

South Korean monks recite prayers to mark "Buddha's Day," which falls in April or May and is widely celebrated throughout the Buddhist world (see p.191).

THE LIFE OF THE BUDDHA

The Buddhist tradition has its origins in the life of the Buddha, Siddhartha Gautama, also known as Shakyamuni or "the Sage of the Shakya Clan," who was born in the Himalayan foothills at the end of the sixth century BCE. From a Buddhist point of view, the story of the Buddha begins with the story of his previous lives as a *bodhisattva* or "future *buddha*." According to the ancient doctrine of rebirth (*samsara*), a person's life is the result of a long series of actions (*karma*) accumulated over a process of many lifetimes, and Siddhartha Gautama was no exception. A body of traditional texts known as the *Jataka* tales (see box, opposite) tells us that he prepared for his final life as a *buddha* by passing through many lifetimes, in which he received teaching from previous *buddhas* and exhibited many of the great moral virtues of the Buddhist tradition.

According to the accepted scholarly chronology, Siddhartha Gautama was born in 566BCE and died aged eighty in 486BCE, although southeast Asian Buddhists accept 623BCE for his birth and 543BCE for his death or *parinirvana* ("final *nirvana*"). There is little disagreement about the basic facts of his birth or about the legend that grew up around his life. He was born at Lumbini in what is now southern Nepal to royal parents of an Indian people, the Shakya. He spent most of his years in the central Ganges basin, in the vicinity of Varanasi, Patna, and Vaishali (see map, p.165).

SIDDHARTHA'S MIRACULOUS BIRTH

The Buddha's birth is associated with a series of supernatural omens and events that portended the significance of his career. According to the *Buddhacharita* ("Acts of the Buddha"), an account of the Buddha's life by the poet Ashvaghosha (second century CE), when the future Buddha was conceived, his mother, Queen Maya, dreamt that a white elephant painlessly entered her side. When the time came for the young Siddhartha to be born, he sprang from his mother's side, took seven steps, and said: "I have been born to achieve awakening (*bodhi*) for the good of the world: this is my last birth."

Siddhartha's father, Shuddhodana, asked his court sages to interpret these marvels. The sages saw wheels on the palms of the child's hands and on the soles of his feet. Siddhartha, they said, would therefore grow up to be a *Chakravartin* ("Wheel-Turner"), quite literally a "revolutionary": either a great conquering king or a great religious teacher.

The wondrous birth and first 7 steps of the Buddha (see sidebar, above); a Tibetan painting of the 18th century.

Buddhist tradition relates that Siddhartha was raised at Kapilavastu in the palace of his father, King Shuddhodana, and married a princess, Yashodhara, who bore him a son, Rahula. In his early thirties, Siddhartha became curious about life beyond the palace, which he had never left, and asked to go beyond its walls. In the park just outside the palace, he witnessed three sights that brought home the reality of human suffering: a person in old age, a sick man, and a corpse.

On another trip outside the royal residence, Siddhartha saw a fourth sight—a wandering ascetic (*shramana*)—and vowed to follow his example and seek release from the world of suffering. At first his father tried to restrain him, but Siddhartha Gautama left the palace—according to legend with the help of the gods, who cast a pall of sleep over the court—and gave up his princely identity in order to assume the life of a wanderer. This event, known as the Pravrajya ("Going Forth"), is reenacted in Buddhist communities whenever anyone decides to take up the life of a monk or a nun.

The earliest stages of Siddhartha Gautama's withdrawal from society were marked by strenuous fasting and self-denial—so much so that he almost died. Convinced that this route to salvation was unproductive, he accepted a gift of food from a young woman and began to follow what is known in Buddhist tradition as the "Middle Way," a mode of discipline

THE STORY OF VESSANTARA

The *Jataka* ("Birth") tales tell of the Buddha's previous lives before his final rebirth as Siddhartha Gautama. The story of Prince Vessantara, the paragon of generosity, is one of the most popular of the tales. Vessantara, it is said, ruled a kingdom blessed by the presence of a white elephant with magical powers that brought abundant rain to the land. One day, the ruler of another kingdom sent messengers to ask for the elephant as a gift. With extreme generosity, Vessantara gave the elephant away. In protest, his subjects drove him into the forest together with his wife and children. There, an evil *brahmin* (member of the priestly caste) called Jujaka asked for Vessantara's children as slaves. The prince happily consented.

Fearing that Vessantara would even give away his wife, the god Sakka assumed human form and asked for her. Vessantara handed her over, but Sakka returned her to the prince at once, explaining that, because she was a gift from a god, Vessantara must now keep her forever. Vessantara's fortunes soon began to turn. His children were ransomed from the evil brahmin and soon the prince's kingdom was also restored and he returned with his family in triumph.

Like other *Jataka* tales (such as the account of the Buddha's incarnation as a deer that offered itself in sacrifice to save a doe), the story of Vessantara is widely venerated throughout southeast Asia as an example of the virtue of generosity. This quality is particularly important for the Buddhist laity in their role as donors and patrons of monasteries. Vessantara's munificence and exile in the forest also anticipated the act of renunciation that set Siddhartha on the road to *nirvana*.

A Tibetan tangka *(portable icon) of ca. 1700CE illustrating stories of the previous incarnations of the Buddha, who sits on a pedestal in the center.*

that seeks to avoid the extremes of self-indulgence and self-denial. Siddhartha's wanderings eventually brought him to a tree on bank of the Nairanjana river at Bodh Gaya that became known as the Bodhi Tree or "Tree of Awakening." He seated himself beneath the tree for a final, determined effort to win freedom from death and rebirth (see pp.192–3). He was assailed by the evil god Mara, the Buddhist tempter (see illustration, p.164), who sent his voluptuous daughters to distract him and his fierce sons to frighten him away. But Siddhartha withstood Mara's onslaught and, during one final night of meditation, became enlightened about the *dharma* ("truth," "law") of human existence (see sidebar, opposite). With this he could properly be called a *buddha* ("awakened one").

At first, it is said, the Buddha wanted to keep his insights to himself and sat in meditation for several weeks before resolving to pass on his newly found wisdom. He walked to the deer park at Sarnath near Varanasi, where he met five former companions on the spiritual quest. He taught them a sermon, or discourse (*sutra*), known as the "First Turning of the Wheel of the Dharma [Law]" (Dharmachakrapravartana). The story of Buddhism as an organized religious tradition begins with the serene and newly wise teacher conveying the results of his awakening to a handful of

REPRESENTATIONS OF THE BUDDHA

The earliest representations of the Buddha are symbols or scenes associated with the Buddha's life without actually depicting his physical form. Two of the most common symbols of the Buddha in these so-called "aniconic" images are the Wheel of the Dharma (representing the first sermon; see illustration, opposite) and the throne beneath the Bodhi Tree, where he achieved his Awakening. Aniconic representations of the "Great Departure," when Siddhartha left his palace to become a wandering ascetic, show an empty horse shielded by a parasol, with a group of lesser Indian deities muffling the sound of the horse's hooves, according to one legend. A common example of this early type of representation is simply the mark of the footprints left behind by the Buddha.

Early in the Common Era, Buddhists began to represent the Buddha's physical form. In the region of Gandhara, on the present-day border between Pakistan and Afghanistan, figures of the Buddha were very strongly influenced by the Hellenistic art of the Greek kingdoms of Afghanistan and western Central Asia. In the region of Mathura, in the middle reaches of the Ganges river, the Buddha was represented in a robust, down-to-earth style derived from the traditional Indian decorative arts. These two styles coalesced during the period of the Gupta dynasty of Indian rulers (320–540CE) to produce the classic representations of the Buddha that have had such wide impact throughout the Buddhist world. The Gupta style is also evident in the paintings on the wall of the Buddhist caves at Ajanta in western India and in the serene, elegant, sensuous, but otherworldly depiction at Sarnath of the Buddha teaching.

Hellenistic influence is striking in the expression, stance, musculature, and drapery of this 2nd-century CE *schist statue of the Buddha from Gandhara. The "wisdom bump" on the head is a specifically Buddhist element, and the hands, now missing, were probably shown in raised and lowered open-palmed gestures of blessing.*

companions, who formed the nucleus of the Buddhist *samgha* ("community"). For the remaining forty-five years of his life, the Buddha wandered the roads of northern India, preaching the Dharma and expanding the boundaries of the community. He is even said to have ascended to heaven to teach the Dharma to his late mother. Finally, in the town of Kushinagari, he delivered a closing discourse (the *Mahaparinirvana Sutra*) to his disciples, lay down between two trees, and died; or, in Buddhist terms, achieved his "final nirvana" (*parinirvana*), never to be reborn.

Following the Buddha's own instructions, a group of lay followers cremated his body, distributed his ashes as relics, and enshrined them in funerary mounds, or *stupa*s (see pp.186–7). The veneration of these remains provided the model for the tradition of Buddhist worship, which came to be directed not only at relics but also at other objects, images, and sites sanctified through their association with events in the Buddha's life. In Buddhist tradition these constitute the Buddha's "Form Body," while his teaching is known as his "Dharma Body" (see p.179). In the two types of "body" (often understood quite differently in different parts of the Buddhist world), the Buddha continues to be a presence in the wider Buddhist community.

THE "FOUR NOBLE TRUTHS"

The first of the Buddha's profound insights at Bodh Gaya was the knowledge of his previous births. This was followed by the knowledge of the births of others, and finally by the knowledge of the "Four Noble Truths": the "truth of suffering," the "truth of the origin of suffering," the "truth of the cessation of suffering," and the "truth of the Path." This can be explained as follows. The Buddha's "awakening" began with his realization that all life is filled with suffering, in particular the suffering that comes from seeing a beloved person, object, or experience pass away, as it inevitably must. He perceived that the origin of suffering lies in desire, and that desire comes from an ignorant misconception about the nature of things, in particular the nature of the self.

With his discovery of the Four Noble Truths came the conviction that he, Siddhartha, had brought suffering to an end. According to the Buddha, suffering ceases when the process that generates it is reversed, bringing about *nirvana*, an end of desire and ignorance (see pp.192–3). The Buddha believed that *nirvana* could be attained through the "Noble Eightfold Path" (see p.184).

Flanked by deer, this ornate "Wheel of the Dharma" adorns the roof of a temple in Lhasa, Tibet. It represents the the Buddha's sermon in the deer park near Varanasi (see main text).

A Gandhara sculpture of the 3rd century CE *depicting the Buddha emaciated as a result of fasting during the ascetic stage of his quest for enlightenment (see p.169).*

SCHOOLS AND VEHICLES

Most of the evidence for the early history of the Buddhist community, the *samgha*, comes from texts written five centuries or more after the Buddha's death. It is therefore difficult to establish for certain how the *samgha* grew from a small band of disciples around a single charismatic leader to become a major force in India and beyond. However, Buddhist tradition records several stages of institutional development that made it possible for the religion to play an important role in the development of Asian civilization.

A short time after the Buddha died in 486BCE (or 543), a "First Buddhist Council" is said to have been held in the city of Rajagrha. In one account, the Buddha's disciple Kashyapa was traveling with a group of monks when he heard that his master had died. One monk openly rejoiced, saying that the death of the Buddha freed them from the constraint of monastic rules. Fearing a breakdown in discipline, Kashyapa proposed the calling of a council to restate the Buddha's teaching and monastic regulations and set down a common body of doctrine and practice to guide the Buddhist community. The council produced what was to become the nucleus of the Buddhist canon.

Another tradition tells of a second council, called about a century later in the city of Vaishali to discuss variations to the monastic code introduced under the pressure of the community's regional expansion. However, the issues were not fully resolved and gave rise to Buddhism's first big schism, between the Sthaviras ("Elders") and Mahasamghikas ("Great Community"). This was the start of the fragmentation of the *samgha* into the Eighteen Schools (*nikaya*s), and anticipated the eventual split between Hinayana ("Lesser Vehicle") Buddhism and Mahayana ("Greater Vehicle") Buddhism (see sidebar, opposite).

The expansion of the early community owed much to royal patronage, both within India and beyond. The great Mauryan emperor Ashoka (268–239BCE), who ruled northern India from his capital at Pataliputra (modern Patna), made an explicit and public conversion to Buddhism. As part of his policy of "righteous conquest" (*dharmavijaya*), he promulgated Buddhist values throughout his kingdom and actively supported the spread of the religion beyond his frontiers. For example, his son Mahendra (Pali: Mahinda) is said to have gone to Sri Lanka at the head of a mission.

At this time it seems there were also Buddhist monks in the region of Afghanistan and central Asia, where they came into contact with Hellenic kingdoms established after Alexander the Great's invasion of India in 327–325BCE. At least one Greek king, Menander (Pali: Milinda), is said to have converted to Buddhism. The religion also received support from the Sakas, a Scythian tribe who invaded Afghanistan ca. 130BCE, and from

BUDDHISM'S DECLINE IN INDIA

In India, by the thirteenth century CE, the rise of Hindu devotionalism (see pp.132–3) seems to have undermined the appeal of Buddhism to the common people, while centuries of Buddhist and Hindu interaction at a popular level had apparently eroded the differences between the two traditions. The position of India's monasteries was also precarious, because they were vulnerable to persecution by the enemies of the kings and princes on whom they relied for support. When Muslim invaders destroyed the monasteries of Nalanda in 1197 and Vikramashila in 1203, Buddhism's active influence on Indian culture effectively ended. A few monks clung on in the ruined monasteries, but from this time until the twentieth century (see p.197), Buddhism was of little significance in the land of its origin.

King Kanishka, who dominated parts of northern Afghanistan ca. 100CE. In southern India, the support of the Satavahana dynasty (220BCE–236CE) produced a flourishing Buddhist culture in what is now Andhra Pradesh.

For the first six or seven centuries CE Buddhism was central to a great flowering of Indian culture, notably in the period of the Gupta dynasty (320–540CE) and the reign of King Harsha (606–646). Buddhist monasteries were sophisticated centers of learning, training monks in philosophy, religion, medicine, astronomy, and grammar. Later, as northern India came under growing pressure from foreign invaders, the focus of monastic life shifted down the Ganges toward Bihar and Bengal. Under the Pala dynasty (ca. 800–1200CE), monastic centers such as Nalanda and Vikramashila continued to elaborate the traditions of earlier times.

The history of Buddhism in southeast Asia goes back to Ashoka's missionaries in Sri Lanka. For a thousand years or more, the Buddhism of this region was an eclectic mix of traditions that mirrored the diversity of Indian Buddhism. From the eleventh century CE, when the influence of Indian monasteries began to wane (see sidebar, opposite), a number of Buddhist monks and kings in Myanmar and Thailand turned to Sri Lanka for guidance. In the reign of Sri Lanka's King Narapatisithu (1173–1210CE), Theravada (one of the Eighteen Schools) came into the ascendancy. Following the example of Sri Lanka, the Theravada orthodoxy was adopted

A Buddhist stupa *at Mihintale, where Mahendra (Mahinda), the missionary son of King Ashoka, is said to have preached the first Buddhist sermon in Sri Lanka. Theravada Buddhism spread from the island to southeast Asia in the 13th century* CE.

MAHAYANA BUDDHISM

Around the beginning of the Common Era, in circumstances that are still poorly understood, a Buddhist reform movement appeared that called itself Mahayana, or "Great Vehicle," in contrast to what it considered the Hinayana, or "Lesser Vehicle," of the Eighteen Schools (see main text).

Mahayana tradition traces its history back to the Buddha himself. According to Mahayana texts, the Buddha held a special assembly at the Vulture Peak in Rajagrha and delivered a sermon known as "the Second Turning of the Wheel of the Dharma" to a select group of disciples. This teaching, it is said, remained hidden for a period and was then revealed to the rest of the Indian Buddhist community.

Whether the Mahayana emerged in one region of India or developed in several different centers is uncertain. But it is clear that its emphasis on the *bodhisattva* ideal (see pp.176–7, 184) incorporated the interests of lay Buddhists, both men and women, in a new way. A *bodhisattva* did not seek to renounce the world to attain *nirvana*, as in the traditional monastic ideal, but returned to the world out of compassion for ordinary humanity.

Mahayana Buddhism developed a mythology of celestial *buddhas* and *bodhisattvas* that shows kinship not only with forms of worship found in Iranian and Middle Eastern religion but with the emerging mythology of Hinduism.

Pagan, the ancient Burmese capital, where the remains of more than 5,000 sacred Buddhist buildings have been found. The city flourished for 2 centuries until it fell to the Mongols in 1287.

in Thailand and Myanmar, and this branch of Buddhism predominates in the region to this day. In the nineteenth and twentieth centuries, southeast Asian Buddhists were confronted by European colonialism, but generations of reformers rose to the challenge and developed a distinctively "modern" Buddhism (see pp.196–7).

Buddhism came to Tibet in two waves, known as the "First" and "Second Diffusion of the Dharma." The first began in the seventh century CE, when the wives of the Tibetan king Srong-btsan-sgam-po (Songtsen Gampo) brought images of the Buddha to the capital, Lhasa. The first monastery was established at bSam-yas (Samye) in the late eighth century CE with the collaboration of the Indian Tantric saint Padmasambhava, the Indian scholar Shantarakshita, and the Tibetan king Khri-srong-lde-btsan (Thrisong Detsen). The history of Tibetan Buddhism is characterized by the elements that these three founders represent: Tantric ritual and meditation (see sidebar, left); monastic intellectual discipline; and royal secular power.

This "First Diffusion" came to an end during a period of persecution that began in the reign of King Glang-dar-ma (Langdarma, 838–842CE). Buddhism was reintroduced to Tibet at the end of the tenth century CE in what is known as the "Later Diffusion," and by the end of the eleventh century the four main sects of Tibetan Buddhism had been clearly distinguished. One, the rNying-ma-pas (Nyingmapa), traced its origin back to Padmasambhava. The others, the Sa-skya-pas (Sakyapa), bKa'-gdams-pas (Kadampa), and bKa'-rgyud-pas (Kargyupa), claimed to be rooted in the saints and scholars who came after the great persecution. From the bKa'-gdams-pas sect sprang the dGe-lugs-pa (Gelukpa) lineage that eventually produced the Dalai Lamas (see box, opposite).

Buddhism entered China in the first (or possibly second) century CE along the Silk Road (see map, p.201). As in southeast Asia and Tibet, the religion's greatest initial challenge was how to express the richness and complexity of Indian Buddhism in an indigenous form. However, by the time of the Tang dynasty (618–907CE), Buddhism had become thoroughly acculturated and was playing an important role in Chinese civilization. This period saw the emergence of the classic Chinese Mahayana schools, including the meditation tradition of Chan (from Sanskrit *dhyana*, "meditation") and the philosophical schools of Tiantai and Huayan. Chinese Buddhism was also deeply influenced by the Mahayana tradition of celestial *buddhas* and *bodhisattvas*, especially Amitabha (Amituo Fo), Avalokiteshvara (Guanyin; see p.211), and Maitreya (Mile Fo; see pp.176–7).

As a "foreign" faith, Buddhism was occasionally persecuted, even in its Tang heyday (see p.206), and the Neo-Confucian revival of the Song dynasty (960–1279CE; see p.205) ensured that Buddhism never regained the dominance it had enjoyed in Tang times. But it remained important as one of China's revered "Three Teachings" (see p.200).

TANTRIC BUDDHISM

Mahayana Buddhism spawned a movement that seemed to challenge the most fundamental commitments of the tradition. It is known as Tantra from the name of the texts that convey its teachings, and also as the Mantrayana ("Vehicle of Sacred Chants") and Vajrayana ("Vehicle of the Thunderbolt").

Tantric Buddhism stresses ritual and symbolism, especially the *mandala* or "sacred circle" (see p.177), and promotes practices aimed at achieving an immediate experience of "awakening." The radical quality of this awakening is most vividly expressed in Tantric art by the depiction of the Buddha as a "wrathful deity." A Tantric *siddha* or "saint" understands that there is ultimately no difference between peacefulness and anger, and that the awakening experience is present in even the most basic of human emotions.

The Chinese variety of Buddhism was introduced to Korea in the fourth century CE and to Japan in the sixth century CE (see p.243). Vietnam also came to adopt Chinese Buddhist traditions, although the religion may originally have penetrated the region as early as the second century CE. A form of Chan Buddhism (Japanese: Zen), with its emphasis on meditation and the experience of "awakening," occurs in all three lands, as does a degree of devotion to celestial *buddha*s and *bodhisattva*s.

By the mid-twentieth century, almost all of the major Buddhist schools and traditions had also come to be represented in the West, both among immigrant communities and Western converts (see sidebar, right). In monasteries, temples, and meditation halls from Scotland to San Francisco, Buddhism has put down vigorous roots in environments quite different from that of the middle reaches of the Ganges, where it came into being.

BUDDHISM COMES TO THE WEST

Scarcely known in the West except to scholars before ca. 1850, Buddhism had begun to spread actively by 1900, partly owing to an ex-US Army colonel, Henry S. Olcott (1832–1907), and a Russian mystic, Helena Blavatsky (1831–91). They took up the cause of reviving Theravada Buddhism in colonial Sri Lanka, and their own Theosophical Society owed much to Buddhist precepts. The faith's profile was also raised by the World Parliament of Religions (Chicago, 1893), attended by many important Asian Buddhist figures.

THE PRIEST-KINGS OF TIBET

The title Dalai Lama (literally "Ocean Teacher," the first word presumably meaning "Ocean of Wisdom") was first given to the Tibetan king bSod-nams rGya-mtsho (Sonam Gyatso, 1543–88CE) by the Mongol chief Altan Khan. However, Tibetan Buddhists consider bSod-nams rGya-mtsho to be the third in a line of reincarnations that leads back to the monk dGe'dun-grub (Gendun Dup, 1391–1475), who is therefore regarded as the true "first" Dalai Lama.

During the reign of the "Great Fifth" Dalai Lama, Ngag-dbang-blo-bzang rGya-mtsho (Ngawang Losang Gyatso, 1617–82), the Dalai Lamas became the full secular and religious leaders of Tibet. Under their leadership, Tibetan Buddhists maintained their traditional way of life until the Chinese invasion of Tibet (1950) forced bsTan-'dzin rGya-mtsho (Tenzin Gyatso), the fourteenth Dalai Lama, into exile. Since that time, he has been the focus of efforts to preserve Tibetan culture, both in Tibet and among communities of converts and exiles around the world (see also p.194).

The Potala Palace in Lhasa, built by the "Great 5th" Dalai Lama, Ngag-dbang-blo-bzang rGya-mtsho, in the 17th century and the seat of the priestly rulers of Tibet until 1950.

CELESTIAL BEINGS

The bust of a bodhisattva *from Gandhara. In Mahayana literature, a* bodhisattva *is portrayed as one who looks down on the world, feels its suffering, and saves beings from danger.*

Theravada Buddhism insists that Siddhartha Gautama was very definitely a human being, who achieved a final *nirvana* and died never to be reborn. When a Theravada devotee makes an offering to an image of the Buddha, this is not the act of divine worship but a means to gain karmic merit and to be reminded of the Buddha's virtues, which one should strive to cultivate.

However, this does not mean that Buddhism has nothing resembling the divinities of, for example, ancient Indian tradition. In the Mahayana tradition, those who progress to the highest stages of the path to *buddha*-hood—the *bodhisattvas* ("*buddha*s-to-be," or "future *buddha*s")—are said to accumulate such power from their many works of compassion and wisdom that they acquire the ability to act in a quasidivine manner. These extraordinary figures are known as "celestial *bodhisattva*s." They can intervene miraculously in this world, and can even create heavenly realms where people may be reborn into bliss for reasons that depend as much on the compassion of the *bodhisattva*s as on the merit of the individual worshipper. At the end of their careers as *bodhisattva*s they become "celestial *buddha*s" and attain even more remarkable powers. But many *bodhisattva*s deliberately postpone their *buddha*-hood in order to assist ordinary devotees on the path to *nirvana*.

The concepts of the celestial *bodhisattva* and *buddha* made it possible for Mahayana Buddhism to develop an elaborate "pantheon" of quasi-deities. One of the most important is the *bodhisattva* Avalokiteshvara ("Lord Who Looks Down"), who has been called the personification of the compassionate gaze of the Buddha. Avalokiteshvara's compassion is invoked by pronouncing the *mantra* "*Om Mani Padme Hum*" ("O Jewel in the Lotus"; *Om* and *Hum* are untranslatable sacred syllables; see p.140).

In Indian Buddhism, Avalokiteshvara became associated with a female *bodhisattva* called Tara, who embodied the feminine side of his compassion. In China, where Avalokiteshvara is worshipped under the name Guanyin, the *bodhisattva*'s male and female identities became compounded, and Guanyin came to be worshipped mainly in female form (see p.211). Tibetans feel a special kinship with Avalokiteshvara (in Tibetan, Spyan-ras-gzigs, or Chenrezig). They claim that he has taken a vow to protect the nation of Tibet and is manifested in the person of every Dalai Lama.

Important celestial *bodhisattva*s also include Maitreya, the "*buddha* of the future age," who will be the next *bodhisattva* to enter the world to become a *buddha* (see illustration, p.163). Like Avalokiteshvara, Maitreya is said to rescue people in danger: in China, where he is called Mile Fo, messianic movements have at times proclaimed his imminent arrival and the transformation of society on Buddhist lines. Other celestial *bodhisattva*s are

SIDDHARTHA THE *BODHISATTVA*

The line between a *bodhisattva* and a *buddha* can be indistinct. According to the *Lotus Sutra* (see p.181), the Buddha himself was merely the manifestation of a great *bodhisattva* whose long career has not yet ended. Realizing that people in this world needed an example of a fellow human being who had experienced the process of attaining *nirvana*, he manifested himself as Siddhartha Gautama and went through a show of achieving *parinirvana* (final *nirvana*). But this was not the end of his career: he continues to manifest himself in a compassionate way as long as there are others who need his help.

Manjushri, the *bodhisattva* of wisdom, and Kshitigarbha, the consoler of the dead and protector of travelers, pilgrims, and children. (See also p.184.)

The best known celestial *buddha* is Amitabha ("Infinite Light"), who is said to have established a paradise, the "Pure Land," on becoming a *buddha* (see p.193). Anyone who chanted his name with faith, especially at the moment of death, would be reborn in the Pure Land and come face to face with Amitabha himself. Amitabha Buddha had a great impact in China and Japan, where he is called Amituo Fo and Amida Butsu respectively (*fo* and *butsu* = *buddha*). Indeed, during the Kamakura era (1185–1333CE), Amida became one of the most important elements in Japanese Buddhist life. The great reformer Shinran (1173–1263) made a radical claim about reliance on the grace of Amida rather than on one's own efforts (see p.254).

Other important figures include the physician-*buddha* Bhaishajyaguru ("Teacher of Healing") and the "Sun Buddha" Vairochana ("Radiant"), the central *buddha* in many Tantric *mandalas* (see box, below). He is identified with the sun and was important in the acculturation of Buddhism to Japan, where the sun goddess (see pp.246–7) heads the Shinto pantheon.

POPULAR DIVINITIES

Buddhism has always found room for the reverence of local deities and spirits. The Buddha himself is said to have been protected by a *naga* (in Indian tradition, a *naga* is a snake deity that controls the rain; in Buddhism, *nagas* also guard the treasures of the tradition). *Stupas* (see p.186) are often associated with *yakshas* (gods of wealth and good fortune) and *yakshis* (fertility goddesses). In southeast Asia, Hindu gods such as Indra and Vishnu are important Buddhist guardian figures, and the faith embraces many regional deities in China, Korea, Japan, and Tibet.

TANTRIC *MANDALAS*

In Tantric Buddhism, the universe is often represented as a *mandala*, or "sacred circle," that symbolizes the macrocosm and the microcosm: it represents both the universe and the mind and body of the individual practitioner. *Mandalas* are used in ritual and meditation to help the devotee to unify his or her vision of the cosmos; to contemplate the integration of the self and the world; and to overcome the distinction between *nirvana* and the realm of death and rebirth.

One of the most common of these sacred images is known as the "*Mandala* of the Five Buddhas" and plays a central role in the Tantric Buddhism of Tibet and in the Shingon tradition of Japan. It takes as its starting point a configuration of five celestial *buddhas*: Vairochana in the center, Amitabha in the west, Amoghasiddhi in the north, Akshobhya in the east, and Ratnasambhava in the south. The *mandala* is expanded and elaborated by a process of symbolic association to include five colors, five personality traits, five wisdoms, and so on, with each element of every pentad associated with one of the five *buddhas*. The *buddhas* are also associated with five goddesses located at the center of the mandala and at the four intermediate points of the compass.

A Nepalese mandala *of 1860 depicting Vairochana in the central circle and the 4* buddhas *in the corners of the square. The* mandala *also depicts numerous other sacred beings.*

WORDS OF THE DHARMA

After the Buddha's death, his followers are said to have called the First Buddhist Council to reiterate his teaching, the Dharma (see p.172). The council established a procedure for memorization and recitation that allowed the teaching to be transmitted orally for almost five centuries before it was committed to writing. Written versions of the canonical collections exist in all Buddhist cultures and are often treated with great reverence, but the oral tradition is still of central importance throughout the Buddhist world.

Owing in part to this ancient practice of oral transmission, Buddhism has no single canon of scripture. Different schools and traditions regard different collections of texts as authoritative, representing the various ways of understanding the Dharma down the ages. The Pali canon of the Theravada tradition (see box, below) contains much very ancient material from the

THE PALI CANON

The most conservative canon of Buddhist writings are the *Tipitaka* ("Three Baskets") of the Theravada tradition. Written in Pali, an old Indian language closely related to Sanskrit, they are often referred to simply as the Pali canon. The *Tipitaka* (Sanskrit *Tripitaka*) is said to have been written down in 29BCE under King Vattagamani of Sri Lanka.

The three "baskets" are the three sections of the canon: the *Sutta* (Sanskrit *Sutra*) *Pitaka*, *Vinaya Pitaka*, and *Abhidhamma* (Sanskrit *Abhidharma*) *Pitaka*. The *sutras* of the *Sutta Pitaka* generally consist of the Buddha's doctrinal discourses and range from short poems to long prose narratives about the Buddha's previous lives. It also contains verses attributed to the Buddha's earliest followers: the *Theragatha* ("Verses of the Male Elders") and *Therigatha* ("Verses of the Female Elders"). The *Vinaya Pitaka* is concerned with rules of discipline, including a commentary on the *Patimokkha* ("Monastic Precepts") and stories intended to illustrate Buddhist moral principles. The *Abhidhamma Pitaka* provides a systematic analysis of the categories of Buddhist thought.

Portions of the canonical collections of some of the other Eighteen Schools (see p.172) have also survived. For example, the school of Sarvastivadin ("Those who hold the doctrine that all things exist") has left behind parts of its own "Three Baskets," in Chinese and Tibetan translations as well as the original Sanskrit. These often vary quite substantially from the *Pitakas* of the Pali canon.

The traditional interpretation of the Pali canon owes a great deal to the monk Buddhaghosa, who came to Sri Lanka from India in the fifth century CE. He collected and translated a large body of Sinhalese commentaries on the Pali texts and his most important work, the *Visuddhimagga* ("Path to Purification"), is an authoritative guide to the practice of Theravada Buddhism.

The first printed version of the Pali canon was made at the instigation of King Chulalongkorn of Thailand in 1893. The version most commonly used by Western scholars was produced in London by the Pali Text Society, founded in 1881 to disseminate the texts of the Theravada tradition.

A section of the Pali canon inscribed in Burmese on a strip of gold. Dating from 5th century CE, it is the oldest extant Buddhist text from Myanmar (Burma).

A Buddhist devotee turns a "prayer wheel" in a temple at Kyicho, Bhutan. Each "wheel" is a cylinder containing sacred prayer texts, which are believed to be activated when the cylinder is spun by the worshipper. Prayer flags function in a similar manner (see p.163).

earliest stages of the oral tradition alongside texts possibly composed in the second century BCE. The Chinese and Tibetan canons contain a wide range of Mahayana literature from as late as the twelfth century CE. Even where a canon is formally closed (as with the Pali canon), its contents may exist in different versions. For example, some texts in the Burmese version of the Pali canon are noncanonical for Sri Lankan Buddhists.

While Buddhist canonical literature is variable and new texts have often been added, it is still considered a source of authority, not only because it provides a record of the Buddha's teaching but because it provides access, in a certain sense, to the Buddha himself. Buddhist sacred texts represent the most important, enduring aspects of the Buddha, what Buddhists refer to as his "Dharma Body" (see p.171). A line in the Pali *Samyutta Nikaya* says: "What is there, Vakkali, in seeing this vile body? He who sees the Dhamma [Pali for "Dharma"] sees me; he who sees me sees the Dhamma." The Dharma/Dhamma functions as the continuing presence of the Buddha in the Buddhist community, and is as worthy of respect as the Buddha himself. Buddhist texts are often recited or copied as acts of devotion, and it is not uncommon, especially in the

"Perfection of Wisdom" sutras *written on palm leaves threaded together ("thread" is the literal meaning of* sutra*).*

THE "PERFECTION OF WISDOM"

The *sutra* portions of the Chinese and Tibetan canons both include a section called the "Perfection of Wisdom" (Sanskrit *Prajnaparamita*), which provides some of the most basic accounts of the *bodhisattva* ideal (see p.184) and the concept of "Emptiness." Taking a fairly short text as their starting point, the Perfection of Wisdom *sutras* range from one hundred thousand lines to brief texts such as the *Diamond* and *Heart sutras*.

Attempts to give a systematic account of the doctrine of Emptiness in the Perfection of Wisdom literature gave rise to the two major schools of Mahayana philosophy: the Madhyamaka ("Middle Way") and the Yogachara ("Practice of Yoga"). The Madhyamaka, which predominates in Tibet, interpreted Emptiness to mean that all things are empty of any real identity and that their "reality" is only conventional or illusory. The Yogachara, prominent in China and areas of Chinese influence such as Vietnam, understood Emptiness to signify that the mind is empty of any real distinction between subject and object.

Mahayana tradition, for texts to be placed on altars as objects of worship, alongside, or even instead of, images of the Buddha.

The development of the Mahayana tradition is intimately connected with the evolution and dissemination of its scriptures. The earliest Mahayana texts can be dated on linguistic grounds to the first century BCE. Important Mahayana writings were translated into Chinese as early as the second century CE, and texts that came to assume canonical status were produced in India after 1100CE. India never produced a Mahayana canon that was as clearly fixed as the Pali canon, although informal Mahayana collections existed as early as the second century CE.

The oldest extant catalog of Chinese Buddhist canonical literature dates from 518CE. The first printed version of the Chinese *Tripitaka* was made during 972–983CE, at the beginning of the Song dynasty. The Tibetan canon was collected by the scholar Bu-ston (1290–1364CE) and was first printed in its entirety in Beijing in the early fifteenth century.

The Chinese and Tibetan canons each give the impression of being a codification of a monastic library. Clearly, for both canons, the concept of "canonicity" was quite loose. There was a core of literature (known in Sanskrit as *sutra* and in Tibetan as *bKa'*) that bore the direct authority of the *buddhas* and *bodhisattvas* (see sidebar, left). Around this core accumulated a body of doctrinal, philosophical, and interpretive literature known in Sanskrit as *shastra* and in Tibetan as *bsTan*, or "teaching."

The most extensive collection of Tantric texts is found in the Tibetan canon. Like other Buddhist canonical literature it ranges widely in form, from the simple songs of the Indian Tantric saints to elaborate commentaries on Tantric ritual, meditation, and symbolism. The Tibetan tradition generally classifies Tantric texts in four categories: ritual (*kriya*), practice (*charya*), discipline (*yoga*), and highest discipline (*anuttarayoga*). The

Mahavairochana Tantra ("Tantra of the Great Vairochana"), a text that had central significance in Chinese and Japanese Tantra, belongs to the *charya* category. To the *anuttarayoga* category belong texts such as the *Hevajra Tantra* and *Guhyasamaja Tantra* that focus on the immediate realization of Emptiness. Buddhist Tantric literature in India evolved gradually from the seventh to the twelfth centuries CE.

Other important Mahayana collections are the *Buddhavatamsaka* and the *Ratnakuta* ("Heap of Jewels"). The *Buddhavatamsaka* contains the *Gandavyuha Sutra* that tells the story of Sudhana, a young pilgrim whose journey is illustrated on the wall of the great *stupa* at Borobudur in Java. The *Ratnakuta* contains the *sutras* that inspired the Mahayana tradition of devotion to the *buddha* Amitabha ("Infinite Light").

The enormous range and variety of Buddhist scripture has led to many controversies about scriptural authority and interpretation. Members of the Eighteen Schools (see p.172) attacked the validity of the Mahayana by claiming that its *sutras* were not the actual teaching of the Buddha. The Mahayana responded by saying that the teaching of the Schools was merely a preparatory teaching, which the Mahayana superseded. Within the Mahayana, the Madhyamaka school argued that only certain Mahayana texts were definitive in meaning (*nitartha*), while others had a meaning that required interpretation (*neyartha*). The Chinese and Tibetan traditions produced several complex schemes of classification to reconcile contradictions and determine which texts could be relied on for the most definitive teaching. The Tantric tradition dealt with issues of interpretation by insisting that the meaning of the *tantras* was deliberately veiled and could be correctly interpreted only by a qualified teacher (Sanskrit *guru*; Tibetan *lama*).

Young monks learning the Buddhist scriptures at Kurje temple, Bhutan.

THE *LOTUS SUTRA*

The *Lotus Sutra* has functioned in east Asia almost as a compendium of Mahayana doctrine and is one of many texts that have had a wide impact on the religious and philosophical development of the Mahayana tradition, but are not part of any standard subdivision of the canon. The *sutra* is the source of a famous parable in which the Buddha is represented as a father who lures his children out of a burning house by promising them different "vehicles." When the children get outside, he gives them "one vehicle," the "great vehicle" of the Mahayana. This parable provides an image of the relationship between Mahayana teaching and that of the "lesser" vehicles associated with the earlier schools.

The *Lotus Sutra* also advocates devotion to the text itself as a way of expressing devotion to the Dharma Body of the Buddha. This practice has had particular significance in Japan, most notably among the devotees of Nichiren (see also pp.251, 254–5).

IN THE MASTER'S FOOTSTEPS

A novice monk in debate with his teacher (left) at Labrang monastery in northeastern Tibet.

To be a "sacred person" in the Buddhist tradition is above all to imitate the Buddha. The most basic way to do this is to embark, like the Buddha, on a monastic life in pursuit of *nirvana* (see pp.184–5). The greatest exemplars of the monastic ideal were the Buddha's first followers, such as his chief disciple, Shariputra (in Pali, Sariputta), who was born into an Indian *brahmin* family in Nalanda. Shortly after his conversion by the Buddha, he became an *arhant*, or "worthy one"—one who, like his master, had attained *nirvana*. Shariputra had a great reputation for wisdom and is often depicted in Mahayana *sutras* as one of the first to ask the Buddha a question. Converted at the same time as Shariputra was his friend Maudgalyayana (Pali, Moggallana), who also came from a *brahmin* family. He was reputed to possess the magical ability to quell the hostile forces of nature and to travel at will to the highest levels of the cosmos. He became popular in Chinese Buddhist legend as Mulian, who traveled to Hell to intercede for his mother.

One of the most remarkable of the Buddha's disciples was Angulimala ("Garland of Fingers"), who is revered as a prime example of how one can make a radical break with the past on taking up a monastic life. Before he met the Buddha, it is said, Angulimala was a mass murderer who wore his victims' fingers as a necklace. Yet he became a monk and attained *nirvana*.

The Indian monasteries of later centuries also produced personalities renowned for their courage, learning, or meditative attainments. Among the products of the sophisticated monastic culture of Bihar and Bengal were the Mahayana philosophers Shantarakshita, who presided over the

SACRED KINGSHIP

One of the most important institutional developments of the *bodhisattva* ideal was its extension to include a form of sacral kingship, a tradition that has existed in Buddhism since the third century BCE and the time of the emperor Ashoka (see p.172), who assumed a special status for Buddhists as protector of the Dharma.

As the Mahayana tradition developed, revered Buddhist princes and kings came to be regarded as *bodhisattvas*. Such figures include Prince Shotoku, who played a crucial role in the introduction of Buddhism to Japan (see p.243), and the Dalai Lamas of Tibet (see p.175), whom Tibetan Buddhists venerated as the incarnation of the celestial *bodhisattva* Avalokiteshvara (see p.176). The respect accorded to their status as *bodhisattvas* enabled the Dalai Lamas to assume responsibility for the secular as well as the religious governance of Tibet.

foundation of the first Tibetan monastery, and Atisha, who helped reintroduce Buddhism to Tibet during the "Later Diffusion" (see p.174).

The development of Buddhism in east and southeast Asia and Tibet is inseparable from the activity of Buddhist monks. An Indian monk, Buddhaghosa, shaped Theravada Buddhism in Sri Lanka (see p.178); the monks Shenxiu and Huineng founded respectively the Northern and Southern schools of Chan in China; the Japanese monk Dogen gave classic form to Zen (see p.252); and the Tibetan monk Tsong-kha-pa (1357–1419) formulated the dGe-lugs-pa tradition that produced the Dalai Lamas. Monastic engagement continues today with such widely revered figures as Thich Nhat Hanh (1926–), a Vietnamese monk who headed the Buddhist Peace Delegation during the Vietnam War and has preached the Buddhist virtue of "mindfulness" in the West. For many, Buddhists and non-Buddhists alike, perhaps the most visible living example of the "Buddha ideal" is the Fourteenth Dalai Lama (see p.194).

The Mahayana idea of the *bodhisattva* (see pp.176–7, 184) is also in principle open to any ordinary devotee in any age, including laypeople as well as monks and nuns. Some of the most influential Mahayana *sutra*s gave vivid accounts of the lives of lay *bodhisattva*s, such as Vimalakirti, who demonstrated that there is no real difference between the attainments of a monk and a layperson. His example had particular appeal in China, where the Buddhist idea of cutting family ties to join a monastery sat uneasily with Confucian concepts of filial piety (see caption, p.219).

BUDDHIST HOLY WOMEN

Not all examples of the monastic ideal have been men. The Buddha agreed to ordain women and create an order of nuns, and the early tradition contains many moving songs attributed to these first nuns. Today the lineage of nuns has died out in most Buddhist countries, but there are active female orders in China, and movements are afoot in other countries to revive orders there as well.

Among the Buddhist laywomen revered as *bodhisattva*s is Queen Shrimala, protagonist of the *Shrimala-devisimhanada* ("The Lion's Roar of Queen Shrimala") *Sutra.* She expresses similar ideas to those of the male *bodhisattva* Vimalakirti (see main text).

TANTRIC MONKS AND SAINTS

In the Tantric tradition, especially in Tibet, there has been a complicated interaction between the ideal of the scholar-monk in a monastic community and that of the solitary *siddha* or "saint." The Indian Tantric tradition tells of *siddha*s, such as Maitrigupta (or Maitripa), who achieved their meditative breakthroughs on the fringes of civilization, working with unconventional and charismatic *gurus*. Padmasambhava, the Indian Tantric saint who shared in the foundation of the first Tibetan monastery, is pictured as a solitary figure with extraordinary powers. His consort, Ye-shes-tsho-gyal, was a powerful figure in her own right.

The Tibetan "saint" Mi-la-ras-pa (or Milarepa; 1040–1123) worked for many years with the irascible guru Mar-pa before he achieved his great insights and retired into the mountains to live as a solitary *siddha*.

Tantric practices have also been drawn into the life of the monastery in ways that enrich but do not contradict traditional monastic values. Tibetan monks often bring the practices of a Tantric *siddha*, a Mahayana *bodhisattva*, and a traditional monk together in the complex fabric of a single life.

A large copper gilt figure of the Tantric "saint" Padmasambhava, cofounder of Tibet's earliest monastery at bSam-yas (Samye). He is shown in dhyanasana *("meditation posture"), with his legs crossed in the lotus position.*

THE PATH TO *NIRVANA*

The spirit of Buddhist ethics is expressed in the story of a man named Malunkyaputta, who confronts the Buddha and tells him that he will not listen to his teaching until he has answered a series of speculative questions, such as "How was the world created?" and "Will the Buddha exist after death?" The Buddha responds by comparing Malunkyaputta to a man who has been shot by a poisoned arrow but refuses to let it be pulled out until the physician can tell him what the arrow is made of, who shot it, and so on. For Buddhists, all speculation is subject to one practical principle: it is valuable only if it can directly help a person to remove the "arrow of suffering" and find the way to *nirvana*. Any other type of speculation, like Malunkyaputta's questioning, is incidental.

The basic guide to the attainment of *nirvana* is the "Noble Eightfold Path," a process of discipline with eight components: "right understanding," "right thought," "right speech," "right action," "right liveli-

THE *BODHISATTVA* IDEAL

In the Mahayana lands of north and east Asia, the ethical ideal of the *bodhisattva* became the central principle of moral practice for Buddhist monks as well as laypeople. The *bodhisattva* cultivates the virtues of compassion (*karuna*) and wisdom (*prajna*). These two principles are expressed in the "*bodhisattva* vow": "May I attain *buddha*-hood for the sake of all other beings!"

The first principle is an active ideal, centered on relieving the suffering of others. This includes helping others to attain *nirvana*, even to the extent of postponing one's own entry into *nirvana* in order to do so. The second ideal is more contemplative. It focuses on seeing through the "veil of illusion" that shrouds ordinary experience, thereby becoming free from suffering oneself.

A monk sits in contemplation of Buddhist scriptures at the great temple complex of Angkor Thom, Cambodia.

hood," "right effort," "right mindfulness," and "right concentration." Alternatively, the fundamental prerequisites for *nirvana* can be expressed as three principles: abstention from harmful actions (*shila*, "moral conduct"; see sidebar, right); a disciplined mind (*samadhi*, "mental concentration"); and a proper understanding of the self and the world (*prajna*, "wisdom"). These principles are related to the traditional Buddhist understanding of the law of *karma*, or moral retribution, that governs the process of death and rebirth. A person should abstain from harmful actions because they will lead to punishment in a future life and thus make it doubly difficult to escape the cycle of death and rebirth. "Mental concentration" helps remove the desires and hatreds that lead to harmful actions. And "wisdom" removes the false sense of self that feeds the whole process of desire, hatred, and harmful action.

Buddhist accounts of the law of *karma* insist that all rewards are related in kind to the actions that produced them. Thus sin causes a person to suffer in the next life; good actions bring happiness; and an action that is a mixture of good and bad will bring results that are a mixture of suffering and happiness. When monks come to a layperson's home on their morning begging round to receive donations of food, the more generous a person can be, the more he or she will prosper in a future life. People who are angry or cruel, disrespectful to parents or elders, or who cause dissension or strife, will suffer in future lives as a consequence. The model for this lay ideal is the Buddha, not so much as the ideal monk, but in his previous lives as an ordinary layperson, when he prepared for *buddha*-hood by performing actions of extraordinary loyalty, self-sacrifice, or generosity (see p.169).

The practice of "mental concentration" (*samadhi*) can take many different forms in the Buddhist tradition. One of the most basic techniques is to sit in a stable position, with a straight back and crossed legs, and cultivate "mindfulness" (Sanskrit *smrti*, Pali *sati*) of one's breathing. The purpose is to calm the mind, diminish harmful emotions, and become more fully aware of the flow of reality that makes up the self and the world. Other forms of concentration or meditation involve a deliberate cultivation of mental images, often of *buddha*s or *bodhisattva*s, to serve as the focus of worship.

The cultivation of "wisdom" (*prajna*) also takes many forms. In the Theravada tradition it is associated with the study of the *Abhidhamma*, the third section of the Pali canon, and its key concept is the doctrine of "No-Self." To be wise (or, in the words of the Noble Eightfold Path, to have "right views") is to see that there is no permanent identity in the self that endures from one moment to the next. To understand this truth in a deep and practical sense is to be freed from the selfish illusions that feed the cycle of death and rebirth.

A 12th-century Chinese painting depicting disciples of the Buddha giving alms to the poor, an example of a "good action" that will aid the soul's progress toward the attainment of nirvana.

THE "FIVE PRECEPTS"

For Theravada Buddhist laity, and indeed most other Buddhists, "moral conduct" is summarized in the Five Precepts: no killing, no stealing, no abusive sex, no lying, and no intoxicating beverages. Novice Theravada monks observe five further precepts: no eating after midday, no use of ornaments, no attending entertainments or shows, no use of money, and no use of soft beds. However, once fully ordained, monks are bound by more than two hundred rules found in the *Vinaya Tipitaka*, the section of the Pali canon (see p.178) dealing with monastic discipline.

The earliest Buddhist temples were established in natural caves, where many shrines may be found today. These images of the Buddha are in the sacred Pak Ou caverns in Luang Prabang province, Laos.

PLACES OF DEVOTION

In his final instructions to his disciples, as recorded in the Pali *Mahaparinibbana Sutta*, the Buddha requested that his body should be cremated and the remains enshrined in a series of *stupa*s, or funerary mounds, to serve as focal points for worship and meditation. The basic form of a Buddhist shrine replicates one of these early *stupa*s, with a large central mound surrounded by a railing and topped by a square structure with a central post holding a series of parasols. In the earliest *stupa*s, the relics of the Buddha were housed in the square structure, but later they were enshrined inside the central mound. As the form of the *stupa* evolved in India, the mound came to be decorated with representations of the Buddha, events of his life, or important stories from Buddhist texts. To pay homage to the Buddha at one of these traditional shrines, a worshipper could make offerings in the same way a Hindu devotee might make offerings to an image of a Hindu god, with flowers, candles, incense, and so on; or a person might walk around the *stupa* in an act of ritual circumambulation.

The basic *stupa* was elaborated in many different ways in different lands. In southeast Asia, shrines commonly retain the low, rounded shape of a traditional *stupa*. In Tibet, the *stupa* has been elongated vertically into the shape of a *mchod-rten* (*chorten*) or "offering place." In China, Korea, and Japan, the soaring shape of a pagoda is derived from the graceful parasols that used to grace the top of *stupa*s in India.

SHAMBHALA: THE SACRED LAND

The apocalyptic *Kalachakra* ("Wheel of Time") *Tantra*, one of the last Tantric texts to appear in India, tells the story of a mythical kingdom named Shambhala, which lies hidden in the mountains to the north of India and is ruled by a righteous Buddhist king. The text prophesies a time when the forces of evil have conquered the world. Shambhala will then become visible and the righteous king will emerge from his citadel, surrounded by his armies, to defeat the forces of evil and reestablish the rule of the Dharma.

The prophecy of the *Kalachakra* represents a type of messianic speculation that has had important influence at certain stages of Buddhist history. For Tibetans, it serves not just as an image of an ideal Buddhist kingdom but also as an idealized symbolic goal for a *yogi* to attain through the process of meditation.

As the utopia of "Shangri-la," Shambhala has become bound up in the Western imagination with the idea of Tibet itself as an idealized Buddhist paradise, its ancient and sacred way of life preserved for centuries from outside influence by the impregnable mountain barrier of the Himalayas.

At the great Buddhist temple at Borobudur in Java, the simple path of circumambulation has been elaborated into a series of ascending galleries, decorated with the story of Sudhana, a young Mahayana pilgrim in search of enlightenment. On the top of the structure, the worshipper is confronted by an open platform with an array of individual *stupa*s, each revealing an image of the seated Buddha. In the center of the platform stands a large, vacant *stupa* representing, it seems, the empty clarity of the Buddha's awareness. There are few more elegant and powerful representations of the Buddha's awakening in all of the Buddhist world.

Indian Buddhists established a tradition of temple-building following the Hindu style. The earliest Buddhist temples were created in caves in western India. Typically, the cave entrance led into a large open space where worshippers could sit or stand in front of a small *stupa* or an image of the Buddha. Sometimes the Buddha-image was in a separate room similar to the *garbha-grha* or "womb-house" of a Hindu temple. In recent years there have been efforts to rebuild some of the important Indian Buddhist temples that were destroyed in the twelfth and thirteenth centuries. For example, a Buddhist organization called the Mahabodhi ("Great Awakening") Society has led the restoration of the temple at Bodh Gaya, on the site where the Buddha achieved his awakening.

Indian Buddhist temple architecture was highly influential throughout the Buddhist world. The Temple of the Tooth in Kandy, Sri Lanka, and the Temple of the Emerald Buddha in Bangkok, Thailand, are sacred to the royalty of both countries and have served as symbols of royal power. The Jokhang in Lhasa is said to house the oldest image of the Buddha in Tibet and has functioned for centuries as an active center of Buddhist pilgrimage. The great temple at Nara, Japan, played a

THE SACRED LANDSCAPE

In India and elsewhere the definition of a Buddhist temple or shrine could be quite fluid, and a place that was sacred on account of its association with the Buddha did not have to be marked by a major architectural monument. Many travelers' tales from ancient India tell of small but unusual features of the landscape that were linked with the life of the Buddha. It was claimed that marks on rocks in a stream near Sarnath had been made by the Buddha's robe as he crossed the stream. A ravine in a town near Shravasti had opened up, it was said, to swallow one of the Buddha's enemies.

In many places there has been a lively cult of the Buddha's supposed footprints, most notably perhaps at Adam's Peak in Sri Lanka. According to Theravada tradition, the Buddha used his magical power to fly to Sri Lanka, and left the footprints as a mark of his visit.

The great Buddhist temple of Borobudur on the island of Java, Indonesia. It is at once a representation of the cosmos in 3 dimensions and one of the most remarkable transformations of the traditional Buddhist stupa.

A worshipper performs a ritual cleansing of a statue of the Buddha at the Shwe Dagon temple in Yangon, Myanmar (Rangoon, Burma).

decisive role in establishing the relationship between Buddhism and the Japanese imperial dynasty.

In the twentieth century, Buddhist temples have become common sights in Europe and North America. Los Angeles is sometimes called the most complex and varied Buddhist city in the world, and its many sacred sites include the sprawling Hsi Lai temple complex, established by a thriving Taiwanese Buddhist community.

The holy space created by Buddhist sacred architecture can be understood on a cosmic scale. For example, the central dome of a *stupa* stands for Mount Meru, the Buddhist cosmic mountain that marks the center of the world, and the parasols that rise above the *stupa*'s central axis represent the levels of heaven occupied by different categories of gods in ancient Indian tradition. Above the parasols, in the empty space of the sky, lies the formless realm attained by Buddhist "saints" in the highest levels of meditation, and the "*buddha*-fields"—the dwelling places of celestial *buddha*s and *bodhisattva*s of Mahayana tradition. Thus to perform a ritual circumambulation of a *stupa* is not simply to recall and venerate the life of the Buddha, but also to orient oneself firmly at the center of the cosmos.

In Indian tradition, the concept of the sacred center was particularly associated with the throne of the Buddha's awakening, or *bodhimanda*, at Bodh Gaya. According to Indian popular legends, all *buddha*s come to the same throne to achieve their awakening. The stone structure now visible under the Bodhi Tree at Bodh Gaya was said to be the top of a diamond throne extending down to the middle of the earth. The concept of the sacred "seat of enlightenment" can also be applied to sacred mountains, such as Mount Kailasa in Tibet and Mount Wutai in China, which are revered as the thrones of powerful *buddhas* or *bodhisattvas*.

Conversely, the idea of the sacred seat also serves to sanctify the simple space in which the ordinary Buddhist sits to meditate. Devotees of Zen habitually remind themselves that the spot upon which they sit for meditation is the throne of all the *buddhas* of the past and future.

In the Buddhist tradition, the bodily relics and physical images of the Buddha that are venerated in shrines constitute his "Form Body." His teaching, known as his "Dharma Body," is also the object of veneration, often quite literally. Some of the early Mahayana *sutras* say that any place where the Dharma is expounded should be treated as a "shrine" (*chaitya*) of the Buddha, and classical Indian writings describe shrines where a copy of a Mahayana scripture is set up with great pomp and ceremony to serve as the focus of worship. Archaeology has shown that many Indian *stupas* contained sacred texts in place of the relics of the Buddha. Reverence for the physical scripture is also seen in Tibetan temples, where copies of the Mahayana *sutras* lie on or around the altars, and in the esteem and power accorded to the *Lotus Sutra* by the Japanese sects tracing their origins to Nichiren (see p.254).

PILGRIMAGE SITES

For centuries, the sacred sites of the Buddhist tradition have been the object of pilgrimage. As indicated by the Chinese story *The Journey to the West* (see p.217), places in northern India associated with the Buddha's life attracted pilgrims from as far away as China until the destruction of Indian Buddhism made such journeys impossible. Buddhists throughout southeast Asia make pilgrimages to sites sacred in their tradition, such as Adam's Peak in Sri Lanka.

Tibetans journey to central Tibet to the holy sites of Lhasa, and they make the grueling journey to the west of the country to circumambulate Mount Kailasa. Other mountains are also regular pilgrimage destinations. Chinese Buddhists make a journey to Mount Putuo on a small island off the coast of Zhejiang Province to pay homage to the *bodhisattva* Guanyin, who is said to reside there, and seek her favor. In Japan, Mount Fuji is venerated by many Buddhist sects (see p.261).

The history of Japanese Buddhism is rich with the recollections of well-known pilgrims. Some, like the Zen founders Eisai and Dogen (see p.252), traveled to China to pursue their quest for the Dharma. Others, like the poet Matsuo Basho (1644–94), lived out their quest for awakening on the roads of Japan.

Adam's Peak in Sri Lanka, at the top of which is a depression in a rock that is traditionally said to be a "footprint" of the Buddha. The mountain is a popular destination for pilgrims.

A Burmese boy has his head shaved prior to entering a monastery for a period of training as a novice monk.

MONASTIC ORDINATION

In the Theravada countries of southeast Asia, monastic ordination often serves as a rite of passage for young men in their early teens to symbolize their transition from childhood to adulthood. Once ordained, a youth may spend no more than a few months or years in the monastery, just long enough to learn the rules of monastic practice, or how to read and write, or—in the lore of Thai Buddhism—to become "ripe" for marriage. However, he may decide to take the necessary vows and become a permanent member of the monastery. The ordination ritual reenacts the events of the Buddha's own renunciation. Amid communal festivities, the young man has his head shaved, dons monastic robes, and pronounces the phrases that indicate his entry into the order.

In the Mahayana lands, there is less stress on ordination as a coming-of-age ritual. But for the few young men or (in China) women who choose the monastic path, it is an equally decisive transition into another way of life.

HONORING THE WAY

Many Buddhist festivals are closely associated with events in the life of the Buddha or with the history and doctrines of Buddhism. The most important Buddhist holiday throughout the Theravada world is "Buddha's Day," which commemorates the Buddha's life (see sidebar, opposite). Tibetans also celebrate the key events of the Buddha's career, but on separate occasions at different times of the year. Most significant is the festival of the Buddha's conception, or incarnation, on the fifteenth day of the first lunar month, one of a range of events that mark the Tibetan New Year.

Celebrations may also center on personal relics of the Buddha. At Kandy, Sri Lanka, Buddhists turn out in July or August to witness the procession of what is believed to be one of the Buddha's teeth in a great festival that is more than a thousand years old (see illustration, opposite). Faxian, a ninth-century Chinese pilgrim, wrote one of the earliest eyewitness accounts of this ancient celebration.

There are festivals in many Buddhist countries to honor important Buddhist teachings or scriptures. Theravada devotees celebrate the Buddha's first sermon on the full moon of the eighth lunar month, a date that coincides with the beginning of the monsoon season, when monks go on an annual retreat. In Laos, the story of the generous Prince Vessantara, one of the Buddha's previous incarnations (see p.169), is celebrated annually. Tibet celebrates the *Kalachakra Tantra* (see p.186) every year, and Chinese and Japanese Buddhists have annual festivals in honor of Buddhist *sutras*, most notably the *Lotus Sutra.*

Theravada lands also mark significant events in the history of Buddhism. The beginning of the *samgha*, the Buddhist community, is widely celebrated on the full moon of the third lunar month. Individual countries commemorate the arrival of Buddhism on their own shores, while monasteries honor the date of their foundation.

The end of the monks' annual monsoon retreat is marked by a big, lively festival in which laypeople join the monks and make offerings to provide clothing and other necessities to sustain the monastic community for the coming year.

Rites of passage are as important to Buddhists as they are in other religious traditions. People in Theravada countries observe a series of rituals as a child moves from birth to adulthood. In Myanmar there is a whole string of special childhood rites, including a pregnancy ceremony; a birth ceremony; a head-washing ceremony after the child is born; a naming ceremony; an ear-piercing ceremony for girls; and a hair-tying ceremony for boys. Frequently there is little in such ceremonies that can genuinely be said to owe its origin to Buddhism, although it is not uncommon for Buddhist monks to be present to recite chants or prayers.

The same ambiguity often pertains to "Buddhist" weddings. It is difficult to look to the Buddha himself as an affirmative model of marriage, since he left his wife and family to take up the life of a wandering monk. In southeast Asia, Buddhist monks are often invited to weddings to receive offerings and chant auspicious texts, but the specifically Buddhist element in the ceremonies seems peripheral, if not entirely absent. In China, even for Buddhists, the ritual of marriage is traditionally governed by the indigenous values of filial piety and reverence for ancestors (see p.226). In Japan, traditional weddings, and indeed several other rites of passage, usually take place in a Shinto, rather than Buddhist, context (see p.264).

However, funerals are a different matter. The Buddha's renunciation of his home and earthly comforts was provoked by a vision of old age, sickness, and death, and the rituals surrounding death are decisively linked to Buddhist values. In China, Korea, and Japan, people turn to Buddhist monks and priests to perform their funerals, and family ties with particular temples are often reinforced by yearly acts of offering and remembrance in honor of the deceased. In southeast Asia, funerals frequently last for several days and involve offerings and the chanting of *sutras*. These are intended to bestow extra merit on the deceased for their benefit in the next life.

"BUDDHA'S DAY"

In Sri Lanka and other Theravada countries of southeast Asia, the most important Buddhist festival is "Buddha's Day," or Vishakha Puja, which falls on the day of the full moon in the lunar month of Vishakha (April–May). The festival commemorates the birth, enlightenment, and death of the Buddha.

Devotees mark the occasion by visiting monasteries, venerating shrines or images of the Buddha, and listening to traditional sermons about his life.

Worshippers in Kandy, Sri Lanka, celebrate during the annual festival in which the sacred relic of a tooth allegedly belonging to the Buddha is paraded through the streets.

A wallpainting from the monastery at Taisicho Dzong, Bhutan, depicting the "Wheel of Life"—a visual representation of the cycle of samsara.

THE CYCLE OF REBIRTH

Buddhists have a tradition of reflection on death that began when Siddhartha Gautama viewed the "Four Sights"—a sick man, an old man, a corpse, and an ascetic—that led him to renounce his royal life (see p.169). His vision of renunciation held out the promise that, with moral and spiritual discipline, the problem of death could be overcome.

Traditional Buddhist ideas about death are predicated on the ancient Indian doctrine of *samsara*, variously translated as "reincarnation," "transmigration," or simply "rebirth," but literally meaning "wandering" from one lifetime to another. By the time of the Buddha, Indian religion had come to view existence as cyclical: a person is born, grows old, dies, and is then reborn in another body to begin the process again. Rebirth can be as a human being, deity, ghost, or animal; or else a person may be reborn to punishment in Hell.

The nature of an individual's reincarnation depends on *karma*, or the law of moral retribution. The greater the merit accumulated in the course of a life, the higher the form in which one will be reborn, and the reverse applies to those who acquire more sin than merit. Before they can be reincarnated in a different form, the worst offenders have to eradicate their demerits by suffering in one of the layers of Hell, which are ranked according to the severity of their punishments. The lowest and worst level is reserved for people who have killed their parents or teacher. Just as the inhabitants of Hell can wipe out their sins and be reborn as a human once more, those who rise to divinity can exhaust their merit and slip back into the human realm. No state is permanent.

Traditionally, people endeavor to avoid evil deeds and to accumulate merit through acts of worship or donations to monks, in the hope of receiving a better birth in the next life. But Siddhartha Gautama saw *samsara* as an eternal grind of deaths and potential suffering and set out to break the cycle. His act of liberation, the cessation of rebirth, is known as *nirvana*, literally the "blowing out" of the fire of ignorance and desire, which the Buddha perceived to be the "fuel" of *samsara* and the source of suffering (see p.171). According to Buddhist tradition, the Buddha achieved *nirvana* in two stages. Under the Bodhi Tree, at the moment of his "awakening" (see p.170), he realized that he was no longer fueling *samsara* by performing karmic actions—in other words, all desire in him had ceased. Decades later, at the moment of his death, known as his *parinirvana* or "final (or 'complete') *nirvana*," all the Buddha's residual *karma* was exhausted and he was completely released from *samsara*, never to be reincarnated. With this death, he ceased to exist.

Monks and nuns have attempted to follow the Buddha's example and

ZEN POEMS ON THE THRESHOLD OF DEATH

Japanese Zen Buddhism has a tradition of composing a poem at the moment of death. This poetry often gives powerful expression to the sense of wisdom and detachment that infuses the story of the Buddha's own death. One Zen warrior, forced to commit suicide out of loyalty to his feudal lord, wrote of death as the sharp-edged sword that cut through the void, and compared it to a cool wind blowing in a raging fire. It was as if his own sword were the sword of the Buddha's wisdom that cut through the illusions of life and blew out the fire of existence, just as the Buddha's own *nirvana* had "blown out" the fire of death and rebirth.

achieve the same liberation from rebirth by renouncing their own attachment to the pleasures and responsibilities of lay life and practicing meditation and good moral conduct. For all Buddhists, the way to *nirvana* involves following precepts such as the "Noble Eightfold Path" (see pp.184–5).

Buddhist funerals are intended to assist the deceased into a better birth. Tibetan funerals go a step further, aiming if possible to ensure the person's liberation from *samsara* (see box, below). This practice seems to be directed as much at the living as the dead. It helps mourners to come to terms gradually (over seven weeks) with their loss, and to prepare themselves for their own transition out of this life. (See also pp.156–7.)

THE *BOOK OF THE DEAD*

One of the best-known Buddhist funeral texts is the Tibetan *Book of the Dead.* Over a period of as long as forty-nine days—said to be the length of time it takes for a person to be reborn in another life—a *lama* chants the words of the text, at first in the presence of the corpse and later before a picture of the deceased.

The text describes an array of benevolent and wrathful *buddhas* who will appear to the deceased in the "intermediate realm" (*bar-do*) between death and rebirth, and explains that a person should recognize these forms as nothing but manifestations of his or her own mind. According to the book, it is possible for the deceased to unite with these forms and thereby be liberated from the cycle of death and rebirth. For those who are not successful in uniting with the *buddha* forms, the *Book of the Dead* goes on to explain how to achieve a positive incarnation in the next life.

An 18th-century Tibetan image of the Buddha in parinirvana, *dying never to be reborn. The* Book of the Dead *seeks to help the deceased to attain this state.*

THE "PURE LAND"

The tradition of Pure Land Buddhism, which is found principally in China, Japan, and Tibet, holds that if a believer chants with faith the name of the celestial *buddha* Amitabha (Chinese Amituo; Japanese Amida), the latter will visit the believer at the moment of death, together with a throng of celestial *bodhisattvas*. Amitabha will then convey the devotee to rebirth in Sukhavati, the heavenly "Pure Land," or "Western Paradise" where he reigns. Here, free from earthly distractions, the devotee can prepare for *nirvana*, which is guaranteed to all who attain the Pure Land.

The belief and practice of Pure Land Buddhism, or Amidism, has its roots in the ancient Indian idea that meditation on a particular deity at the moment of death will help ensure rebirth in that deity's celestial domain. Amidism continues to dominate the understanding of death in some of the most popular forms of Japanese Buddhism (see pp.253–4).

His Holiness bsTan-'dzin rGya-mtsho (Tenzin Gyatso), the 14th Dalai Lama, in exile. His spiritual authority remains largely undiminished among Tibetan Buddhists, both at home and abroad.

ROLES AND RELATIONSHIPS

The Buddhist community, or *samgha*, has four traditional divisions: monks, nuns, laymen, and laywomen. The monks and nuns attempt to follow the Buddha's example by renouncing the duties of ordinary lay people and living lives of simplicity. The laity take responsibility for maintaining the fabric of a Buddhist society. They marry and have families; grow crops; accumulate wealth and distribute its benefits; fight wars and maintain order; and do all the things that make it possible for the inhabitants of the monasteries to pursue *nirvana*. The simple divisions of Buddhist society are made more complex, however, by the different roles that exist within the monastic community; by the complexity of occupations and functions within the lay community; and by the shifting relationships that bind the two orders of society, monastic and lay, together.

The monastic community began as a group of wanderers who followed the Buddha as he went through the towns and villages of northern India. As time went on, the monks and nuns adopted a more settled mode of life. The monsoon rains that come to northern India during the months of July and August made roads impassable, and the monastic community adopted the practice of staying in a fixed location during the period of the rains. Out of this practice grew the institution of the monastery (*vihara*), which in time became the central institution in Buddhist life. Supported by the patronage of kings and wealthy donors, the great Indian monasteries became centers of learning, not just in Buddhist philosophy and ritual, but in secular arts such as literature, medicine, and astrology. The Buddhist lands of southeast Asia in particular developed sophisticated monastic traditions that often were closely linked to royal power. Sometimes this link has been quite direct, as in the case of King Mongkut of Thailand (see p.196).

The tradition of Buddhist kingship looks back to Ashoka, a ruler of the Maurya empire in northern India in the third century BCE (see p.172), as the ideal *dharmaraja* or "righteous king." According to tradition, Ashoka converted to Buddhism after a particularly bloody military campaign and attempted to promote a policy of *dharmavijaya*, "righteous conquest," by means of the Dharma rather than by force of arms. Buddhist monarchs have traditionally viewed themselves as "righteous rulers" in the style of Ashoka and have protected the monasteries in return for monastic recognition to legitimate their rule.

The most unusual variant of the institution of Buddhist kingship (see

PERSECUTION IN TIBET

Traditional Buddhist life continued in Tibet much as it had for centuries until 1950, when the newly founded People's Republic invaded the country to enforce its claims to hegemony. The Fourteenth Dalai Lama, bsTan-'dzin rGya-mtsho (Tenzin Gyatso), a youth of sixteen, remained in office but was forced to acknowledge Chinese overlordship.

In 1959 an uprising against Chinese rule provoked harsh intervention and the Dalai Lama fled to India. From this time, the Tibetan monasteries suffered severe persecution and many were destroyed, especially during the Cultural Revolution (1966–76). However, in the 1980s, controls on religious activities were relaxed and monastic life began again in some of the traditional monastic centers.

From exile in India, the Dalai Lama has continued to call for peaceful efforts to preserve Tibet's culture and autonomy. He was awarded the Nobel Peace Prize in 1989. But China has been unreceptive to his appeals and seeks to control Tibetan religious affairs, notably in the selection of its own approved "reincarnations" of such figures as the Panchen Lama and other high-ranking monastic officials.

p.182) occurred in Tibet, where the "Great Fifth" Dalai Lama took advantage of the weakness of his rivals to become the country's full secular *and* religious leader, a position perhaps analogous to that of the papacy before the loss of its temporal realm in the nineteenth century. Tibet was governed by this distinctive combination of monastic and royal leadership until the Chinese invasion in the 1950s (see sidebar, opposite, and p.175).

While respecting the large and socially influential monasteries, Buddhists also retain a reverence for the individual "saint" who retires in solitude or with a small group of companions to seek *nirvana* away from the affairs of society. The forest-saints of Sri Lanka or Thailand are often treated as the great heroes of the tradition and provide an important counterweight to, and critique of, life in the major monasteries and society as a whole. When Dogen, the founder of the Soto Zen sect in Japan (see p.252), rejected the requests of an imperial envoy to involve himself in the life of the Japanese court, and threw the envoy out of his monastery, he was enacting an ancient Buddhist ideal of withdrawal from the affairs of state.

The relationship between monks and ordinary laypeople is best seen in the ancient practice of the morning begging round, still observed in southeast Asia. Each day, monks leave the monastery and go from house to house to beg their food for that day. This simple ritual ties the monks and laity together in a network of mutual support. The monks receive

Young monks line up to receive their morning alms from a Bangkok householder.

A worshipper at Thien Hao pagoda in Ho Chi Minh City (Saigon), Vietnam.

the alms that aid their quest for *nirvana*, and laypeople are offered a daily opportunity to practice generosity and thereby accumulate merit that will lead them to a better rebirth in the next life. This reflects the broader idea of "interdependent causation" taught by the Buddha. According to this, every person has a distinct role to play in the framework of Buddhist society, but all are bound together in a network of mutual dependence.

In the nineteenth and twentieth centuries, the traditional structures of Buddhist society in southeast Asia have been shaken by the challenges of European colonialism, secularism, Communism, and modern science. Under the influence of the modernist and scientific vision of Buddhism developed by the Theosophical Society (see p.175), the Sri Lankan monk Anagarika Dharmapala (1864–1933) led an important movement in the early part of the twentieth century to rationalize Buddhist practice, strip away "superstitious" aspects, and mobilize the Buddhist community in a struggle against British colonial rule. Since Sri Lanka (as Ceylon) gained independence in 1948, Buddhist institutions have flourished there, but not without struggle. Ethnic violence between Buddhist Sinhalese and Hindu Tamils has introduced an element of religious conflict into modern Sri Lankan society that seems difficult to reconcile with the image of Buddhist tolerance and peace.

Myanmar is particularly notable for its distinctive vision of the active relationship between Buddhism and politics. After independence (as Burma) from Britain in 1948, the first prime minister, U Nu (1907–95), promulgated a program of reform referred to as "Buddhist Socialism." U Nu said that a true socialist state should promote equality, discourage acquisitive instincts, and provide enough leisure so that the people may

REFORM IN THAILAND

Of all the Buddhist royal lineages, that of Thailand (formerly Siam) has survived most vigorously into the twentieth century. Spared the difficulties of European colonial rule, Thailand charted its own distinctive route into the modern world under the guidance of its monarchs. King Mongkut (1804–68) spent twenty-five years as a monk before assuming the throne, in which period he became a supporter of a reformist branch of Buddhism known in Thai as Thammayut (from Pali Dhamma-yuttika, "Those who adhere to the Dharma"). As king (from 1851), he continued to support the Thammayut reform program, characterized by efforts to modernize and tighten the discipline of the Thai monastic community.

Mongkut's son Chulalongkorn (ruled 1868–1910) continued his father's policy of promoting a form of Buddhism consistent with modern Western science (Chulalongkorn is the bicycling monarch depicted in the musical *The King and I*). To this day, the Thai king continues to play a central role in his country's political and religious life.

devote time to meditation and the pursuit of *nirvana*. Ousted by the military in 1962, U Nu lived in exile in India for a number of years before returning to Myanmar in 1980 and becoming a Buddhist monk.

More recently, Aung San Suu Kyi has brought Buddhist principles to bear in a campaign to restore Burmese democracy (see box, below). As her career demonstrates, it is possible for women to play an important role in the political life of the modern Buddhist countries of southeast Asia. But traditional ideas of male dominance are still deeply rooted in the culture of this and other regions.

Outside Tibet, Buddhism has also faced the challenges of living under secularizing Communist regimes in Indochina, where the degree of religious oppression has varied considerably. In Vietnam, for example, Buddhist institutions have remained fairly active, but in Cambodia they suffered massively from the devastation wrought nationally by the Khmer Rouge government of 1975–79 and are still recovering.

The twentieth century has also seen an attempt to revive Buddhism in its homeland of India as part of a critique of the traditional caste system. Dr. Bhimrao Ramji Ambedkar (1891–1956), an "Untouchable" from the Indian state of Maharashtra, saw in Buddhism an ideal of equality and social justice that could relieve the oppression of the disadvantaged castes in Indian society (see p.159). He created an important social movement based on Buddhist principles that continues to play a role in Indian religious life and politics.

AUNG SAN SUU KYI

Modern Myanmar (formerly Burma) provides one of the most celebrated examples of a woman bringing Buddhist religious values to bear on secular affairs. In July 1988, the Burmese ruler General Ne Win, head of the Myanmar Socialist Programme Party, held a national referendum on Myanmar's political future. Popular opposition to the authoritarian military rule crystallized around the figure of Aung San Suu Kyi. Her father, Aung San, was a colleague of U Nu (see main text) and had led the movement for national independence until his assassination in 1947.

Aung San Suu Kyi's political writings, gathered in a collection called *Freedom From Fear*, speak eloquently of a modern quest for democracy and human rights and of the traditional Buddhist values of truth, fearlessness, righteousness, and loving kindness. In recognition of her campaign for peaceful democratic reforms, she was awarded the Nobel Peace Prize in 1991.

Aung San Suu Kyi and supporters at a press conference at the gate of her home in Yangon (Rangoon), from where—under a state of effective house arrest— she headed the movement for democratic reform in Myanmar.

Chapter Six

CHINESE TRADITIONS

Jennifer Oldstone-Moore

An 18th-century depiction of students sitting an examination to qualify as civil servants. The test required a thorough grounding in the Confucian precepts that formed the basis of Chinese government for two millennia.

OPPOSITE *Pilgrims climb to the temple on Taishan (Mount Tai, or the "Great Mountain"), a peak of central importance to Chinese religion since ancient times. It is one of many sacred mountains in China* *(see map on p.201).*

INTRODUCTION

The three formal traditions of Confucianism, Daoism, and Buddhism, as well as the pervasive popular religion, have shaped Chinese culture and history for millennia and remain an important aspect of Chinese civilization. The traditional religions thrive in Taiwan and Hong Kong as well as in Singapore and other overseas Chinese communities. Hong Kong aside, they have a more muted presence in the People's Republic, where practices persist in the face of official discouragement and occasional persecution.

China's religious traditions rest on two fundamental principles: the cosmos is a sacred place; and all aspects of it are interrelated. The central purpose of Chinese religion is to uphold this sacredness by maintaining harmony among human beings and between humanity and nature. This is reflected in the indigenous formal traditions of Daoism and Confucianism, as well as in the popular religion. Buddhism, introduced from India, also came to accommodate the Chinese perspective.

The main octagonal motif on this child's hat depicts the circular yin-yang *symbol surrounded by the eight trigrams used in traditional divination (see sidebar, p.213).*

Buddhism has proved by far the most successful of the international religions to have entered China, although Islam has also had an impact, notably in the west (see illustration, p.119). But elsewhere in China neither Islam nor Christianity has had a significant impact, partly at least because the exclusivity of both faiths sits uncomfortably with the strongly syncretic nature of Chinese religious practice. Confucianism, Daoism, and Buddhism, which are known as the "Three Teachings," are seen as complementary rather than exclusive, and a person will usually practice all three simultaneously. While the traditions have their own distinctive histories and specialists, for most Chinese the saying "the Three Teachings merge into One" holds true.

Traditional Chinese religion is underlain by an ancient understanding of how the cosmos functions. According to this, everything that exists, including Heaven, Earth, human beings, and deities, is made up of the same vital substance, or *qi* (*ch'i*: see note on transliterations, opposite). *Qi* is manifested most basically as two complementary forces, *yin* and *yang*. These terms originally signified the shady side of a hill (*yin*) and the sunny side (*yang*), but very early on they came to be used more symbolically. Thus *yin* denotes that which is dark, moist, inert, turbid, cold, soft, and feminine, and the complementary *yang* denotes that which is bright, dry, growing, light, warm, hard, and masculine. All things consist of both *yin* and *yang* in varying proportions.

The *yin-yang* view of the cosmos functions in conjunction with the cycle of the "Five Phases," which furnishes a more detailed structure for understanding how vital forces interact. The phases are represented by "fire," "wood," "metal," "water," and "earth," but rather than concrete

SACRED CHINA

The Chinese religious landscape is characterized by sacred mountains and temples. Some locations have been considered holy since ancient times, such as the Five Sacred Peaks (Taishan, Hengshan [north], Songshan, Huashan, and Hengshan [south]); others became sacred as religious leaders and schools emerged and became identified with a particular peak (such as Mount Tiantai [Tiantaishan], the home of the eponymous Buddhist sect, and Putuoshan, a mountain sacred to the Buddhist deity Guanyin).

Wherever the traditional religion is practiced, from the tiniest village to the capital, there are a multitude of temples. In the People's Republic, important temples are given official sanction largely on account of their value as tourist attractions, although there is also religious activity.

Other sites of special religious interest shown on the map include Anyang (the site of many oracle bone discoveries); Qufu (the birthplace of Confucius); and Chang'an (the Tang dynasty capital, where many Buddhist scriptures were first translated into Chinese and where China's first Christian community was established in the seventh century CE).

[Note: Throughout this chapter and elsewhere the modern pinyin romanization of Chinese words is used. For certain terms that remain familiar in the older Wade-Giles transliteration, the latter is also given in parentheses.]

Key

- Site of special religious significance
- Other site
- Sacred mountain
- Historical routes of the silk trade
- Other transmission routes of Buddhism to and from China
- Great Wall

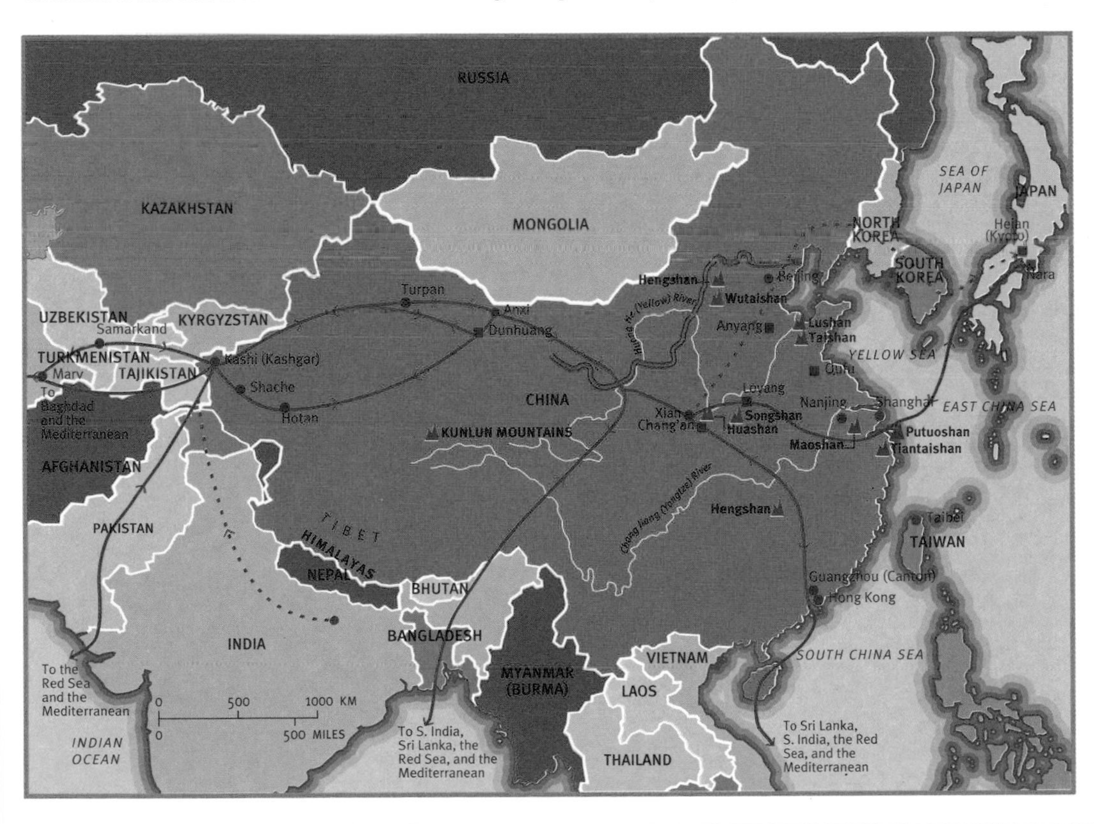

elements these are to be understood as metaphysical forces, each exercising a dominating influence at any one time. The phases reflect the *yin-yang* system (fire and wood are *yang*; metal and water are *yin*; earth is neutral) and are ordered in two cycles. In the first sequence (wood, fire, earth, metal, water), each phase is said to produce the next. In the second cycle (fire, water, earth, wood, metal), each element destroys its predecessor. Everything in the universe—the changes and patterns in nature, the heavenly bodies, time, natural phenomena, and human society—is linked by its participation in these cycles of transformation as well as by its varying proportions of *yin* and *yang*. The relationship between each of the Five Phases is paralleled in countless other pentads (groups of five) that express the nature and interaction of Heaven, Earth, and human beings. These include the directions (north, east, south, west, center), deities, animals, numbers, planets, seasons, and colors.

The major spiritual traditions express, in various ways, the ideal of furthering cosmic harmony. Confucianism, based on the teachings of a sixth-century BCE sage, Master Kong (Kong Fuzi, latinized in the West as "Confucius"), focuses on the relationships between people and the creation of a harmonious society founded on virtue. The pivotal virtue is *ren* ("benevolence," "humaneness," or "humanity"). According to Confucius, the primary relationship is that between parent and child, specifically between father and son, ideally characterized by the virtue of *xiao*, filial piety. Through the maintenance of this bond the family, community,

CHRONOLOGY

LEGENDARY PERIOD *(all dates traditional)*

The "Culture Heroes"

2852BCE • Fu Xi
2737BCE • Shen Nong
2697BCE • Huang Di

The "Sage Kings" and Xia Dynasty

2357BCE • Yao
2255BCE • Shun
2205BCE • Yu (founder of Xia dynasty)
2205–1766BCE • Xia dynasty

HISTORICAL PERIOD

Shang Dynasty (ca. 1766–1050BCE)
- Divination; ancestor worship and worship of the "Lord on High" (Shang Di)

Zhou Dynasty (1050–256BCE)
- Worship of Heaven (Tian); idea of Mandate of Heaven formulated; Chinese Classics written; "100 Schools" founded by Confucius (551–479BCE), Mencius (371–?289BCE), Laozi (?b.604BCE), and others; *qi* and *yin-yang* theories articulated; shamanism practiced

Qin Dynasty (221–207BCE)
- Emperor Qin Shihuangdi persecutes scholars

Han Dynasty (206BCE–220CE)
- Confucianism becomes basis for state religion; Buddhism enters China; popular religious movements emerge, such as "Yellow Turbans" and "Celestial Masters"

Era of Division (220–589CE)
- Religious Daoism emerges; Buddhism well established

Sui Dynasty (581–618CE)

Tang Dynasty (618–907CE)
- Buddhism, Daoism ascendant (but Buddhists persecuted, 841–5); Pure Land and Chan Buddhism develop; Nestorian Christian church founded 635CE; Islam arrives (8th century); Judaism, Manicheism, Zoroastrianism present

"Five Dynasties" (907–970)

Song Dynasty (960–1279)
- Rise of Neo-Confucianism; formation of Buddhist devotional societies; popular religion develops

Yuan Dynasty (1276–1386)
- Mongols rule China

Ming Dynasty (1368–1644)
- Neo-Confucian Wang Yangming (1472–1529); Catholic missionaries arrive (16th century)

Qing Dynasty (1644–1911)
- Christianity suppressed early in dynasty; in 19th century, China is "opened" by Western powers and Christian missions return

MODERN PERIOD

Republic of China (1911–49; 1911–present on Taiwan)
- Traditional religions flourish; some Christian missionary activity

People's Republic of China (1949–present)
- Atheistic state ideology suppresses religious activities; cult of Mao Zedong; persecution of religions during Cultural Revolution (1966–76); some easing of restrictions on religious activity following death of Mao in 1976

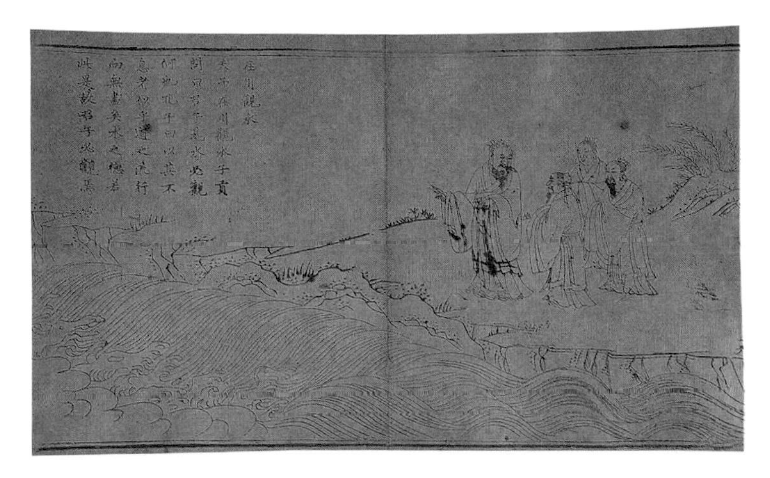

Confucius with a group of followers. An illustration from an anonymous 16th-century work, the Book of the Life of Confucius.

state, and ultimately the cosmos would be transformed (see pp.216–7).

Daoism (Taoism), traditionally said to date from the sixth century BCE but primarily based on works of the fourth and third centuries BCE, is less concerned with interpersonal harmony than on concord between human beings and nature. The term Dao ("Way") signifies the natural pattern underlying all cosmic change and transformation, the way in which *qi* is endlessly created and dissolved to form the myriad phenomena of the universe. Daoism is centered on the concept of *wu wei*, "noninterference" with the Dao. To achieve order and harmony in one's own life and in the cosmos, a person must learn to perceive the Dao in nature and to act—or refrain from acting—in accordance with it. Over time, the idea of strengthening oneself through attunement with natural forces was applied to the preservation of the human body through the quest for longevity.

Buddhism arrived in the first century CE and soon attracted many adherents. It brought with it the allure of the foreign and exotic, a fascinating and complex Indian cosmology, and the promise of universal salvation—ideas not present or relatively undeveloped in the indigenous traditions. But Buddhism in China also developed distinct forms, seen most notably in the fusion of Daoism and Buddhism that produced the Chinese Buddhist school of Chan ("Meditation"; see p.219).

Chinese religions are often characterized as this-worldly and practically oriented, and this is certainly evident in the popular tradition. It reflects the major concerns of the Three Teachings, but has no systematic set of beliefs and focuses on improving this life by securing health, long life, prosperity, domestic harmony, children to continue the family line, and protection from disasters. A reciprocal relationship between the living and the spirits (ancestors, deities, and ghosts) is central to popular practice. It is assumed that if humans play their part, the spiritual world will respond in kind, granting blessings or—in the case of ghosts—doing no harm.

The head of the Buddha, part of a massive statue carved into a rock face at Leshan in Sichuan province. While it enhanced the native Chinese traditions, Buddhism in China was greatly changed from its south Asian form. As at Leshan, this sinicization is also evident in Chinese Buddhist art.

A WEALTH OF TRADITIONS

Many core beliefs and themes of Chinese religion were present as early as the Shang and Zhou dynasties (eighteenth to third centuries BCE), and form a common basis for Confucianism, Daoism, Buddhism, and the popular tradition. Reverence for ancestors became marked during the Shang era, and the dead were buried with sumptuous grave offerings. People used "oracle bones" for divination (see box, below). A high god, Shang Di ("Lord on High"), was occasionally invoked, but was perceived to be remote from humanity and during the Zhou dynasty came to be replaced by Tian ("Heaven"), which presided over the spirits of the dead. As the worship of Tian developed, it was considered to bestow the "Mandate of Heaven" on the person or dynasty deemed worthy to rule. Tian's displeasure with a ruler was manifested in disorder, such as rebellion, famine, and natural disasters. If conditions became intolerable, Tian was deemed to have withdrawn its Mandate and the ruler could legitimately be deposed.

The Chinese cosmological system of *qi*, *yin-yang*, and the Five Elements (see pp.200–203) was also established during the Zhou dynasty. In the same period, various practices, arts, literary works, and exemplary deeds were distilled into the Six Classics, which were to become foundational texts for Confucianism (see pp.212–13).

ORACLE BONES

Divination with "oracle bones" was an important practice during the Shang dynasty. The royal house employed it to receive guidance on a range of concerns, from forecasting the weather and determining the cause of a toothache to the right time to wage war, the likelihood of success in hunting, and the abundance of the harvest. Many oracle bones have been discovered at Anyang in northeast China (see map, p.201).

Bones were used to respond to questions requiring a simple "yes" or "no" answer, which were posed to supernatural beings—usually ancestors, who were considered a source of blessing or misfortune, particularly concerning the fertility of humans. Questions might sometimes also be put to the high god Shang Di, as well as to natural forces.

As a question was intoned, a heated rod was placed on the scapula (shoulderblade) of an ox or sheep or the shell of a turtle. A diviner would interpret the cracks made by the hot rod to reveal the answer to the question.

An "oracle bone," part of a sheep's scapula. The question and its answer are inscribed on the bone, as was common practice.

By the sixth century BCE, the political authority of the Zhou rulers had declined, and the ensuing period of disorder saw the formulation of numerous theories of government aimed at restoring harmony and peace. The many teachings that arose in this period are collectively known as the "Hundred Schools," of which Confucianism and Daoism are the most famous. Born in 551BCE at Qufu in modern Shandong province, Confucius (Kong Fuzi) came from a poor but respectable family. After serving in the government of the state of Lu, he spent thirteen years traveling the various Chinese states and asking their rulers to put into practice his ideas about government. He returned home disappointed and spent the rest of his days, until his death in 479BCE, teaching students and editing the Six Classics.

The three towering figures in China's religious and philosophical traditions are brought together in this 18th-century painting. Laozi (left) looks on as Confucius cradles the infant Buddha.

Basically, Confucius asserted that government must be founded on virtue, and that all citizens must be attentive to the duties of their position. His great follower, Mencius (Mengzi, 371–?289BCE), elaborated Confucius' teachings about human virtue and good government, proclaiming the original goodness of human nature and the right of the people to rebel against a wicked ruler. The third great Confucian thinker of ancient times, Xunzi (active ca. 298–238BCE), offered a very different view of human nature. He claimed that humans were originally evil and become good only through strict laws and harsh punishments. Xunzi's views were taken to extremes by the "Legalists," who formed another of the "Hundred Schools." They have been reviled in Chinese history for their role in the brutal reign of the first emperor of all China, Qin Shihuangdi (221–209BCE), whose rule was characterized by mass book-burnings and the execution of many Confucian scholars.

The Han dynasty (206BCE–220CE) witnessed a synthesis of Confucianism, Legalism, and *yin-yang* cosmology. But the era was most notable for the formation of the Chinese imperial bureaucratic system that ran the country until the twentieth century with men trained in Confucian virtues.

Over the following centuries, the popularity of Daoism and Buddhism sapped the vitality of Confucianism, but the Song dynasty (960–1279CE) saw a revival known as Neo-Confucianism. The most renowned scholar of this period, Zhu Xi (1130–1200CE), propounded a metaphysical system based on Confucian morality. He posited that all things, including human nature, have an ordering principle, *li* (not the same word as *li* meaning "ritual"), that shapes the vital material called *qi* (see p.200). Humans must "investigate things" to understand their underlying principles, and cultivate themselves so as to base their actions on the appropriate principles of human behavior. The Neo-Confucian advocacy of "quiet sitting" (meditation) as a technique of self-cultivation reflects Buddhist influence.

Tradition holds that Laozi, the legendary founder of Daoism, was born in 604BCE after a miraculous gestation and birth. He served in the imperial bureaucracy and promoted a *laissez-faire* theory of government,

A portrait of Matteo Ricci (1552–1610). The Italian missionary had a phenomenal memory and during his stay in China impressed the imperial court by reciting long passages of classical Chinese.

but became disillusioned and retired to the mountains. However, on the way, a guard at the western pass begged him to write down his teachings. The result was Daoism's foundational text, the *Dao De Jing*. There are two distinct Daoist traditions, "philosophical" Daoism and "religious" Daoism. Philosophical Daoism, represented by Laozi and Zhuangzi (fourth century BCE), is concerned with perceiving and following the *Dao*, the force and pattern behind the natural order. Zhuangzi asserted that peace and harmony are the natural state of things until humans interfere, and that one should see the relativity of all values and points of view.

Religious Daoism began in the second century CE with such movements as the "Yellow Turbans" and "Celestial Masters" (also known as the "Way of Five Bushels of Rice"). These groups combined ancient practices and beliefs, such as the pursuit of long life, with their own scriptures, divinities, rituals, and, quite often, millenarian expectations, which were perceived as a threat by the government. Over time, religious Daoism developed a canon of revealed scripture, a pantheon of divinities, a literate priesthood, and established rituals.

Buddhism has been part of the Chinese religious landscape since the first century CE. In its heyday in China (third–ninth centuries CE), it held out the prospect of universal salvation in a time of political instability, and offered an intricate and colorful view of the afterlife. Buddhism proved to be highly adaptable, the most successful schools being those most attuned to Chinese sensibilities. Tiantai Buddhism, by organizing the range of Buddhist teachings into levels of relative truth, appealed to the Chinese inclination to harmonize and accommodate divergent points of view. "Pure Land" Buddhism had a broad popular appeal and met the needs of uncertain times in its devotionalism and promise of a happy rebirth (see p.193). The critique of language and rational discourse that characterized the Meditation school, or Chan, resonated with philosophical Daoism, which shared its goal of understanding the true nature of reality, even if that reality was differently described. (Tiantai, "Pure Land," and Chan were all to exercise great influence on the Buddhism of Japan; see pp.252–3.)

However, Buddhism has always been identified as a "foreign" religion and has suffered several persecutions. After the worst (841–5CE), when thousands of monasteries were closed, Buddhism remained an important force in Chinese religious life, but never regained its former stature. Of the numerous schools, only "Pure Land" and Chan continued to thrive.

The basic structure of the Chinese popular tradition was in place by 1000CE. It includes many ancient indigenous practices, such as shamanism (see sidebar, opposite), divination, and veneration of ancestors. It has also incorporated Buddhist ideas of *karma* and rebirth, and its cosmologies of heavens and hells, *buddha*s, and *bodhisattva*s, together with the Daoist hierarchy of deities. Confucians have scorned popular religious

THE JESUITS IN CHINA

The Jesuit mission to China in the sixteenth century was the first attempt by Europeans to seek to understand Chinese religions from the inside. A leading figure in the mission was Matteo Ricci (see illustration, above), who landed in Macao in 1582. In order to win approval from Confucian officials, and thereby gain access to the emperor, Ricci and his colleagues learned Chinese and adopted the dress, manners, and learning of the educated élite.

The Jesuits favored accommodation of Confucian rituals with Christianity, for example permitting the veneration of ancestors, but as an act of remembrance rather than worship. Ricci believed that the ancient Chinese had worshipped the one God in the form of Shang Di (see p.204), but that subsequent religious degeneration had eroded their original monotheism. However, despite the missionaries' acculturation and readiness to be accommodating, the Chinese found the religion of the West far less compelling than they did Western astronomy, mathematics, and machines.

practices, while the role of Buddhist and Daoist priests is to conduct rituals rather than explain doctrine to the masses. They are brought in to perform particular ceremonies at temples run by neighborhood organizations and are not permanently affiliated to temples of the popular religion.

Chinese religious traditions have faced tremendous challenges in the last two centuries arising from both cultural and military encounters with the West. The traditions have been seen by intellectuals and governments as the cause of Chinese weakness, and as "unmodern" in comparison to Western science and rationalism. This attitude is reinforced in the official policies of the Communist regime, and it is difficult to assess the strength of traditional religion on the mainland today. However, it is observable that whenever government pressure eases, religious practices are very quick to reappear.

SHAMANS

Shamans are a vehicle for communication with the spirits: in a trance, the shaman has the experience of leaving the body and traveling to the spirit world. In ancient China, shamans took part in sacrificial rituals at court and served as channels of sacred power, invoking the gods and goddesses, pleading for rain, healing, and exorcising demons. Their official role had ceased by ca. 400CE, but in the popular religion shamans still act as mediums, healers, exorcists, and dream interpreters.

THE CAVES OF DUNHUANG

A group of artificial caves in the remote northwest of China provide remarkable evidence of the early flowering of Buddhism in China and its transformation from an Indian to a Chinese context. Dunhuang was an outpost for Chinese pilgrims and merchants on the Silk Road that linked China to India, the Middle East, and Europe (see map, p.201). The road brought Buddhism to China, and it was the way taken by Chinese pilgrims to India in search of scripture, such as the monk Xuanzang (see p.217).

From the fourth to the fourteenth centuries CE, pilgrims carved the "Caves of a Thousand Buddhas" into the soft stone of a sheer cliff at Dunhuang. Temples, shrines, and lodgings were hewn from the rocks, and their walls were adorned with colorful murals. The iconography at Dunhuang illustrates how Indian Buddhism transmuted into Chinese Buddhism over the centuries as Chinese themes were incorporated.

The caves included a library of many thousands of precious manuscripts of Buddhist literature (see illustration, p.213). The library was sealed shut in the eleventh century for protection against raiders and thus remained intact until it was reopened in 1900.

The caves at Dunhuang, northwest China. Their remoteness ensured that they remained untouched by various eruptions of anti-Buddhist sentiment in China, including the persecution of 841–5CE and, more recently, the Cultural Revolution.

An early 20th-century print of the Kitchen God surrounded by his divine family.

ZAO JUN, THE KITCHEN GOD

The kitchen area of the home is the defining object of the family unit, for related families may share an altar but never a stove. Just as Tudi Gong is the god of the neighborhood (see main text), so Zao Jun, the Kitchen God, is the god of the family, and its link with the celestial bureaucracy. On the 23rd or 24th of the last month of the year, Zao Jun is sent off to Heaven—an image or effigy of the god is burnt—to make an annual report on the family to the Jade Emperor (see main text). Before he goes, the family feeds him treats made of sweet, sticky ingredients so that he will have only sweet things to say about the family—or so that his lips will be glued shut and his words rendered incomprehensible.

THE CELESTIAL EMPIRE

The Chinese preoccupation with the divine takes two main forms. On the one hand there is a wide range of active deities and spiritual beings, many of which are venerated at shrines and temples. On the other, much religious activity focuses on ordering principles—cosmic forces and concepts of ultimate reality—that are the subject of contemplation rather than worship. For most people, contact with the divine takes the form of acts of worship and offerings to those gods and goddesses who may help them with everyday matters or provide protection from danger. However, philosophical Daoists, Confucians, and Buddhists of intellectually-oriented sects such as Chan, concentrate on the pursuit of insight and enlightenment rather than on worship or supplication.

Chinese deities are ranked in a celestial bureaucracy that is modeled on the bureaucracy of imperial China. The pantheon embraces Daoist figures, *buddhas* and *bodhisattvas*, and a host of personalities from Chinese folklore and legend. Each deity has a specific function, and a supplicant chooses the appropriate one for a particular need. There are different divinities to heal particular illnesses, grant offspring to the childless, protect soldiers or sailors, and bring fortune and good luck to a community. One may appeal to gods and goddesses to assist ancestors or to control dangerous and disorderly ghosts.

High-ranking deities have authority over those in the earthly bureaucracy who are of equivalent rank to their own celestial juniors, and vice versa. Depending on their performance, deities, like mortal civil servants, may be promoted or demoted. Those who do not carry out their duties properly may be punished by their superiors in the celestial bureaucracy, or by human officials who outrank them. For example, a god who fails to bring rain during a drought may be removed from a temple and left in the sun to see how he likes being hot and dry. Those who give exemplary service will be rewarded with promotion.

The lowest official in the celestial bureaucracy is one's local god, Tudi Gong, the "God of the Earth." Every neighborhood or village has its own Tudi Gong, who is likened to a village policeman or magistrate. It is his job to keep the peace, to quell local ghosts who cause trouble, and to be aware of what goes on in the area. Residents of small villages might report incidents and important events such as births, deaths, and marriages both to Tudi Gong and to the local (mortal) police station. Tudi Gong passes on any relevant happenings to his superior in the celestial hierarchy.

Tudi Gong resides in a small shrine where people can make frequent simple offerings on the second and sixteenth days of each lunar month (that is, just after the new and full moons), and perhaps a daily offering of incense. More elaborate offerings are made on the god's birthday, which falls on the second day of the second lunar month.

At the top of the hierarchy of Heaven is the high god known as the Jade Emperor, a figure of uncertain origin whose cult appeared in the ninth century CE and was fully developed by the tenth century. He is the supreme judge and sovereign of Heaven, the overseer of the administrative hierarchy, who authorizes the promotion and demotion of his infe-

MAZU, THE EMPRESS OF HEAVEN

Mazu, or Tian Hou (Empress of Heaven), is one of the most popular deities of southern China and Taiwan. Her story illustrates important aspects of the Chinese pantheon: the human origin of the gods; their particular function and appeal; and the way in which they are promoted for merit.

According to legend, Mazu was born with auspicious portents in the eleventh century to a family of fisherfolk in Fujian Province in south China. The child Mazu displayed supernatural powers. One day, knowing that her father and two brothers were in danger in a storm at sea, her soul left her body to rush to their aid and began to pull their two boats to shore. But her mother found the apparently lifeless body of Mazu and, terrified, shook her arm, causing the soul to release her father's boat. Her brothers returned home, weeping that their father had nearly been saved, but then was lost; they also reported seeing Mazu's shape on the waves.

After Mazu died at the age of twenty-eight, local boats began to carry an image of her for protection at sea. After two centuries of popular veneration, she was officially recognized as a goddess and was subsequently promoted in the celestial hierarchy. Finally, in the seventeenth century, Mazu became Empress of Heaven, a consort of the Jade Emperor (see pp.209–10).

A ceremony at a temple of Mazu in northern Taiwan. The goddess remains a patron of those who make a living at sea.

THE GOURD OF CHAOS

In philosophical Daoism, the Absolute is represented by the original state of primal perfection, the time of chaos and of boundless potential. The symbolic story of Hundun, the "cosmic gourd," describes the destruction of that paradisial state, when what was natural and spontaneous became prescribed and defined.

Hundun ("Chaos"), the king of the Center, had none of the seven apertures of other living creatures. His generosity to King Fast of the North and King Furious of the South was spontaneous and natural, and this troubled them. They fretted about how they would keep face if they failed to repay Hundun's kindness. Finally, they decided to bore seven holes into Hundun, to give him the orifices that all other people have. Fast and Furious therefore paid him a visit, and each day bored a hole into Hundun. But on the seventh day Hundun died.

In the story, Hundun is envisaged as a faceless, lumpy gourd, an irregularly-shaped container of seeds that symbolizes the creative potential of chaos. This is in contrast to Fast and Furious, who, rather than accepting Hundun's gifts with the joy and spontaneity with which they were given, were obsessed with rules and protocol. They assumed, wrongly, that Hundun would appreciate the social "face" by which they allowed themselves to be defined and restricted, and thus brought about the death of creative spontaneity. In the Daoist view, the two kings acted contrary to the Dao.

An 18th-century lacquer vase adorned with lapiz lazuli, jade, and other stones and made in the shape of a gourd. The vegetable has long been associated with Daoism; Daoist immortals are often shown with a gourd full of potent herbs.

riors. He wears the robes and headdress of the old Chinese emperors. There are some temples for the Jade Emperor, but not many—for the average person, as well as for lowly gods such as Tudi Gong, the Jade Emperor is a remote figure and it is possible to communicate with him only through intermediaries.

Apart from the fact that they dwell in Heaven, deities differ from humans mainly in terms of power and function. Humans who live exemplary lives are appointed to the celestial hierarchy after death as a reward, as, for example, in the case of Mazu (see p.209). The life stories and personalities of the gods and goddesses are well known through Chinese operas and folktales, and from communication via spirit mediums. A deity's birthday is an important celebration.

The relationship between worshipper and deity is based on reciprocity. It is understood that when a god or goddess is offered incense, money, and food, the deity has a certain obligation to respond. However, Chinese deities are not omnipotent, not even the Jade Emperor, and there is a limit to what can be requested or given. Requests must go through the proper channels: an ordinary person cannot petition the

Jade Emperor directly, any more than a commoner in imperial China could petition the emperor.

While the Jade Emperor is at the apex of the celestial hierarchy, he is only the mouthpiece for a trinity of primordial Daoist beings known as the Three Pure Ones. Although they may be represented on the temple altar, they are rarely worshipped. The Three Pure Ones stand for the undifferentiated, abstracted power of the Dao. They are remote cosmic powers who are not asked for favors, but are invoked by Daoist priests in liturgies of cosmic renewal.

In Confucian thought, the expression of the Ultimate is "Heaven" itself (Tian). Before Confucius, in the Shang and Zhou dynasties, the high gods called the Lord on High (Shang Di) and Tian (see p.204) were thought of in anthropomorphic terms, but were rarely approached in divination, being considered too distant. Confucius' understanding of Heaven was somewhat different: he spoke of it as the moral order that underpins the cosmos. He was convinced that, while he personally was not successful in his mission to make virtue the basis for ruling, he was doing the will of Heaven, which was manifest in the celestial Mandate bestowed upon or withdrawn from the terrestrial emperor (see p.204). In imperial China, only the emperor, who was known as the Son of Heaven, was permitted to perform acts of worship to Heaven. This demonstrated his authority under the Mandate, which gave the emperor a pivotal role as mediator between Heaven and Earth.

The mystical naturalism of philosophical Daoism is not concerned with virtue and morality, but rather the movement and creation of all things in accordance with the Dao, the "Way" of nature and cosmos. It is the source and pattern for all things which are formed from, and dissolve into, the primal vital material, or *qi* (see p.200). Daoists express reverence for the infinite subtlety and scope of the Dao, which permeates all things. The Dao is silent and imperceptible, impartial and all-encompassing. But it is not divine, and therefore cannot be worshipped as Heaven and the deities can.

Mahayana Buddhism, the tradition that took root in China, recognizes a number of revered savior figures known as celestial *buddhas* (in Chinese, *Fo*) and *bodhisattvas* (in Chinese, *pusa*), who can bestow blessings on human beings from their heavenly realms (see pp.176–7). Although not originally considered to be divine in nature, a number of these figures have become enshrined in the popular Chinese pantheon, such as the historical Buddha (Shakyamuni, Chinese Shijiamouni), Amitabha Buddha (Amituo/Emituo Fo), Maitreya (Mile Fo), and Avalokiteshvara (Guanyin), a male *pusa* who has metamorphosed into the popular Chinese goddess of mercy (see sidebar, above right).

GUANYIN THE MERCIFUL

The Buddhist *bodhisattva* Guanyin ("Hearer of Cries") is the goddess of mercy and one of the most beloved and frequently approached figures in Chinese popular religion. She has various aspects. In particular, Guanyin is the special guardian of women and children, and the goddess to whom women pray for offspring: she is often depicted holding a baby. She is commonly portrayed either as a *bodhisattva* with a thousand eyes and arms (symbolizing her unbounded ability to look favorably on her devotees and dispense compassion); or as a slender figure in a white robe holding a willow branch and a vase of nectar, symbols of heavenly benevolence. (See also pp.177, 248.)

A large wooden figure of Guanyin of the Ming dynasty (1368–1644) or earlier.

THE *DAO DE JING*

The *Dao De Jing*, attributed to Daoism's founder, Laozi, advocates finding one's place in nature and learning to practice *wu wei* (see p.203) in order to create a harmonious life. In abbreviated, mystical language, he extols the strength of the apparently weak, such as the water that can conquer stone drop by drop. The *Dao De Jing* paradoxically asserts that words and names are not to be trusted, and are impediments to gaining insight into the nature of the Dao. In the Daoist view, words are simply a convenient means to indicate something which is in constant flux and unnameable.

WORDS OF THE SAGES

Sacred scripture in the formal Chinese religious traditions is made up primarily of writings that are not considered to represent the word of the divine. Rather, numerous ancient texts of central importance have acquired canonical status for one or more, or all, of the main traditions. At the center of these stand the Confucian scriptures. Although until recently only a small percentage of Chinese have been literate, the ideas and values embodied in the Confucian canon have been so influential that they are an intimate part of the cultural identity of the Chinese people. They were the basis of China's civil service examinations—and hence government—for two millennia. The scholar-officials who ran the empire applied lessons gleaned from the works of the canon to contemporary problems.

The overarching concern of the Confucian canon, which consists of the "Six Classics" and "Four Books," is harmony in the social order. Confucius saw himself not as a creator, but as a mediator of the wisdom of the sage kings of antiquity. For him, this wisdom was accessible primarily through the study of six classic texts: the *Book of Changes* (*Yi Jing*; see sidebar, opposite), the *Classic of History*, the *Classic of Poetry*, the *Spring and Autumn Annals*, the *Book of Rites*, and the lost *Classic of Music*. Traditionally, Confucius is credited with writing the *Spring and Autumn Annals* and a commentary on the *Yi Jing*, and editing the other texts. According to modern scholarship, these texts were compiled throughout the Zhou dynasty (1050BCE–256CE), the *Classic of History* perhaps even earlier. Confucius drew moral lessons and examples of good government from the *Classic of History* and the *Annals*. He also asserted that to be a cultivated, "superior person," one must be steeped in music, poetry, cosmology, divination, and etiquette, as presented in the other classics.

Confucius' own prescriptions for an ideal society are preserved in the *Analects*, a record of his sayings recorded by his students. In it, he demonstrates how the rites (*li*) of early Chinese rulers—from state ceremonies to etiquette—provide a template for effortless and appropriate human interaction. The remaining three books, the *Mencius*, the *Great Learning*, and the *Doctrine of the Mean*, also describe ways to achieve virtuous government and a harmonious society. All of these Confucian texts are written in the terse, refined language of classical Chinese, which has given rise to a tradition of commentary to elucidate their meaning.

Ink-stamps of individual maxims from Confucius' Analects *have been popular since ancient times and constitute a minor artistic genre. This one reads: "Be courteous, magnanimous, sincere, diligent, and clement."*

The foundational texts of Daoism, the *Dao De Jing* (see sidebar, above left) and the *Zhuangzi*, have been as influential in forming the Chinese ethos as the Confucian canon. They too teach the way to find harmony, but look to the force of the Dao for pattern and order, not to an ancient golden age. Like the *Dao De Jing*, the *Zhuangzi*, named after its

Buddha preaching to his aged disciple Subhuti; a woodblock illustration to a scroll of the Diamond Sutra *(see p.180), one of many Buddhist scriptures found at Dunhuang (see p.207). It dates from the Tang dynasty (618–907CE).*

author (see p.206), advocates harmony with nature. It delights in nature's ever-shifting forms, and refutes standards of worth created by humans and imposed upon its endless variety. Death and life are a part of nature's process, to be embraced with equal joy and enthusiasm. The *Zhuangzi* tells stories of curious people and things, and revels in flights of fancy.

Religious Daoism has a vast scriptural collection of over a thousand works, and is still growing. This canon includes treatises on various topics, including rituals, alchemy, exorcism, the lives of past Daoist worthies, and revelations. These are consulted by Daoist priests and adepts in ministering to others or in their own quest for enlightenment and longevity.

Chinese Buddhist scriptures reflect the effort to adapt the foreign tradition of Buddhism to a very different context. The first Buddhists in China were faced with a huge preexisting corpus of scripture. The *Lotus Sutra,* a text of great significance in all East Asian branches of Buddhism (see also pp.181 and 251), accounts for Buddhism's diverse and often contradictory teachings and asserts that all the Buddhist schools ultimately teach the truth that leads to enlightenment. Another key text, the *Platform Sutra,* is purely Chinese in origin, and describes the enlightenment of Huineng, the sixth patriarch of the Meditation school, or Chan.

The popular religion is by and large without sacred texts, although various sectarian movements have had their own scriptures. The ancient *Songs of the South* (fourth century BCE), describes shamanic flight and other practices and beliefs that have continued in the popular tradition (see p.207). With the advent of printing in the eighth century CE, inexpensive morality texts drawn from the various religious traditions became widely popular.

THE *YI JING*

The tremendous importance of the ancient practice and theory of divination is captured in the Confucian classic the *Yi Jing* (*I Ching*), the *Book of Changes,* which developed over several hundred years beginning in the early Zhou dynasty. Although a part of the Confucian canon, it is universal in its appeal and importance in Chinese religions. Its popularity is due in part to its cosmological speculation, which appealed to the élite, and especially its use as a manual of divination, which continues today.

The *Yi Jing* system of divination is based on combinations of eight trigrams, devices made up of broken and unbroken lines that represent the opposing yet complementary forces of *yin* (broken) and *yang* (unbroken) (see pp.200–203). The trigrams are combined in pairs, in all possible combinations, to form a total of sixty-four hexagrams. These hexagrams are taken to represent all possible situations and developments in the constantly changing universe. In addition to giving judgments on the individual hexagrams and the lines of which they are composed, the *Yi Jing* provides commentaries and explanations to assist in interpreting the results of divination.

A silk funerary banner of the 6th or 7th century CE depicting Fu Xi intertwined with Nü Gua, a goddess who features in Chinese mythology as the creator of humanity from mud.

SAINTS AND HEROES

Many real, legendary, semilegendary, and mythical figures have acquired heroic or saintly status as founders or exemplars of the ideals expressed in the Chinese religious traditions. Confucian heroes are associated with the establishment of the fundamentals of civilization, or the perfection of social norms. These include the quasimythical culture heroes and sage kings of antiquity, who are the earliest figures in traditional Chinese history. There are also records of extraordinary individuals who displayed great self-sacrifice in their devotion to Confucian-inspired virtue. Daoist heroes, by contrast, are those who have perfected their knowledge of the workings of the Dao. However, both Confucian and Daoist heroes are revered for contributing to the goal of universal harmony.

Heroes were often canonized as deities to become part of the celestial hierarchy (see pp.208–211). Perhaps the most famous example of this is the widely popular Guan Di, a military hero of the Han era (206–220CE). Throughout the centuries, he was promoted by imperial decree through the ranks of the celestial hierarchy, and continues today to be the patron god of many trades and professions.

The most noted of the culture heroes—semimythical figures who are said to have brought humanity the basics of civilization—are Fu Xi, Shen Nong, and Huang Di. Fu Xi, the Ox-tamer, is credited with inventing nets for catching animals and fish, as well as with domesticating animals. He established the art of divination by devising the Eight Trigrams (see sidebar, p.213) and invented marriage and thus the family. Shen Nong, the Divine Farmer, invented the plow and hoe and taught humanity the skills of agriculture. He discovered the rudiments of medicine and pharmacology by determining the therapeutic and toxic qualities of all plants. Huang Di, the Yellow Emperor, invented warfare and defeated "barbarians" to secure what became the heart of the Chinese empire.

Chinese tradition considers the period following the culture heroes as the golden age of antiquity, the time of the "sage kings" and perfect government. Kings Yao, Shun, and Yu were referred to by Confucius as exemplary rulers. Yao determined that all of his sons—ten in number—were not worthy to rule, and therefore searched for the most virtuous man in the kingdom to succeed him. His criterion of virtue was filial piety, which was demonstrated by Shun, who continued to honor and serve his father and stepbrother without complaint, despite their attempts to murder him. Shun became king and later also bypassed his sons, handing the succession to Yu (see box, opposite).

In every dynasty there were heroes and heroines who embodied such ideals as the virtuous and selfless public servant, the filial child, and the chaste and devoted wife. Their stories are recounted in texts used as primers over centuries, such as the *Classic of Filial Piety* and *Biographies of Heroic Women*, as well as in accounts reported in local gazettes and dynastic histories. Such stories include that of Laizi, who pretended to be a child even when he was more than seventy, so that his aged parents would not feel old; others tell of girls who committed suicide at the death of their fiancés in order to be loyal to their betrothed, and of the secondary wife who ran into a burning house to rescue the children of her husband's primary wife, leaving her own to perish.

In contrast to the ethical, virtuous, and altruistic cast of the Confucian hero, who upholds morality and legitimacy, Daoist heroes exemplify those who practice intense self-cultivation to absorb the teachings of Daoism, in order to acquire magical powers and, above all, achieve immortality. These figures are admired, but they also have a countercultural air. For example, the scabby-headed Daoist monk, free from society's expectations and bonds, laughing uproariously and irreverently, is a recurrent literary image.

THE DUKE OF ZHOU

Much praised by Confucius, the duke of Zhou (died 1094BCE) has long served as a model of the exemplary public servant who did his duty to uphold order and his dynasty, but without seeking the throne for himself. The duke was the brother of King Wu, founder of the Zhou dynasty. After Wu died, the duke acted as regent for Wu's young son for seven years, never attempting to usurp the throne, in spite of accusations—subsequently disproved—to the contrary. This heroic role model proved so enduring that "duke of Zhou" was a popular nickname for the respected Communist premier Zhou Enlai (1898–1976).

YU, THE CONTROLLER OF FLOODS

From the Chinese perspective, the ideal state is characterized by good government and just rulers who strive to bring about a state of order and harmony between nature and humanity. This is exemplified by the story of Yu, one of the "sage kings" of antiquity and the founder of the legendary Xia dynasty (traditional dates: 2205–1766BCE), whose worthiness was demonstrated in his ceaseless labor to protect the people from flooding—throughout history China's most frequent form of natural disaster.

In the time of Yu, the people were cursed with a great flood that destroyed all in its path. Yu sluiced off the great river that had caused the flood, creating nine provinces and making the land habitable. So great was Yu's dedication to this task that for ten years he did not visit his own home, even when he passed by so closely that he could hear the cries of his young children.

Yu worked until his hands had no nails and his shanks no hair, and persevered even when he contracted so many debilitating illnesses that his body had shriveled to half its size, his internal organs had ceased to function effectively, and his legs were in such a poor state that he could barely walk.

Yu is praised for his great concern for, and dedication to, the welfare of the "black-haired people." The great flood motif is a common one in world mythology; it is telling that in the Chinese version, humanity is saved solely by the agency of a dedicated human hero rather than by a powerful deity.

Yu the Great, third of the exemplary sovereigns of Chinese legend known as the "sage kings" and founder of the traditional first dynasty. His reputed tomb can be seen today near Shaoxing in Zhejiang province.

IN QUEST OF CONCORD

Chinese ethics evince a remarkable ability to synthesize diverse strands of religious teachings into a comprehensive system. Elements derived from the distinctive traditions of Confucianism, Daoism, Buddhism, and the popular religion are embraced without apparent conflict. The underlying ethical concern of all the traditions can be summed up as the pursuit of concord: living harmoniously within the family, society, and nature.

Ethical teaching is important in Daoism, but not necessarily central. Philosophical Daoism stresses the pursuit of spontaneous, natural action, while the focus of religious Daoism is the pursuit of longevity and immortality. Buddhism has its own distinctive ethical system, related to its principal concerns of enlightenment and salvation. It has accommodated itself to the older Confucian and Daoist ethos, and the indigenous traditions in turn have incorporated such Buddhist ideas as the practice of meditation.

Confucianism places the strongest emphasis on ethical teachings. Confucian ethics are directed toward the creation of a harmonious society and

A 12th-century wall hanging of children paying their respects to their elders, in accordance with the Confucian ideal of filial piety, which demands respect and obedience from the child and care and concern from the parent.

a virtuous, benevolent state. These can be brought about, Confucians believe, if everyone is reflective and sincere, and practices *ren*, "humanity," a deep-seated altruism. Confucius described *ren* as treating all people with respect, and living according to the golden rule (see right).

Confucianism demands that all persons be treated with humanity, but within a well articulated hierarchy. Filial piety—the duty, love, and respect due to parents—is a central Confucian virtue, as is behaving appropriately according to one's rank. The most important relationships are those of father and son, emperor and minister, husband and wife, elder brother and younger brother, friend and friend. Only the last is considered to be between people of equal rank. An ordered, harmonious society depends on each person playing his or her part appropriately and with good intent.

*This ink-stamp, or "chop," contains Confucius' version of the golden rule: "Do not unto others what you would not have them do to you"(*Analects *12.2).*

Confucian ethics pay little attention to reward or punishment beyond this world. However, to a great extent, the Confucian virtue of filial piety became integral to concepts of salvation in the popular tradition, especially in the cult of ancestors. Ideally, in order to become a contented and benevolent ancestor, rather than a potentially malign ghost, one must have living male descendants to perform the necessary sacrifices after one's death.

Like Confucianism, philosophical Daoism is not concerned with salvation, but rather with an acceptance of the constant flux of the universe. For philosophical Daoists, there is no state of being from which to be

THE *JOURNEY TO THE WEST*

The Chinese classic novel *Journey to the West*, written in 1592 by Wu Chengen and based on a true story, is hilarious, bawdy, irreverent, and highly entertaining. But it can also be read as an allegory of Neo-Confucian mind-cultivation, Daoist physiological alchemy and pursuit of immortality (see p.221), and Buddhist enlightenment and redemption.

In the story, the monk Xuanzang (who lived ca. 596–664CE) sets off on a hazardous trip to India in search of Buddhist scriptures with companions who are celestial beings and have gained their powers through Daoist practices. Under the orders of the Buddha, and guided and protected by Guanyin (see p.211), their progress is charted by the Daoist Laozi and the Jade Emperor, a Confucian figure (see pp.209–11). Having fought off dangers to life, limb, and virtue from various voracious and lascivious monsters, the five pilgrims reach India safely and return with many Buddhist scriptures. In the course of the journey, Xuanzang has attained Buddhist enlightenment; gained fundamental insights into the Dao and achieved physical immortality; and traversed the mental terrain of Neo-Confucian mind-cultivation.

The ultimate reward of the pilgrims is therefore the attainment of the enlightenment and salvation offered by all three teachings. This is a fine articulation of the easy flow which, for the Chinese, exists among these traditions—to the extent that the aims of all three may be embraced by one individual.

A central role in the Journey to the West *is played by Monkey, a trickster of magical powers and great intelligence. He represents the common Daoist and Buddhist metaphor of "the Monkey of the Mind," denoting the restless mind that is so difficult to control.*

saved, because all stages of existence are a part of the natural order of the Dao. The ethic of "noninterference" (*wu wei*) in nature demands that one submit to natural processes and change. To be born, mature, and die are therefore all equally valid, and necessary, parts of the natural process. Criticized for not mourning his wife, the Daoist philosopher Zhuangzi replied: "Originally she had no life; and not only no life, she had no form ... form was transformed to become life, and now life is transformed to become death. This is like the rotation of the four seasons ... For me to go about weeping and wailing would be to show my ignorance of destiny" (Zhuangzi, "The Equality of Death;" Chan, *Source Book*, p.209).

In religious Daoism, by contrast, there is a strong emphasis on the quest for immortality. By understanding the working of the *Dao* one can unlock the secrets of life and death, and use them to advantage. This is attempted through various practices: diet, sex, gymnastics, and meditation. In these practices Daoists seek to reverse the flow of essential fluids in the body, and thus grow younger and nurture within them an "embryo of immortality" that will survive after death. Adepts of these practices should purify their minds and hearts as well as their bodies, and must employ any magical powers that they acquire only to benefit others.

Buddhist ethical teaching, particularly the ancient Indian concept of *karma* (see pp.156–7), is very much integrated into the Chinese religious sensibility. Knowledge of the laws of *karma* encourages acts of merit and compassion, which include distributing scripture, releasing captive animals, and giving food to beggars, including Buddhist monks and nuns.

In Chinese Buddhism, salvation and enlightenment may be seen as two

THE ART OF ENLIGHTENMENT

Art is one means by which Chan Buddhists may articulate truths learned in meditation without resorting to words. Enlightenment comes in a lightning flash, in which all distinctions between the self and the rest of the cosmos dissolve; this experience is captured in the rapid, intense brushwork of Chan artists, who seek to record the insight in its full intensity. Where words might fail, the finished work of art jolts the viewer into a similar realization of ultimate truth.

Muqi (active in the first half of the twelfth century), one of the most famous of the Chan Buddhist painters, is a master of this spontaneous style. He painted a wide variety of subjects, but his work always encourages the viewer to identify with the inner nature of his subject and dissolve the boundary of "self" and "other."

Six Persimmons, *by Muqi. In this masterpiece of Chan art, Muqi has transformed his fleeting, powerful insight into black ink on paper, on which, to quote sinologist Arthur Waley, "passion has congealed into stupendous calm."*

forms of the same goal. For the average person, for whom the rigor of the monastery and meditation are too great or unaffordable, salvation is attained through devotional "Pure Land" Buddhism. In this the devout invoke the name of Amitabha Buddha (Amituo Fo in Chinese), the *bodhisattva* who has promised to help all those seeking enlightenment. Having chanted "Hail to you, Amitabha Buddha" with a sincere heart, a devotee will be saved from reincarnation in Hell and be reborn instead in the Pure Land, or "Western Paradise," where Amitabha presides (see p.193).

The Chan (Sanskrit *dhyana*, "meditation") school of Chinese Buddhism stresses enlightenment rather than salvation. Enlightenment is the flash of intuition that reveals the essential emptiness of all things. Chan asserts that all human beings may become enlightened, because all living creatures are endowed with "*buddha*-nature." This can be accomplished in this lifetime through meditation. In order to gain the great moment of insight, and to force the mind to break from its usual path of discursive thought, the Chan master may employ what is termed the "public case" (*gong an*, whence Japanese *koan*), a question-and-answer session between the master and disciple that may include shouting, beating, and apparently nonsensical statements. Through this process, the disciple is pushed to let go of the mundane perception of reality and grasp ultimate truth.

Meditation is also an important aid to enlightenment in Daoism and Confucianism. In Daoism, immortality is achieved by those who have both preserved their bodies and acquired true insight into the Dao. A tradition of "quiet sitting," or meditative reflection on Confucian teachings, developed in medieval China with a similar aim of attaining true insight.

Buddhist monks at a Shanghai monastery. From the traditional Chinese ethical perspective, Buddhist monks and nuns were seen as parasitical because they begged, and unfilial because they were celibate. Tales such as that of Mulian, a disciple of the Buddha who rescues his mother from Hell, helped to teach that a Buddhist may still be a filial child.

ETHICS AND GOOD GOVERNMENT

Both Confucianism and Daoism are concerned with good government, but have very different ideas about what constitutes an ethical ruler. Confucius' *Analects* envision the ruler as an active exemplar of virtue: "If you desire what is good, the people will be good. The ... ruler is like the wind and ... the people [are] like grass. In whatever direction the wind blows, the grass always bends" (*Analects* 12.19; Chan, *Source Book*, p.40). The *Dao De Jing* expresses Daoism's more passive approach to rule: "I do not interfere and the people are transformed by themselves. I prefer peace and the people correct themselves. I do nothing and the people of themselves have abundance. I have no desires and the people become simple by themselves" (*Dao De Jing*, chapter 57).

Chinese bureaucrats were once selected on the basis of their mastery of the Confucian classics (see illustration, p.199). They were urged to be loyal and virtuous, to the extent of chastising the emperor himself if his rule strayed from virtue, and withdrawing from service rather than serve a despot. As Confucius put it: "When the [good] way prevails in the empire, then show yourself; when it does not, then hide" (*Analects* 8:13; Chan, *Source Book*, p.34). After the invading Mongols founded the Yuan dynasty in 1279, for example, many courtiers chose "virtuous retirement" in preference to serving the "barbarian" foreign ruler.

A HALLOWED COSMOS

In Chinese religion the sacred may be encountered in temples and shrines, in the home, and in nature. The temple is the site for community worship and sacrifice to gods and goddesses. Temples of the popular religion are designated "Daoist," but generally speaking they are not exclusively so. Indeed, many temples incorporate statues of Buddha, the *bodhisattva* Guanyin (see p.211), and Confucius, as well as deities of the popular religion. Worship at these temples is usually informal, with the worshipper offering food, incense, and "spirit money" (see p.232). At other times, the community will gather at a temple for important festivals and sacrifices, such as Chinese New Year, the spring and autumn Earth God ceremonies, the Hungry Ghost festival (see p.232), and the *jiao*, or "great offering," an elaborate ritual of renewal for the community (see p.226). Some temples are also popular pilgrimage sites, especially on the birthday of a deity.

Temples are built by private donations, and managed by a temple association made up of local laypeople. Religious specialists, such as Daoist and Buddhist priests, are hired to perform special ceremonies. The temple community often includes spirit-mediums who write or speak on behalf of a particular deity, and exorcists. Temples also function as community centers. They may be a place to discuss village affairs, or to enjoy music and theatre, and are frequently used as somewhere for local social clubs and cultural associations to meet.

In Daoist and popular belief, deities are ranked in a hierarchy paralleling the civil service of the Chinese empire (see pp.208–11). Similarly, the

THE *WESTERN INSCRIPTION*

The Neo-Confucian scholar Zhang Zai (1027–77) was the author of a tremendously influential theory of the nature of the universe. In this brief text, called simply the *Western Inscription*, Zhang explains the fundamentally interrelated nature of the cosmos and evokes the holiness and completeness of the created order:

> "Heaven is my father and Earth is my mother, and even such a small creature as I finds an intimate place in their midst. Therefore that which fills the universe I regard as my body and that which directs the universe I consider as my nature. All people are my brothers and sisters, and all things are my companions. The great ruler [the emperor] is the eldest son of my parents [Heaven and Earth], and the great ministers are his stewards ... In life I follow and serve [Heaven and Earth]. In death I will be at peace."

(Chan, *Source Book*, pp.497–8.)

Part of the roof of a monastery temple in the Forbidden City, the old imperial palace complex, in Beijing. The roof of a Chinese temple is likened to a sacred mountain, and may be "populated" with creatures and characters from Chinese myth, such as famous immortals.

temples where these celestial officials reside are modeled on the buildings of the imperial bureaucracy, with features such as curved eaves; pillars and doors painted an auspicious red; and stone lions guarding the entrances. The temple also mirrors the cosmos: its base is square, like the Earth, and the ceiling may be domed to evoke the vault of Heaven (see p.222).

Buddhist and Confucian temples also form part of the religious landscape of China. The former are usually monasteries, with Buddhist monks and nuns in residence. In Confucian temples, members of the (earthly) state bureaucracy traditionally honored Confucius—as a human being, not a god—in twice-yearly sacrifices on the equinoxes. These temples are also built on a square base, and internally they are completely symmetrical, each wall a mirror image of the one opposite, conveying the order and rationality associated with Confucian thought.

Natural features of the landscape, such as rivers, caves, and mountains, are believed to possess spiritual power. Taishan (Mount Tai), the most

THE BODY: A HOLY MICROCOSM

Certain Daoist meditative practices require the adept to look inward and observe the "country of the body." The "country" is a familiar terrain, for it is a microcosm, a faithful duplication of the universe. For example, reflecting the ancient Chinese cosmological premise that Heaven is round and Earth is square, the human head is Heaven and the "square" feet are Earth. This corporeal cosmos is also said to contain the sun and moon, constellations, mountain ranges, bridges, lakes, and pagodas. The inner country is inhabited by a large population, administered in the same way as the imperial Chinese state.

The interplay between microcosm and macrocosm is a constant theme in Daoism. When a Daoist priest performs the actions and liturgy of the *jiao* ceremony (see p.226), he simultanously employs a technique of meditation on the bodily microcosm known as "physiological alchemy." In this, vital essences and fluids of the body are believed to be purified and transmuted. It is employed in tandem with dietary, sexual, gymnastic, and other practices, in the search for longevity or even immortality.

Physiological alchemy became the dominant activity for seekers after long life during the Tang and Song dynasties and is still practiced today. Before then, they employed a more conventional form of alchemy involving substances outside the body, creating elixirs from metals and other ingredients that they consumed in the hope of promoting long life. Physiological alchemists also endeavor to produce elixirs, but seek to do so internally, by exercising transformations on the substances within their own bodies.

The use of parallels between the macrocosm of the universe and the microcosm of the human body reflects the underlying principles of the Chinese cosmos, and of Daoism: that all things derive from the same source, and that once the underlying pattern of the universe—the Dao—has been perceived, it can be applied for personal benefit.

A late 19th-century painting on silk, one of many depictions of Daoist esoteric sexual practices that aimed to further the preservation of the "internal cosmos." Daoism holds that, just as the universe is holy and eternal, the microcosm of the human body can also be made eternal through the practice of alchemical transformation on one's sacred interior.

THE TEMPLE OF HEAVEN

South of the emperor's palace in Beijing is a large sacred complex that was one of the holiest sites of imperial China: the Temple of Heaven. Here, the emperor would perform rituals such as the annual sacrifices on the winter solstice when *yin* energy was at its peak and *yang*, bringing growth, warmth, and light, was just beginning to reemerge. As the Son of Heaven, the sole intermediary between Heaven (Tian) and the empire (Tian Xia, "All under Heaven"), he alone could perform this sacrifice. The regular, predictable movements of the heavenly bodies demonstrated the ability of Heaven to regulate the cosmos. Through his sacrifices, the emperor of China called upon Heaven to guarantee the order of the empire.

The Temple of Heaven was sacred ground—commoners were not allowed even to watch the silent procession of the emperor and his entourage from the imperial palace to the temple. At the sacrifice on the winter solstice, the emperor offered incense, jade, silk, and wine. He sacrificed a red bullock, symbolizing *yang*, and prostrated himself nine times (nine is considered the most *yang* of numbers) before the altar to Heaven.

The emperor received Heaven's mandate to govern (see p.204) on the basis of his proper performance of the rituals, and his continued virtuous rule for the benefit of the people. His fulfillment of his duty ensured the successful growth of crops and the continuation of order in the empire. But if Heaven was not satisfied with the emperor, the harmony and regular rhythms of the natural and human world would be disrupted. Portents of chaos such as inundations, earthquakes, famine, drought, and uprisings indicated Heaven's displeasure. If they continued they could ultimately legitimate the replacement of the dynasty.

The ceiling of the Temple of Heaven, Beijing. Like all the buildings in the temple complex, it has a square base and round vaulted ceiling, symbolizing Earth and Heaven. The configurations of individual elements of each structure are based on a complex numerology.

Family members worship at a domestic altar at Dali at Yunnan province, south China. For most Chinese, the home is the most frequently used religious space, in particular the "home altar," which may be freestanding or a simple niche in the wall (see also p.230).

important of five sacred mountains (see illustration, p.198), was seen as a provider of fertility, a preventer of natural disasters, and a symbol of stability. It was worshipped in spring and autumn to ensure a successful planting and an abundant harvest. Chinese people still make pilgrimages to these sacred peaks and perform acts of worship at mountaintop temples.

Sometimes a part of the landscape may take on spiritual power as the site of an unnatural death. For example, roadside shrines might be built at the scene of a fatal motoring accident to propitiate the angry ghost who is considered to linger there and threaten the safety of the living.

The sacrality and latent power of the physical world is expressed in the ancient art of *fengshui*, Chinese geomancy, which is still practiced today and has become popular in the West. *Fengshui* (literally "wind and water") is the art of fixing the most auspicious place for graves, buildings, and even cities, in order to make the most of the sacred power present in the natural environment. Through *fengshui*, it is believed, human beings are able to live harmoniously with and within the natural order. The *fengshui* master uses a special compass to take bearings on the site and on visible features of the surrounding landscape, such as mountain peaks, watercourses, paths, and prominent rocks. In this way, the master is able to detect the celestial and earthly forces, the interaction of which determines the auspiciousness of the site.

Employing *fengshui* to determine the siting of graves is extremely important, because a peaceful resting place ensures the comfort and hence benevolence of one's ancestors. *Fengshui* can also be used to decide the position of doors, windows, furnishings, and so on, in order to create a prosperous and harmonious space within the home or workplace.

An array of fruit, cakes, and other foodstuffs at a Daoist festival in Taiwan.

FESTIVE FOODS

The food consumed at Chinese festivals is often chosen for its symbolism and associations. Many foods pun on New Year wishes. "Peanut" is a homophone of "life"; dates (*zao*) and chestnuts (*lizi*) together suggest "early son" (*zaozi*); "lotus seeds" sounds like "many children"; and kumquat sounds like "gold." Other foods are more purely symbolic, such as peaches (the fruit of longevity in myth), pomegranates (its many seeds represent many sons), and bamboo shoots (their rapid growth symbolizes a rapid rise in one's profession). Some foods have auspicious names, such as the steamed bread called "gold ingots" and the noodles called "threads of longevity."

The roundness of many foods symbolizes completion, perfection, and the presence of the whole family circle at the holiday. Examples are the giant pork meatballs ("lion heads") and rice flour balls (*yuanxiao*) of New Year; and the round fruits and mooncakes of the Mid-Autumn festival, which also represent the full moon (see p.266).

SEASONS OF WORSHIP

The Chinese calendar incorporates lunar reckoning of time (see box, p.227) and many religious festivals coincide with the important phases of the moon. Others are derived from the agricultural cycle, since farming has been the primary Chinese economic activity since antiquity. The annual festivals also reflect ancient *yin-yang* cosmology, as evident in the waxing (*yang*) and waning (*yin*) phases of the moon and the seasonal round of growth and decay.

Other themes underpin the major festivals of the Chinese religious year: the importance of the family and the respect shown for forebears; the pursuit of longevity; the desire for blessings; and the propitiation and warding off of potentially malevolent forces. Many of these themes are also expressed in the worship of the gods and goddesses of the popular religion, particularly in the celebrations to mark their birthdays. The importance of Confucian teaching is marked on Confucius' birthday (September 28th), also designated Teachers' Day, celebrated today at Confucian temples in Taiwan with traditional costumes, music, and dance.

The Chinese New Year, or spring festival (see box, opposite), is celebrated to mark the end of the ascendancy of *yin* power, which reaches its peak at the winter solstice, and the onset of *yang*. It is a time for families to come together and renew their bonds. The Clear and Bright festival (Qingming), which follows two weeks after the spring equinox, also unites the family, but in this case the focus is on renewing ties with the dead. The spirits of the deceased are also central to the Hungry Ghost festival, which falls on the fifteenth day (full moon) of the seventh month (see p.232).

Two other major festivals are still widely celebrated: the Double Fifth and Mid-Autumn festivals. The Double Fifth falls on the fifth day of the fifth lunar month, close to the summer solstice, when *yang* powers are said to be at their annual peak. In former times this hot season was regularly the time of epidemics, and on the Double Fifth prophylactic herbs and grasses are still hung on front doors. Plants that are pungent and possess sharp points or leaves are believed to be the most efficacious in warding off disease; the pointed leaves of the sweet flag plant, for example, are considered to act as "demon-slaying swords."

Five is an important number in Chinese cosmology, and the Double Fifth is rich in the imagery of pentads (see p.202), especially the "Five Poisons" (centipede, snake, scorpion, toad, and lizard) and the "Five Colors" (blue, red, yellow, white, and black). At the time of the festival, images of the Five Poisons are displayed on clothing, food, and amulets. They are auspicious creatures, thought to repel noxious and dangerous attacks with their potent toxins. The Five Colors evoke the creative power of the Five Elements (see pp.200–202).

The Double Fifth festival also celebrates dragons, water, and the poet Qu Yuan. In agricultural terms, the season of the Double Fifth is when rice seedlings are transplanted into the paddies, which are watered by heavy rains at this time. In Chinese tradition, this rain is caused by dragons that live in clouds and water and bless the Earth with fertility. The famous "dragon boat" races that take place on the Double Fifth reflect this lore as well as the legend of Qu Yuan, a celebrated poet who served in the government of Chu, a small kingdom of the Zhou dynasty during the third century BCE. This conscientious and wise minister gave unpopular advice and was sent into exile. Heartsick, he wandered the land. Finally, after composing his most famous poem, *Li Sao* ("Encountering Sorrow"), which summarized his ideals and his life, he threw himself into

CHINESE NEW YEAR

The New Year, or Spring Festival, is the most important holiday of the Chinese calendar. It begins on the first day of the first lunar month, usually between January 21st and February 19th. Beforehand, the house is thoroughly cleansed of the old year's dirt and "inauspicious breaths." All the family returns home, debts are paid, and quarrels settled. An account of the old year is sent off to Heaven with the Kitchen God (see p.208).

The lucky color red is seen everywhere. Doorways are decorated with fresh images of the traditional door gods and auspicious words. On New Year's Eve, the family gathers for a meal, the table also being set for dead family members, who are present in spirit. The family talks through the night, carefully avoiding unlucky or negative topics or words. Traditionally, the doors might be sealed before midnight to keep out the evil spirits and reopened on New Year's Day. For the first two days of the year no one is to work, and there are prohibitions on sweeping or using blades for fear of "brushing away" or "cutting off" the good luck of the New Year.

The final night of the New Year celebrations is the Lantern Festival on the first full moon of the New Year. Happy, noisy crowds gather amid displays of beautiful lanterns to watch stiltwalkers, lion dancers, and people in traditional costumes.

Costumed stiltwalkers are among the crowds celebrating the Chinese New Year on the streets of Beijing.

THE *JIAO*

A great Daoist sacrificial ceremony, the *jiao*, is still practiced today at temples on Taiwan. It is conducted at irregular intervals by Daoist priests on behalf of a community in order to renew its connection with the Three Pure Ones, the highest cosmic powers (see p.211). The whole community prepares for the *jiao* by fasting, but only priests, musicians, and prominent benefactors of the temple witness the ritual itself. However, the people make bountiful offerings at the temple and take part in lively festivities that accompany the *jiao*.

the Miluo river in present-day Hunan province. People raced out in boats but failed to save him, so they threw rice into the water so that the fish would eat this instead of Qu Yuan's body. Tradition has it that today's dragon boat races reenact the frantic search for Qu Yuan. The rice thrown to the fish is represented today by *zongzi*, sticky rice dumplings wrapped in bamboo leaves and tied with strings of the Five Colors.

The Mid-Autumn festival falls at full moon in the eighth lunar month. It is a harvest festival that also celebrates the moon and the quest for immortality. In Chinese myth, the moon is home to a rabbit that pounds special herbs to make the elixir of immortality, and to the moon goddess, Chang E. For this festival, a table is set up outdoors and laden with round (full moon-shaped) fruit such as oranges, melons, and pomegranates, and "moon cakes." People gather to watch the harvest moon and to recite stories and poems on lunar themes.

Chinese religious celebrations focus on family and community rather than the individual. Other than death, when a person becomes an ancestor (see pp.230–32), the most significant Chinese rite of passage is marriage, which assures the continuation of the family through the promise of descendants. Traditionally, a marriage became official when the couple bowed before the ancestral tablets of the groom, introducing the bride to her husband's forebears. Such practices maintain the link between the living and the dead, represent proper filial behavior, and thus ensure the blessings of the ancestors on the family. There are also coming of age cer-

Dragon boat racers during the Double Fifth festival on the Miluo river in Hunan, in which the poet Qu Yuan is said to have drowned. The boats, adorned with a dragon's head and tail, may be over 30 meters (100 feet) long, with as many as 80 rowers.

THE CHINESE CALENDAR

The Chinese religious year combines solar and lunar calendars. The lunar calendar consists of twelve lunar months, with intercalary months added every two or three years to keep the lunar and solar calendars in step. The solar year, in which the solstices and the equinoxes determine the beginning of seasons, is divided into twenty-four periods of approximately fifteen days, called "nodes," or "breaths." They are derived from observation of the climate and the heavens, and reflect the passage of the agricultural year.

Eight of the periods are named after the equinoxes, solstices, and starts of seasons. Others evoke agriculturally and meteorologically significant phenomena, and have names such as "Insects Awaken" (early March); "Clear and Bright" (early April, hence the name of the festival that falls at this time); "Limit of Heat" (end of August); and "Frost Descends" (end of October).

Familiar to many outsiders is the cycle of twelve years based on the animals of the Chinese zodiac. This scheme forms one element of a wider system of cycles. For example, a longer cycle of sixty years involves the zodiac animals, the Five Colors (see pp.224–5), and two sets of symbols, the Ten Heavenly Stems and Twelve Earthly Branches. Each animal is associated with one Branch, and each color correlates to two Stems. Thus 2000 is the year of the White Dragon; 2012 will be the year of the Black Dragon. The first year of the sixty-year cycle is *jiazi*, the year of the Blue Rat, most recently 1984.

The animals of the Chinese zodiac: rat, ox, tiger, rabbit, dragon, snake, horse, ram, monkey, rooster, dog, and pig. A 19th-century bronze disc.

emonies for boys and girls, but these are not of primary importance, and over time they came to be celebrated just before marriage rather than at a particular age. Also significant is a person's sixtieth birthday, which symbolizes the completion of a basic cycle of time (see box, above).

Acts of worship of the great cosmic forces, particularly Heaven and Earth, were the privilege and responsibility of the emperor alone. The proper observance of these rituals ensured that nature remained beneficial. In the imperial capital, the emperor made offerings at the Temples of the Sun on the spring equinox; at the Temple of Earth on the summer solstice; at the Temple of the Moon on the autumn equinox; and at the Temple of Heaven (see p.222) on the winter solstice. He also performed rites at the start of each season. During Qingming, he sacrificed to his own ancestors, to those of all past emperors, and to the culture heroes (see p.214).

All other rites and festivals in the empire were carried out in accordance with an annual almanac of predicted celestial events issued by the official Bureau of Astronomy, a department of the Ministry of Rites. Imperial foreknowledge in such matters indicated harmony between the emperor and Heaven; any unexpected cosmic event could be interpreted as a sign of imminent loss of the sovereign's mandate to rule (see p.204).

OVERLEAF *A girl and lion dancers take part in a traditional New Year parade in China.*

A home altar in Beijing with offerings of incense before portraits of ancestors. In wooden tablets on the altar reside the spirits of the ancestors, to whom the family burns incense and offers food and drink. At the altar the ancestors are also informed of important events in the lives of the family, such as births, deaths, betrothals, trips, and business ventures.

ANCESTRAL TABLETS

The home altar is in many ways the locus of family unity, encompassing all generations, alive and dead. It is here that the tablets are kept in which the ancestral spirits are believed to reside. Generally speaking, the tablets record the names, birth and death dates, and number of sons of each ancestor. The ancestors are addressed and treated as close family members. In theory it is the family of the senior male in the family that is represented on the altar, but under certain circumstances other tablets may be present. For instance, in a family with no sons, a woman may put her own ancestor tablets on the family altar of her husband.

The tablets go back three to five generations. As each generation passes away, the oldest tablets are removed from the altar and placed in an ancestral hall used by several households of the same extended family. Here, devotion takes place to the ancestors as a group; emotions are more formal, and indicative of gratitude to the host of forebears rather than of filial love toward the more recently departed.

THE IMMORTAL BODY AND SOUL

Chinese concepts of death and the afterlife reflect ideas drawn from all the major traditions. Most ideas and rituals may be identified as those of religious Daoism, Buddhism, or the popular religion. Confucianism is not directly concerned with belief in an afterlife, although the Confucian virtue of filial piety is crucial to understanding the life of the dead and the responsibility of the living toward them. Buddhism has its own distinctive teachings about one's fate after death; over many centuries, these have merged with and shaped the indigenous Chinese ideas. In general, Chinese funerary and other practices are more important than the beliefs that lie behind them, because the rituals represent great expressions of family unity and ethical behavior toward others.

The Chinese feel the dead to be near, and to exercise a great influence on the living. Deceased members of a family have a powerful role in that family's continued well-being. Filial piety demands that deceased family members receive a proper burial and regular sacrifices. Thus treated they become ancestors, a source of blessings and fertility (that is, progeny) for the family. This idea dates from at least as early as the Shang dynasty (see p.204). Those not properly cared for after death—through neglect or a lack of descendants—and those who die prematurely or by violence, become ghosts: dangerous, malevolent forces that need to be placated.

The material boundaries between the living and the dead are fluid and vague. Those who reside in this world and the next are composed of the same vital material (*qi*) in its *yin* and *yang* forms (see p.200). Every person has two souls, a *hun* soul, made up of *yang qi*, and a *po* soul, made up of *yin qi*. At death, the *hun* soul, which represents the spiritual and intellectual aspect of the soul, departs from the body and ascends, due to its *yang* nature; it ultimately comes to reside in the ancestral tablets that are to be found on the domestic altar of a traditional Chinese home (see sidebar, left). The *po* soul, as *yin* energy, sinks into the ground. It remains with the body so long as it has been buried with the proper rites and is propitiated by tomb offerings.

If the burial is not performed correctly, or the death was early or violent, or the soul is not "fed" adequately (see below), the *hun* soul will not rise to reside in the ancestral tablets and nor will the *po* soul descend into the grave. Instead, the spirit of the deceased will haunt the living as a ghost until it has been propitiated.

It is the responsibility of the living to provide the things the dead need to be comfortable: food, money, and other amenities. At the most basic level, the care of ancestors consists of offering incense twice a day at the family altar. On the new moon and full moon, offerings may include food and "spirit money" (see p.232) as well as incense.

When offered food, ancestors are believed to consume the "essence" and leave the coarse material part for the family to enjoy. During the funerary ritual, the dead are provided with useful items such as cars, servants, houses, cash, and domestic furnishings—all made of paper and burned so that they ascend to the ancestors in the smoke. Ancestors are offered incense twice a day on the family altar; on holidays and the anniversary of an ancestor's death, food, drink, and spirit money are

IMMORTALS

There is a long history in Chinese civilization of attempting to perfect the human body in order to live forever: immortality as understood by the Chinese was not possible without a physical body. Techniques to produce longevity, and the belief that some people had perfected these techniques, are a part of Chinese history from as early as the Zhou dynasty. Such techniques included tempering the physical body (see box, p.221), but also purifying one's heart and mind, as there was no radical dichotomy between body and soul: any means of purification and preservation would assist the quest for immortality.

In ancient times, people sought the elixir or pill of immortality, either in their own laboratories (where "potable gold" was made from various substances including cinnabar), or from figures who lived in legendary places at the edges of the known Chinese world. Two such places, Penglai island and Kunlun mountain, were the objects of quests by royalty and commoners alike. Penglai was reported to be inhabited by immortals and situated off the coast of south China. Qin Shihuangdi, the first emperor of the Qin dynasty (221–209BCE), sent expeditions in search of Penglai and the legendary medicine of immortality that could be found there. Mount Kunlun, in the northwestern border area between China and Central Asia (see map, p.201), was thought to be the royal abode of the Queen Mother of the West, a goddess who could bestow immortality. The Queen Mother of the West also cultivates peaches of immortality, produced by her trees once every three thousand years. Peachwood ornaments are still popular in China as tokens of the wish for longevity.

A 20th-century depiction of the "Eight Immortals" of Daoism. The accounts of how each of these celebrated figures attained eternal life constitute a popular element of Daoist mythology.

Those who attained immortality would live in the outer boundaries of the cosmos, flying among the stars and wandering the Earth in perfect serenity, nourished by eating the wind and drinking the dew. Some immortals are depicted as "bird men," sprouting feathers and flying away. Others would apparently suffer death like ordinary mortals, but after burial, if their coffin were to be exhumed and opened, it would be found empty except for some personal token such as a cane or a sandal.

offered in addition to incense. Rituals practiced for the dead ensure blessings for the living; they also proclaim the unity and strength of the family through time and space. Offerings show that ancestors, as family, are accorded appropriate respect and love (see also box, below).

The strongly syncretistic tendency of Chinese religion is illustrated by its ability to encompass numerous—and in some cases, apparently contradictory—notions of the fate of the soul after death. Thus the *po* soul of the deceased is also believed to descend into the Chinese underworld, or Hell, to be judged and tried for its sins by the infernal judiciary before being punished and, eventually, reincarnated. This is an ancient belief, well established before the coming of Buddhism to China in the first century CE. Buddhism added its own concepts to the existing framework: the idea of

FESTIVALS FOR THE DEAD

There are two special holidays each year in which the dead are propitiated. One, the Clear and Bright festival (Qingming) in the spring, is designated for ancestors. The other, the Feast of the Hungry Ghosts (Gui Jie) on the fifteenth day of the seventh lunar month, aims to placate potentially malevolent spirits.

Qingming falls two weeks after the spring equinox. On this day families unite to visit the family graves for a celebration picnic. Weeds are cleared and inscriptions repainted. After lighting incense and red candles, the family makes offerings to the deceased of rice, wine, tea, food, paper clothes, and "spirit money."

The Feast of the Hungry Ghosts on the fifteenth day of the seventh lunar month is not directed at family unity but rather at communal protection. During the seventh lunar month, the gates of Hell are opened, and its residents are free to wander where they will. Those with no descendants to care for them, euphemistically called "the good brethren," are malevolent, unhappy, and potentially dangerous ghosts. The Feast of the Hungry Ghosts is designed to placate such ghosts with things they need, such as sustenance and amusements (music and theater). On Hungry Ghost day, a community celebration at an outdoor altar is performed by Buddhist and Daoist priests to propitiate the ghosts. The priests exhort the ghosts to repent and enter the Buddhist Pure Land. Ghosts who do not repent are sent back to Hell after the ceremony to continue their sufferings.

The food offerings presented to ghosts and ancestors on these and other occasions symbolize their respective relationships to the living. Ancestors are part of the family and are offered food in the home or at the ancestral hall or graveside. Their food is carefully prepared, cooked, and seasoned like that of the living; certain ancestors who are particularly revered may be offered food that they especially enjoyed when alive.

In contrast, ghosts are fed at the back door or outside the house altogether, and their food is generic and coarse—a reluctant, fearful bribe rather than a caring gesture to beloved family members.

The remains of an offering of "spirit money." It is specially printed in various denominations and is used to sustain the dead in the afterlife; like other offerings, it is burned and sent to the ancestor in the smoke.

karma (an individual's balance of accumulated merits and demerits); the figure of Yama, the king of Hell; and the different punishment levels of Hell, in which sinners suffer to redress their karmic imbalance before being reincarnated on Earth. On entering Hell, souls are judged by the Ten Magistrates, depicted in the costumes of the old Chinese imperial judiciary, who preside over the Ten Tribunals of Hell, each of which tries different crimes. After judgment, the soul pays for its past crimes by passing through various layers of Hell, where it undergoes torments appropriate to the crimes committed. At last, the soul reaches the final court of Hell where, having atoned for its shortcomings in the life just past, it is reincarnated in accordance with all the merits it has accumulated in every previous existence. Families can speed the passage of their loved ones in Hell through offerings and good works, such as the chanting of Buddhist *sutras*.

The "books of life and death," in which every person's allotted days are recorded, are also kept in Hell. Chinese folklore contains many accounts of bureaucratic mistakes that result in a person being wrongly consigned to Hell until the error is discovered.

The soul of an exceptionally virtuous person may, rather than be reincarnated, enter the heavenly bureaucracy as a deity. The celestial bureaucracy mirrors every aspect of a typical earthly civil service (see p.208), including its potential shortcomings: error, incompetence, corruption, nepotism, tedious formalities, and reams of paperwork.

Chinese concepts of what happens after death also include the teachings of "Pure Land" Buddhism. Devotees of Amitabha (Amituo Fo), the *buddha* of the "Pure Land," anticipate rebirth in this paradise as a prelude to attaining *nirvana* and escaping the cycle of rebirth altogether (see p.193).

An 18th-century painting on silk depicting the 4 kings who guard the register of judgments made in Hell.

DEATH AND PHILOSOPHICAL DAOISM

Although Chinese religious traditions place much emphasis on longevity and immortality (see box, p.231), those who were more philosophically inclined had a different attitude toward death and afterlife. Rather than seek immortality to escape death, philosophical Daoists reveled in the creative possibilities of the endless shifting patterns of the Dao. They welcomed death as the time when the *qi* of which they were made would be transformed miraculously into something else in creation.

THE STATE, THE FAMILY, AND THE INDIVIDUAL

The formal teachings of Confucianism, Daoism, and Buddhism have had a role in shaping Chinese society, with the popular tradition reflecting the ethics and concerns of all three traditions. However, Confucianism has played the most obvious role in forming Chinese social expectations and norms, so much so that many cultural attitudes derived from Confucian precepts are designated simply "Chinese."

Confucianism has been the ordering principle for the two most influential entities shaping Chinese life: the State and the family. The ideal expressed in Confucianism—virtuous rule for the benefit of the people—was the basis of the theory of statecraft in imperial China. Autocratic emperors knew that their reigns would be judged on the basis of Confucian ethics and recorded in dynastic histories for posterity to evaluate. Ministers and bureaucrats were chosen on the basis of their knowledge of Confucian teachings and their adherence to Confucian virtues.

The relationship between emperor and subject was considered analogous to the primary relationship of Chinese society: that between parent and child, or more specifically father and son. Children owed their parents absolute loyalty and obedience. They were expected to care for them in their old age and to produce descendants who would continue to care for their spirits when dead (see pp.230–233). Traditional Chinese law reflected this relationship: for example, a father was within his rights to kill a disobedient child, and a son could be executed for striking his father.

Traditional Chinese society was authoritarian and hierarchical. In Confucian thought, each member of the family and of society had a specific role. Women were considered embodiments of *yin* energy and therefore passive and nurturing, in contrast to the dynamic *yang* of males. According to this scheme, they were subordinate to men, and were expected to live in obedience to their fathers when girls, to their husbands when married, and to their sons when old. A married woman was supposed to show filial devotion to her husband's parents, with whom the couple often lived.

In the modern age, the strong emphasis on family unity and the relationship between child and parent continues, although it has lessened in degree. In China it came under severe strain during the Cultural Revolution (1966–76), when Mao Zedong encouraged children and juniors to denounce the ways of their elders and seniors as bourgeois and counterrevolutionary. This experience, so profoundly opposed to the tradition of filial piety, undoubtedly left deep psychological scars. Even in the officially egalitarian People's Republic, there is still a marked preference for

Buddhist nuns invoking the name of Amituo Fo (Amitabha Buddha) at a temple on Drum Mountain, near Fuzhou in China's Jiangxi province.

A WORD FOR "RELIGION"

Until recently, the Chinese language had no word for "religion" in the Western sense of a particular set of beliefs, doctrines, and rituals. The Chinese have never seen Confucianism, Daoism, and Buddhism as exclusivistic, and traditionally refer to them simply as "teachings." However, one result of increased contact with the West from the nineteenth century onward (see box, opposite) was the need to render the sense of "religion" as applied to a belief system such as Christianity. The neologism *zongjiao* was adopted at the turn of the twentieth century; it literally translates as "ancestral (or clan) teachings."

But many Chinese practices and beliefs cannot be categorized as *zongjiao*. For the Chinese, the ways of the "Three Teachings" are reflected in many aspects of everyday life, not simply in formal "religious" rites and acts of worship. These include dealing with officials, relationships, the arts, and even cooking.

sons over daughters—the Communist policy of allowing couples only one child to counter overpopulation has given rise to a range of methods to ensure that the child is male.

Daoism and Buddhism have provided complementary or alternative outlooks to that of Confucianism. Daoism furnished a contemplative strain and the ideal of retreat to nature to escape urban or official life. The Daoist quest for longevity is reflected in arts such as *taiji-chuan* (*t'ai-chi ch'uan*) and *qigong* (*chi kung*), still widely practiced in China and elsewhere, which aim to strengthen the body and sharpen the mind. Many other arts, such as painting, cooking, and medicine, are influenced by Daoist teachings of harmony and balance. For women, Daoism also provides an alternative vision to Confucian male domination. Philosophical Daoism favors the female over the male, and there have been Daoist nuns and adepts for centuries.

Buddhism has colored, more than created, Chinese traditions. Buddhist monks are associated with Chinese funerary rites, reciting *sutras* to help speed souls through Hell. With its promise of universal salvation, Buddhism has also provided a refuge for many, notably women, from the rigidity of Confucian hierarchical ideals. It is not uncommon for widows or women whose children have left home, to become lay Buddhists or nuns.

WESTERN ENCOUNTER

In the nineteenth century, China's relations with the West largely took the form of humiliating military defeats, one-sided treaties, and an unwanted influx of missionaries, diplomats, and traders. This experience, as well as the impact of Western views of Chinese culture, shattered China's perception of itself as the arbiter of civilization and had a profound effect on its understanding of, and attitude toward, its religious traditions.

Confucianism, the theoretical basis for government and morality for two millennia, came under attack as stiflingly traditional and as the underlying cause for China's political and military weakness. As the quest for modernization and industrialization became more urgent, Buddhism, Daoism, and popular traditions were criticized as superstitions and barriers to progress. But tradition proved too strong to be broken altogether, in spite of the sometimes severe strains put on it. In the twentieth century, traditional Chinese thought has come to accommodate modernity, not only in Taiwan, Hong Kong, and overseas communities with Western-style capitalist economies, but also in the rest of China, where Communism has imposed its own pressures, often in the form of severe persecution.

In China, the foreign philosophy of Marxism-Leninism has been shaped to fit a Chinese context. For example, although successive Communist leaders have vilified traditional Confucianism, official rhetoric about working for the good of the state, party, or collective is not different in kind from the traditional Confucian emphasis on the group over the individual.

Neon dragons and other emblems from Chinese traditional religion adorn Hong Kong skyscrapers to mark its return to China in 1997.

聚樂
神輿伴揃

Chapter Seven

JAPANESE TRADITIONS

C. Scott Littleton

A statue of the Buddha at Kamakura, Japan. He is depicted seated zazen *(in the lotus position), the ideal posture for meditation, according to Zen Buddhists.*

OPPOSITE *Worshippers in the traditional dress of a pilgrim bow before a Shinto shrine at Karatsu on Kyushu island during the annual Kunchi festival in November* *(see also p.262).*

INTRODUCTION

*Offerings left by pilgrims on Koya-*san *(Mount Koya), the headquarters of Shingon, founded by Kobo-daishi in the ninth century* CE *(see p.243) and one of the major sects of Japanese Buddhism.*

The inhabitants of Japan simultaneously espouse two major faiths, Shinto and Buddhism, which have coexisted and influenced one another for the past fifteen hundred years. Shinto is indigenous to Japan, while Japanese Buddhism is a branch of a world religion that commands the devotion of hundreds of millions of people throughout east and southeast Asia and in the West.

Japan's indigenous religion is called the "Way of the Gods (or Spirits)," which is expressed both by the native phrase *Kami no Michi* and the synonymous term Shinto, a Japanese articulation of Chinese *shen* ("spirit") and *dao* ("way"). Both phrases are written with the Chinese characters for *shen* and *dao*. Shinto has been the more usual expression since the resurgence of the religion in the eighteenth and nineteenth centuries—ironically, since the promoters of the revival tended to be anti-Chinese (see p.255).

The roots of Shinto lie deep in Japanese prehistory. Its most ancient and fundamental concept, that of the *kami* ("spirit," "divine being," or "god/goddess"; see pp.246–9), is still central to the Japanese religious consciousness. Buddhism's ultimate source was far from Japan, in India (see chapter 5). However, like most trappings of Japanese civilization, the new faith arrived by way of China, the great mother-civilization of east Asia, whence it was brought to Japan, via Korea, in the mid-sixth century CE. At this time Japan had no writing, but Buddhism brought literacy in its wake. The Buddhist scriptures were available only in Chinese translations, so the newly converted Japanese aristocrats—it would be several centuries before Buddhism spread widely throughout the population—were obliged to learn to read Chinese characters.

Confucianism and Daoism also made their appearance in Japan in this period, and both had a profound impact on Shinto and the development of Japanese Buddhism. But only rarely (such as at the Tokugawa court ca. 1700CE) did they attain the status of true religious sects.

Despite the huge impact of Chinese religious beliefs, philosophy, and arts, Japan always remained distinct from its neighbor across the sea. The nation's deep-rooted tendency to readapt and transform what it borrows from other cultures soon manifested itself. Hence the Mahayana Buddhist sects that took root or emerged in Japan—the "Nara Schools," Tendai, Shingon, Jodo-shu and Jodo-shinshu, Nichiren-shu and Nichiren-shoshu, Zen, and others—soon became, and have remained, uniquely Japanese. Thus, the line between Buddhism and Shintoism can sometimes be somewhat hazy—as demonstrated by the fact that many Buddhist deities came to be worshipped as Shinto *kami* (see p.249).

In more recent years, Japan has witnessed the establishment of the

SACRED JAPAN

There are many hundreds of places of religious significance all over Japan, and some of the most important are shown on the maps on this page. As well as formal places of worship such as Buddhist temples (*otera*) and Shinto shrines (*jinja*), countless natural features, for example Mount Fuji and Mount Koya, are also revered for their sacred significance and are the objects of pilgrimage.

Key

- Sacred mountain
- Site of special religious significance
- Other town or city

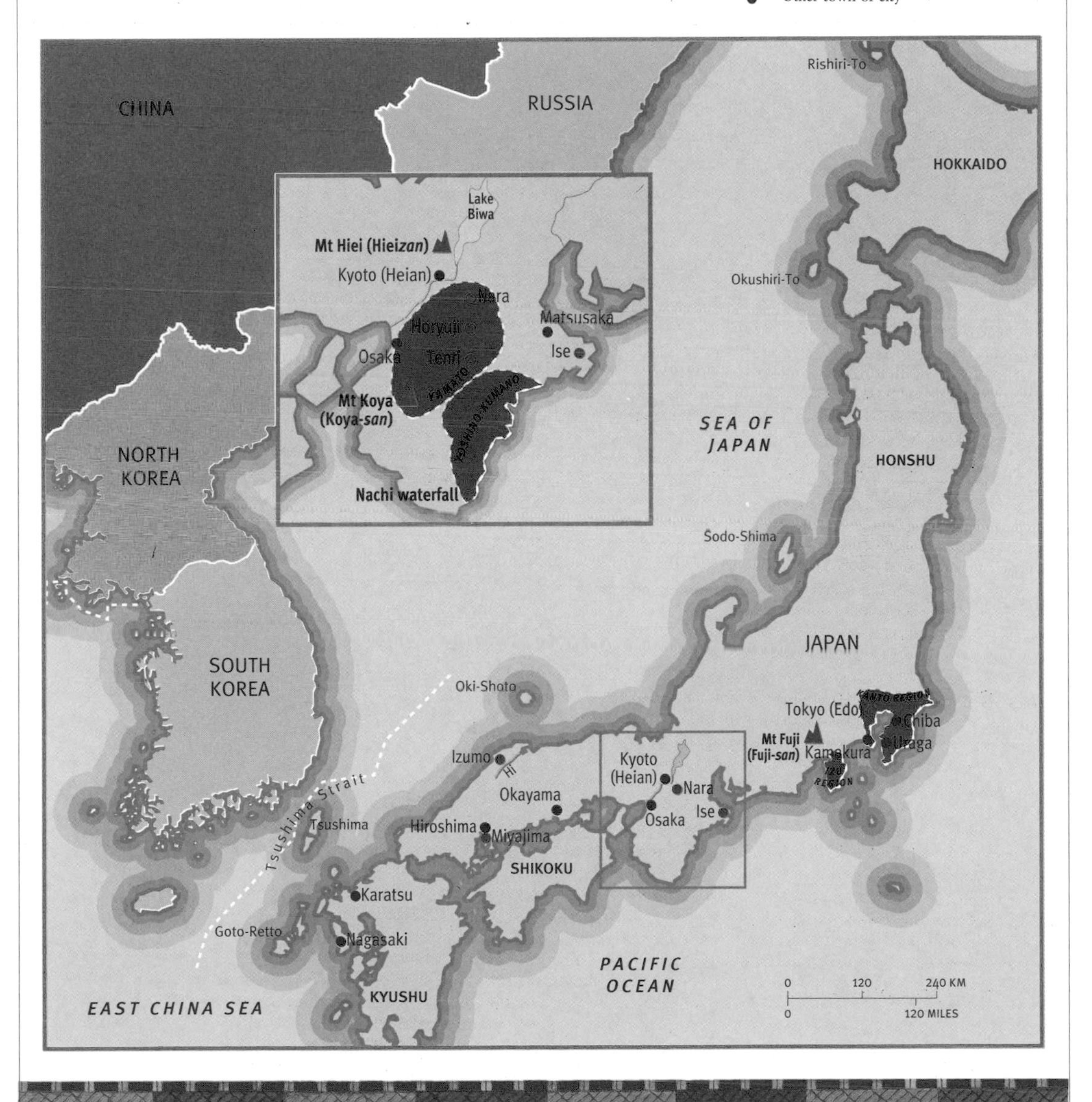

so-called "New Religions" (see pp.270–71), and the reemergence of Christianity, which first came to Japan in the sixteenth century but was subsequently suppressed (see p.244). The growth of these faiths was stimulated respectively by the social chaos of the last three decades (1837–67) of the Tokugawa shogunate and by the rapid economic development that followed the Second World War. But in each case the end result has been quintessentially Japanese, a relatively seamless blend of foreign and indigenous ideas, customs, rites, and beliefs.

Syncretism, the fusion of disparate beliefs and practices into a single system, has long since been a feature of religious life in Japan, together with what in the West might be considered a high degree of "ambiguity tolerance." With some important exceptions, most Japanese people would probably consider themselves to be both Shintoists and Buddhists and would perceive no contradiction in practising two faiths with such radically different roots. Many might put it this way: Shinto is the "life religion" and Buddhism is the "death religion." Thus, for example, by far the majority of Japanese weddings are held according to Shinto rites, while an equally overwhelming majority of funerals are Buddhist and most cemeteries are attached to Buddhist temples. Broadly speaking, Shinto focuses

CHRONOLOGY *All dates are* CE, *except where stated*

PREHISTORIC PERIOD

Jomon Era (ca. 11,000–300BCE)
- Earliest fertility cults

Yayoi Era (ca. 300BCE–300CE)
- New people arrive from southeast Asia; beginnings of Shinto

Kofun Era (ca. 300–552)
- ca. 400 • Mounted nomads from central Asia introduce *kofun* (tumulus) burials and *haniwa* figurines

HISTORIC PERIOD

Asuka Era (552–646)
- 552 or 538 • Introduction of Buddhism
- 592 • The regent Shotoku makes Buddhism the court religion

Hakuho Era (646–710)
- Four of the six "Nara Schools" of Buddhism founded

Nara Era (710–794)
- Other two "Nara Schools" founded; first great flowering of Japanese Buddhism
- 712 • Ono Yasumaro compiles *Kojiki*
- 720 • Composition of *Nihonshoki*

Heian Era (794–1185)
- 804–06 • Kobo-daishi and Dengyo-daishi, founders of Tendai and Shingon, visit Buddhist sites in China
- 850–1000 • Tendai and Shingon spread throughout Japan

Kamakura Era (1185–1333)
- Honen (1133–1212) founds "Pure Land" sect (Jodo-shu) of Japanese Buddhism; Eisai (1141–1215) introduces Rinzai sect of Chan (Zen) Buddhism from China; Shinran (1173–1263) founds "True Pure Land" sect (Jodo-shinshu) of Buddhism; Dogen (1200–53) introduces Soto sect of Chan from China; Nichiren (1222–82) founds Nichiren-shu sect of Buddhism

Ashikaga Era (1333–1568)
- 1549 • Jesuit mission of Francis Xavier inaugurates Japan's "Christian century"

Momoyama Era (1568–1603)
- 1571 • Oda Nobunaga destroys the great Tendai Buddhist temple complex on Mount Hiei; he flirts with Catholicism
- 1596 • *Shogun* Toyotomi Hideyoshi bans Christianity; novices killed

Tokugawa Era (1603–1868)
- 1615 • Christian missionaries expelled
- 1638 • *Shogun* Iemitsu enforces anti-Christian edicts; Buddhism ascendant
- mid–1700s • Beginnings of Shinto revival
- early 1800s • "New Religions" begin to appear (e.g. Tenrikyo, 1838)

Meiji Era (1868–1912)
- 1872 • Emperor Meiji repeals anti-Christian edicts; beginnings of "State Shinto;" Buddhism persecuted for a brief period

Taisho Era (1912–26)
- Revival of Buddhism

Showa Era (1926–1989)
- 1945 • Following Japan's defeat in the Second World War, the US occupying powers enforce the abolition of State Shinto and Emperor Hirohito's renunciation of divine status of the Japanese imperial line
- 1950s–60s • "New Religions," such as Soka Gakkai, flourish

Heisei Era (1989–)
- 1995 • Gas attack by Aum Shinrikyu sect on Tokyo subway

on matters relating to this world, on procreation, the promotion of fertility, on spiritual purity, and physical well-being. Buddhism, on the other hand, although it does not reject the real world, has always placed far greater emphasis on salvation and the possibility of an afterlife. Indeed, the "Pure Land" sects took shape specifically to meet this need.

Any assessment of the role played by religion in ancient or modern Japan must take into account certain fundamental aspects of Japanese culture. Most important is the subordination of the individual to the group, epitomized in the Japanese expression "the nail that sticks up will be hammered down." Many scholars believe that this ethos has its roots in the close cooperation and collective decision-making necessitated by wet-rice cultivation, until very recently Japan's prime source of sustenance. The rice paddy, introduced to Japan in the late first millennium BCE, is extremely labor-intensive; before mechanization, each rice plant had to be individually inserted into the wet ground. Even in modern times, all members of a household subordinate their personal inclinations to work together for the good of the crop—and, by extension, for mutual survival. At a broader level, it is a village affair, in which a cluster of households assist one another in planting, weeding, and harvesting.

Such social cooperation, and the concomitant absence of marked individualism, have characterized both Shinto and Japanese Buddhism from the outset. Over the centuries, both religions have always made a prime virtue of subordination to the well-being of the larger social unit, whether that unit be a household, a rice-growing village, a feudal domain dominated by a close-knit *samurai* élite, or the body of "salarymen" employed by a modern multinational corporation.

Gankakeema *(prayer tablets) left by devotees at the Kiyomizu Buddhist temple at Kyoto. The city was Japan's imperial capital from 794CE (when it was called Heian) until 1868 and one of the most important centers of Japanese Buddhism.*

FAITH AND COEXISTENCE

A hanniwa *figurine of a warrior—perhaps engaged in an act of devotion to a deity or lord—found at Yamato-mura in Ibaraki prefecture, eastern Honshu.*

The origins of Shinto lie deep in prehistory. It is open to question whether the prehistoric Jomon culture (ca. 11,000–300BCE) possessed a faith centered on the reverence of *kami*, at least in anything like the form known today. These preliterate, seminomadic foragers and fisherfolk produced *dogu*, stylized female figurines that emphasized the hips and breasts. The precise nature of the beliefs surrounding *dogu* is unknown, although they probably reflect the existence of a fertility cult. *Dogu* were often placed in or near graves after being deliberately broken, perhaps ritually "killed" in order to release the spiritual "essence" of the *dogu*. But whether this "essence" was conceived in terms of anything resembling a prototypical Shinto *kami* remains entirely a matter of speculation.

However, strikingly Shintoistic iconographic evidence begins to appear with the arrival of the more complex Yayoi culture (ca. 300BCE–300CE). Among the grave goods associated with the Yayoi—rice cultivators whose homeland probably lay somewhere in southeast Asia or south China—are small images of grain storehouses that are remarkably similar to the architecture of the shrine of Ise, which has remained unaltered for at least twelve hundred years (see p.258). Female fertility images also occur, as well as stone clubs that appear to have a phallic symbolism. The introduction of paddy rice agriculture seems to have brought with it rituals associated with sowing and harvesting that were probably fundamentally similar to rice-related Shinto rituals that persist to this day in rural Japan.

Closely associated with the Yayoi fertility cult are comma-shaped jewels called *magatama,* ceremonial mirrors, and sacred swords, all of which play a significant role in Shinto mythology and form part of the imperial regalia to this day. Many scholars suspect that the majority of the *ujigami*, the tutelary deities associated with the most ancient recorded Japanese *uji* (clans), date from this period. The most important *ujigami* was (and is) Amaterasu, the sun goddess (see p.247), the mythological progenitor of the Yamato *uji* ("Sun clan"), that is, the Japanese imperial family.

In the fourth century CE, Japan was conquered by horse-riding nomads from central Asia—almost certainly a ruling élite rather than an invading population—and a new form of chieftain's tomb appeared: the *kofun*, or tumulus. *Hanniwa*, votive figurines of horses and warriors, were often placed around the periphery of these massive, keyhole-shaped mounds to accompany the deceased warlord on his journey to the afterworld.

By the beginning of the sixth century CE, the Yamato emperor, based in the region that still bears this name, exercised authority over most of the country to the south and west of the Kanto plain (see map, p.239). It was to this embryonic state that the first substantial contingent of Buddhist missionaries traveled, in 552CE according to tradition, although scholars think 538CE a more likely date. According to the *Nihonshoki* of 720CE (see p.250), the recently converted king of Paekche in southwest Korea sent missionaries to the Yamato court recommending the new religion from far-off India to his Japanese "brother."

Many Yamato courtiers enthusiastically embraced the new religion—albeit for the most part in a highly Shintoistic way, worshipping statues of the Buddha as manifestations of a powerful *kami*—while others resented its intrusion. However, in 592CE, the regent Shotoku declared Buddhism the official religion of the imperial court.

In the following two centuries, Buddhism rapidly expanded its influence among the imperial aristocracy. But most Japanese remained untouched by the religion until the early Heian era (794–1185CE). In 806CE, the monks Kobo-daishi and Dengyo-daishi returned from sojourns in China to found two new sects on Chinese models, respectively Shingon (from Chinese *Zhen yan*, "True Word") and Tendai (from Tiantai, a mountain and sect in eastern China). Both had their headquarters on mountains near the new capital of Heian (Kyoto)—Shingon on Mount Koya and Tendai on Mount Hiei. From these bastions, mis-

THE NARA SCHOOLS

Between 625 and 738, six important schools of Buddhism were founded in or near Nara, the first Japanese capital, by Japanese monks who had studied in China: Jojitsu (625), Sanron (625), Hosso (654), Kusha (658), Kegon (736), and Ritsu (738). Each of these "Nara Schools" had links with a parent temple in China. The best known of the Nara Schools is probably Kegon, whose massive wooden headquarters, the Todai-ji temple in Nara, houses a huge bronze statue of the Buddha and is one of the most famous buildings in Japan.

PRINCE SHOTOKU

The second son of the emperor Yomei, Prince Shotoku (Shotoku Taishi), was born in 574CE, barely two decades after the arrival of the first Buddhist missionaries. His father was one of the first emperors to embrace the new faith and saw to it that his son was exposed to Buddhist ideas almost from the time he was born.

In 587 the future of Buddhism in Japan was assured when the Soga clan, which championed the new faith, defeated a conservative coalition headed by the Mononobe family. Subsequently, after the young Shotoku was appointed regent on behalf of his aunt, the empress Suiko, he was able in 592 to declare Buddhism the official religion of the Yamato court.

Shortly thereafter he founded (and perhaps designed) a major Buddhist temple complex at Horyuji, near Nara, and throughout his reign he worked tirelessly to advance the Buddhist cause. For this reason, Shotoku is often described as the "founder of Japanese Buddhism."

But his contribution to the development of Japanese religion were not limited to his activities on behalf of Buddhism. He was also steeped in the Chinese classics and did as much as anyone to introduce Confucianism and Daoism to Japan. In 604 he promulgated his famous "Seventeen Article Constitution," which drew heavily on both Buddhist and Confucian ethical principles. By the time of Shotoku's death in 622, Japan had moved from being a peripheral, barely literate proto-state to become a civilized and highly sophisticated empire closely modeled on that of China.

Prince Shotoku: a hanging scroll of ca. 1850. The founder of Buddhism in Japan, the prince himself became the object of popular veneration.

sionaries from the new sects journeyed through the countryside, and the number of converts to Buddhism rose rapidly in the ninth and tenth centuries. Later, Kyoto became the headquarters of the Zen sects introduced from China during the twelfth and thirteenth centuries (see p.252).

Buddhists did not attempt to undermine or supplant Shinto, but simply founded their temples next to Shinto shrines and proclaimed that there was no fundamental conflict between the two faiths. Toward the end of the Heian era, this sense of inclusiveness led to the development of Ryobu Shinto, or "Double Shinto," in which Shinto *kami* and Buddhist *bosatsu* (*bodhisattvas*; see pp.176–7) were formally combined into single divine entities. This theological fusion was often visually represented by images of

CHRISTIANITY IN JAPAN

In 1549, Francis Xavier, a Portuguese priest and a founder of the Jesuit order, arrived in Japan at the head of a Christian mission, just four years after the visit of the first Portuguese merchant ships. The new religion was supported, at least implicitly, by the powerful *daimyo* (warlord) Oda Nobunaga (1534–82), who made effective use of European weaponry. The new faith spread rapidly and, by the early 1580s, virtually all of the *daimyo* of Kyushu island had converted, along with their subjects. There were also large pockets of Christians in other regions, including the capital, Kyoto, and the total number of converts cannot have been far short of a million. There is no firm evidence that Nobunaga himself converted to Catholicism, but one of the last portraits of him depicts him wearing a crucifix.

The monument to the "Japanese Martyrs" in Nagasaki—formerly, as today, the seat of the Roman Catholic church in Japan. They were put to death during the persecution of Christians under Toyotomi Hideyoshi.

In 1582, Nobunaga was assassinated by a subordinate. He was succeeded by his chief general, Toyotomi Hideyoshi (1536–98), who in 1587 reversed the policy of tolerance. A number of Japanese Jesuit novices were crucified—the "Japanese Martyrs"—and missionaries were expelled. Christianity was officially banned in 1596. The persecution became less intense under Tokugawa Ieyasu (1542–1616), Hideyoshi's successor and founder of the Tokugawa shogunate that governed Japan from 1603 to 1867. But Ieyasu's grandson, Shogun Tokugawa Iemitsu, was zealous in his efforts to stamp out the faith. For example, suspected Christians who refused to trample on an image of the Virgin were summarily executed. Faced with such repression, most Christian *daimyo* and their subjects renounced the faith. By 1640, Japan's so-called "Christian century" had come to an end.

A handful of Japanese Catholics continued to practice in secret, mostly in and around Nagasaki. By the time the anti-Christian edicts were repealed in 1872, they had had no contact with Rome for over two centuries and much of their practice had become far removed from mainstream Christianity (for example, devotion to Jesus and Mary had come to resemble the worship of powerful Shinto *kami* or Buddhist *bosatsu*). Most refused to rejoin the Catholic church, and this Christian offshoot now forms a tiny piece of the Japanese religious mosaic. Today, there are about 600,000 Christians in Japan, out of a population of almost 130 million.

kami in human form "dreaming" of their *bosatsu* counterparts.

The last years of the Heian era were marked by a bloody civil war that culminated in the appointment of Minamoto no Yoritomo to the new imperial office of *shogun*, or "generalissimo." Four centuries of almost constant internal strife followed, leading many priests to suspect that *mappo*, the Mahayana Buddhist "age of chaos" (see pp.266–7), had come. Early in the Kamakura era (1185–1333CE), three sects arose in response to the spiritual challenge: Jodo-shu (the "Pure Land sect"), Jodo-shinshu ("True Pure Land sect"), and Nichiren-shu ("Nichiren sect"). The founders of these new strands of Buddhism, respectively Honen (1133–1212), Shinran (1173–1263), and Nichiren (1222–82), were all trained at the great Tendai Buddhist complex on Mount Hiei.

The most significant religious development of the Ashikaga and Momoyama eras (1333–1603CE) was the arrival of Christianity in 1549, but its initial gains were reversed following the death of its early patron, Oda Nobunaga (see box, opposite). Under the Tokugawa shogunate (1603–1868), Buddhism was in the ascendant, especially the "Pure Land" sects. The Tokugawa also espoused the hierarchical philosophy of Chinese Neoconfucianism (see p.205); Tokyo's only Confucian temple was founded in 1690 by the fifth Tokugawa *shogun*. Daoism also came to occupy an important position, at least among the court intelligentsia.

In the late eighteenth century, the efforts of Motoori Norinaga (1730–1800) and other Shinto scholars led to a renewed interest in the *Kojiki*, *Nihonshoki*, and other ancient Shinto texts (see p.250). A century later, this Shinto revival, which strongly emphasized the imperial cult, was a major factor in the collapse of the by then economically moribund shogunate and the restoration in 1868 of imperial power under the emperor Meiji. In the years immediately following the Meiji restoration, Shinto became the official religion of Japan (known as "State Shinto") and Buddhism went into a brief eclipse (see sidebar).

In the 1870s, missionaries from a variety of Christian denominations returned to a newly tolerant Japan, but few Japanese saw any merit in switching from Shinto, a faith closely associated with the imperial regime and hence also with the growing prosperity that was the result of the government's policy of Western-style industrialization. Today only around six hundred thousand Japanese profess the Christian faith.

An important phenomenon in the recent history of Japanese religion is the growth of the Shinko Shukyo ("New Religions"), a term used to cover the many new sects that began to arise in the early nineteenth century amid the social chaos that marked the collapse of *shogun* feudalism. For the most part, these sects were blends of Shinto and Buddhism, but since the Meiji restoration some have adopted elements of Christianity and other faiths (see pp.270–71).

THE BUDDHIST PERSECUTION

The triumph of Shinto after the Meiji restoration resulted in a backlash against Buddhism, which had been favored by the shogunate. Long-standing Buddhist symbols and practices were forcibly removed from major shrines by the new imperialist regime, and in the 1870s the Buddhist clergy dramatically lost the influence it had enjoyed under the Tokugawa. Museums and collectors in Europe and America provided a ready market for priceless artifacts looted from temples by anti-Buddhist zealots, with the authorities often turning a blind eye.

However, in the late 1880s, the imperial government put an end to the backlash, and the Buddhist establishment made a rapid comeback. Shinto remained the state religion until 1945, but the historic balance between the two faiths was restored and persists to the present. State Shinto was disestablished after the end of the Second World War, and since then no faith has enjoyed official status.

An 18th-century map of the Tendai Buddhist complex on Hieizan (Mount Hiei) near Kyoto. Many great founder figures of Japanese Buddhism trained here, including Honen, Shinran, Nichiren, Eisai, and Dogen (see pp.252–5).

Jimmu Tenno on the quest that will establish him as the first emperor of Japan. A 19th-century print.

A WORLD OF SPIRITS

The Japanese word *kami* is often translated as "deity" (a god or goddess), but in reality it designates an extremely wide range of spirit-beings together with a host of mysterious and supernatural forces and "essences." In the *Kojiki* (see p.250), it is said that there are eight million *kami*, which in Japanese is another way of saying that the number is infinite. They include countless vaguely defined tutelary divinities of clans, villages, and neighborhoods (*ujigami*); "spirits of place"—the essences of prominent geographical features, including mountains, rivers, and waterfalls; and other natural phenomena, such as the *kamikaze* ("divine wind"), the typhoon that saved Japan from a seaborne Mongol invasion in the thirteenth century. Some *kami* are *oni*, demonic, vengeful spirits (see p.248); others are compounded of benign imported Buddhist and Daoist deities.

Ancestral spirits form another important category of *kami*. In Shinto, a person's soul is believed to become a *kami* after the death of its mortal "host," and the *kami* of a family's ancestors are revered at household shrines. Some ancestral *kami*, such as the spirits of the modernizing emperor Meiji (1867–1912) and other rulers, may become the foci of more widespread cults. For example, Meiji's shrine is the most important Shinto shrine in Tokyo. The *kami* of all Japan's war dead since 1872 continue to be worshipped at Tokyo's controversial Yasukuni shrine (see p.268).

The most widely known *kami* are the anthropomorphic gods and goddesses who emerged during what ancient texts call the "Age of the Gods" (see box, opposite). These are the "heavenly *kami*" (*amatsukami*), such as the widely venerated sun goddess, Amaterasu, and the "earthly *kami*" (*kunitsukami*), such as the popular Okuninushi, the guardian god of Japan and its emperors (see sidebar). Okuninushi is venerated at Izumo Taisha, the second most important Shinto shrine after that of Amaterasu at Ise.

Other major *kami* include Inari, the rice god, widely venerated as the deity who ensures an abundant rice harvest and, by extension, general prosperity. His cult is thus especially important to shopkeepers, merchants, and artisans. Inari's messenger and guardian is the fox, and images of this animal are prominent at all the god's shrines. In ancient times, Inari was also considered to be the patron of swordsmiths.

The so-called "Seven Lucky Gods" embody a variety of desirable characteristics. The most popular are Daikokuten and his son Ebisu, both of whom represent material abundance and are often enshrined together. Daikokuten, typically depicted with a large sack over his left shoulder, is particularly revered by cooks and restaurateurs. He is frequently assimilated to Okuninushi, who is also known as Daikokusama. Ebisu carries a fishing rod in his left hand and a sea bream under his right. The other five

THE IMPERIAL MYTH

The Izumo region of Japan made an important contribution to Shinto myth, in particular the story of the establishment of the rule of Jimmu Tenno, the first emperor, and the Japanese imperial line.

After Susano's banishment from heaven (see box, opposite), he descended to "the Reed Plain" (earth), where he saved a beautiful maiden from a dragon. Susano found a fabulous sword, Kusanagi, in one of its eight tails and gave it to his sister, the goddess Amaterasu, as a peace offering. He married the maiden, built a palace near Izumo, and fathered a dynasty of powerful deities who came to rule the earth. The greatest was Okuninushi, the "Great Lord of the Country." Alarmed at Okuninushi's power, Amaterasu sent her grandson Honinigi to reestablish her sovereignty over the earth. A compromise was reached: beginning with Honinigi's descendant, Jimmu Tenno, the earthly scions of Amaterasu would rule the earth as emperors, while Okuninushi would be the perpetual divine guardian of the land.

"THE AGE OF THE GODS"

The stories of the great gods and goddesses of Shinto are told in the epics the *Kojiki* and the *Nihonshoki* (see pp.250–51). They give an account of the primeval era known as "the Age of the Gods," when deities were active on earth before establishing the rule of their mortal descendants, the emperors, and then withdrawing to the heavenly domain.

In the beginning, when the world was a fluid, turbulent, formless chaos, there arose seven successive generations of invisible *kami*. In the eighth generation, the god Izanagi and the goddess Izanami came into being and, standing on the "Floating Bridge of Heaven" (probably to be interpreted as a rainbow), they dipped a jeweled spear into the jelly-like mass and created an island, Onogoro. This was the first land.

Izanagi and Izanami descended to the island. At this point they became aware of their gender difference and had sexual intercourse. But Izanami's first offspring was a "leech-child" (that is, a monster), and the couple sought help from the older *kami*. Izanami then gave birth to an array of *kami* and also islands—the Japanese archipelago. But the birth of her last child, the fire god, caused her such severe burns that she died and went to Yomi, the land of the dead (see p.267).

Izanagi ventured into Yomi in a vain attempt to retrieve his beloved wife, but he disregarded her plea not to look upon her. He saw that Izanami had become a rotting, hideous demon, and fled in horror, pursued by Izanami and the so-called "Hags of Yomi." He barely escaped with his life.

To purify himself of Yomi's pollution, Izanagi bathed in the Hi river (see map, p.239). As he washed, the sun goddess Amaterasu was born from his left eye, the moon god Tsuku-yomi from his right eye, and the storm god, Susano, from his nose. Izanagi then retired to northwest Kyushu island, where today there are a handful of shrines to him and Izanami. Before retiring, Izanagi handed power to his offspring: Amaterasu was to be supreme deity, Tsuki-yomi became lord of the night, and Susano lord of the sea.

But Susano was jealous of his sister and raged through heaven, causing chaos. Amaterasu's response was to shut herself away in the "Heavenly Cave of Darkness," making matters worse by depriving the world of sunlight and causing the crops to wither. She was eventually tricked into reappearing, and as she did so the sunlight returned.

After the sun goddess's reemergence, Susano was banished and Amaterasu's sovereignty was confirmed. Her descendant Jimmu became the first emperor (see sidebar), and with the establishment of the imperial line, the "Age of the Gods" came to an end.

A 19th-century triptych showing Amaterasu, the sun goddess, emerging from the "Heavenly Cave of Darkness" in a blaze of light. She left the cave only after the other deities had tricked her into believing that her reflection in a mirror—a sacred Shinto symbol—was a more powerful sun goddess. It has been suggested that this episode was based on a solar eclipse.

are Benten (god of skill in music and other arts), Fukurokuju (god of popularity), Hotei (god of magnanimity), Jurojin (god of longevity), and Bishamonten (god of benevolent authority).

Japanese Buddhism, following the Mahayana tradition, venerates a broad array of sacred beings known as *butsu* (Sanskrit *buddha*) and *bosatsu* (Sanskrit *bodhisattva*; see pp.176–7). Three of these divine beings loom especially large in Japanese Buddhism: Amida, Kannon, and Jizo. Of these, the most important is the *butsu* Amida (Sanskrit Amitabha), who presides over the "Pure Land," or Western Paradise, which plays a central role in the Tendai sect and its Pure Land offshoots (see p.193).

After Amida, the most popular Buddhist divinity is Kannon, who derives directly from the Chinese goddess Guanyin (see p.211) and ultimately from the Indian male *bodhisattva* Avalokiteshvara (see p.176). Variously depicted as male or female, Kannon is the protector of children, dead souls, and women in childbirth; it is also the *bosatsu* to whom worshippers turn for mercy and forgiveness. Kannon is often depicted as "Kannon of the Thousand Arms," based on the idea that the deity possesses limitless compassion to dispense to the believer. Temples dedicated to Kannon are found in almost every Japanese community.

The *bosatsu* Jizo is also concerned with children, particularly with the souls of those who have died (including, in recent times, aborted fetuses). Tiny Jizo-*yas*, or temples to Jizo, are to be found everywhere in Japan, and are readily identifiable by their cluster of little images of the *bosatsu* wearing a red scarf and, often, a piece of clothing from a deceased child. Jizo is

EVIL SPIRITS

In Japanese tradition, most evil spirits or *oni* ("demons") are invisible. Some are thought to be animal spirits who have the capacity to possess a person. Among the most feared is the fox spirit, possession by which can bring about all sorts of calamities, including illness and death. In parts of rural Japan, especially in the north, where old customs and beliefs tend to linger, the *yamabushi* ("mountain warriors"; see p.260), are considered particularly adept at exorcising such spirits and thereby restoring the victim to good health.

Another variety of evil spirit is the *obake*, or ghost. These entities, too, are believed capable of causing considerable harm, and they can be driven off with appropriate rituals.

TENJIN: THE DIVINE BUREAUCRAT

A prime example of a historical figure who became a major Shinto *kami* is Sugawara no Michizane, otherwise known as Tenjin, or "Heaven Person." A brilliant administrator and scholar, Tenjin (845–903CE) was at the peak of his career as a member of the Heian (Kyoto) court when several jealous colleagues conspired against him. Falsely accused of misconduct in office, Tenjin was banished from his native city and spent the rest of his life as a restless political exile.

After his death, Heian was devastated by fires and pestilence. The imperial authorities were convinced that this was divine retribution for their treatment of Tenjin and sought to appease his angry spirit by building a major shrine to his *kami*—the Kitano Temmangu shrine, which remains one of the most important Shinto shrines in modern Kyoto.

According to the story, conditions in Heian immediately improved. Thereafter, Tenjin became an important member of the Shinto pantheon, venerated throughout Japan. He is considered especially helpful in matters relating to education, and he is still regularly invoked by students who are about to take important examinations, and by scholars seeking divine help in their research.

the protector of all who suffer pain, and he is believed to be able to redeem souls from Jigoku ("Hell;" see p.267) and lead them to the Pure Land.

In popular worship, the distinction between Shinto *kami* and Buddhist *bosatsu* and *butsu* is very blurred. At times in the past Shinto priests have used the phrase "*kami*-nature" in a fashion analogous to the Buddhist "*buddha*-nature." Both *kami* and *bosatsu* are seen as essentially complementary, and a number of divinities are important to both faiths, such as Hachiman (see sidebar). Kannon and Jizo are also worshipped as *kami* by vast numbers of Japanese.

Hachiman is not the only deity with historical or quasihistorical roots. Others include Tenjin (see box), while the most recent include the emperor Meiji. Japanese Buddhists sometimes invoke the spirits of the Buddhist masters Honen, Shinran, and Nichiren (see pp.253–5) much as if they were *kami*—although they have never become the focus of major cults.

HACHIMAN

The Shinto *kami* Hachiman is an important warrior god largely derived from the semilegendary emperor Ojin (ca. 300CE). Hachiman is widely worshipped throughout Japan at both Buddhist temples and Shinto shrines. Most notably, he is the tutelary deity of the Todaiji temple in Nara (which also houses the largest statue of the Buddha in Japan) and of the Hachiman shrine in Kamakura.

Hachiman shrines are favorite venues for the ritual called *omiyamairi* in which infants—primarily boys in the case of Hachiman—are taken to shrines for the first time and purified (see p.264). At the same time, Hachiman's image is to be found in a great many Buddhist temples, where he is venerated as a *bosatsu.*

A statue of Hachiman by the sculptor Kaikei, who worked at Nara in the 13th century. The striking realism of this figure was typical of the Kamakura era (1185–1333). The god is represented in the habit of a Buddhist monk.

A Buddhist master calligrapher in Tokyo at work on a scroll. Calligraphy was introduced from China and became a major art form, especially after a simplified Japanese script was devised in the 9th century CE *(see p.253).*

THE *NIHONSHOKI*

The leading Japanese clans were apparently dissatisfied with the *Kojiki* even before Ono had completed it (see main text), largely because it emphasized the history of the imperial clan at the expense of their own. The court responded to their dissatisfaction by commissioning the *Nihonshoki* ("Chronicles of Japan") from a committee of courtiers.

Ono had produced a relatively straightforward narrative, but the authors of the *Nihonshoki* felt compelled to retell each important mythological event from a variety of perspectives, reflecting the versions sacred to the several major clans. The result was a jumble of compromises, redundancies, and even contradictions. Nonetheless, the *Nihonshoki* is a treasure trove of tales that shed a great deal of light on the range and diversity of ancient Shinto mythology and its *kami*.

Unlike the *Kojiki*, the *Nihonshoki* is written in classical Chinese, although it includes poetic sections in archaic Japanese. Wherever possible, the authors presented the myths from a Chinese perspective, and the text contains a great many Chinese mythological themes and references. A good example is the Pan Gu story, a Chinese creation myth that recurs in almost identical form at several points in the *Nihonshoki*.

CHRONICLES AND HOLY WRITINGS

The most ancient and important written sources for Shinto are two epics of the early eighth century CE: the *Kojiki* and *Nihonshoki*. Neither of these texts can be called "scripture" in the sense of divine revelation. Rather, they are both genealogically based chronicles that extend well into the early historic period. The *Kojiki* ("Record of Ancient Matters"), the oldest surviving text in Japanese, was compiled and edited in 712CE by the scholar-courtier Ono Yasumaro from a number of earlier sources. These sources, some written (and unfortunately long since lost) and others oral, were for the most part genealogies of the several powerful *uji*, or clans, that dominated Japanese political life in the Nara period (710–794CE), the most important being the imperial Yamato clan. Each genealogy traced the descent of the *uji* in question back to a particular *kami* (god or goddess).

At this period Japan was actively borrowing almost every conceivable cultural trait from China. Inspired by the Chinese genre of "imperial chronicle" that served to legitimize the ruling dynasty, the Japanese court commissioned Ono to compile a coherent Japanese chronicle that would establish for all time the supremacy of the Yamato clan. The early part of Ono's text contains the primary account of Shinto cosmology and theogony: the creation of the islands of Japan by the primordial deities Izanagi and Izanami; the birth of the sun goddess Amaterasu; the extension of her authority to the "Reed Plain" (Japan); and the appearance of her descendant Jimmu, the first emperor (see pp.246–7).

The *Kojiki* and *Nihonshoki* (compiled in 720CE as a sort of corrective to the *Kojiki*; see sidebar) are by no means the only sources of Shinto beliefs. Other writings include the *Manyoshu* (ca. 760CE), a vast anthology of poetry that embraces poems on religious, mythological, and secular themes; the *Fudoki*, provincial chronicles commissioned in 713CE that include legends of local *kami*; and the *Engishiki*, which dates from the late tenth century CE and includes a large body of *norito*, or ritual prayers for public ceremonies.

By far the most important text in Japanese Buddhism is the *Lotus Sutra* (*Hokkeyo*; see box). Next in significance is the *Dainichi-kyo*, or *Sun Sutra*, which underpins the Shingon sect introduced to Japan by Kobo-daishi (774–835CE). According to the *Sun Sutra*, the entire cosmos emanated from Vairochana, the Sun Buddha, and the goal of the worshipper is to understand the inner meaning of this process. Like the *Lotus Sutra*, the *Sun Sutra* holds that "*buddha*-nature" is inherent in every person and that one can become enlightened in a single lifetime. However, the *Sun Sutra*'s route to salvation is via the esoteric knowledge contained in a highly complex *mandala* (a symbolic representation of the cosmos; see p.177), rather than via professions of faith in the *bodhisattvas*.

The many other revered texts in Japanese Buddhism include the original writings of great masters such as Kobo-daishi, Dengyo-daishi, Honen, Shinran, Nichiren, and the founders of Zen, Eisai and Dogen (see p.252). Zen is also noted for the *koan* (sacred riddle, from Chinese *gong an*), a *mantra*-like statement or enigmatic, sometimes seemingly impossible, question for contemplation. One famous *koan* is "What is the sound of one hand clapping?"

THE *LOTUS SUTRA*

Purportedly based on sermons preached by the Buddha himself, the *Lotus Sutra* is one of the most important religious texts in the Mahayana Buddhist tradition (see also p.181). The *Lotus Sutra* came to Japan with the first Buddhist missionaries in the mid-sixth century CE, but it did not achieve supreme importance until the introduction of the Tendai (Chinese Tiantai) sect from China by Dengyo-daishi (762–822CE). All the major Japanese sects that sprang from Tendai are rooted in the *Lotus Sutra*, including the Pure Land sects preached by Honen and Shinran and especially the sect founded by Nichiren (see pp.254–5).

The central thesis of the *Lotus Sutra* is that all life contains, to a greater or lesser degree, "*buddha*-nature." This can be understood as the capacity for an all-embracing compassion, coupled with the serenity that comes with having renounced all desire. Salvation is possible only if one's "*buddha*-nature" can be fully realized, and to achieve this the worshipper must be devoted to a life of prayer and meditation, and seek the help of a variety of *bodhisattvas* (see pp.176–7). The realization of "*buddha*-nature" brings the devotee closer to the ultimate goal: *nirvana*, permanent release from the endless cycle of death and rebirth.

丘功德悉成滿當得斯淨土賢
事我今但略說
二百阿羅漢心自在者作是
未曾有若世尊各見授記如
亦快乎佛知此等心之所念
千二百阿羅漢我今當現前
多羅三藐三菩提記於此衆
陳如比丘當供養六万二千
為佛号曰普明如來應供正
遍世間解無上士調御丈夫
其五百阿羅漢優樓頻螺迦
提迦葉迦留陀夷優陀夷阿
劫賓那薄拘羅周陀莎伽陀
多羅三藐三菩提盡同一号
世尊欲重宣此義而說偈言

Verses from the Lotus Sutra *inscribed with gold ink in Chinese script on indigo paper. This very fine manuscript is believed to form part of a copy of the* sutra *produced, probably at Kyoto, for the emperor Go-Mizunoo (ruled 1611–29).*

LIGHTS OF WISDOM

In the last two thousand years great contributions to Japanese religious development have been made by individuals ranging from priests and monks to bureaucrats, princes, and emperors. Most of these revered figures have been Buddhists—the founders of new sects and schools. Between them, they established the religious framework that still governs Japanese Buddhism and has also had a profound impact on the evolution of Shinto, as the two faiths have sought to find common ground. Those who have featured prominently in the history of Shinto include scholars such as Ono Yasumaro (see p.250) and Motoori Norinaga (see p.255), who strove tirelessly to preserve the ancient stories of the *kami* faith.

Prominent among early Buddhist masters are Saicho (762–822CE) and Kukai (774–835CE), better known respectively as Dengyo-daishi and

THE FOUNDATION OF ZEN

The Kamakura era witnessed the emergence of Zen—the branch of Japanese Buddhism that is best known outside Japan. Its founders were Eisai (1141–1215) and Dogen (1200–53), both of whom trained at the Tendai "seminary" on Mount Hiei (Hiei*zan*).

Eisai became disillusioned with what he considered the lax monastic discipline on Hiei and in 1168 set out on a five-month pilgrimage to China, visiting the major temples of the Tiantai sect (from which Tendai had sprung) and collecting sacred texts as yet untranslated into Japanese. On a longer pilgrimage (1187–91), he became acquainted with Xu'an Huaichang, master of the Linji sect of Chan, a school of Buddhism centered on intensive meditation (the word "Chan" derives from Sanskrit *dhyaṅa*; see p.219).

Inspired by Xu'an's teachings, Eisai returned to Japan to preach the doctrines of Linji Chan, or "Rinzai Zen" in the Japanese articulation. He left Hiei*zan* and went to Kamakura, where he gained the patronage of the shogunate and produced several important writings, including *Shukke Taiko* ("Essentials of the Monastic Life," 1192), *Kozen Gokku ron* ("The Promulgation of Zen as a Defense of the Nation," 1198), and *Nihon Buppo Chuko gammon* ("A Plea for the Revival of Japanese Buddhism," 1204).

Eisai, the founder of Rinzai Zen. Rinzai spread rapidly among Japan's samurai *élite, who found that the mental discipline of Zen made them better fighters.*

Dogen, the founder of the Soto Zen sect, also studied on Hiei*zan*, and like Eisai he became disenchanted with what he saw as its spiritual laxity. His doubts led Dogen to leave for nearby Kenninji, a Rinzai Zen monastery. Six years later, Dogen also made a pilgrimage to China, where he studied under a master of the Cuotong sect of Chan.

Dogen returned home to establish a Japanese sect of Cuotong Chan ("Soto Zen" in Japanese). Soto Zen is characterized by its emphasis on sitting *zazen*, that is, cross-legged in the "lotus position," as a prerequisite for attaining *satori*, or enlightenment. Unlike Eisai, who advocated the study and contemplation of *koans* (see p.251), Dogen felt that the key to spiritual enlightenment lay in individual discipline focused on an intense understanding of one's own "*buddha*-nature." He elaborated this idea in *Fukan Zazengi* ("A Universal Promotion of *Zazen* Principles," 1227), one of his many influential treatises.

Kobo-daishi, the founders of the Tendai and Shingon sects (see p.243–4). Both are still revered as sages by Japanese Buddhists generally—not just the members of their own sects—and Kobo-daishi is also traditionally credited with inventing *hiragana* and *katakana*, scripts that greatly simplified the writing of Japanese, based on the sounds represented by fifty-one Chinese characters.

The Kamakura era (1185–1333) produced several important Buddhist figures who received their fundamental religious training at the great Tendai temple complex on Mount Hiei, for centuries Japan's principal Buddhist "seminary." These figures include the great masters Eisai and Dogen, who introduced Chan (Zen), the Chinese meditation school of Buddhism, as a major force in Japan (see box, opposite).

This modern print depicts the haloed figure of Honen, who established "Pure Land" Buddhism, seated on a high pedestal in the form of a lotus. He holds a rosary for chanting.

The first of the revered alumni from Mount Hiei in this period was Genku (1133–1212), better known as Honen, founder of the "Pure Land" sect (Jodo-shu). Honen became a Tendai monk at the age of fifteen but over the years he became dissatisfied with orthodox Tendai dogma. In the late 1170s he founded a new sect based on doctrines that had originated in China several centuries earlier and centered on the "Pure Land," a celestial paradise presided over by Amida Buddha (see p.193). Reflecting on the social chaos of the time, Honen asserted that all human beings were inherently too wicked to achieve salvation on their own, even if they lived ostensibly perfect lives. The only hope, he asserted, was to throw oneself on the mercy of Amida. One could reach the Pure Land through *nembutsu*—the Tendai practice of reciting the phrase "*namu Amida Butsu*" ("I put my faith in Amida Buddha")—as well as the teachings of the Chinese masters Daochuo, Shandao, and Zhiyi.

Honen's theology was predicated on the concept of *mappo*, the Mahayana Buddhist notion that the world had entered an age in which the power of the law (*dharma*) had declined, and faith rather than meditation had become the key to salvation. Honen preached that if one practiced *nembutsu* repeatedly, and especially just before death, Amida would take pity on the supplicant's soul and cause it to be reborn in the "Pure Land." (See also pp.266–7.)

From 1207 until a few months before his death, Honen was banished from Hiei and went to live on the remote island of Shikoku. Most of his important works, including *Senchaku hongan nembutsu-shu* ("Treatise on the Selection of the *Nembutsu* of the Primal Vow"), which stresses the supreme importance of *nembutsu*, were written during this period of exile. Honen's sect eventually received formal recognition by the Tendai establishment and Jodo-shu became a major force in the subsequent history of Japanese spirituality.

An even more influential doctrine was preached by Honen's chief disciple, Shinran (1173–1263), the founder of Jodo-shinshu, the "True Pure

SHINRAN: THE GREAT REFORMER

A watercolor on silk depicting Shinran, who advocated faith in a personal relationship between the worshipper and Amida rather than reliance on the nembutsu, *as advocated by Honen.*

Few details are known of the early life of Shinran (1173–1263), the founder of Jodo-shinshu, the "True Pure Land" sect—at present Japanese Buddhism's largest single sect. It is known that he began his monastic training at the age of eight and served as a *doso* (low-ranking monk) on Mount Hiei until 1201. He subsequently fell under the influence of Honen (see main text) and accompanied him into exile from 1207–11.

After Honen's death in 1212, Shinran received a pardon from the authorities. By this time, Shinran's own interpretation of the doctrine of *nembutsu* (see p.253) had begun to diverge from that of his master, and he had also rejected the doctrine of priestly celibacy. During his exile with Honen, he had become the first Buddhist priest to marry and raise a family (today, following Shinran's example, many other Japanese Buddhist sects permit their priests to marry).

Shinran decided to migrate eastward to the Kanto region, gathering his own band of disciples in the process, and this period marks the beginning of Jodo-shinshu. Some years later, in 1235, Shinran returned to Kyoto, where he remained until his death at the age of ninety.

What sets Shinran apart from Honen is his emphasis upon what he called the "Primal Vow," that is, an absolute commitment to Amida Buddha (see p.177) as one's "personal savior," to borrow a phrase from Christian theology. Shinran held that an all-embracing, intensely personal faith in the power of the divine—Amida—was the key to salvation (an idea remarkably similar to the Protestant doctrine of "justification by faith" formulated three centuries later by Martin Luther). Ultimately, what counted was this compact between the supplicant and Amida, and everything else was fundamentally peripheral: hence it did not matter how often one recited *nembutsu*, or whether one uttered it just prior to death, as Honen preached. A single, intensely fervent *nembutsu*, in which the supplicant opened his or her heart to Amida, was all that was required to gain eventual rebirth in the "Pure Land."

Land" sect (see box). Initially, Jodo-shinshu was a loosely organized set of congregations that Shinran had founded in the course of his travels around Japan, each of which interpreted their master's teachings in its own way. The sect was only organized into a tightly-knit, hierarchical community some two centuries after Shinran's death by the monk Rennyo (1414–99), who is known as Jodo-shinshu's "second founder."

A third, and far more controversial, master to emerge from Hiei*zan* during this period was Nichiren (1222–82). From an early age Nichiren entertained many doubts about "Pure Land" beliefs—in particular the power of *nembutsu*—as well as those of the Zen sects (see p.252). He came to regard a single text, the *Lotus Sutra*, with its doctrine of universal salvation, as the supreme spiritual authority (see p.251). He imputed such awesome power to it that he encouraged his followers to chant the phrase known as the *daimoku*: "*Namu myoho renge kyo*" ("I take my refuge in the *Lotus*

On his voyage into exile in the isles of Izu (about 160 km [100 miles] south of Tokyo), Nichiren calms the sea as the crew cower in terror. In this woodblock print by Kuniyoshi (1797–1861), Nichiren's sacred chant, the daimoku *(see main text) appears in the waves.*

Sutra"). Nichiren rejected all other Buddhist tenets, including the belief that Amida possessed the power to save souls.

In 1253, after leaving Hiei*zan*, Nichiren began to preach against the "Pure Land" and Zen sects, and was exiled by the authorities to Izu—the first of a series of banishments and incarcerations. In 1268, Nichiren asserted that an impending Mongol seaborne invasion would be averted only if Japan adopted his doctrines as its sole religion. His denunciations of the government became so virulent that he was sentenced to death for treason—a penalty that was later revoked. (In the event, the Mongol fleet was destroyed by a typhoon hailed as a *kamikaze* or "divine wind.")

Quarrelsome, charismatic, fanatical and ultra-patriotic, Nichiren cut against the Japanese grain. No other Buddhist claimed to preach the only truth, and this aspect of his teaching was widely resented from the beginning. As a result, the two sects based on his teachings, Nichiren-shu and the later Nichiren-shoshu, remained relatively insignificant until this century, when the latter, supported by an organization called the Soka Gakkai (the "Value-Creating Society"), launched a campaign to revive the teachings of Nichiren. Since the Second World War, Soka Gakkai and Nichiren-shoshu have gained millions of supporters, but remain controversial among mainstream Buddhists and Shintoists (see p.271).

Since Nichiren, Japan has produced many more religious thinkers and scholars, both Buddhist and Shinto, including the great eighteenth-century Shinto scholar Motoori Norinaga (see sidebar, right). However, none rival the stature of the galaxy of seminal figures who appeared in the century and a half between the birth of Honen and the death of Nichiren.

THE SHINTO REVIVAL: MOTOORI

The greatest of all Shinto scholars was probably Motoori Norinaga (1730–1801), who was largely responsible for bringing about the Shinto revival known as Kokugaku ("National Learning Movement") from the late 1700s. Motoori studied medicine before devoting himself to the study of Japanese mythological classics, especially the *Kojiki* and the *Nihonshoki* (see p.250). He was inspired by the Shingon Buddhist monk Keichu (1640–1701) and, more immediately, Kamo no Mabuchi (1697–1769). Both had sought to define Japanese national identity with reference to the ancient Shinto texts.

Motoori spent the rest of his life interpreting the *kami* faith and attracted a wide following. His masterpiece, the monumental, forty-four-volume *Kojiki den* ("Interpretation of the *Kojiki*," 1798) is both an exhaustive exegesis of the *Kojiki*, and a vast compendium of knowledge about ancient Japan.

Motoori came to believe that Chinese influence—including Buddhism—had long obscured the essential Japanese character. Neither Motoori nor his two intellectual predecessors explicitly renounced Buddhism, but their attitude toward it was generally negative. Motoori attacked Buddhists and Confucian scholars for seeking to "know the unknowable."

Anti-Chinese sentiment and the importance of the Shinto *kami*—both of which Motoori tirelessly promoted—were significant elements in Kokugaku and profoundly influenced the men who engineered the Meiji restoration in 1868.

A Zen priest in meditation. The adept of Zen (see sidebar, below) seeks to achieve intense mental focus, tranquility, and a paring down of extraneous thought.

HARMONY AND ENLIGHTENMENT

It has sometimes been said that the Japanese rely in all cases on their Buddhist heritage for ethical guidance. However, this can be disputed. At the core of Shinto theology lies the idea that a benign harmony, or *wa*, is inherent in nature and human relationships, and that anything that disrupts this state is bad. This helps to explain the widespread and deeply rooted Japanese belief that the individual is less important than the group, be it family, school, or workplace. Rules governing human behavior are considered necessary for the maintenance of *wa*, without which both society and the natural world would disintegrate into chaos.

Confucian and Daoist ideas imported from China also claimed that chaos would follow if social nonconformity were tolerated, but these concepts served principally to reinforce the existing Shinto ethic, which sprang from the clan-based society of prehistoric and ancient Japan. This ethic revolves around two fundamental and intimately related concepts: the need to maintain the "face" (*tatemae*) that a person presents to the outside world; and the extended household (*ie*), that includes all the ancestral spirits (see p.246). The idea that Japanese ethics are based on shame rather than guilt has been exaggerated, but it is nonetheless true that conformity is enforced to a large degree by the loss of *tatemae* that an individual—and consequently his or her *ie*, school, employer, or other social group—would suffer as a result of violating part of the social code. Depending on the seriousness of the loss of face, a person may atone by bowing deeply, through a ceremonial act of gift-giving, or by committing suicide (*jisatsu*). Even today, suicide is often blamed on a person's inability to cope with the shame of, say, failing an examination.

If a whole group is stigmatized, a collective act of atonement is made. For example, when Japan's famous Shinkansen "Bullet Train" is late, every employee from the engineer to the conductor, hostesses, and ticket sellers, feels responsible and will apologize profusely to delayed passengers. Once atonement is made, the shame and guilt cease and are not passed on.

The Shinto ethic reached its apogee during the "State Shinto" era (1872–1945), when obedience to the emperor became the noblest form of behavior—up to and including sacrificing one's life for his benefit. It is very much a "this-worldly" phenomenon, with little or no emphasis placed on reward or punishment in the afterlife (see pp.266–7). However, the state of the soul after death is very much the concern of Japan's Buddhist traditions. From the outset, Mahayana Buddhism has had a well-defined concept of inherent human wickedness, and the

ZEN AND *SATORI*

Rinzai Zen and Soto Zen are exceptions to the general Buddhist rule in that they are less concerned with achieving enlightenment (Sanskrit *bodhi*) as a step to *nirvana* and salvation (see main text), than with applying it to the demands of the present world. Such "practical enlightenment" is called *satori* ("spiritual awakening"), in which mind and body subjectively disappear in the course of meditation, and a direct awareness of the inner self is achieved.

Rinzai and Soto differ in the manner in which *satori* is attained. In Rinzai, the emphasis is on the *koans* (see p.251): *satori*, it is believed, often arrives in a flash, at the moment that the mind penetrates the inner meaning of one of these *mantra*-like sayings. However, Soto places primary emphasis on the meditation process itself, in other words, sitting *zazen* (in the lotus position). As the novice becomes more adept, the mind frees itself—gradually rather than in an instant of insight—from what the late Alan Watts (1915–73), one of the first Western practitioners of Zen, called "the internal conversation." Once this freedom is achieved, *satori* soon follows.

Buddhist's ultimate goal is to achieve salvation in the form of *nirvana*, or "release," from the cycle of birth, death, and rebirth. This cycle is fueled by the accumulation of merit and demerit, the concept known as *karma* (see pp.156, 192). In the Buddhist view, demerit springs from desire, and the loss of desire is thus the key to salvation.

In Mahayana Buddhism, the attainment of *nirvana* essentially depends on adherence to the "Noble Eightfold Path" (see pp.184–5). From the point of view of the "Pure Land" schools, there are simply two paths to salvation. The first, or "hard" way, involves leading a morally perfect life—avoiding the selfishness that lies at the root of desire and performing good works—and engaging in intense meditation in order to reach the state of enlightenment that is a prerequisite for *nirvana*. In Japan, the Buddhist insistence on suppressing personal desire complements the Shinto ethical tradition that demands subordination to the group in such a way that harmonious relationships (*wa*) are maintained.

The second, or "easy" way to grace, advocated by the "Pure Land" sects, reasons that the effort required to achieve salvation is too great for anyone living in this troubled and distracting world. It recommends professing utter faith in the Amida Buddha, who will lead the soul after death to the paradise of the "Pure Land," where salvation may be more easily pursued (see pp.266–7).

A Zen garden at Ryoanji Zen temple, Kyoto. Over the centuries, the discipline required to attain satori *(see sidebar, opposite) inspired the Japanese aesthetic of "quiet and simple elegance"* (shibui, or wabi-sabi*) that may be seen in a wide range of Japanese arts, such as* ikebana *(flower arranging),* haiku *(a genre of poetry in which an idea or image is expressed in a mere 17 syllables),* chanoyu *("tea ceremony," a precise ritual for serving tea), and garden design. The harmonious and simple design of the typical Zen garden is an ideal environment for contemplation.*

A LANDSCAPE OF SANCTUARIES

The two principal types of sacred building in Japan are the Buddhist temple (*otera*) and the Shinto shrine (*jinja*). There is also a considerable, though far smaller, number of Christian churches (*kyokai*), located mainly in the larger towns and cities.

China provided the prototypes for Japan's Buddhist temples. The first Japanese monks considered their temples to be the offspring of those they had visited in China, and followed the Chinese custom of building them on mountains. Hence, the word *san* or *zan* ("mountain"), from the Chinese *shan*, occurs frequently in the names of Japanese temples—even those on level terrain—in honor of the mountain-top location of their Chinese parent institution. Famous hilltop temples include the great Tendai complex on Mount Hiei (Hiei*zan;* see p.245) and the Shingon holy places that adorn Mount Koya (Koya-*san*; see p.238).

THE ISE SHRINE

Part of the Naiku, or Inner Shrine, of Amaterasu at Ise, before which stands the torii *or sacred gateway (see p.260). Ise was last completely rebuilt in 1993.*

The destination of Japanese pilgrims for over a millennium, Ise is a grand complex of shrines near the coast southeast of Nara in Mie prefecture (see map, p.239). The site's most ancient shrine—and Shinto's holiest place—is the Naiku ("Inner Shrine"), dedicated to the sun goddess, Amaterasu. The complex also includes the Geku ("Outer Shrine") of the rice goddess, Toyouke-omikami.

What makes Ise truly unique is the fact that, since the seventh century CE, all the buildings in the shrine complex have been replaced every twenty years by replicas that are exact copies down to the last wooden peg. Thus Ise is at once old and always new. The symbolism here is extremely important: with each rebuilding both the sun goddess (the divine ancestor of the imperial house) and the rice goddess acquire renewed vigor, and this by extension ensures the continuing vitality of both the imperial line and the rice crop, without either of which the nation could not survive.

At the end of the twenty-year cycle, the new shrine buildings are erected on a site alongside the old ones. For a brief period, the visitor might be forgiven for experiencing a sense of double vision, because the complex and its copy stand side-by-side until the sacred images have been ritually transferred to the new shrine by the distinctively clad Ise priests. Only then are the old structures dismantled and the ground cleared, to be carefully maintained until the rebuilding cycle comes around again. The dismantled buildings continue to be imbued with the powerful sacred essence of the goddesses and are not destroyed. Instead, pieces are distributed to shrines throughout Japan and incorporated into their walls, thereby spiritually reinvigorating the entire Shinto universe.

Otera, like their Chinese Buddhist counterparts, typically consist of a complex of buildings, rather in the manner of a medieval Christian monastery. The *kondo*, or main hall, contains sacred images of the Buddha, together with other *buddhas* and *bosatsus*. In addition there is a *daikodo*, or lecture hall, and various treasuries, storehouses, priestly residences, and, usually, a five-story pagoda (*goju no to*), which traditionally houses sacred relics and is derived from the ancient *stupa* (see p.186). Wherever local geography allows, the complex is surrounded by a garden, some parts of which, like the famous Zen garden at Kyoto's Ryoanji temple, are themselves sacred places and foci of devotion. One of the first and most notable temple complexes was built in 607CE by Shotoku Taishi (see p.243) at Horyuji, near Nara, which is held to be the oldest surviving group of wooden buildings in the world. The complex includes ten major structures, several of which are officially designated "national treasures" by the Japanese government.

The typical Shinto *jinja* is also a complex of several buildings and, with the exception of the tiny shrines sometimes found on the roofs of department stores and other modern high-rise buildings, they are almost always

The Ryoanji otera *(Buddhist temple) at Kyoto. It was founded in the mid-15th century by the Hosokawa, one of many powerful contending dynasties of* daimyo *(feudal warlords) during this period.*

located in natural settings, even if this consists of only a few trees shading an urban open space. The oldest *jinja* were open-air sacred precincts, perhaps around a revered natural object such as a tree or stone. Enclosed shrines began to appear early in the Common Era. Many of these were for the veneration of rice deities and were modeled on thatched rice storehouses. The two most ancient are also the most sacred: those of Ise (see p.258) and Izumo. Dedicated to the patron god of the Izumo region, Okuninushi, "the Great Lord of the Country" (see p.246), the Izumo shrine is built of wood and thatch and, like Ise, has been rebuilt frequently to an identical design, although not at regular intervals.

During the Nara period (710–794CE), many Shinto shrines began to incorporate elements of Chinese design, such as upturned gables and bright vermilion paint instead of natural, unadorned wood. An important early example of the new Chinese style is the Kasuga-*jinja* in Nara. From this time on, *jinja* and *otera* came to look very similar. However, just as the presence of a pagoda is a common way of identifying an *otera*, the *jinja* is instantly recognizable by its ceremonial sacred gateway, or *torii*. In its simplest form, as at Ise (see p.258), this consists of a pair of posts topped by two crossbars, one of which extends beyond the uprights. The *torii* serves to mark the boundary between the impure

SYNCRETISM AND SACRED ARCHITECTURE

It may be no coincidence that, as Shinto shrines adopted more Chinese architectural characteristics in the Nara period, and thus came to resemble Buddhist temples in appearance (see main text), the process of syncretism between the two faiths proceeded accordingly. Indeed, almost every major Buddhist temple (*otera*) includes at least one small Shinto shrine (*jinja*).

A curious result of this process was the movement known as Shugendo ("Way of the Mountain"), which took shape in the Heian period (794–1185CE). Spread by mystics known as *yamabushi* (literally "mountain warriors"), it involved a fusion of Buddhist *bosatsu* and Shinto *kami* (see pp.246–7), especially the *kami* believed to live on mountains. Shugendo survives to this day in parts of northern Japan and is practiced in sacred buildings that are at once *otera* and *jinja*.

The famous "floating" ceremonial gateway, or torii, *to the shrine of Itsukushima on Miyajima island in the bay of Hiroshima. Visitors must pass through the gateway by boat before entering the shrine, a great pilgrimage destination for many centuries. The Chinese-influenced design of the* torii *may be compared with the more ancient and simpler style of the gateway to the Inner Shrine of Ise (see p.258).*

secular world and the sacred confines of the shrine. In passing through it, a visitor to the shrine symbolically undergoes a ritual purification of the pollution accumulated in the outer world.

Beyond the *torii*, the principal building of the *jinja* is the *honden* (main hall), where the sacred image is kept of the *kami* to which the shrine is dedicated. There will also be one or more storehouses, an outer building before which worshippers pray and make offerings, and a stone water tank for the ritual ablutions—rinsing the hands and mouth—required before one approaches the image of the *kami*.

Several mountains have become sacred to one or other (and sometimes both) of Japan's two main faiths (see box, below), and countless other natural features are also held to be sacred. Indeed, almost every distinctive rock outcrop, river, hill, and waterfall is likely to have some association with a local temple, shrine, or both. One example is the magnificent Nachi waterfall in Wakayama prefecture (see map, p.239), which, like Fuji-*san*, is widely conceived to be a powerful *kami*.

Whole regions are also considered sacred from their association with particular Shinto deities. For example, the Yamato region is revered as the homeland of the imperial dynasty, which according to Shinto myth is of divine descent (see p.246).

HOLY MOUNTAINS

A fascination with the sanctity of mountains pervades both Buddhism and Shinto. Two of the most important Buddhist sects, Tendai and Shingon, have their headquarters in temple complexes on Hiei*zan* and Koya-*san* (mounts Hiei and Koya) respectively (see p.258).

However, the most famous of all Japanese sacred mountains is Mount Fuji, or Fuji-*san* (see map, p.239), which is traditionally considered an important *kami* in its own right. It has long been a place of mass pilgrimage, and each year thousands of devotees climb it to worship at the small Shinto shrine at the summit. In the nineteenth century, when travel was more difficult, a "Fuji cult" developed that involved erecting small replicas of the mountain at local Shinto *jinja* in many parts of Japan. Those unable to climb the real mountain would walk up the replica in a symbolic act of pilgrimage.

Fuji-*san* is also sacred to a number of Japanese Buddhist schools, such as Nichiren-shu (see p.254). The main temple of this sect stands in the foothills of the mountain at Minobu in Yamanashi prefecture.

The snow-capped peak of Mount Fuji, revered as a Shinto deity in its own right by the many thousands of Japanese pilgrims who annually ascend to the shrine at its summit. Climbing the 3,800-meter (10,335-ft) high dormant volcano is in itself considered to constitute an act of worship.

SHARING IN THE SPIRIT

Perhaps the most outstanding feature of Japanese religion is its great abundance of local festivals and rituals, both Shinto and Buddhist. In addition to such widespread observances as the Japanese New Year (see sidebar, opposite) and the Obon ancestor festival (see p.264), each Shinto shrine and almost every Buddhist sect and temple has its own calendar of special rituals and ceremonies (see sidebar, left). The same is true of the "New Religions" (see pp.270–71). Other common rituals include funerals, almost all of which are conducted according to Buddhist rites, the chief exception being imperial obsequies, which are totally Shinto in form (see p.266).

As far as most communities are concerned, by far the most important Shinto ritual is the annual (or, in some cases, biennial) local festival or *matsuri*. Virtually every Japanese town, neighborhood, village, or *buraku* (village quarter) has such a festival, which centers on the shrine to the local Shinto *kami*. There are two basic types of *matsuri*. The first, an "ordinary festival," or "shadow *matsuri*," does not directly involve the local *kami*, but is still centered on the shrine, and culminates in the festive procession of a portable shrine, a *mikoshi*, around the neighborhood. The second type of *matsuri* is a *taisai*, or "big festival," during which the

THE REALM OF HOLY PURITY

A good example of a ritual that is unique to a single Buddhist sect is the famous *goma*, or fire purification ceremony, which occupies a central place in Shingon worship. It is accorded a special reverence by the Japanese due to its great antiquity: like most Buddhist rites it was brought to Japan from China, but it originated in India in Vedic times and is thought by some scholars to be related to the ancient Indian *soma* ceremonial (see p.131). *Goma* focuses on the purification of the worshippers, who seek to be transported symbolically to a higher realm of consciousness by the flames. The Shingon priests pile up small strips of wood in a square, each strip inscribed with a prayer or passage from a sacred Buddhist *sutra*. As the priests intone holy chants, the pile is ignited, and sacred *goma* (sesame seed oil) is poured onto the flames, making them leap and dance.

As the sacred smoke rises, the priests fumigate various everyday objects handed to them by members of the congregation—photographs of loved ones, wallets, purses, drivers' licenses, and so on—thereby rendering them pure and, it is believed, safe from harm. At the close of the ceremony, each member of the congregation receives a dab of sesame seed oil on the forehead as a mark of purification and of his or her exposure to the esoteric realm symbolized by the flames and smoke.

An enormous lacquered fish is hauled through the streets of Karatsu on Kyushu island during the city's annual Kunchi matsuri. *Giant colorful floats of various creatures are a feature of this 300-year-old festival (see also illustration, p.236.)*

Traditional gigaku *(sacred dance theater) performers at the Meiji*-jingu, *the shrine of the emperor Meiji in Tokyo. Millions of Japanese visit the shrine during Shogatsu Matsuri, the Japanese New Year festival (see below).*

mikoshi contains the sacred image of the local *kami. Taisai* typically occur every three years, although they may occur more frequently and even annually at certain major shrines. In both types of *matsuri*, the three groupings that represent the local community—the merchants' association (*shotenkai*), the neighborhood residents' association (*chokai*), and the shrine elders' association (*sodaikai*)—cooperate to present a positive image of the local community, and at the same time to reinforce their own sense of social solidarity and local pride (see box on p.265).

In addition to participating in communal household rites and local festivals, a great many Japanese go to temples and shrines individually to seek the blessings of the local *bosatsu* or *kami*, especially when faced with some personal crisis. In a Buddhist temple, this usually involves burning a stick of incense as an offering to the deity and wafting the smoke over oneself. At a shrine, the worshipper first performs a purifying ablution, rinsing out the mouth and washing the hands, before approaching the outer part of the shrine and dropping an offering, usually money, into a collection box.

Then, in order to alert the deity to his or her presence, the worshipper claps twice or pulls a rope to ring a bell, or both. Next, with head respectfully bowed and hands clasped, the supplicant makes a request for assistance. For example, a mother might ask the *kami* to help her child pass an entrance examination. Other requests might include asking the *kami* to heal a sick infant or ensure the fertility of a marriage. The worshipper claps again to signify that the request has been made and leaves the shrine. If the request is granted, good manners dictate that the petitioner should return to the shrine in order to thank the *kami* for his or her beneficence.

THE NEW YEAR FESTIVAL

The three-day Japanese New Year festival, Shogatsu Matsuri, has been celebrated from January 1–3 since Japan abandoned the Chinese lunar calendar in favor of the Gregorian on January 1, 1873. In the days immediately preceding the New Year, people scrub their houses clean in order to begin the year with as little pollution as possible. There are family meals (*osechi*) that include a special soup (*ozoni*) and pounded rice cakes (*mochi*); and gifts are given to superiors as tokens of appreciation.

But the most important activity of Shogatsu Matsuri is a ceremonial visit to a shrine or temple to make an offering and pray for prosperity and good health in the coming months. In some Shinto cults, the miniature household shrines, which sit atop *kamidana* and the tablets bearing the names of family ancestors (see sidebar, p.264), are ritually burned and replaced with new ones.

One of the most common Shinto rites of passage is the birth ritual known as *omiyamairi*, literally "honorable shrine visit" (*omiya* is a synonym for *jinja*), when the infant is welcomed into the community of its family. Some months after the birth, the parents take the child to a shrine to be purified by the *kannushi* (Shinto priest). Typically, the child's extended family—grandparents, uncles, aunts, and so on—are also present, and afterward there will be a festive meal. At major shrines, such as the Meiji-*jingu* in Tokyo, the party is held in a special room in the shrine grounds.

Oharai, the act of ritual purification, forms a central part of most Shinto ceremonies. Waving a sacred branch of *sakaki* ("prospering tree," *cleyera ochnacea*, an evergreen bush of the pine family) and chanting appropriate prayers (*norito*), the *kannushi* or *guji* (senior priest of a shrine) seeks to remove any spiritual pollution contaminating the person, place, or thing. This pollution can include possession by evil spirits, or *oni* (see p.248).

Purification of the bride and groom is central to traditional Japanese wedding ceremonies, which are typically performed by Shinto priests. However, for the most part these take place not at shrines but in hotels and "wedding palaces" built for that purpose.

THE RETURN OF THE DEAD

One of the most widely celebrated of all Japanese festivals is Obon, the Buddhist celebration of the annual return of the dead to their ancestral homes in mid-August. At Obon, the date of which is still determined by the lunar calendar, people return to their own hometowns if possible and clean family gravestones. They say prayers for the dead, especially the newly departed, and join in Bon-odori, a traditional dance to honor the deceased.

At other times of the year, regular ancestor rites take place in the home. From the Shinto standpoint, the souls of the dead become a low level of deity; from the Buddhist they are souls seeking salvation. But both concepts are accepted, reflecting Japanese "ambiguity tolerance" in spiritual matters.

Some domestic ancestor rituals, especially during Obon, involve burning incense on the *butsudan*, the domestic Buddhist altar, and offering small dishes of rice to the souls of the family's ancestors. Seven days after death, the soul is given a "death-name" (*kaimyo*) that is inscribed on one of the ancestral tablets (*ihai*) kept in the *butsudan*. The same ancestral souls are also revered as Shinto *tama* (see p.266) or *kami*, represented by tablets on the *kamidana*, the domestic "god-shelf," often directly above the *butsudan*. Offerings are also made to these family *kami*. Most domestic rites are performed in the early morning, a time considered sacred in both Buddhism and Shinto.

A Shinto priest intones prayers as part of the annual Saigusa Matsuri (Lily Festival) at the Isagawa shrine in Nara. During the festival, which dates back to the 8th century CE*, offerings of lilies are made as charms against disease.*

A TYPICAL TOKYO *TAISAI*

The local *matsuri* (festival) celebrated in the northwest Tokyo neighborhood of Nishi-Waseda (in the district 3-*chome*) is a triennial *taisai* ("big festival") in honor of the sun goddess Amaterasu, who is the *kami* of the local shrine, the Tenso-*jinja*. It is one of thousands of shrines to the goddess throughout Japan, the most important being at Ise (the Ise-*jingu*; see p.258).

The *matsuri* traditionally takes place over a two-day period in early September. On the morning of the first day, children carry a children's *mikoshi*, a portable shrine about a quarter of the size of the adult version, around the neighborhood. The Tenso-*jinja* is too small to have its own *guji* (senior Shinto priest, as opposed to an ordinary priest, or *kannushi*), so the *taisai* organizers call upon the services of a *guji* from another shrine nearby. In the afternoon, assisted by the local *sodai* (shrine elders), the acting *guji* performs a ceremony in which he chants Shinto prayers and purifies the shrine and its contents by waving a branch of *sakaki* (sacred pine tree; see main text, opposite).

Later, in the evening, there is public entertainment in the grounds of the shrine. In some years this might be performed by a traditional dance group, and in others by a Shinto theater troupe, who stage *kagura*, sacred Japanese theater (see p.268). Itinerant *matsuri* concessionaires, called *roten*, set up their stalls and sell souvenirs and traditional festival foods, such as *okonomiyakai*—an egg dish prepared on a grill—and fried noodles.

In this photograph taken by the author, the children's mikoshi *procession prepares to depart on the first morning of the Nishi-Waseda festival. The involvement of boys and girls in the* taisai *is considered essential for passing on the traditions of the festival to a new generation. The* mikoshi *processions were originally all-male affairs, but girls and young women have participated since 1978 (see p.269).*

Early the next morning the *guji* removes the sacred (and rarely seen) image of Amaterasu from the inner precincts of the shrine and places it in the waiting *mikoshi*. Then, rotating teams of thirty or forty young men and women carry the portable shrine up one narrow street and down another, chanting "*Wa shoi! Wa shoi!*" (an untranslatable cry somewhat like "Hurrah!"). The procession, which halts frequently for liquid refreshments, is led by the *guji* and includes singers, a drummer, a young man impersonating Tengu—the guardian demon of the shrine—and the *sodai*. After about six or seven hours, the procession finally returns to the grounds of the shrine, and the priest removes the image from the *mikoshi*. He returns it to its place in the inner shrine, where it will remain until the next *taisai*.

The fundamental purpose of this ritual is to sanctify the neighborhood served by the *jinja* by periodically exposing it to the sacred aura emitted by the divine image paraded in the *mikoshi*, which also, of course, sanctifies the *mikoshi* bearers. A *matsuri* is therefore a joyous occasion, one in which the participants feel that they partake of the divine essence of the local *kami*. In the process, they may experience feelings close to ecstasy.

After a final prayer by the priest, the *mikoshi* carriers share a meal at the *mikisho*, or festival headquarters, which stands in the grounds of a small Buddhist temple to the *bosatsu* Jizo (see p.248), some distance from the Tenso-*jinja*.

HEAVENS AND HELL

In this 18th-century woodblock print, a devotee of Amida Buddha experiences a vision of Amida enthroned in the celestial "Pure Land."

It has been noted that, for the Japanese, Shinto is essentially the "life religion" and is primarily concerned with the here and now, the abundance of nature, and human and animal fertility. Since the advent of Buddhism, specifically Shinto ideas of life after death and the salvation of the soul have become confined to the belief that a person's spirit persists after death and remains effective for the benefit of the living. The ancestral spirits, or *tama*, are considered part of the social group to whom one is duty-bound not to fall into a state of shame (see p.256). The *tama* of the newly deceased are therefore nourished with offerings at the domestic Shinto shrine, or *kamidana* (see p.264); in return, they are expected to bless and protect the living.

Matters of death and what happens afterward are central to most of Japan's Buddhist traditions. There are numerous Buddhist "heavens," of which the most pervasive is the "Pure Land" (see p.193). For the "Pure Land" Buddhist sects, the route to ultimate "salvation" (*nirvana*, the release from the cycle of life and death; see p.257) lies in rebirth in the eponymous "Pure Land," a celestial region where, free from earthly disturbances, the deceased will be able to attain enlightenment and eventually *nirvana*. The "Pure Land" is thus a sort of "half-way heaven" between the pain and suffering of the mortal world and final and perpetual release. The key to being reborn in this paradise is absolute faith in the figure of Amida Buddha, expressed in the utterance of the *nembutsu* (see pp.253–4). Amida is believed to possess an almost unbounded compassion for human beings, to the extent that although he has himself attained the enlightened state of a *buddha*, he has undertaken to refrain from entering *nirvana* in order to help others to reach the haven of the "Pure Land."

It is still theoretically possible for a person to achieve *nirvana* directly via the "hard path" of intense meditation and attention to spiritual cleansing. But Honen, the founder of the "Pure Land" sect (see p.253), was convinced that faith in Amida is necessary because most human beings are so inherently wicked that even a near-perfect spiritual life in this world is probably not enough to achieve ultimate salvation.

The assistance of Amida was made more necessary by the widespread assumption on the part of most Buddhist clergy that the universe had reached its "third age," the epoch of increasing chaos known in Japanese as *mappo*. In this period, growing confusion, disorder, and evil would make it difficult for more than a handful of people to find the peace necessary to enable them to follow the "hard" path to salvation. If they failed, they might (in the "Pure Land" view) be consigned to the

BIDDING FAREWELL TO THE DEAD

Professing faith in Amida Buddha was to become a vital part of the Japanese way of death, and today the great majority of Japanese choose to be cremated with Buddhist rites and to have their ashes interred in a Buddhist cemetery. Almost all Japanese cemeteries are attached to temples, especially those of the "Pure Land" sects (Jodo-shu and Jodo-shinshu).

However, it is possible to be buried according to Shinto rites, and there are at least two Shinto cemeteries in Tokyo. One of them is reserved for the imperial family, whose funerals are traditionally Shinto in form. The most recent was that of the late Showa emperor (Hirohito) in 1989, which was presided over by Shinto priests (*kannushi*) from Ise and other important shrines.

fires of the Buddhist Hell, Jigoku (see box, below). "Pure Land" Buddhists rely on Amida to aid the mass of the faithful to avoid this fate.

According to the "Pure Land" sects, anyone who has not been "saved" by Amida can look to another important figure in Buddhist eschatology, the *bodhisattva* Maitreya ("Benevolent One," Japanese Miroku), the "*buddha* of the future age." Maitreya, it is said, will come to restore the teachings of the Buddha (the Dharma) and create an earthly Buddhist paradise when the current world-age ends, at the conclusion of *mappo*. No one can say when this apocalypse will be, but some Buddhist-based "New Religions" have made apocalyptic predictions, most recently (and notoriously) the Aum Shinrikyu group that carried out fatal sarin gas attacks on the Tokyo metro system in 1995.

LANDS OF THE DEAD

Japan's prehistoric religion appears to have had a well-developed concept of an afterlife. A great deal of attention was paid to the disposition of the body, and during the Kofun period (ca. 300–552CE) elaborate tumuli were constructed to house the spirits of dead emperors. Ancient Shinto does seem to have possessed the concept of a Hades-like infernal region, as seen in the image of Yomi in the *Kojiki*, but save for the celebrated episode in which the primal god Izanagi visits this subterranean realm in a vain attempt to retrieve his dead spouse (see p.247), there is no further mention of the place and it plays no role in modern Shinto theology.

Buddhist ideas have superseded most Shinto concepts of regions of the dead, but not entirely. After thirty-three years, the *tama*, or spirit of a deceased ancestor (see main text), is believed to lose its individual nature and to merge with the collective body of family ancestral spirits or *kami*. These are said to dwell on a sacred mountain, often in the Kumano, Yoshino, or another mountainous region of the heartland of ancient Japan. The amorphous family *kami* are also invoked in ritual, but at a more abstract level than the *tama* of a family member who has recently passed away (see also p.264).

The Buddhist sects introduced a number of afterworld concepts, including paradisial regions presided over by the Buddha himself (the Nichiren sects), the Vairochana Buddha (the Shingon sect), the Maitreya, and Kannon. They also introduced the concept of divine judgment, in which, forty-nine days after death, the soul is assessed by a being called Emma (Sanskrit Yama). Depending on his judgment, the soul is assigned either to a paradise, or to one of the demonic regions of Jigoku (Hell), or to rebirth as a beast, a deity, or a new human being. However, the most pervasive Buddhist afterworld concept was that of the "Pure Land," a paradise where souls could escape the torments of Jigoku and eventually achieve permanent release, *nirvana*.

The Shintoist belief in the soul as both *tama* and *kami* is held simultaneously with the Buddhist belief that the soul is assigned to hell or paradise and reincarnation. As so often, Japanese religion sees no conflict in embracing both notions, however contradictory they may at first appear.

Emma, the lord of Jigoku (top), judges the karma *(balance of merits and demerits) of the dead; those with excess demerit are consigned to a punishment region. An 18th-century print.*

OLD FAITHS IN THE MODERN WORLD

Ancient Japanese society was organized into *uji*, or clans, and the roots of Shinto were intimately intertwined with the collective values fostered by this all-encompassing social unit. Indeed, the tutelary *kami* enshrined in a local Shinto shrine is still called the *ujigami*, or "clan deity," despite the fact that the *uji* system, as a major force in Japanese life, has been defunct for more than a millennium. More recently, the *ie*, or extended household, which supplanted the *uji* as the dominant social unit as feudalism took hold after ca. 1185CE, has given rise to a deep-seated emphasis on the family in both Shinto and the more popular Buddhist sects (see p.256). Shrine or temple membership is still determined by a person's *ie*, a fact that has contributed to the rise of the so-called "New Religions" (see pp.270–71).

For centuries, women have played a relatively minor role in the country's religious life, although there were reigning empresses until well into the early historic period: Shotoku Taishi was regent for one (see p.243), and the *Kojiki* (see p.250) was commissioned by another. There were also high priestesses of Ise, the shrine of the sun goddess (see p.258). But by ca. 800CE the impact of Chinese Confucianism and its heavily patriarchal ideology had effectively put an end to this early equality of status. Since that time all emperors and most priests have been male, even though Amaterasu remains Shinto's most revered deity.

In recent years, the worldwide women's movement has begun to exert an influence on traditional Japanese beliefs and practices. An increasing number of Shinto shrines now permit young women to carry *mikoshi* (portable shrines) during festivals (see box, opposite). There has also been

THE YASUKUNI SHRINE

The specter of Japan's militaristic past occasionally raises its head in the context of the Yasukuni shrine in Tokyo. The *kami* enshrined in this *jinja* are the souls of Japan's war dead from the creation of the Imperial Army in 1871 to the end of the Second World War. As such, the shrine continues to be the center of controversy, especially when prominent members of the government—sometimes even the prime minister—call to pay their respects.

Such occasions may not be common, but they always receive heavy coverage in the Japanese media. The Japanese Left, evoking prewar State Shinto (see p.245) and its intensely nationalist ideology, accuses politicians involved of violating Japan's 1947 constitution, which clearly prohibits the state from involvement in any religion. The Right counters with the claim that the Yasukuni shrine is a private religious institution and that those who pray there do so as private individuals.

Complicating matters is the fact that in recent years there have been repeated attempts to turn the Yasukuni-*jinja* into Japan's equivalent of a "tomb of the unknown soldier," a place where visiting foreign dignitaries may lay wreaths. But the sensitivities of the Left on this issue resonate across much of the Japanese political spectrum, and so far the measure has failed to receive sufficient backing in the Japanese Diet (parliament).

Female dancers taking part in kagura, *sacred Shinto theater, at a shrine in Nara. Women have long taken part in Shinto ceremonies as musicians or dancers, but until recently they were largely excluded from officiating as priests.*

an increase in the number of women Shinto priests, in spite of opposition from the more conservative shrines. In 1996, out of 21,091 priests, ten percent were women, compared with nine percent in 1993.

Shinto's past association with the state militarism that existed until 1945 still occasionally gives rise to controversy (see sidebar, opposite). However, while the Buddhist sects have generally steered clear of politics, they have also been less responsive to the kind of pressure for change that has led to women entering the Shinto priesthood. Japanese Buddhism has few, if any, women priests. There have been Buddhist nuns for centuries, but they constitute a very conservative element of Japanese religious life.

The one Buddhist sect that has become controversial in modern times is Nichiren-shoshu (see p.255), or more particularly its lay organization, Soka Gakkai ("Value-Creating Society"; see p.271).

WOMEN SHRINE BEARERS

The act of carrying the *mikoshi*, or portable shrine, during a local festival or *matsuri* (see p.262–3) is regarded as a considerable privilege, especially on those occasions when the *mikoshi* contains the image of the deity from the local Shinto shrine. Traditionally, the task of *mikoshi* bearing was reserved for young men: women were expected to play a supportive role in *matsuri* processions, providing refreshments for *mikoshi* bearers and cooking dinner after the portable shrine had been returned to the main shrine.

Female shrine bearers are now a common sight at local Shinto festivals. These women are taking part in a matsuri *at Asahikawa on Hokkaido island.*

However, this began to change in the late 1970s, with women in one neighborhood after another gaining the right to join their brothers and husbands in carrying the *kami* through the streets.

In the Tokyo neighborhood of Nishi-Waseda (see p.265), this change occurred in 1978. In March of that year, six months before the annual "shadow *matsuri*," (see p.262) a member of the women's committee of the neighborhood residents' association (*chokai*)—the head of which has overall responsibility for the festival—pointed out that young women were carrying *mikoshi* in nearby *matsuri*, and suggested that the time had come for their own neighborhood to follow suit.

The process of decision-making that followed was typically Japanese, with courteous discussion rather than polarized argument. The idea was considered by the main bodies involved in organizing the *matsuri*: the *chokai*, the shrine elders' association, and the local merchants' association (most of the would-be shrine-bearers were shopkeepers' daughters). The *guji* (chief priest) of a neighboring shrine, who regularly officiated during the Nishi-Waseda *matsuri*, was also consulted. He approved the change, citing as a precedent the fact that there were once high priestesses of Amaterasu at Ise (see main text)—Amaterasu is also the local deity of Nishi-Waseda.

Several months later, after every important group involved had discussed the proposal informally and approved it, the change was formally agreed by the head of the *chokai*. A week or so before the *matsuri* a group of young women were duly incorporated into the roster of *mikoshi* bearers.

THE "NEW RELIGIONS"

Since the early nineteenth century, Japan has spawned a host of spiritual movements that have collectively come to be called the "New Religions" (Shinko Shukyo). The great majority of these are derivatives of Shinto, although most are heavily infused with ideas drawn from a variety of sources, including Buddhism, Chinese traditions such as Confucianism and Daoism, Christianity, and, in modern times, even Western occultism. Despite occasional excesses and sometimes garbled theological underpinnings, the New Religions provide vivid evidence that the ancient impetus to religious innovation is very much alive and well in modern Japan.

The first New Religions arose against the background of growing social chaos that accompanied the breakdown of the Tokugawa shogunate. At this time, a number of successful new sects sprang up, usually led by charismatic individuals. Their success continued in the Meiji period (1868–1912), by the end of which thirteen Shinto-based sects, including Tenrikyo (see box, below), had been recognized by the Japanese government. Several movements have also arisen directly from Buddhist traditions, the most influential being Soka Gakkai ("Value Creating Society"),

THE TENRIKYO SECT

In 1838, while nursing her sick son, Miki Nakayama (1798–1887) was possessed by a *kami* who identified himself as Ten-taishogun, the "Great Heavenly Overlord." In the course of the next few years, Ten-taishogun told Nakayama that he and his nine subordinate entities were the only true *kami*, and that they had chosen her to spread what came to be called the "Heavenly Truth," or *tenri*. Thus was born the Tenrikyo sect.

Devotees at Tenrikyo's main sanctuary in Tenri City, or Oyasato, the "Parental Home." In Tenrikyo belief, it is here that "God the Parent" created humanity.

The *kami*'s message was eventually written down in a long poem, completed in 1883, called the *Ofudesaki*, "The Tip of the Divine Writing Brush." In it can be found the collected revelations the founder received about the nature of heaven and especially of the *kami* who dwell there. Their relationship to human beings was analogous to that of a parent to his or her children. Thus, the prime manifestation of the godhead in the Tenrikyo faith is called the Oyakami, "God the Parent."

By the beginning of the twentieth century, Tenrikyo had become a recognized Shinto sect, and it remains today one of the most successful of the New Religions. Although it is primarily rooted in the Shinto concept of a hierarchy of *kami*, the religion founded by Miki Nakayama (or Oyasama, "Honored Parent") incorporates concepts borrowed from "Pure Land" Buddhism, including the concept of "salvation" through an intense profession of faith, in this instance in the power of Oyakami, and a well-defined afterworld.

From its base at Tenri City, near Nara, the faith spread throughout Japan and in recent years it has been carried to Hawaii, North America, Brazil, and other countries with sizeable Japanese immigrant populations.

A contemporary woodblock print by the artist Yoshitoshi depicting one of Commodore Matthew C. Perry's US Navy warships off Uraga, Edo (Tokyo), in 1853. The end of the shogunate began when Perry's "Black Ships" forcibly broke Japan's two-centuries-old self-imposed blockade. From this time, Japan was once more receptive to outside influences, which lent great impetus to the burgeoning New Religions. Many of the latter sprang up in response to conditions in the last decades of the shogunate, when organized Shinto and Buddhism had grown stagnant and unresponsive to changing social conditions.

founded in the late 1920s by Makiguchi Tsuesaburo (1871–1944) and closely linked to the existing Nichiren-shoshu sect. By the Second World War, Tsuesaburo and his disciple, Toda Josei (1900–58), had only attracted a few thousand disciples before their devotion to the teachings of Nichiren (see p.255) led to their suppression. But after 1945, under Toda, the movement grew rapidly, spurred by the social upheavals that accompanied Japan's rapid post-war economic growth (see sidebar, right).

Soka Gakkai's appeal was primarily to the masses who had migrated to the cities from rural areas and had lost touch with the social networks that are so important to Japanese life. Attendance at a temple or shrine was based on one's *ie*, or family (see p.256), so those new to an area often found it difficult to join a place of worship. Many New Religions arose to meet the spiritual needs of such people. The more "mainstream" New Religions, such as Tenrikyo, have become much like the older Japanese sects in their promotion of "family values." However, a small minority of new sects have been accused of behaving like the more notorious cults in the West, for example targeting and "brainwashing" susceptible young people. One such was Aum Shinrikyo, an apocalyptic Buddhist-based sect responsible for a gas attack on the Tokyo metro in 1995 that killed several people.

According to one estimate there are some two hundred thousand New Religions today, although many have tiny followings. A good example of a smaller movement is Shukyo Mahikari, or "Divine Light," founded in the early 1960s. It emphasizes healing and has an extraordinarily broad-based theology that draws on Shinto, Buddhism, and a host of other elements—including the legend of Atlantis. Like other New Religions, Shukyo Mahikari demonstrates the continuing vitality of the Japanese genius for blending elements of many different spiritual and cultural traditions.

SOKA GAKKAI

By the late 1960s, led by Toda Josei's successor, Daisaku Ikeda (1928–), Soka Gakkai had attracted over eleven million members. The movement has also recruited many non-Japanese members, particularly in the United States.

Soka Gakkai's strict hierarchy, quasimilitary organization, mass rallies, and demand for almost total commitment from its members raised suspicions that it was a front for militarist subversives. This suspicion—subsequently proved totally incorrect—was fueled when it launched Komeito, the "Clean Government Party," in the 1960s. Komeito was widely seen as an attempt to politicize Nichiren-shoshu or even seize power. This sentiment lingers, despite the fact that Komeito severed all official connections with Soka Gakkai over twenty years ago (and, indeed, recently dissolved itself).

Another source of unease is Soka Gakkai's intense efforts to win converts, which goes against the grain of Japan's traditional inclusivist attitude toward different religions. But in spite of a recent decline in membership, financial scandals, and a rift with the Nichiren priesthood, Soka Gakkai remains an important force in Japanese religious life.

GLOSSARY

bodhisattva Sanskrit, "future *buddha*," "*buddha*-to-be"(literally "enlightenment being"). In Buddhism, an individual who attains enlightenment (*bodhi*) but opts to defer *nirvana* (see below) in order to assist others in their spiritual quests.

bosatsu Japanese, "*bodhisattva*" (see above).

buddha Sanskrit, "enlightened one." In Buddhism, one who has attained enlightenment and *nirvana* (see below). Used as a title ("the Buddha"), the term refers to Siddhartha Gautama, the founder of Buddhism.

Chan Chinese *chan*, "meditation," from Sanskrit *dhyana* (see below). A school of Chinese Buddhism in which the pursuit of enlightenment centers on the practice of meditation.

Davidic Of or pertaining to David, king of Israel ca. 1000–960BCE, and his lineage.

dharma Sanskrit, "truth," "order," "righteousness," "duty," "justice." The term is used in both Hinduism and Buddhism; as a proper noun ("the Dharma"), it refers specifically to the "truth" about human existence discovered and taught by the Buddha.

dhyana Sanskrit, "meditation," whence Chinese *chan* (see above), and Japanese *zen* (see below).

dualism A belief that the cosmos is controlled by twin opposing forces (for example, good and evil), which have different sources (for example, God and the devil). This idea is rejected in strict monotheism, in which God is viewed as the source of all phenomena.

eschatology Greek, *eschatos*, "last." Doctrine or doctrines relating to the end of the world.

guru Sanskrit, "teacher." In Hinduism, a revered male or female religious teacher.

Hadith Arabic, "report." An account, or the body of accounts, recording the words, teachings, and deeds of the Prophet Muhammad.

halakhah The entire body of Jewish law.

imam Arabic, "leader." The person selected to lead the regular Friday prayer session in a mosque. As a proper noun (Imam), the term refers to one of the persons regarded in Shiism as the only legitimate heirs of Muhammad on earth.

karma Sanskrit, "action." In Hinduism and Buddhism, the balance of merit and demerit accumulated by an individual, which determines the nature of one's next reincarnation.

mantra In Hinduism and Buddhism, a word or short verse spoken or chanted repeatedly as an aid to meditation.

Mosaic Of or pertaining to Moses, and especially to the laws recorded in the first five books of the Hebrew Bible or Old Testament as having been transmitted through Moses by God to Israel.

nirvana Sanskrit, literally "blowing out." In Buddhism, a state free of all ignorance and desire, in which one ceases to accumulate *karma* (see above) and thus achieves liberation from the cycle of death and rebirth.

Patristic Of or pertaining to the "Church Fathers," the (male) theologians of the early Christian centuries (ca. 200–500CE) who helped shape fundamental Christian doctrine.

Prophet, the The Prophet Muhammad.

Pure Land Sukhavati, the "Western Paradise" where the *buddha* Amitabha (known as Amituo in China and Amida in Japan) reigns; it is a place of bliss and tranquility where his devotees, after death, can pursue enlightenment and *nirvana* (see above). Belief in the Pure Land is strong in east Asian Buddhism.

rabbinic Of or pertaining to the rabbis of Judaism and their teachings, especially those of the "rabbinic age" (see below).

rabbinic age, rabbinic period In Judaism, the term given to an era (generally considered to last from the late first century to the early seventh century CE) marked by the writings of great rabbis (teachers) such as Yohanan ben Zakkai, Akiva, and Judah the Prince. This period saw the production of the great collections of Jewish law, the Mishnah (ca. 200CE) and the Talmud (Jerusalem Talmud, ca. 400CE; Babylonian Talmud, ca. 500CE).

Sufi Of or pertaining to Sufism (Islamic mysticism); an Islamic mystic.

talmudic age, talmudic period The era of Jewish literary history in which the writings constituting the Talmud were produced (ca. 200–500CE) (see also **rabbinic age,** above).

Tantra The name given to ancient sacred texts and the movements to which they were foundational in Hinduism (from ca. 500CE) and Buddhism (from ca. 7th century CE). Hindu Tantra centers on the harnessing of male and female divine energies; Buddhist Tantra stresses ritual, symbolism, and rapid enlightenment involving the concept of "wrathful deities." The use of *mandalas* (circular representations of the cosmos) is common to both forms.

Trinitarian Of or pertaining to the Christian doctrine of the Trinity (God as Father, Son, and Holy Spirit).

ulama Arabic, "learned ones." In Islam, the body of religious and legal experts who constitute the highest scholarly authority in religious matters.

Vedic Of or pertaining to the sacred Sanskrit texts known collectively as *Veda*, the ancient sacrificially-based religious practices to which they were central, or the period during which they were compiled (ca. 1750–600BCE).

Zen Japanese *zen*, "meditation," from Chinese *chan* and ultimately Sanskrit *dhyana* (see above). A school of Japanese Buddhism focusing on the practice of meditation.

BIBLIOGRAPHY

GENERAL BIBLIOGRAPHY

Bowker, John. *The Oxford Dictionary of World Religions*. New York: Oxford University Press, 1997.

Brandon, S. G. F. *A Dictionary of Comparative Religion*. London: Weidenfeld & Nicolson, 1970.

Eliade, Mircea. *The Sacred and the Profane: The Nature of Religion*. Translated by Willard R. Trask. New York: Harcourt Brace, 1959.

——, ed. *The Encyclopedia of Religion*. 16 vols. New York: Macmillan, 1987.

Freedman, David Noel, ed. *The Anchor Bible Dictionary*. 6 vols. New York: Doubleday, 1992.

Hastings, James, ed. *Encyclopaedia of Religion and Ethics*. 12 vols. New York: Charles Scribner's Sons, 1913.

Hick, John. *Philosophy of Religion*. 4th ed. Englewood Cliffs, NJ: Prentice-Hall, 1991.

Hinnells, John R., ed. *A Handbook of Living Religions*. New York: Viking, 1984.

James, William. *The Varieties of Religious Experience*. Cambridge, MA: Harvard University Press, 1985 (orig. 1902).

Leeuw, G. van der. *Religion in Essence and Manifestation*. 2 vols. New York: Harper & Row, 1963.

Ludwig, Theodore M. *The Sacred Paths: Understanding the Religions of the World*. 2nd ed. Upper Saddle River, NJ: Prentice Hall, 1996.

Metzger, Bruce M. and Michael D. Coogan, eds. *The Oxford Companion to the Bible*. New York: Oxford University Press, 1993.

Noss, David S. and John B. Noss. *A History of the World's Religions*. 9th ed. New York: Macmillan, 1993.

Otto, Rudolf. *The Idea of the Holy*. Translated by John W. Harvey. 2nd ed. New York: Oxford University Press, 1958.

Porter, J.R. *The Illustrated Guide to the Bible*. New York and Oxford: Oxford University Press, 1995.

Sharma, Arvind, ed. *Women in World Religions*. Albany: State University of New York Press, 1987.

Smart, Ninian and Richard D. Hecht. *Sacred Texts of the World: A Universal Anthology*. New York: Crossroad. 1982.

Smith, Jonathan Z., ed. *The HarperCollins Dictionary of Religion*. San Francisco: HarperSanFrancisco, 1995.

Smith, Wilfred Cantwell. *The Meaning and End of Religion: A New Approach to the Religious Traditions of Mankind*. New York: Macmillan, 1963.

Sullivan, Lawrence E., ed. *Enchanting Powers: Music in the World's Religions*. Cambridge, MA: Harvard University Press, 1997.

Wach, Joachim. (ed. J.M. Kitagawa). *The Comparative Study of Religion*. New York: Columbia University Press, 1961.

Willis, Roy, ed. *World Mythology: The Illustrated Guide*. New York: Simon & Schuster, 1993.

Young, Serenity, ed. *Encyclopedia of Women and World Religion*. New York: Macmillan, 1998.

CHAPTER 1 JUDAISM

Carl S. Ehrlich

Avineri, Shlomo. *The Making of Modern Zionism: The Intellectual Origins of the Jewish State*. New York: Basic Books, 1981.

Baskin, Judith R., ed. *Jewish Women in Historical Perspective*. Detroit: Wayne State University Press, 1991.

Ben-Sasson, H. H., ed. *A History of the Jewish People*. Cambridge: Harvard University Press, 1976.

Bialik, Hayim Nachman and Yehoshua Hana Ravnitzky, eds. *The Book of Legends (*Sefer Ha-Aggadah*): Legends from the Talmud and Midrash*. Translated by William G. Braude. New York: Schocken, 1992.

Borowitz, Eugene B. *Choices in Modern Jewish Thought: A Partisan Guide*. 2nd ed. West Orange, NJ: Behrman House, 1995.

Carmi, T., ed. *The Penguin Book of Hebrew Verse*. New York and London: Penguin Books, 1981.

Cohen, Arthur A. and Paul Mendes-Flohr, eds. *Contemporary Jewish Religious Thought: Original Essays on Critical Concepts, Movements, and Beliefs*. New York: Free Press, 1987.

Dawidowicz, Lucy S. *The War against the Jews, 1933–1945*. Toronto and New York: Bantam, 1986.

Elbogen, Ismar. *Jewish Liturgy: A Comprehensive History*. Translated by Raymond P. Scheindlin. Philadelphia: Jewish Publication Society, 1993.

Epstein, I., ed. *The Babylonian Talmud*. 18 vols. London: Soncino Press, 1961 (orig. ca. 1935–48).

Friedman, Richard Elliot. *Who Wrote the Bible?* New York: Summit, 1987.

Green, Arthur, ed. *Jewish Spirituality*. (*Vol. 1: From the Bible through the Middle Ages; Vol. 2: From the Sixteenth Century Revival to the Present.*) New York: Crossroad, 1988.

Heschel, Abraham Joshua. *God in Search of Man: A Philosophy of Judaism*. Northvale, NJ: Jason Aronson, 1987 (orig. ca. 1955).

Holtz, Barry W., ed. *Back to the Sources: Reading the Classic Jewish Texts*. New York: Summit, 1984.

Idelson, A. Z. *Jewish Music: Its Historical Development*. New York: Dover, 1992 (orig. ca. 1929).

Klein, Isaac. *A Guide to Jewish Religious Practice*. New York: Jewish Theological Seminary of America, 1979.

Kugel, James L. *The Bible as It Was*. Cambridge, MA: Harvard University Press, 1997.

Leviant, Curt, ed. *Masterpieces of Hebrew Literature: A Treasury of 2000 Years of Jewish Creativity*. New York: Ktav, 1969.

Marcus, Jacob R. *The Jew in the Medieval World: A Source Book, 315–1791*. Westport, CT: Greenwood, 1975 (orig. ca. 1938).

Mendes-Flohr, Paul and Jehuda Reinharz, eds. *The Jew in the Modern World: A Documentary History*. New York: Oxford University Press, 1980.

Plaskow, Judith. *Standing Again at Sinai: Judaism from a Feminist Perspective*. San Francisco: Harper & Row, 1990.

Plaut, W. Gunther, Bernard J. Bamberger and William Hallo. *The Torah: A Modern Commentary*. New York: Union of American Hebrew Congregations, 1981.

Roth, Cecil, ed. *Encyclopaedia Judaica*. 16 vols. New York: Macmillan, 1972.

Scholem, Gershom. *Major Trends in Jewish Mysticism*. New York: Schocken, 1961 (orig. ca. 1954).

Seltzer, Robert M. *Jewish People, Jewish Thought: The Jewish Experience in History*. New York: Macmillan, 1980.

Strassfeld, Michael, ed. *The Jewish Holidays: A Guide and Commentary*. New York: Harper & Row, 1985.

Tanakh: A New Translation of the Holy Scriptures According to the Traditional

Hebrew Text. Philadelphia: Jewish Publication Society, 1985.
Trachtenberg, Joshua. *The Devil and the Jews: The Medieval Conception of the Jew and Its Relation to Modern Anti-Semitism*. 2nd ed. Philadelphia: Jewish Publication Society, 1983.
Urbach, Ephraim E. *The Sages: Their Concepts and Beliefs*. Translated by Israel Abrahams. Cambridge, MA: Harvard University Press, 1987.
Werblowsky, R.J. Zwi and Geoffrey Wigoder, eds. *The Oxford Dictionary of the Jewish Religion*. New York: Oxford University Press, 1997.
Wigoder, Geoffrey, ed. *Jewish Art and Civilization*. New York: Walker, 1972.

CHAPTER 2 CHRISTIANITY
Rosemary Drage Hale

Appiah-Kubi, Kofi and Sergio Torres, eds. *African Theology en route*. Maryknoll, NY: Orbis, 1979.
Brown, Peter. *The Rise of Western Christendom: Triumph and Diversity, 200–1000AD*. Oxford: Blackwell, 1997.
Brown, Schuyler. *The Origins of Christianity: A Historical Introduction to the New Testament*. rev. ed. New York: Oxford University Press, 1993.
Carson, D. A., Douglas J. Moo and Leon Morris. *An Introduction to the New Testament*. rev. ed. Grand Rapids, MI: Zondervan, 1994.
Chadwick, Henry. *The Early Church*. New York: Pelican, 1964.
Clark, Elizabeth and Herbert Richardson. *Women and Religion: A Feminist Sourcebook of Christian Thought*. New York: Harper and Row, 1977.
Copleston, Frederick. *A History of Christian Philosophy in the Middle Ages*. London: Sheed and Ward, 1978.
Cross, F. L. and E. A. Livingston, eds. *The Oxford Dictionary of the Christian Church*. 3rd ed. Oxford: Oxford University Press, 1997.
Cross, Lawrence. *Eastern Christianity: The Byzantine Tradition*. Philadelphia: E. J. Dwyer, 1988.
Dillenberger, John and Claude Welch. *Protestant Christianity: Interpreted Through Its Development*. 2nd ed. New York: Macmillan, 1988.
Jedin, Hubert. *The Church in the Modern World*. New York: Crossroad, 1993.
Johnson, Paul. *A History of Christianity*. New York: Atheneum, 1976.
Kazhdan, Alexander P., ed. *The Oxford Dictionary of Byzantium*. 3 vols. New York: Oxford University Press, 1991.
Knowles, David. *Christian Monasticism*. New York: McGraw-Hill, 1969.
Lossky, Vladimir. *The Mystical Theology of the Eastern Church*. London: James Clarke, 1968.
McGinn, Bernard. *The Foundations of Mysticism*. New York: Crossroad, 1992.
McGrath, Alister E. *Christian Theology: An Introduction*. Oxford: Blackwell, 1996.
McKenzie, Peter. *The Christians, Their Beliefs and Practices: An Adaptation of Friedrich Heiler's Phenomenology of Religion*. Nashville: Abingdon, 1988.
McLaren, Robert Bruce. *Christian Ethics: Foundations and Practice*. Englewood Cliffs, NJ: Prentice-Hall, 1994.
McManners, John, ed. *The Oxford Illustrated History of Christianity*. Oxford: Oxford University Press, 1992.
Meyendorff, John. *Byzantine Theology: Historical Trends and Doctrinal Themes*. New York: Fordham University Press, 1974.
Porter, J. R. *The Illustrated Guide to the Bible*. New York and Oxford, Oxford University Press, 1995.
Quebedeaux, Richard. *The New Charismatics: The Origins, Development, and Significance of Neo-Pentecostalism*. New York: Doubleday, 1976.
Raitt, Jill, ed. *Christian Spirituality*. 3 vols. New York: Crossroad, 1985–1989.
Self, David. *High Days and Holidays: Celebrating the Christian Year*. Oxford: Lion, 1993.
Southern, R. W. *Western Society and the Church in the Middle Ages*. New York: Penguin, 1970.

CHAPTER 3 ISLAM
Matthew S. Gordon

Abbott, Nabia. *Aishah, The Beloved of Muhammad*. New York: Arno, 1973 (orig. 1942).
Al-Ghazzali, Abu Hamid Muhammad. *The Alchemy of Happiness*. Translated by Claud Field (revised by Elton L. Daniel). London: M. E. Sharpe, 1991.
Ali, A. Yusuf. *The Koran: Translation and Commentary*. Washington, D.C.: American International Printing, 1946.
Ali, Muhammad. *A Manual of Hadith*. London: Curzon, 1977.
Arberry, A. J. *The Koran Interpreted*. New York: Macmillan, 1955.
Armstrong, Karen. *Muhammad: A Biography of the Prophet*. San Francisco: Harper San Francisco, 1992.
Daniel, Norman. *Islam and the West: The Making of an Image*. Edinburgh: Edinburgh University Press, 1960.
Denny, Frederick M. *An Introduction to Islam*. New York: Macmillan, 1985.
Dunn, Ross. *The Adventures of Ibn Battuta: A Muslim Traveller of the Fourteenth Century*. Berkeley: University of California Press, 1986.
Ernst, Carl W. *The Shambhala Guide to Sufism*. Boston: Shambhala, 1997.
Esposito, John L. *Islam and Politics*. Syracuse: Syracuse University Press, 1987.
——. *The Oxford Encyclopedia of the Modern Islamic World*. 4 vols. New York: Oxford University Press, 1995.
——. *Islam: The Straight Path*. 3rd ed. New York: Oxford University Press, 1998.
Fernea, Elizabeth. *In Search of Islamic Feminism: One Woman's Global Journey*. New York: Doubleday, 1998.
Gibb, H. A. R. and J. H. Kramers, eds. *Shorter Encyclopaedia of Islam*. Leiden: E. J. Brill, 1991.
Guillaume, A. *The Life of Muhammad: A Translation of Ibn Ishaq's Sirat Rasul Allah*. London: Oxford University Press, 1967.
Ibn Khaldun. *The Muqaddimah: An Introduction to History*. Translated by Franz Rosenthal. 3 vols. New York: Bollingen Foundation, 1958.
Khomeini, Ruhollah. *Islam and Revolution: Writings and Declarations of Imam Khomeini*. Translated by Hamid Algar. Berkeley: Mizan, 1987.
Lapidus, Ira M. *A History of Islamic Societies*. Cambridge: Cambridge University Press, 1988.
Malcolm X. *The Autobiography of Malcolm X*. Written with the assistance of Alex Haley. New York: Grove, 1965.
Momen, Moojan. *An Introduction to Shi'i Islam*. New Haven: Yale University Press, 1985.
Nanji, Azim A., ed. *The Muslim Almanac: A Reference Work on the History, Faith, Culture, and Peoples of Islam*. New York: Gale Research, 1996.
Rahman, Fazlur. *Islam*. Chicago: University of Chicago Press, 1979.
Renard, John. *Seven Doors to Islam: Spirituality and the Religious Life of Muslims*. Berkeley: University of California Press, 1996.
Robinson, Francis, ed. *The Cambridge Illustrated History of the Islamic World*. Cambridge: Cambridge University Press, 1996.
Robinson, Francis. *Atlas of the Islamic World since 1500*. New York: Facts on File, 1982.
Rodinson, Maxime. *Europe and the Mystique of Islam*. Translated by Roger Veinus. Seattle: University of Washington Press, 1987.
Said, Edward. *Orientalism*. New York: Vintage, 1979.

CHAPTER 4 HINDUISM
Vasudha Narayanan

Baird, Robert D., ed. *Religion and Law in*

Independent India. New Delhi: Manohar, 1993.
Basham, Arthur L. *The Wonder That Was India: A Survey of the History and Culture of the Indian Sub-continent before the Coming of the Muslims*. 3rd ed. London: Sidgwick and Jackson, 1967.
Danielou, Alain. *Hindu Polytheism*. New York: Bollingen Foundation, 1964.
Doniger, Wendy and Brian Smith, translators. *The Laws of Manu*. Harmondsworth: Penguin, 1991.
Eck, Diana L. *Darsan: Seeing the Divine Image in India*. Chambersburg, PA: Anima, 1981.
Erndl, Kathleen M. *Victory to the Mother: The Hindu Goddess of Northwest India in Myth, Ritual, and Symbol*. New York: Oxford University Press, 1993.
Gandhi, Mahatma. *An Autobiography: The Story of My Experiments with Truth*. Ahmedabad: Navjivan Publications, 1959.
Gold, Ann Grodzins and Gloria Goodwin Raheja. *Listen to the Heron's Words: Reimagining Gender and Kinship in Northern India*. Berkeley: University of California Press, 1994.
Hart, George. *Poets of the Tamil Anthologies: Ancient Poems of Love and War*. Princeton: Princeton University Press, 1979.
Hawley, John S. and Donna M. Wulff, eds. *Devi: Goddesses of India*. Berkeley: University of California Press, 1996.
Hawley, John S. and Mark Juergensmeyer. *Songs of the Saints of India*. New York: Oxford University Press, 1988.
Hiriyanna, Mysore. *The Essentials of Indian Philosophy*. London: Allen and Unwin, 1960.
Kane, P. V. *History of Dharmasastra*. 5 vols. Poona, India: Bhandarkar Oriental Research Institute, 1953–1974.
Leslie, Julia, ed. *Roles and Rituals for Hindu Women*. Rutherford, NJ: Fairleigh Dickinson University Press, 1991.
Lutgendorf, Philip. *The Life of a Text: Performing the Ramcaritmanas of Tulsidas*. Berkeley: University of California Press, 1991.
Miller, Barbara Stoler, ed. and trans. *Love Song of the Dark Lord: Sayadeva's Gitagovinda*. New York: Columbia University Press, 1977.
Miller, Barbara Stoler, trans. *The Bhagavad Gita: Krishna's Counsel in Time of War*. New York: Columbia University Press, 1986.
Narayan, R. K. *The Ramayana*. New York: Viking, 1972.
Narayan, R. K. *The Mahabharata*. New York: Viking, 1978.
Narayanan, Vasudha. *The Vernacular Veda: Revelation, Recitation and Ritual*. Columbia: University of South Carolina Press, 1994.
O'Flaherty, Wendy Doniger. *Hindu Myths: A Sourcebook*. Baltimore: Penguin, 1975.
O'Flaherty, Wendy Doniger, ed. *Karma and Rebirth in Classical Indian Traditions*. Berkeley: University of California Press, 1990.
Olivelle, Patrick, trans. *The Upanisads*. New York: Oxford University Press, 1996.
Pandey, Raj Bali. *Hindu Samskaras: Socio-religious Studies of the Hindu Sacraments*. Delhi: Motilal Banarsidass, 1982.
Peterson, Indira Viswanathan. *Poems to Siva: The Hymns of the Tamil Saints*. Princeton: Princeton University Press, 1990.
Rajagopalachari, C. *Mahabharata*. Bombay: Bharatiya Vidya Bhavan, 1953.
Ramanujan, A. K., trans. *Speaking of Siva*. Harmondsworth: Penguin, 1973.
Ramanujan, A. K., trans. *Hymns for the Drowning: Poems for Viosonu*. Princeton: Princeton University Press, 1981.
Sax, William S. *The Gods at Play: Lila in South Asia*. New York: Oxford University Press, 1995.
Singer, Milton B. *Krishna: Myths, Rites, and Attitudes*. Honolulu: East-West Center Press, 1966.
Tharu, Susie and K. Lalita. *Women Writing in India 600BC to the Present*. 2 vols. New York: The Feminist Press at the City University of New York, 1991.
Waghorne Joanne P., Norman Cutler and Vasudha Narayanan. *Gods of Flesh, Gods of Stone: The Embodiment of Divinity in India*. Chambersburg, PA: Anima, 1985.
Yocum, Glenn E. *Hymns to the Dancing Siva: A Study of Manikkavacakar's Tiruvacakam*. New Delhi: Heritage, 1982.
Young, Katherine. "Hinduism" in *Women in World Religions*. (ed. Arvind Sharma). Albany: State University of NY Press, 1987.

CHAPTER 5 BUDDHISM
Malcolm David Eckel

Bechert, Heinz and Richard Gombrich, eds. *The World of Buddhism: Buddhist Monks and Nuns in Society and Culture*. New York: Facts on File, 1984.
Conze, Edward, ed. *Buddhist Scriptures*. New York: Penguin, 1959.
Eckel, Malcolm David. *To See the Buddha: A Philosopher's Quest for the Meaning of Emptiness*. Princeton: Princeton University Press, 1994.
Gombrich, Richard F. *How Buddhism Began: The Conditioned Genesis of the Early Teachings*. London: Athlone, 1997.
Gombrich, Richard and Gananath Obeyesekere. *Buddhism Transformed: Religious Change in Sri Lanka*. Princeton: Princeton University Press, 1988.
Horner, I. B. *Women Under Primitive Buddhism: Laywomen and Almswomen*. London, 1930; repr. Delhi: Motilal Banarsidass, 1975.
Kitagawa, Joseph M. *Religion in Japanese History*. New York: Columbia University Press, 1966.
Lamotte, Etienne. *History of Indian Buddhism from the Origins to the Saka Era*. Translated by Sara Webb-Boin. Louvain-la-Neuve: Institut Orientaliste, 1988.
Nakamura, Hajime. *Indian Buddhism: A Survey With Bibliographical Notes*. Delhi: Motilal Banarsidass, 1987.
Paul, Diana Y. *Women in Buddhism: Images of the Feminine in the Mahayana Tradition*. 2nd ed. Berkeley: University of California Press, 1985.
Rahula, Walpola. *What the Buddha Taught*. New York: Grove, 1974.
Rhie, Marylin M. and Robert A. F. Thurman. *Wisdom and Compassion: The Sacred Art of Tibet*. New York: Harry N. Abrams, 1991.
Snellgrove, David and Hugh Richardson. *A Cultural History of Tibet*. Boulder, CO: Prajna Press, 1980.
Suzuki, Daisetz T. *Zen and Japanese Culture*. Princeton: Princeton University Press, 1959.
Tambiah, S. J. *Buddhism Betrayed? Religion, Politics, and Violence in Sri Lanka*. Chicago: University of Chicago Press, 1992.
Tambiah, S. J. *World Conqueror and World Renouncer: A Study of Buddhism and Polity in Thailand against a Historical Background*. Cambridge: Cambridge University Press, 1976.
Aung San Suu Kyi. *Freedom From Fear and Other Writings*, rev. ed. New York: Viking, 1991.
Tenzin Gyatso, the Fourteenth Dalai Lama. *Freedom in Exile: The Autobiography of the Dalai Lama*. New York: HarperCollins, 1990.
Tweed, Thomas A. *The American Encounter with Buddhism, 1844–1912: Victorian Culture and the Limits of Dissent*. Bloomington: Indiana University Press, 1992.
Williams, Paul. *Mahayana Buddhism: The Doctrinal Foundations*. London: Routledge, 1989.
Wright, Arthur F. *Buddhism in Chinese History*. Stanford: Stanford University Press, 1959.
Zwalf, W., ed. *Buddhism: Art and Faith*. London: British Museum, 1985.

CHAPTER 6 CHINESE TRADITIONS
Jennifer Oldstone-Moore

Birrell, Anne. *Chinese Mythology:*

An Introduction. Baltimore: Johns Hopkins University Press, 1993.
Chan, Wing-tsit. *A Source Book in Chinese Philosophy*. Princeton: Princeton University Press, 1963.
Chen, Kenneth. *Buddhism in China: A Historical Survey*. Princeton: Princeton University Press, 1964.
Confucius. *The Analects*. Translated by D. C. Lau. New York: Viking, 1979.
De Bary, William Theodore, Wing-tsit Chan and Burton Watson, eds. *Sources of Chinese Tradition*. Vol. 1. New York: Columbia University Press, 1960.
Fingarette, Herbert. *Confucius: The Sacred as Secular*. New York: Harper & Row, 1972.
The I Ching. Translated by Richard Wilhelm, and from German to English by Cary F. Baynes. 3rd ed. Princeton: Princeton University Press, 1967.
Lao-Tzu. *The Tao Te Ching*. Translated by D. C. Lau. Baltimore: Penguin, 1963.
Lopez, Donald S., Jr. *Religions of China in Practice*. Princeton: Princeton University Press, 1996.
Jordan, David. *Gods, Ghosts, and Ancestors: The Folk Religion of a Taiwanese Village*. Berkeley: University of California Press, 1972.
Martin, Emily. *The Cult of the Dead in a Chinese Village*. Stanford: Stanford University Press, 1973.
Mencius. *The Mencius*. Translated by D. C. Lau. Harmondswoth: Penguin, 1970.
Overmyer, Daniel L. *Religions of China: The World as a Living System*. San Francisco: Harper & Row, 1986.
Overmyer, Daniel L.; Alvin P. Cohen; N. J. Girardot and Wing-tsit Chan. "Chinese Religions." Vol. 3. pp. 257–323 in *The Encyclopedia of Religion* (ed. Mircea Eliade) New York: Macmillan, 1987.
Saso, Michael. *The Teachings of Taoist Master Chuang*. New Haven: Yale University Press, 1978.
Schipper, Kristofer. *The Taoist Body*. Translated by Karen C. Duval. Berkeley: University of California Press, 1993.
Stepanchuk, Carol and Charles Wong. *Mooncakes and Hungry Ghosts: Festivals of China*. San Francisco: China Books and Periodicals, 1991.
Thompson, Laurence. *Chinese Religion: An Introduction*. 5th ed. Belmont, CA: Wadsworth, 1998.
——. *The Chinese Way in Religion*. 2nd ed. Belmont, CA: Wadsworth, 1998.
Tu Wei-ming. *Confucian Thought: Selfhood as Creative Transformation*. Albany: State University of NY Press, 1985.
Watson, Burton. *Chuang Tzu: Basic Writings*. New York: Columbia University Press, 1996.
Welch, Holmes. *Taoism: The Parting of the Way*. Boston: Beacon, 1974.
Wolf, Arthur P., ed. *Religion and Ritual in Chinese Society*. Stanford: Stanford University Press, 1974.
Wright, Arthur F. *Buddhism in Chinese History*. Stanford: Stanford University Press, 1959.
Yampolsky, Philip B. *Platform Sutra of the Sixth Patriarch*. New York: Columbia University Press, 1978.

CHAPTER 7 JAPANESE TRADITIONS

C. Scott Littleton

Ashkenazi, Michael. *Matsuri: Festivals of a Japanese Town*. Honolulu: University of Hawaii Press, 1993.
Aston, W. G., trans. *Nihongi: Chronicles of Japan from the Earliest Times to AD697*. Rutland, VT: Charles E. Tuttle, 1972 (orig. 1896).
Blacker, Carmen. *The Catalpa Bow: A Study of Shamanistic Practice in Japan*. London: Allen and Unwin, 1975.
Bloom, Alfred. *Shinran's Gospel of Pure Grace*. Tucson: University of Arizona Press, 1965.
Boxer, C. R. *The Christian Century in Japan: 1549–1650*. Berkeley: University of California Press, 1951.
Brannen, Noah S. *Soka Gakkai: Japan's Militant Buddhists*. Richmond, VA: John Knox Press, 1968.
Davis, Winston Bradley. *Dojo: Magic and Exorcism in Modern Japan*. Stanford, CA: Stanford University Press, 1980.
Dumoulin, Heinrich. *Zen Buddhism: A History*. Translated by James W. Heissig and Paul Knittnerr. 2 vols. New York: Macmillan, 1988; 1990.
Earhart, H. Byron. *Japanese Religion: Unity and Diversity*. 3rd ed. Belmont, CA: Wadsworth, 1983.
Foard, James H. "In Search of a Lost Reformation: A Reconsideration of Kamakura Buddhism." *Japanese Journal of Religious Studies* 7 (1980): pp.261–291.
Hall, John Whitney. *Japan from Prehistory to Modern Times*. New York: Delacorte, 1970.
Hardacre, Helen. *Shinto and the State, 1868–1988*. Princeton, NJ: Princeton University Press, 1989.
Littleton, C. Scott. "The Organization and Management of a Tokyo Shinto Shrine Festival." In *Ethnology* 25 (1986): pp.195–202.
——. "Shinto." in *Eastern Wisdom: An Illustrated Guide to the Religions and Philosophies of the East*. ed. C. Scott Littleton, pp.144–61. New York: Henry Holt, 1996.
Matsunaga, Daigan and Alicia Matsunaga. *Foundation of Japanese Buddhism*, Vol. 1. Los Angeles: Buddhist Books International, 1974.
McFarland, H. Neil. *The Rush Hour of the Gods: A Study of New Religious Movements of Japan*. New York: Macmillan, 1974.
Nelson, John K. *A Year in the Life of a Shinto Shrine*. Seattle: University of Washington Press, 1996.
The Nichiren Shoshu Sokagakkai. Tokyo: Seikyo Press, 1966.
Ono, Sokyo. *Shinto: The Kami Way*. Rutland, VT: Charles E. Tuttle, 1962.
Philippi, Donald L., trans. *Kojiki*. Princeton: Princeton University Press, 1969.
Reader, Ian. *Religion in Contemporary Japan*. Honolulu: University of Hawaii Press, 1991.
Sadler, A. W. "Carrying the Mikoshi: Further Notes on the Shrine Festival in Modern Tokyo." In *Asian Folklore Studies* 31 (1976): pp.89–114.
Saso, Michael R. *Tantric Art and Meditation: The Tendai Tradition*. Honolulu: University of Hawaii Press, 1970.
Suzuki, D. T. *Zen and Japanese Culture*. 2nd ed. New York: Pantheon, 1959.
Takahatake, Takamichi. *Young Man Shinran. A Reappraisal of Shinran's Life*. Waterloo, Ontario: Wilfrid Laurier University Press, 1987.
Tanabe, George J. and Willa J. Tanabe. eds. *The Lotus Sutra in Japanese Culture*. Honolulu: University of Hawaii Press, 1989.
A Short History of Tenrikyo. Tenri, Japan: Tenrikyo Kyokai Honbu, 1958.
Watts, Alan. *The Way of Zen*. New York: Pantheon. 1957.
Yamasaki, Taiko. *Shingon: Japanese Esoteric Buddhism*. New York: Random House, 1988.

INDEX

Page references in *italics* are to captions

A

B

C

D

E

F

G

H

I

J

N

O

P

Q

R

S